T0303313

The Story of God Bible Commentary Series Endorsements

"Getting a story is about more than merely enjoying it. It means hearing it, understanding it, and above all, being impacted by it. This commentary series hopes that its readers not only hear and understand the story, but are impacted by it to live in as Christian a way as possible. The editors and contributors set that table very well and open up the biblical story in ways that move us to act with sensitivity and understanding. That makes hearing the story as these authors tell it well worth the time. Well done."

Darrell L. Bock

Dallas Theological Seminary

"The Story of God Bible Commentary series invites readers to probe how the message of the text relates to our situations today. Engagingly readable, it not only explores the biblical text but offers a range of applications and interesting illustrations."

Craig S. Keener

Asbury Theological Seminary

"I love The Story of God Bible Commentary series. It makes the text sing, and helps us hear the story afresh."

John Ortberg

Senior Pastor of Menlo Park Presbyterian Church

"In this promising new series of commentaries, believing biblical scholars bring not only their expertise but their own commitment to Jesus and insights into today's culture to the Scriptures. The result is a commentary series that is anchored in the text but lives and breathes in the world of today's church with its variegated pattern of socioeconomic, ethnic, and national diversity. Pastors, Bible study leaders, and Christians of all types who are looking for a substantive and practical guide through the Scriptures will find these volumes helpful."

Frank Thielman

Beeson Divinity School

"The Story of God Bible Commentary series is unique in its approach to exploring the Bible. Its easy-to-use format and practical guidance brings God's grand story to modern-day life so anyone can understand how it applies today."

Andy Stanley

North Point Ministries

"I'm a storyteller. Through writing and speaking I talk and teach about understanding the Story of God throughout Scripture and about letting God reveal more of His story as I live it out. Thus I am thrilled to have a commentary series based on the Story of God—a commentary that helps me to Listen to the Story, that Explains the Story, and then encourages me to probe how to Live the Story. A perfect tool for helping every follower of Jesus to walk in the story that God is writing for them."

Judy Douglass
Director of Women's Resources, Cru

"The Bible is the story of God and his dealings with humanity from creation to new creation. The Bible is made up more of stories than of any other literary genre. Even the psalms, proverbs, prophecies, letters, and the Apocalypse make complete sense only when set in the context of the grand narrative of the entire Bible. This commentary series breaks new ground by taking all these observations seriously. It asks commentators to listen to the text, to explain the text, and to live the text. Some of the material in these sections overlaps with introduction, detailed textual analysis and application, respectively, but only some. The most riveting and valuable part of the commentaries are the stories that can appear in any of these sections, from any part of the globe and any part of church history, illustrating the text in any of these areas. Ideal for preaching and teaching."

Craig L. Blomberg
Denver Seminary

"Pastors and lay people will welcome this new series, which seeks to make the message of the Scriptures clear and to guide readers in appropriating biblical texts for life today."

Daniel I. Block
Wheaton College and Graduate School

"An extremely valuable and long overdue series that includes comment on the cultural context of the text, careful exegesis, and guidance on reading the whole Bible as a unity that testifies to Christ as our Savior and Lord."

Graeme Goldsworthy
author of *According to Plan*

PROVERBS

The Story of God Bible Commentary

PROVERBS

Ryan P. O'Dowd

Tremper Longman III & Scot McKnight
General Editors

ZONDERVAN®

ZONDERVAN

Proverbs
Copyright © 2017 by Ryan O'Dowd

This title is also available as a Zondervan ebook.

Requests for information should be addressed to:
Zondervan, *3900 Sparks Dr. SE, Grand Rapids, Michigan 49546*

ISBN 978-0-310-49113-2

Unless otherwise indicated, Scripture quotations are taken from The Holy Bible, New International Version®, NIV®. Copyright © 1973, 1978, 1984, 2011 by Biblica, Inc.® Used by permission of Zondervan. All rights reserved worldwide. www.Zondervan.com. The "NIV" and "New International Version" are trademarks registered in the United States Patent and Trademark Office by Biblica, Inc.®

Any Internet addresses (websites, blogs, etc.) and telephone numbers in this book are offered as a resource. They are not intended in any way to be or imply an endorsement by Zondervan, nor does Zondervan vouch for the content of these sites and numbers for the life of this book.

Cover design: Ron Huizinga
Cover image: iStockphoto®
Interior composition: Kait Lamphere

Printed in the United States of America

17 18 19 20 21 22 23 24 25 26 27 /DHV/ 15 14 13 12 11 10 9 8 7 6 5 4 3 2 1

To Calum Carmichael

Old Testament series

New Testament series

Contents

Acknowledgments

Τ here is no more time to lick this whelp," Douglas Templeton commented on a recently completed book. It is a fitting proverb for writing: the thing must eventually take on a life of its own. I owe a great debt to those who have contributed to this final version.

The people at Chesterton House center for Christian Study at Cornell and Bread of Life Anglican Church patiently encouraged me in my writing and supported my travel to present papers where I tested ideas. Thanks to those who commented on papers I presented at meetings of the Society of Biblical Literature Annual Meeting, the Institute of Biblical Research, and the Harvard Divinity School Ways of Knowing Conference.

I gratefully acknowledge Karl Johnson for supporting my scholarship and encouraging me to create a course on Proverbs for students at Chesterton House.

Tremper Longman III, George Athas, Nancy Erickson, and the rest of the editing staff at Zondervan maintained joy and anticipation of this commentary all the while laboring to correct its faults and strengthen its conclusions. It is a rare scholar who can examine another's work with such a critical eye while remaining humble and enthusiastically supportive of the writing. These are a few great examples.

Thanks to the many friends who carefully edited chapters of the commentary: Scott Brodie, Angela Brodie, Trina Garrison, Emily Honeycutt, and Alicia Anderson. Thanks also to Matt Garrison for his literary and pop-cultural allusions and a constant spark of imagination.

My children, Patrick, Annie, Aidan, and Emma Clare, endured countless random attempts to explain the contemporary significance of some individual saying or another. Thank you. Your lives are part of every sentence in this book. My wife Amy is the *eshet hayil* of Proverbs 31 and the living waters of Proverbs 5. Always supportive, she listened to thousands of small sections of writing as I sought to find the words and style that seemed just out of reach. I wish I had the beautiful, effortless style of her writing. She is amazing in every way.

Calum Carmichael has been a tutor and a friend these last seven years. To those who know him he is a man of prodigious learning and tireless wit. Along with countless jokes, he taught me to be the last person to be convinced by my own arguments; to pursue every matter from every possible angle; to tinker with my writing until someone takes it away from me; and to find pleasure in the process. This book is dedicated to him.

The Story of God Bible Commentary Series

Why another commentary series?

In the first place, no single commentary can exhaust the meaning of a biblical book. The Bible is unfathomably rich and no single commentator can explore every aspect of its message.

In addition, good commentary not only explores what the text meant in the past, but also its continuing significance. In other words, the Word of God may not change, but culture does. Think of what we have seen in the last twenty years: we now communicate predominantly through the internet and email, we read our news on iPads and computers. We carry smartphones in our pockets through which we can call our friends, check the weather forecast, make dinner reservations, and get an answer to virtually any question we might have.

Today we have more readable and accurate Bible versions in English than any generation in the past. Bible distribution in the present generation has been very successful; more people own more Bibles than previous generations. However, studies have shown that, while people have better access to the Bible than ever before, people aren't reading the Bibles they own, and they struggle to understand what they do read.

The Story of God Bible Commentary hopes to help people, particularly clergy but also laypeople, read the Bible with understanding not only of its ancient meaning, but also of its continuing significance for us today in the twenty-first century. After all, readers of the Bible change too. These cultural shifts, our own personal developments, the progress in intellectual questions, as well as growth in biblical studies and theology and discoveries of new texts and new paradigms for understanding the contexts of the Bible—each of these elements work on an interpreter so that the person who reads the Bible today asks different questions from different angles.

Culture shifts, but the Word of God remains. That is why we as editors of The Story of God Bible Commentary, a commentary based on the New International Version 2011 (NIV 2011), are excited to participate in this new series of commentaries on the Bible. This series is designed to speak to this generation with the same Word of God. We are asking the authors to explain what the Bible says to the sorts of readers who pick up commentaries so they can understand not only what Scripture says but what it means for today. The

Bible does not change but relating it to our culture changes constantly and in differing ways in different contexts.

As editors of the Old Testament series, we recognize that Christians have a hard time knowing exactly how to relate to the Scriptures that were written before the coming of Christ. The world of the Old Testament is a strange one to those of us who live in the West in the twenty-first century. We read about strange customs, warfare in the name of God, sacrifices, laws of ritual purity, and more and wonder whether it is worth our while or even spiritually healthy to spend time reading this portion of Scripture that is chronologically, culturally, and—seemingly—theologically distant from us.

But it is precisely here that The Story of God Commentary Series Old Testament makes its most important contribution. The New Testament does not replace the Old Testament; the New Testament fulfills the Old Testament. We hear God's voice today in the Old Testament. In its pages he reveals himself to us and also his will for how we should live in a way that is pleasing to him.

Jesus himself often reminds us that the Old Testament maintains its importance to the life of his disciples. Luke 24 describes Jesus' actions and teaching in the period between his resurrection and ascension. Strikingly, the focus of his teaching is on how his followers should read the Old Testament (here called "Moses and all the Prophets," "Scriptures," and "the Law of Moses, the Prophets and Psalms"). To the two disciples on the road to Emmaus, he says:

> "How foolish you are, and how slow to believe all that the prophets have spoken! Did not the Messiah have to suffer these things and then enter his glory?" And beginning with Moses and all the Prophets, he explained to them what was said in all the Scriptures concerning himself. (Luke 24:25–27)

Then to a larger group of disciples he announces:

> "This is what I told you while I was still with you: Everything must be fulfilled that is written about me in the Law of Moses, the Prophets and the Psalms." Then he opened their minds so they could understand the Scriptures. (Luke 24:44–45)

The Story of God Commentary Series takes Jesus' words on this matter seriously. Indeed, it is the first series that has as one of its deliberate goals the identification of the trajectories (historical, typological, and theological) that land in Christ in the New Testament. Every commentary in the series will, in the first place, exposit the text in the context of its original reception. We will interpret it as we believe the original author intended his contemporary audience to read it. But then we will also read the text in the light of the death and resurrection of Jesus. No other commentary series does this important work consistently in every volume.

To achieve our purpose of expositing the Old Testament in its original setting and also from a New Testament perspective, each passage is examined from three angles.

Listen to the Story. We begin by listening to the text in order to hear the voice of God. We first read the passage under study. We then go on to consider the background to the passage by looking at any earlier Scripture passage that informs our understanding of the text. At this point too we will cite and discuss possible ancient Near Eastern literary connections. After all, the Bible was not written in a cultural vacuum, and an understanding of its broader ancient Near Eastern context will often enrich our reading.

Explain the Story. The authors are asked to explain each passage in light of the Bible's grand story. It is here that we will exposit the text in its original Old Testament context. This is not an academic series, so the footnotes will be limited to the kinds of books and articles to which typical Bible readers and preachers will have access. Authors are given the freedom to explain the text as they read it, though you will not be surprised to find occasional listings of other options for reading the text. The emphasis will be on providing an accessible explanation of the passage, particularly on those aspects of the text that are difficult for a modern reader to understand, with an emphasis on theological interpretation.

Live the Story. Reading the Bible is not just about discovering what it meant back then; the intent of The Story of God Bible Commentary is to probe how this text might be lived out today as that story continues to march on in the life of the church.

Here in the spirit of Christ's words in Luke 24 we will suggest ways in which the Old Testament text anticipates the gospel. After all, as Augustine famously put it, "the New Testament is in the Old Testament concealed, the Old Testament is in the New Testament revealed." We believe that this section will be particularly important for our readers who are clergy who want to present Christ even when they are preaching from the Old Testament.

The Old Testament also provides teaching concerning how we should live today. However, the authors of this series are sensitive to the tremendous impact that Christ's coming has on how Christians appropriate the Old Testament into their lives today.

It is the hope and prayer of the editors and all the contributors that our work will encourage clergy to preach from the Old Testament and for laypeople to study this wonderful, yet often strange portion of God's Word to us today.

TREMPER LONGMAN III, general editor Old Testament
GEORGE ATHAS, MARK BODA, AND MYRTO THEOCHAROUS, editors

Abbreviations

AB	Anchor Bible
ABRL	Anchor Bible Reference Library
AEL	*Ancient Egyptian Literature*. M. Lichtheim. 3 vols. Berkeley, 1971–1980
BBRS	Bulletin for Biblical Research Supplements
BCOTWP	Baker Commentary on Old Testament Wisdom and Psalms
BTM	*Before the Muses: An Anthology of Akkadian Literature*. B. R. Foster. CDL, 2005
BZAW	Beihefte zur Zeitschrift für die alttestamentliche Wissenschaft
CBQ	Catholic Biblical Quarterly
CC	Continental Commentaries
COS	The Context of Scripture. Edited by W. W. Hallo. 4 vols. Leiden, 1997–2016
DLCPT	Digital Library of Classic Protestant Texts
FRLANT	Forschungen zur Religion und Literatur des Alten und Neuen Testaments
HS	Hebrew Studies
ICC	International Critical Commentary
JANES	Journal of the Ancient Near Eastern Society
JBC	Jerome Biblical Commentary. Edited by R. E. Brown et al. Englewood Cliffs, 1968
NIB	New Interpreter's Bible
NICOT	New International Commentary on the Old Testament
NIDOTTE	New International Dictionary of Old Testament Theology and Exegesis. Edited by W. A. VanGemeren. 5 vols. Grand Rapids, 1997
OTL	Old Testament Library
SBLAIL	Society of Biblical Literature Ancient Israel and Its Literature
SBLSymS	SBL Symposium Series
SJSJ	Supplements to the Journal for the Study of Judaism
WBC	Word Biblical Commentary

Introduction to Proverbs

> For understanding proverbs and parables,
> the sayings and riddles of the wise. (Prov 1:6)

During a visit to a seaside village on the south coast of England, my wife and I were captivated by countless beautiful stones on the shore. We decided to collect some stones to make a small display in our home, reproducing our experience for friends and visitors. Conservationists, rest assured that the stones never made it home, but we still remember looking through what must have been thousands of brightly colored stones, each with some unique glint or curve that caught the eye. Proverbs are like seaside stones: from an ancient past, infinite in variety, and yet rarely seen in their original setting.

Readers will undoubtedly have read and considered a number of these proverbs and probably even have a habit of turning to some favorites on various occasions. The beauty of proverbs is that they can be contemplated one at a time like this.

But such casual study of individual proverbs can be shortsighted, both because it is apt to overlook the endless depth of each saying and also because the sayings take on a whole new life in the larger collection of thirty-one chapters—like stones on a shore. As biblical literary scholar Robert Alter notes, by looking at the whole of the book we are drawn into the rhythm of a "didactic and mnemonic neatness of smoothly matched statements clicking dutifully into place." And yet, despite our sense that "cultivated smoothness" seems to be the norm for sayings in Proverbs, we tend to overlook the unusual sayings.[1]

These uncommon and often contradictory sayings appear like knots in a smooth piece of wood. To a person admiring the wood, the knots add beauty. But when we try to work with this wood, the knots can get in our way and challenge our designs to shape it. Sometimes the knotted sayings in Proverbs reveal the rare wonder and beauty of life. At other times these knots force us to wrestle with problems that are not easily solved—much like life. To get wisdom one must wrangle seriously with all of these proverbial sayings as a collection.

---

1. Robert Alter, *The Art of Biblical Poetry* (New York: Basic Books, 1985), 164.

Composition, Transmission, and Canonicity

Authorship and Date

The date and authorship of Proverbs are uniquely difficult to tie down. We will consider authorship first. Proverbs is most naturally associated with Solomon, as his name appears in the introduction (1:1) and in the second (10:1) and fifth set of sayings (25:1). But other authors and collectors are listed as well (see 22:17; 24:23; 25:1; 30:1; 31:1), among whom only Hezekiah (25:1) is known to us from the Old Testament (2 Kgs 18:1).[2]

Furthermore, 223 of the sayings (24 percent of the book) are repeated exactly or as slightly modified variants. It seems less likely that a single author like Solomon would write with such redundancy than that an editor or editors would use these variant sayings both in an effort to add structural markers to the book and as a way of fitting familiar sayings into a variety of loosely related contexts.[3] Many of these sayings, especially in Proverbs 22:17–24:34, have close or nearly identical parallels in Egyptian and other forms of ancient wisdom writings, which at least suggests that no one person formulated all of these sayings on his own.

Related to this, Longman points out that individual authors do not "typically" write out lists of proverbs; most proverbs originate in public life and then are collected to preserve them for the future.[4] There are some modern examples of sayings written by single authors, such as Francis Bacon, Benjamin Franklin, and François de La Rouchfoucauld.[5] But none of these collections is anything like Proverbs in relation to its sheer size and its repetition of hundreds of sayings.

Furthermore, in Waltke's arguments for Solomonic authorship he is only able to show that Solomon *could* have written or collected the sayings in chapters 1–24, not that he did.[6] The name Solomon most likely serves an honorific purpose, just as Moses does for the Pentateuch and David for the Psalms (half of which are explicitly written by other authors). Though it is not a convention we recognize today, the ancient world naturally associated books with key authority figures, usually kings, in order to emphasize their

---

2. Proverbs 25:1 lists "the men of Hezekiah" who collected proverbs of Solomon.

3. For an in-depth study of repeated sayings see Knut Heim, *Poetic Imagination in Proverbs: Variant Repetition and the Nature of Poetry*, BBRS 4 (Winona Lake, IN: Eisenbrauns, 2013).

4. Tremper Longman III, *Proverbs*, BCOTWP (Grand Rapids: Baker Academic, 2006), 24.

5. François, duc de La Rochefoucauld, *Maxims of La Rochefoucauld*, trans. John Heard Jr.; 1917 (Mineola, NY: Dover, 2006).

6. Though I think he fails to address adequately why this is so important or other problems concerning Solomonic authorship addressed in other commentaries. See Bruce K. Waltke, *The Book of Proverbs: Chapters 1–15*, NICOT (Grand Rapids: Eerdmans, 2004), 31–37.

authoritative status. This is somewhat like our associating a television program with the central actor or character. Waltke helpfully observes that the book of Ecclesiastes is associated with a "Solomon-like figure" for honorific reasons even though the author very clearly avoids naming Solomon.[7] See the commentary on Proverbs 1:1–7 for further discussion of authorship.

As a final note, upon closer inspection we should notice that Solomon is less of a grand author of wisdom in Proverbs than a kind of literary character who had much wisdom and yet failed to live up to the instructions that bear his name. See Reading in the Context of the Old Testament (pp. 39–46).

Second, as should be clear from the discussion of authorship, the dating of these 915 sayings is nearly impossible to tie down, particularly if we are interested in the birth of a particular saying. We discuss the nature of a proverb in more detail under Title and Canonicity (p. 22) and Genre (pp. 23–29) and the commentary at 1:1–7, but we should pause to address the matters of dating related to the structure of Proverbs. That is, the book makes several strong breaks or transitions at 10:1, 25:1, 30:1, and 31:1. The content in chapters 1–9 and 31 also differs significantly from the material in the middle.

The majority scholarly view tends to view the longer poems in Proverbs 1–9 and 31 as "late" wisdom, during what these scholars regard as Israel's monotheistic worship of Yahweh. Assuming Israel became monotheistic as they suppose, this would explain the placement of the majority of the "fear of the LORD" sayings in those chapters. Some scholars also believe that "Yahweh sayings" were then added to parts of chapters 10–29 to make older, secular wisdom fit more neatly within the theological framework of the later material. The late/early wisdom hypothesis still exists in a few circles today, but an increasing number of scholars recognize the great difficulty in dating individual sayings and the weak foundations for assuming that chapters 10–29 arose somewhere in Israel's secular or polytheistic pre-history. We simply have to conclude that we do not know how or when this book came together. But as we will see throughout the commentary, the final editors were very careful to bring unity to the whole and situate the book within Israel's sacred history.

Occasion for Writing

The social origin of these sayings is another of Proverbs' great mysteries. Owing to the nature of a proverb as a "saying current among the folk,"[8] proverbs are in the class of rumors, jokes, and folktales that make their way into

---

7. Ibid., 35.
8. As described by the great folklore scholar Archer Taylor, *The Proverb* (Cambridge: Harvard University Press, 1931), 3.

cultural popularity without anyone knowing when or how. We still need to address several issues related to their being included in the Old Testament.

The first is the matter of schools. We know that schools existed in ancient Egypt and Ugarit and that Israel most likely had some interchange with these cultures and their folklore and literature.[9] But the evidence we have for schools in those cultures cannot be found in Israel's earliest literature and archaeology. It could be that schools were so common that they did not deserve mentioning. But this is unlikely. We also know that when schools did arise in Israel's Second Temple period, "sons" and "fathers" were used to name pupils and their teachers or rabbis. There also seems to be an indication that sages or "wise men" had become a distinct social class by Israel's late monarchy (cf. Isa 19:12; 29:14; 44:24; Jer 8:9; 18:18; 50:35; 51:57). Interesting as these facts may be, they do not show that Proverbs was created within or for schools.

We must also consider whether these sayings were first gathered for use in royal courts to train young men in line for the throne or if they were collected for parents to teach to children at home. The evidence for a royal setting can be seen in the collections of royal sayings in chapters 16 and 25–29, especially the superscription in 25:1, "These are more proverbs of Solomon, compiled by the men of Hezekiah king of Judah." But the sayings in 1:8, 2:1, 4:8, 6:20, etc. may indicate a home setting. While that may be true, we cannot rule out the possibility that this was a royal home. Furthermore, any of the sayings could obviously have been used in both settings, though we can say little more than that.

A final point of interest concerns orality and literacy. Most of these sayings arose in spoken contexts, whether in the home, the marketplace, the craft-maker's shop, the battlefield, or royal and judicial courts. But eventually these sayings were written and collected in the form we have in Proverbs; we no longer have access to this speech in its living performance. Van Leeuwen's concluding thoughts on this are worth bearing in mind as one reads the book.

> It is likely that differing social groups produced and made use of originally independent sections and that the final author-editors collected, augmented, and edited the parts to provide a complex and diverse compendium of wisdom. One group learns from another, borrowing and adapting its wisdom for its own ends. This is entirely in keeping with the amazing mobility of proverbial wisdom.[10]

---

9. I rely here on James L. Crenshaw, *Education in Ancient Israel: Across the Deadening Silence*, ABRL (New York: Doubleday, 1998), 85–113.

10. Raymond C. Van Leeuwen, *The Book of Proverbs*, NIB 5 (Nashville: Abingdon, 1997), 22–23.

While there may be a limit to what we can say about the origin of these sayings in one sense, it should spark our interest in the very beauty, intricacy, and philosophical and theological complexity of the collection as a whole. We expand on the nature of the collection under Genre (pp. 23–29) and Theological Message (pp. 33–39).

Textual Witnesses

This commentary relies primarily on the Masoretic Text (MT) represented by the Leningrad Codex (AD 1008). I will also occasionally refer to the Septuagint (LXX) and only rarely to the Targum, Syriac, and Dead Sea Scrolls manuscripts.

A little more should be said about the LXX (second century BC) and its relationship to the MT. The LXX is obviously a much older text, but it is based on an even older Hebrew text that provides the basis for the MT. In their versions of Proverbs, the MT and LXX have a number of sayings unique to them. In fact, the LXX is 130 lines longer, largely because it adds sayings to bring clarity where the Hebrew is too ambiguous or too difficult for the translators (cf. 1:15; 3:3; 8:5; 28; 9:1, 11; 10:10; 13:15; 18:19; 23:27; 25:7; 28:23; 31:16, 17).

The LXX also changes the order of sayings in the MT a few times between 1:1–24:22 and fairly radically between 24:23–31:31, as chapters 30:1–31:11 in the MT and English translations have been broken up and inserted at various points between chapters 25–29, yielding the following order: 24:1–22; 30:1–14; 24:23–34; 30:15–33; 31:1–9; chapters 25–29; 31:10–31. The reasons for these major changes in order have been debated, with some scholars believing it is a minor issue and others that it is evidence of heavy-handed exegesis by the LXX.[11] On this point, notice that the LXX has removed the superscription to Agur in 30:1 and placed the text next to the Solomonic section ending at 24:22 and changed "Lemuel" in 31:1 to "from God." Dropping these two names shows that the LXX has an interest in preserving Solomonic authorship, since Agur and Lemuel were both unknown and maybe even foreigners. Furthermore, as Clifford has observed, the nature of the loose translation in the LXX owes to the translator's discomfort with the short, pithy, and often intentionally ambiguous language in the Hebrew.[12] Sadly, the same is true of most English translations.

---

11. I refer the reader to longer discussions in Michael V. Fox, *Proverbs 1–9: A New Translation with Introduction and Commentary*, AB 18A (New York: Doubleday, 2000), 360–66, and Waltke, *Proverbs 1–15*, 1–8.

12. Richard J. Clifford, *Proverbs: A Commentary*, OTL (Louisville: Westminster John Knox, 1999), 29.

Title and Canonicity

The title *mishle*, "Proverbs," comes from *mashal*, which describes a number of sayings in the Old Testament, such as riddles, parables, and aphorisms. See more in Genre (pp. 23–29) and the commentary at 1:1–7.

A few medieval rabbis questioned the canonicity of Proverbs based upon its supposed secular origins and the unsettling contradiction in 26:4–5. Aside from these rare cases, most of Jewish tradition in the MT and LXX as well as the early church received Proverbs as a part of the canon.

Our English Bibles follow the order of books in the LXX: Job, Psalms, Proverbs, Ecclesiastes, Song of Songs, etc. In the Hebrew Bible (HB) Proverbs falls into the last of three divisions: law, prophets, and writings, alongside Ruth, Lamentations, Daniel, and others. As can be seen in the table below, the books appear in a different order.

English	Hebrew Bible (The Writings)	
Job	Psalms	
Psalms	Job	Distinct Poetry
Proverbs	Proverbs	
Ecclesiasts	Ruth	
Song of Songs	Song of Songs	
Isaiah	Ecclesiastes	Megillot
etc.	Lamentations	
	Esther	

Longman points out that the Masoretes added special accents to the first three books of the writings—Psalms, Job, and Proverbs—most likely because they read these books as poetry.[13] Among these, the poetry of Proverbs is one of a kind.

After Proverbs, Ruth is the first of the five books known as the Megillot (scrolls), which were read sequentially at the annual Jewish festivals. As I discuss in the commentary on Proverbs 31, Ruth has a great deal in common with the valiant woman, which makes the juxtaposition of these two books all the more significant.

---

13. Longman, *Proverbs*, 23.

Literary Analysis

Genre
What Is a Proverb?

> A proverb is wise; it belongs to many people; it is ingenious in form and idea; and it was first invented by an individual and applied by him to a particular situation.[14]

All proverbs are wisdom, but not all wisdom is proverbial. The book of Proverbs is a unique genre in this light, as narratives can be historical, fictional, or didactic, for example, but the short sayings of proverbs are native to wisdom literature. That said, wisdom is also found in other types of poetry and narrative, as in Job and Psalms. In what follows, I will first discuss matters of proverbial style before turning to the genre of wisdom literature.

Robert Alter called proverbs the "poetry of wit," and Gerhard von Rad, "a sentence filled to the brim with ideas."[15] Earlier, I cited Archer Taylor's definition of a proverb as a "saying current among the folk."[16] Definitions can be helpful guides, but they inevitably fall short. We simply have to resolve that we know a proverb when we hear one: Live and learn; Enough is enough; No fool like an old fool; There is a time for everything; and Don't count your chickens before they hatch. New proverbs emerge everyday: Just believe; Money Talks; Money doesn't grow on trees; Just do it; and Life is like a box of chocolates.

We learn a great deal about proverbs by looking at two sayings that are particularly well known. First, consider John F. Kennedy's famous line, "Ask not what your country can do for you, ask what you can do for your country."[17] This saying is nearly a perfect proverb pair that rings true when we hear it. But the origins of the saying are highly disputed and helpful for understanding how proverbs emerge.

The careful wording is typical of President Kennedy's distinguished speechwriter Ted Sorensen, so many believed he wrote it. And yet we also know that the headmaster at the Choate School, where Kennedy was educated, was known for the saying, "[it is] not what Choate does for you, but

---

14. Archer Taylor, "The Wisdom of Many and the Wit of One," in *The Wisdom of Many: Essays on the Proverb*, ed. Wolfgang Mieder and Alan Dundes (Madison, WI: University of Wisconsin Press, 1994), 3.

15. Alter, *Art of Biblical Poetry*, 163. Gerhard von Rad, *Wisdom in Israel*, trans. James D. Martin (London: SCM Press, 1972), 3.

16. Taylor, *The Proverb*, 3.

17. See Michael V. Fox, *Proverbs 10–31: A New Translation with Introduction and Commentary*, AB 18B (New Haven: Yale University Press, 2009), 492; Louis Menand, "Ask Not, Tell Not: Anatomy of an Inaugural," The New Yorker, November 8, 2004, http://www.newyorker.com/magazine/2004/11/08/ask-not-tell-not.

what you can do for Choate."[18] Now that has a ring of a proverb to it, but it was certainly not commonly known until Kennedy mimicked the famous line during his inauguration.

The interesting life of a proverb can also be found in the familiar phrase "seeing is believing," which demonstrates the modern privileging of sight above our other senses. The saying as we know it, however, has dropped the older parallel line, "but feeling's the truth."[19] The meaning of the longer saying is nearly opposite of the shorter one, coming close to the saying, "Don't judge a book by it's cover." Thus cultural factors, or foundations of one's worldview, also have a role in how sayings come to life. At the very least these sayings reveal that common ideas worded just right and spoken at the right time and circumstance simply *click*. And that is a proverb.

How Do Proverbs Work?

First, almost all of the sayings in Proverbs are recorded in parallel lines.

> When pride comes (A1), then comes disgrace (A2),
> but with humility (B1) comes wisdom (B2). (Prov 11:2)

The annotations above demonstrate the lines and their respective parallels. During the nineteenth and most of the twentieth centuries, it was generally believed that parallelism took one of three forms: synonymous, antithetical, or synthetic. But scholarship in recent decades has shown that the parallels are far more nuanced than first imagined. In fact, according to Knut Heim, uneven or disjointed proverbs are the norm in Proverbs, rather than the exception, leaving us with a broad spectrum of parallels between synonymous and antithetic.[20] Beneath these parallel structures, the sayings have a number of more specific forms that work in a variety of ways.

Type of Saying and Function	Examples
Poems—extended metaphors and outline of worldview	1–9; 30:1–33; 31:1–9, 10–31
Synonymous/semi-synonymous—opening up a concept, emphasizing significant similarities	1:8, 9, 20; 6:1, 2, 4, 17:4, 6; 18:3, 6, 7; 19:2, 5

18. Edward Wyatt, "Two Authors Ask About 'Ask Not,'" New York Times, May 10, 2005, http://www.nytimes.com/2005/05/10/books/two-authors-ask-about-ask-not.html?_r=0.

19. Alan Dundes, "Seeing is Believing," in *Interpreting Folklore* (Bloomington: Indiana University Press, 1980), 89.

20. Heim, *Poetic Imagination*, 642.

Type of Saying and Function	Examples
Antithetical—defining limits and world order	11:1–3 (most of chapters 10–15, 28)
Macarisms—vision, admonishment	3:13; 8:32, 34; 14:21; 16:20; 20:7; 28:14
Litotes—understatement for rhetorical effect	16:9, 29; 17:26; 19:2
Better-than—rhetorical and hermeneutical	15:16–17; 16:8; 17:1; 19:1
Reused or variants—structuring and forming cognitive patterns	12:14; 13:2; 18:20
Pairs—structuring and nuancing ideas	25:16–17
Clusters—structuring, poetry	16:1–9; 25
Numerical—lists as illustrations of broad reality, provocation to further thought	6:16–19; 30:18–31
Disjointed—hermeneutical problems and puzzles	13:5; 28:7; 29:5–6; 30:4, 15, 18–31

Each of these forms is discussed in the commentary.

Thinking of the structure of a proverb, experts known as paremiolgists often begin by describing proverbs as having a "topic" (T) and a "comment" (C). In the saying "money talks," "money" is the topic and "talks" is the comment. The essence of the comment is that money has power to effect change. But it is proverbial precisely because of its poetic form.

Topics and comments also form the structure of an admonition:

If your enemy is hungry, (T)
    give him food to eat. (C) (Prov 25:21a)

Most proverbs follow the order T-C, but on some occasions the order is reversed to comment-topic, usually for emphasis:

Like clouds (C1) and wind without rain (C2)
    is one who boasts of gifts never given. (T) (Prov 25:14)

In a desire to make the meaning more clear, English translations often "fix" these sayings by reversing them to the normal sentence order. Ironically, the opposite results, especially when a powerful and often violent metaphor loses its place at the beginning of the sentence (see ch. 25). What was once a riddle-like saying that prompted the imagination becomes a flat, rote observation.

Hebrew language is also unique in the way it can combine the subject, verb, and object into a single word. Many forms of a Hebrew word can also often be translated as a verb or a noun. Together, these features of Hebrew create punchy sayings that are often full of ambiguity. For example, a flat translation of Proverbs 20:10 reads:

> *Eben waeben; ephah, waephah* (stone and stone; measure and measure)
> Yahweh detests them both.

Most translations emend the first line to "Differing weights and differing measures," which seems to be the sense. But one of the points of a proverb is for the reader to work this meaning out rather than be fed it with a spoon. These simplified translations also obscure other poetic features, such as the parallel repetition only a few verses later:

> "It's no good, it's no good!" says the buyer. (20:14)

As I state under How to Read this Commentary (p. 46), I aim to give back to the reader the work of puzzling through the saying in its language and its meaning—to allow the proverb to *work* as wisdom in order to *yield* wisdom (1:6).

Noticing our human tendency to reduce poetry to more digestible forms of prose, the German philosopher Johann Georg Hamann commented, "This kind of translation, is, more than any other, like the underside of a carpet,

> And shews the stuff, but not the workman's skill;

or like an eclipse of the sun, which can be seen in a bowl of water."[21] Indeed, why substitute a "reflection for the sun in glory"?[22] Theologian Ben Quash echoes this same sentiment about the "provisional" nature of biblical texts, especially of poetry, that resist translation and "definitive interpretive closure."[23] The process of working through this contingency both requires and nurtures a "sapiential" skill—wisdom.[24]

---

21. J. G. Hamann, *Aesthetica in Nuce*, citing the poetry of Wentworth Earl of Roscommon in Ronald Gregor Smith, *J. G. Hamann 1730–1788: A Study in Christian Existence* (London: SCM Press, 1960), 198.

22. Douglas A. Templeton, *The New Testament as True Fiction: Literature, Literary Criticism, Aesthetics* (Sheffield: Sheffield Academic, 1999), 176.

23. Ben Quash, *Found Theology: History, Imagination, and the Holy Spirit* (London: Bloomsbury, 2013), xiv–xv.

24. Ibid., xvi.

Thus proverbs are not mere decoration meant to be decoded once and for all, but creative puzzles meant to engage speaker and hearer in an open and imaginative relationship. Roland Murphy similarly argues that proverbs often sound straightforward when they are not. "The reader is left to qualify it by other contexts, by exceptions, by experiences that run contrary to it . . . [the proverb] provides insight, not only by what is said, but by the process: the reader can be startled, and thus invited to go beyond the proverb itself."[25]

I would go even further to argue that the arrangement of 915 proverbs creates for the reader successive patterns of order, confusion, uncertainty, and recognition. What seems to be a random distribution of sayings actually serves to move us through a relatively limited number of themes, catchwords, and verbal sounds that are applied to an array of contexts that mimic the variety of experiences we meet in daily life. Each time we return to the familiar topics and catchwords, we find them displayed in a new context, which tests our ability to discern wisdom and order.[26] Each test develops the skills of discernment that we call wisdom. In fact, the more than 200 repeated proverbs serve the pedagogical purpose of reinforcement, steadying us amidst new and often challenging sayings in their contexts.

What Is Wisdom?

Wisdom is that essential tool needed to make our way in the world. Obviously, such a broad definition does little to narrow wisdom to a particular genre. And rightly so, for wisdom can be found in proverbs, stories, psalms, parables, riddles, and laments. So then, is not the whole Bible wisdom literature? Scholars have debated this question intensely over the last century, and we will not solve it here, but a few things merit discussion.[27]

Firstly, the label "wisdom literature" is a modern invention and would probably not be recognized by the original authors and early readers of the Bible. It is also true in this light that our divisions of prophecy and poetry in the Bible differ from the ancient Jewish culture that produced these books.

But, secondly, the fact is that the genres we find in any culture, including our own, are fluid categories and always changing. Sneed helpfully speaks to the tension we must live with when he says about wisdom literature,

---

25. Roland Murphy, *The Tree of Life: An Exploration of Biblical Wisdom Literature* (New York: Doubleday, 1990), 20.
26. See von Rad, *Wisdom in Israel*, 4.
27. See the important collection of essays edited by Mark R. Sneed, *Was There a Wisdom Tradition?*, SBL 23 (Atlanta: SBL Press, 2015).

Basically you know it when you see it! That should not perplex us. The conventions of this literature exist, but only as our minds detect the patterns. We cannot enter into the minds of the ancient authors and clearly and definitively detect these conventions. We might grasp the general features, but never the details. This means the boundaries can never be hard and fast and that there may be more than one way to configure them.[28]

In this way, wisdom literature is a helpful genre category for Job, Proverbs, and Ecclesiastes, as well as a few Psalms, all share a unique set of themes and vocabulary that we rarely find elsewhere in the Old Testament. For example, when we search for all of the occurrences of the words "wisdom," "insight," "knowledge," and "understanding" among the books of the Old Testament, we find an overwhelming density among the three "wisdom" books.[29] These books we call "wisdom" are also specifically concerned with the unique intersection of ways of knowing—epistemology and education; ways of living—ethics; and human nature—anthropology. So while the book of Esther, which is sometimes labeled a wisdom book, has a lot to say about wise conduct and unique insight into complex social matters, it is not explicitly concerned with knowledge, ethics, or anthropology as its subject matter. So we might call Esther a book full of wisdom but written more specifically in the genre of a novella or festival reading intended for cultural memory.[30] Psalm 1, meanwhile, which lacks the typical wisdom vocabulary, expresses the themes of "torah" (law) and walking in the ways of Yahweh, so scholars typically label it wisdom. Other books that sometimes attract the label "wisdom literature" include Song of Songs, Daniel, the Joseph story in Genesis, and the biblical laws in the Pentateuch. Each of these provides wisdom in the way they contribute to the tradition that guides the community to navigate life in God's world, but each also fits better into other recognized genres. We should reserve "wisdom literature" for those books to which no other label is more suitable.

Finally we should recognize that human cultures have always accumulated ideas and writings devoted to the meaning of the good life and how to live well. The very existence and diversity of wisdom literature is evidence

---

28. Mark R. Sneed, "'Grasping after the Wind': The Elusive Attempt to Define and Delimit Wisdom" in *Was There a Wisdom Tradition?*, 62–3.

29. For a more thorough discussion of biblical terms of knowing, see Ryan P. O'Dowd, *The Wisdom of Torah: Epistemology in Deuteronomy and the Wisdom Literature*, FRLANT (Göttingen: Vandenhoeck & Ruprecht, 2009).

30. See Michael V. Fox, *Character and Ideology in the Book of Esther*, 2nd ed. (Grand Rapids: Eerdmans, 2001), 142–52.

that wisdom does not come to us naturally and that its ideas are complex and debatable. To be wise, we need instruction, study, and apprenticeship in the midst of lived experiences. Each culture will produce its own wisdom based upon its own wisdom and worldview. As we will see in the comments under Theological Message (pp. 33–39), Israel's wisdom was uniquely ingrained in her religious devotion to Yahweh and his account of the world and its purpose.

Structure

Proverbs deliberately binds together freedom and form. This can first be seen in the macro-structure of the book: chapters 1–9 and 30–31. This outer frame of highly structured poems encloses the free collection of sayings inside, containing them in a worldview in which Yahweh is the creator of the world and author of wisdom.[31]

Second, within this structure human wisdom is pictured as a process of conforming our thoughts and actions to God's design for the world. Chapters 1–9 and 31 in particular portray the *eros* of wisdom as seen in the five women in these chapters. As we will see in 5:1–9:18, Woman Wisdom, Dame Folly, the wife, and the harlot (or strange woman) imagine wisdom tied to the seamless fabric of knowledge and desire. More than that, wisdom (and reason) in these chapters inevitably follows the path of the desires of the heart. In this light, all of the sayings in the book appear as threads in this fabric of wisdom. To know wisdom is to know the smallest part in its relation to the whole, not simply of the book, but of God's reality and human nature. Chapter 31 portrays Woman Wisdom in the concrete life of a woman. Not only is she desirable (31:10), but her works beautifully and dramatically embody the whole of wisdom in chapters 1–30.

We can also see in the structure below that chapters 1–9 present ten parental admonitions that frame the interludes addressing Woman Wisdom and Dame Folly. As a result, the parents' authority is joined to the authority of Woman Wisdom, who gains her expertise directly from the creator (8:1–36). The son (1:8) has every reason to trust these two sources of authority.

Part I: Proverbs	1:1–9:18	The Sayings and Admonitions
	1:1–7	Title and Prologue
	1:8–19	First Admonition: Warning Against Sinners

---

31. See Ryan P. O'Dowd, "Frame Narrative," in *Dictionary of the Old Testament: Wisdom, Poetry & Writings*, ed. Tremper Longman III and Peter Enns (Downers Grove, IL: IVP Academic, 2008), 241–45.

There is a rather intense debate as to how much structure and shaping exists in the sayings in chapters 10–29. On one side, Heim, Waltke, Meinhold, and, to a lesser degree, Murphy identify countless groups of clusters and poems of anywhere from three to ten sayings. They also find macro-structures that organize a whole chapter or more. Longman, Fox, and Clifford, meanwhile, tend to regard these structures and clusters of sayings as speculative. Indeed, there is a psychological phenomenon, known as pareidolia, where people find patterns and structures among things that are completely random. I discuss these issues briefly in the introduction to chapters 10–29 (pp. 175–79) and throughout each of the individual chapters as well.

I add a brief word here as to why I tend to side with the former scholars, grouping sayings when it seems reasonable to do so, whether or not the original author clearly intended to create these groupings. My motivation for doing this is driven by the nature of proverbs as collected *poetry*. Every saying, by virtue of its poetic nature, has a vagueness that can be taken in more than one way.[32] This results in multi-valency in which meaning is thick, straddled among several layers of depth.

There is a danger in pushing this vagueness to the point that we see structures everywhere, making Proverbs 10–29 look like a neat and tidy book. But there is also a danger in pressing the poetry out of the book in search of the scientific comforts of certainty and clarity, since it is not true to the genre. Art is distinct in the way it allows the viewer to experience meaning in the encounter with the artifact. To paraphrase David Foster Wallace's comments on narrative, one could argue that clusters and structures are "reactions to" or an individual's "take" on the poetry. But these reactions and takes *are* the poetry. The reader's life outside the poetry changes the poetry, whether we choose to admit to it or not.[33]

As a final thought, consider the present rise of reality television, where viewers rely on a panel of aesthetic experts to discern for the audience who are the best cooks, dancers, and singers. These judges do not provide lengthy arguments for their judgments. Rather they rely on the intuitive sense they have gained through being embedded in their field for so long.[34] They have the ears and eyes of a master—wisdom. In the end, proverbs are imaginative, poetic creations, full of beauty, wonder, and nuance. I seek to honor that in the chapters that follow.

---

32. As argued by Barbara Kirshenblatt-Gimblett, "Toward a Theory of Proverb Meaning," in *The Wisdom of Many: Essays on the Proverb*, ed. Wolfgang Mieder and Alan Dundes (Madison, WI: University of Wisconsin Press, 1994), 111–21.

33. See Larry McCaffery, "An Interview with David Foster Wallace," *The Review of Contemporary Fiction* 13 (Summer 1993): 141.

34. What Matthew B. Crawford calls a "tacit integration of sensual knowledge": *Shop Class as Soulcraft: An Inquiry into the Value of Work* (New York: Penguin, 2009), 172.

Historical Background

Historical Setting of the Contents of the Book

As we discussed in Authorship and Date (pp. 18–19), the historical setting of Proverbs is largely unknown, except to say that it arose, as in any human culture, in response to the need for counsel and guidance to live out our lives in this world. As von Rad has observed, our lives are so deeply embedded in this cultural wisdom of "practical experience" resident in our stories and traditions that we rarely recognize the way it shapes our beliefs and behavior.[35] Books like Proverbs are evidence that, within every culture, some people recognize the value of these sacred traditions and seek to capture and preserve them for future generations. Where the sayings originated and how this process of collection took place are still almost entirely a mystery to us.

Ancient Near Eastern Background

Despite the fact that we cannot tie down a specific date and occasion for Proverbs, we can still learn a great deal from Israel's neighbors in Mesopotamia and Egypt.[36] Both of these cultures produced a variety of wisdom texts that share many parallels with Job, Proverbs, and Ecclesiastes.

The most consistent parallel with Proverbs is the setting of these sayings in a father's writing to a son. Such preparation for adulthood is common in every human culture. Anthropologists call this a liminal stage, paralleling other major thresholds in human life—birth, adulthood, marriage, parenting, and death. Proverbs' liminal material is most prominent in chapters 1–9 where the young man is repeatedly presented with the choice of two paths, two women, and their two houses. See the commentary in 1:1–7.

Like Proverbs, other ancient wisdom literature works within a paradigm where God, king, humans, and creation exist in a common nexus. With God or the gods as creator in the heavens, the king represents the divine presence on earth and, as such, is the mediator of wisdom for the rest of humanity. Without the burdens of modern secular/sacred dualisms, ancient political life, ethical life, and religious life were thus seen to be part of the fabric of the created order.

This God-king-humanity paradigm is also at work in the metaphor of "house building."[37] Here the divine building of the house of creation "by

---

35. Von Rad, *Wisdom in Israel*, 3.

36. For a longer discussion of this topic, see Craig G. Bartholomew and Ryan P. O'Dowd, *Old Testament Wisdom Literature: A Theological Introduction* (Downers Grove, IL: IVP Academic, 2011), 32–46.

37. Raymond C. Van Leeuwen, "Cosmos, Temple, House: Building and Wisdom in Mesopotamia and Israel," in *Wisdom Literature in Mesopotamia and Israel*, SBL Sym 36, ed. Richard J. Clifford (Atlanta: Society of Biblical Literature, 2007), 67–90.

wisdom" and "by knowledge" (3:19–20) establishes the foundation for us to build our own houses (human lives) "by wisdom" and "by knowledge" (24:3–4). Once again the sacred is present in the mundane or secular by way of wisdom.

One major question that stymies scholars is the degree to which cultures influenced one another. It does seem to us from 1 Kings 4:29–30 that Israel at least knew of other wisdom traditions. But the ideas and themes in wisdom are so common that it is almost impossible to suggest an influence. As Roland Murphy wisely observes, "instruction is a mode of communication that hardly needs a foreign model."[38] Waltke goes even further in saying that the fear of Yahweh makes the distinctive point that this wisdom is not from foreign cultures, but the one true God, parallels aside.[39] This is significant because Egypt in particular had a much stronger confidence in human wisdom and specifically in its dependence on *Maat*, usually thought of as a goddess associated with wisdom, truth, order, and justice. Israel, by contrast, faced the world full of uncertainties and doubts, which continually reinforced reliance on Yahweh, who alone held knowledge and control of the creation.[40] Von Rad claims that "Israel was obliged to remain open, in a much more intensive way, to the category of the mysterious."[41] It is altogether possible that Woman Wisdom was intentionally created as a contrast to the idea of *Maat* and the human self-confidence in Egypt's later wisdom tradition.

Theological Message

Michael Fox claims that Proverbs is "clearly a secular work. It makes no pretense to an origin in divine revelation or inspiration."[42] Fox is correct that God never speaks in Proverbs, but it's not clear that this is all that relevant to the question of whether Proverbs is a theological work.

There is an error in confusing what we know about the life circumstances and cultural origins of proverbial sayings with the book's self-presentation of wisdom in the context of the Old Testament. For one, Proverbs is represented as the wisdom of Solomon (1:1; 10:1), which he received *from God* in response to his request in prayer (cf. 1 Kgs 4:29–32). The editors of Proverbs also carefully frame the book with the motto "the fear of the LORD is the beginning of wisdom" (9:10; cf. 1:7; 31:10), setting the entry point for Israel's

38. Roland E. Murphy, *Proverbs*, WBC 22 (Nashville: Thomas Nelson, 1998), xxii.
39. Waltke, *Proverbs 1–15*, 52.
40. See von Rad, *Wisdom in Israel*, 72.
41. Ibid., 73.
42. Fox, *Proverbs 1–9*, 7.

pursuit of knowledge. Waltke here is on firmer ground in rejecting the idea of proverbs as simply "humanistic" and secular in content and claiming that it "anchors its teachings in 'the fear of the Lord' . . . not in humanity."[43] Oddly, where Fox and others who share his opinion are keen to keep the secular and sacred distinct, Proverbs labors to hold them together, a point emphasized throughout the commentary.

Theology of the Book

Wisdom combines the perspectives of a narrative of a journey and an overall map of the territory covered. This relates the particular human life to the universal framework of God's word.

In the moment of knowing not to touch a hot stove, wisdom seems simple, much like typing a key and watching a letter appear on the computer screen. But when we look beneath the surface we discover that wisdom turns out to be far from simple. Wisdom depends upon a number of fundamental assumptions and the complex inner-workings of the world and our relationship to that world. In what follows, I outline four major epistemological foundations of proverbial wisdom and five tenets that flow from them.

The Major Foundations

1. Wisdom begins with "the fear of the LORD" (1:7; 2:5; 9:10; 31:30). Gerhard von Rad says that "the fear of Yahweh" is "the prerequisite of wisdom and trains man for it. . . . [It] contains in a nutshell the whole Israelite theory of knowledge."[44] Von Rad is making far more than a simple doctrinal affirmation about religion and wisdom. To fear Yahweh means to orient one's whole life, thought, desire, action, speech, and measure of value around the designs and orders of the God who created the world, who redeemed Israel, who gave them the law, and who is redeeming them from their corruption in sin (Ps 111:9–10). What it means to live life in the fear of Yahweh cannot be answered in any simple way; the whole book of 915 sayings is oriented to that task.

2. Wisdom is grounded in tradition, both that of the parents (1:8; 2:1; 6:20, etc.) and cosmic Woman Wisdom, who gets her knowledge from Yahweh (1:20; 8:1; 9:1–12). As we saw in the discussion on Structure (pp. 29–31), these two sources of authority are interwoven, giving the son two witnesses or testimonies, the one practical and momentary and the other theological and trans-temporal.

---

43. Waltke, *Proverbs 1–15*, 51. See Waltke's extensive theological reflection on pp. 50–55, 78–133.
44. Von Rad, *Wisdom in Israel*, 67.

We live in an age when it is common to believe that our knowledge comes to us through objective, individual, private thought—an outworking of Enlightenment Deism. Technology only reinforces the image that our minds operate like computers processing digital data. But actual knowing isn't anything like this. Everything we know comes through the filters of tradition and authority. In other words, anytime we learn some behavior or take something to be true, we are simply conforming ourselves to some standard of authority whether for the process we learn or the measure truth that grounds our understanding. We need not, and usually do not, recognize these sources of authority or tradition as we come to know things.

The philosopher of hermeneutics Hans Gadamer once observed that the "fundamental prejudice of the enlightenment [sic] is the prejudice against prejudice itself, which deprives tradition of its power."[45] Gadamer exposes the anti-tradition Enlightenment epistemology as just another tradition with its own prejudices. The question in the human pursuit of truth and wisdom, therefore, is which tradition will lead the way. See Tradition in Live the Story in chapter 8 (pp. 112–14).

3. Wisdom discerns the whole in relation to its individual parts. Popular cultural understandings of knowledge are often expressed in terms of content where expertise is equated with exhaustive information. But wisdom is based on the recognition that even exhaustive data is inadequate, for it is the relationships between the things that make knowledge most useful. In contrast to content, wisdom is the skill of fitting things into the framework of the whole, the true details of which are infinite.

The very point of knitting parental wisdom together with the cosmic speeches in Proverbs 1–9 is to situate the particular knowledge of human experience within the cosmic order of God's creation. We also see in the parallels between God's way of building the creation (3:19–20) and human ways of building houses (24:3–4) that this relational or ordering knowledge is central to wisdom. This order is *the key* to wisdom. Such wisdom knows little of trivia, and even less of random facts, and far more about the architecture and purpose of the world around us that allows us to solve the puzzles and dilemmas that make up day-to-day life.

4. As a perfect complement to the sense of the whole in Proverbs, the book imagines human life as a journey. Proverbs 1–9 (2–4 in particular)

---

45. Hans-Georg Gadamer, *Truth and Method*, 2nd ed., (New York: Crossroad, 1985), 239–40.

continually appeal to the young man to travel the "path," "road," and "way" to Wisdom and her house rather than the "way," "path," and "road" that lead to the abode of Dame Folly and death. The "bipolarity" of this journey, as Van Leeuwen calls it, undergirds a worldview that believes that God made the world with moral and religious boundaries or limits.[46] As noted above, anthropologists describe such boundaries as liminals where rights of passage and thresholds act as symbols within a worldview that guides a society along its common journey through life.

These epistemological foundations are supported by five tenets of biblical wisdom.

1. Wisdom as mastery of a craft or trade, often as a "spirit of wisdom." This is the sense of wisdom that describes those with refined skills who construct the tabernacle (Exod 28:3; 31:6; 35:25–26; 36:1–2), those in trading (Ezek 28:4), wailing women (Jer 9:17), and sailors (Ezek 27:8–9), as well as those who don't "know Yahweh" and are "skilled in doing evil" (Jer 4:22). The Valiant Woman of Proverbs 31:10–31 is the archetype of wisdom as skill. The chapter shows her expertise in as many as sixteen different activities, most of them with her hands.

2. Wisdom as a skill of discernment. The ancient virtue tradition that started with Aristotle expanded considerably throughout the Middle Ages. Discernment was the skill or virtue known as *prudentia* (Latin) or *phronēsis* (Greek), which was one of the capital intellectual virtues that described the ability to solve problems. Joseph and Daniel are singled out for having discernment of this kind, both knowing how to navigate tricky social and political dilemmas and how to avoid temptations to act immorally. Solomon's skill in deciding the case with the two harlots (1 Kgs 3:16–28) may be described just as much by prudence as justice (see commentary in 4:1–27 and 8:1–36).

    But how does one get discernment? Jacque Maritain rightly points out that *prudentia*, like any virtue, plants its roots in a storied world that gives us a picture of a *telos* or end of things. Prudential decision making is not just a matter of solving puzzles, but choosing between alternatives based upon knowledge of the ultimate purpose of things, whether people, cities, foods, art, marriage, education, markets, etc.[47] To quote Alasdaire MacIntyre, "I can only answer the question 'What

---

46. Raymond C. Van Leeuwen, "Liminality and Worldview in Proverbs 1–9," *Semeia* 50 (1990), 116–17.

47. Jacques Maritain, *Education at the Crossroads* (New Haven: Yale University Press, 1943), 22.

am I to do?' if I can answer the prior question, 'Of what stories do I find myself a part?'"[48]

3. Wisdom as virtue and self-mastery of passions and desires. This commentary continually addresses the central role of love and passions (1:8–19; 3:13–20; 3:21–35; 4:6; 5:15–20; 6:20–7:27; 8:17; 9:1–18; 19:1–29) as well as virtue and vice (23:1–35; 24:1–34). Scholars of Proverbs disagree about the relationship between the concrete women (the wife and adulteress) and cosmic women in Proverbs 1–9. Much of this debate gets off track from the start because of its failure to address the social and anthropological nature of human learning alongside the poetic imagery.

   Holding Proverbs next to Genesis 2 helps explain the point here. A very literal translation of Genesis 2:16–17 yields the following: "Of every tree of the garden, eat, eat! but of the tree of the knowledge of good and evil do not eat, for in the day that you eat of it you will die die."[49] After Adam names all the living animals, God forms Eve out of Adam's rib. Upon seeing the woman, Adam announces, "bone of my bone, flesh of my flesh." Taking note of the unambiguous repetition of these terms "eat," "die," "bone," and "flesh," Genesis ties human knowledge to human passion and virtue. God freely gives food and sexual experiences for human enjoyment, but he gives these gifts with limits that are set for our good: *all* fruit of the trees, but *not* this one; *this* woman and *not* any of the other creatures. With this background, it should be no surprise that wisdom, grounded as it is in virtues, habits, and control of one's passions, is the object of our love and learning and the path to a "tree of life" (Prov 3:18).

4. Wisdom as justice. In the opening words of Proverbs wisdom is, among other things, for "righteousness, justice, and equity."[50] Proverbs frequently weaves together sayings about the justice of Yahweh, the king, and the individual (16:1–33; 20:1–30; 21:1–31; 28:1–28; cf. Gen 18:19; Ps 119:121). This woven fabric reinforces what was said above regarding the connection between God's cosmic ordering of creation and the order within the particularities of daily life. The moral order of the world is not some subjective construction of human beings to keep the peace; it is as firm and certain as the mountains and the seas.

---

48. Alasdaire MacIntyre, *After Virtue: A Study in Moral Theory*, 2nd ed. (Notre Dame: University of Notre Dame Press, 1984), 216.

49. My translation.

50. My translation.

Proverbs is in no way naïve to the fact that the world is full of inequality and unmerited suffering. Van Leeuwen carefully analyzes the variety of sayings as they relate within a system of "character-consequence."[51] The majority of the sayings embody the positive form of "good leads to good and bad to bad."[52] But interlaced within these sayings are dozens of other sayings that observe contradictions where the righteous suffer, fools rule, and the hard worker loses his wealth to natural calamity and theft. Proverbs kindly affirms our sense that our faith will often run counter to reality. Being wise may not yield all that we hope. At the same time, Proverbs strongly affirms Yahweh's justice and power, leaving us with a sense that inequalities and injustices will be righted in the end (cf. 16:1–33; 21:1–31; 27:1–28:28; 29:26).

5. Wisdom as wonder. The scientific age has in many ways catapulted humanity into the great misconception that everything can be known—that there are no limits to our knowledge, moral or other-wise. Scientists of course know that science is often wrong (such is the very lifeblood of new scientific research) and that science hits limits that it cannot surpass. But our cultural training pushes us forward.

Wisdom literature by contrast trains us to have patience and pause at moments of moral uncertainty. The story of Job takes us face to face with the limits of human understanding of God, of nature, and of divine justice: "Surely I spoke of things I did not understand, things too wonderful for me to know." (Job 42:3; cf. 28:1–28; 38:1–42:6). The *locus classicus* of wonder in the Old Testament is Agur's oracle in Proverbs 30.

> [2] Surely I am only a brute, not a man;
>   I do not have human understanding.
> [3] I have not learned wisdom,
>   nor have I attained to the knowledge of the Holy One.
>   (Prov 30:2–3)

Agur begins by confessing his status as a creature and the limits of his learning. He goes on to cite lists of mystery and wonder that quiet our hubris and add virtue to our thirsty pursue of knowledge.

Something should be said here about Proverbs, religion, and the narrative of redemption. Many if not most scholars believe that Proverbs has little or

---

51. Raymond C. Van Leeuwen, "Wealth and Poverty: System and Contradiction in Proverbs," *HS* 33 (1992): 25–36.
52. Ibid., 28.

nothing to say about Israel's covenants, temple life, or God's redemptive work for Israel and the rest of creation. This is only true to a point, as Proverbs almost exclusively uses God's covenant (redemptive) name Yahweh rather than Elohim. Proverbs is also fully in touch with the story of creation and the fall into human rebellion and division as told in Genesis. As Yoram Hazony has said of all the poetic books, "one is hard-pressed to find any of them . . . that do not, once placed within the orbit of the History, speak to issues that are central to the teaching of the great historical narrative."[53]

Proverbs speaks into this world of creation and vulnerable human societies with a combination of honest words to help us get along with life and distinct visions of hope for the future (3:12–20; 8:1–36; 31:10–31). Life might be hard, but wisdom allows us to see that the problems we face day-to-day do not rule our deeper realities. The book instills deep trust and confidence in the creator and the goodness and durability of his creation, whatever it may look like to us in the moment (cf. Pss 37; 73). How else could wisdom lead to a tree of life (3:18), imagine creation as good and worthy of dancing delight (8:30–31), and make a woman laugh at the future (31:25)?

Finally, the notion of paths and journeys demands the cohesive power of story—of past, present, and future. Otherwise, a life of wisdom would be meaningless and hopeless. As Jonathan Wilson observes, "The closest we come to the virtue tradition in the OT is the wisdom literature, especially Proverbs. In passages such as Prov 2:1–11, we can see the telos, practices, community, and narrative of God's redeeming work."[54]

Reading in the Context of the Old Testament

Wisdom and Creation

We have already briefly mentioned the role of wisdom in God's creation of the world. "Wisdom" here is not merely an inert adjective. Rather it speaks to the pattern by which God creates three realms in days 1–3 and then fills them with their appropriate form of life in days 4–6. These patterns of filling and fittingness are drawn out in the hymn of God's care for the variety of spheres of creation in Psalm 104. The song rejoices, "How many are your works, O Yahweh! In wisdom you made them all; the earth is *full* of your creatures" (v. 24, author's translation).

---

53. Yoram Hazony, *The Philosophy of Hebrew Scripture* (Cambridge: Cambridge University Press, 2012), 42.

54. Jonathan R. Wilson, "Virtue(s)," in *Dictionary of Scripture and Ethics*, ed. Joel B. Green et al. (Grand Rapids: Baker Academic, 2011), 813.

The connection between building and filling the creation through wisdom informs God's instructions for the construction of the tabernacle in Exodus 31–36. The tabernacle will stand as a sign of God's redemption of Israel through the great movement of waters over land, echoing Genesis 1, and bring Israel into a new creation. The craftspeople are specifically skilled with "wisdom," a "heart of wisdom," or a "spirit of wisdom, understanding, and knowledge" to carry out their work (Exod 28:3; 31:3, 6; 35:25, 31, 35; 36:1–2). When the work was done, "the glory of the LORD *filled* the tabernacle" (Exod 40:34, emphasis added).

Wisdom and Law

During the upheavals in biblical studies in the nineteenth and twentieth centuries, wisdom was largely set aside as scholars struggled to relate it to Israel's covenants and history of redemption. One exception was the German scholar Franz Delitzsch (1830–1890), who argued that there were many echoes or affinities between Proverbs and Deuteronomy. Delitzsch's theory was largely dismissed in order to support a hypothetical social history of Israel's evolution that imagined law as an older institution that fell away only to be replaced by the more international and less religiously flavored wisdom literature. One problem with this theory is that we have little historical evidence to support the hypothesis. Another problem is that wisdom and torah come to be equated in Israel's Second Temple period.[55] Such a social reconstruction is dubious and motivated by deeper ideological agendas. As we will see in the commentary in 3:1–12 and chapters 28:1–28 and 30:1–33, many recent scholars have turned back to Deuteronomy and Proverbs and the law more generally to argue that law and wisdom are not as opposed as was once believed.[56]

The sermons in Deuteronomy clearly imagine law and wisdom working in harmony:

> [5] See, I have taught you decrees and laws as the LORD my God commanded me, so that you may follow them in the land you are entering to take possession of it. [6] Observe them carefully, for this will show your wisdom and understanding to the nations, who will hear about all these decrees and say, "Surely this great nation is a wise and understanding people." [7] What other nation is so great as to have their gods near them the way the LORD our God is near us whenever we pray to him? [8] And what

---

55. See Bernd U. Schipper and D. Andrew Teeter, *Wisdom and Torah: The Reception of 'Torah' in the Wisdom Literature of the Second Temple Period*, SJSJ 163 (Leiden: Brill, 2013).

56. Cf. Bernd U. Schipper, *Hermeneutik der Tora: Studien zur Traditionsgeschichte von Prov 2 und zur Komposition von Prov 1–9*, BZAW 432 (Berlin: de Gruyter, 2012).

other nation is so great as to have such righteous decrees and laws as this body of laws I am setting before you today? (Deut 4:5–8)

I argue throughout this commentary that wisdom provides insight into the created and moral order of God's world, so it makes perfect sense for it to give way to just laws. If Israel had actually obeyed the law, it would have been clear to the nations that this way of ordering society surpassed their own stories and law codes. Indeed, Deuteronomy has a uniquely humanitarian character to it.

The psalmist confirms that Israel's laws provide wisdom and insight that surpass the insights of others:

⁹⁷ Oh, how I love your law!
   I meditate on it all day long.
⁹⁸ Your commands are always with me
   and make me wiser than my enemies.
⁹⁹ I have more insight than all my teachers,
   for I meditate on your statutes.
¹⁰⁰ I have more understanding than the elders,
   for I obey your precepts. (Ps 119:97–100)

Surely Solomon's reign is one example of a time when wisdom and law attract the interest of surrounding nations. Solomon spoke proverbs (1:1; 10:1; 25:1; 1 Kgs 4:32), built houses by wisdom (24:3–4, cf. 3:19, 1 Kgs 7:14; 10:4), and ruled the people justly (1:3; 1 Kgs 3:16–28).

But Solomon's story has another side as well. In Proverbs the fear of Yahweh is the beginning of wisdom (1:7; 9;10), yet Solomon turned to foreign gods, built altars, and offered pagan sacrifices (1 Kgs 11:1–7). Furthermore, Solomon, who addresses his own son in Proverbs (1:1, 8), clearly failed to listen to his father David, who pleaded with Solomon to follow Yahweh and keep all the laws of Moses (1 Kgs 2:1–4). David's advice is alluded to in Proverbs 4:4.

Solomon also amassed silver and gold (1 Kgs 10:25), violating the Mosaic law (Deut 17:17). Silver and gold show up in Proverbs as inferior to, and in competition with, getting wisdom (3:14; 8:10, 19). Solomon's many wives, another violation of the Mosiac law (Deut 17:17), also turn his heart away from following Yahweh. More significantly, the strange woman, the adulteress, and Dame Folly, like Solomon's wives, are competitors and opponents of both wisdom and Woman Wisdom (2:16–19; 5:1–23; 6:20–35; 7:6–27; 9:1–18)—a biting critique of Solomon's sexual and religious license. In fact, Solomon's love for his foreign wives (1 Kgs 11:2) should have been devoted first to wisdom and to his own wife (4:6; 5:15–19). Also note that the term for "forced labor" (*mas*) in 12:24 is the same word used to describe Solomon's unjust rule over the Israelites some five times in Kings and two in Chronicles (1 Kgs 5:27, 28; 9:15, 21; 2 Chr 8:8), far more than anywhere in the Old Testament.

Wisdom in Crisis

Proverbs is not the only wisdom book. Job and Ecclesiastes also address the intersection of knowledge, ethics, and all the mundane activities of life in the world. The crises in these latter books do not react to the worldview in Proverbs so much as narrow and enhance the more idealistic message of Proverbs. For, as we observed above, Proverbs has a robust view of character and consequence; its world is full of exceptions to the character-consequence relationship, places where the righteous and wise suffer and the wicked and foolish prosper. Chapter 30 makes this point most emphatically. Job and Ecclesiastes react more strongly to the challenges of life in a fallen world.

Job depicts the ultimate example of injustice, a man who "was blameless and upright . . . feared God and shunned evil" (Job 1:1; 2:3; 42:7). And yet Job is tested by God for reasons that are never fully explained. The book is an excellent case for theodicy: How can a good and loving God not only permit, but invite, evil (1:8; 2:3)? Where we might expect the book to respond to this question with a rational justification, Job instead provides a guide for our human response, inviting us to argue with God in prayer. This does not mean that all prayers and arguments are valid; indeed, Job's prayers consistently wrestle with his bleak situation and his faith in God's goodness and sovereignty, and they (the prayers) lead to the appropriate response when his understanding reaches its limits.

God's answer to Job resembles Proverbs 30 and Psalms 37 and 73. Using more than eighty descriptive questions, God demonstrates his power and his design in the creation. These questions manifest God's control and order among those things that would be the most untamed to Job: wild animals, cosmic beasts, and the destructive power of natural calamities. Job is not only reminded in the end that he is not the creator and that there are limits to his knowledge (28:1–18; 42:1–6) but also that the creator acts as a father and mother in giving care and homes to the wildest parts of nature (38:8–9, 19–21, 28–29; 39:5–6, 19, 27–28; 40:15).

Whereas Proverbs most often celebrates the goodness of life, especially chapters 8 and 31:10–31, Ecclesiastes draws out the things that most make human life a burden and a scourge: old age, death, the toil of daily work, the limits of and illusiveness of wisdom, the sense of circularity and lack of progress, the fading of memory, the absence of hope, and the futility of loneliness.

It is common to read Ecclesiastes as a reaction to the optimism in Proverbs. But a few points must be remembered. First, despite clear differences in emphasis and tone, both books have a mixture of optimism, realism, and pessimism. Second, Ecclesiastes takes the reader on a wild journey but ends with the confession that the "conclusion of the matter [is] fear God and keep his commandments" (12:13). The book does not hold back in its expressions of suspicion and despair, but its lament is chiefly aimed at the human condition and its limited understanding of the world, and it refuses to abandon the foundations of wisdom in Proverbs.

Third, what the main speaker Qohelet says in his speeches is not what he always commends for others, or even necessarily what he believes to be true in his own mind. His rhetoric presses against his own pessimism in a way that he can show empathy with the despair and pessimism of the reader but also expose the fault lines of pessimism and narrow humanistic reasoning. Consider two examples of the ironic rhetoric in the book.

First, Qohelet's musings are emphatically internal and individualistic: "I said to myself in my heart" (2:1, 15). At some points 80 percent of the verbs and nouns are in the first-person singular form, far more than anywhere else in the Old Testament.[57] Many of the uses of "I" are grammatically unnecessary. Meanwhile, Qohelet laments those who go through life alone (4:9–12), yet nowhere do we hear him appeal to peers or elders or the wisdom tradition that gives him all of his language. Proverbs refers to the "father" twenty-eight times; Qohelet never mentions him.

Second, Qohelet constantly denies any remembrance of the past or hope for the future (1:4–11; 2:16; 3:15; 5:14, 19; 7:2, 7, 10; 9:3–5, 12, 15; 11:8; cf. 12:1, 6). Qohelet denies any sense of a metanarrative while he forces his own narrative upon us.

Thus, whereas Proverbs looks back at the goodness of creation with a hope that is never fully articulated or justified, Job and Ecclesiastes look forward with desperate hope for relief from the heavenly realms.

Wisdom and Prophets

The prophetic relationship with wisdom is two-sided, expressing critique and expectation. First, many of the prophets are critical of a class known as "the wise" (Isa 5:21; 19:11; 44:24; Jer 4:4; 8:8–9; Obad 1:8). Ezra, Nehemiah, Malachi, Jeremiah, Ezekiel, and Hosea all also describe Israel's broken covenant with Yahweh in terms of marital unfaithfulness to foreign wives, much like Proverbs 6:20–7:27. The prophets also look forward to the coming of a

---

57. 1cs forms make up 80 percent of chapters 1–2; the next highest in the Old Testament is Ecclesiastes 8.

wise messiah: "The Spirit of the LORD will rest on him—the Spirit of wisdom and of understanding, the Spirit of counsel and of might, the Spirit of the knowledge and fear of the LORD" (Isa 11:2). This messiah will bring together the wisdom, hope, and justice of the law and the wisdom literature.

Reading from the Perspective of the New Testament

It is easy to overlook the role of wisdom in the New Testament. Most readers are unaware of the fact that the wisdom tradition was at its peak at the time of Jesus' earthly ministry. Books like Sirach, the Wisdom of Solomon, and Baruch often expressed the Jewish hopes of salvation in terms native to wisdom literature. For example, in the book of Sirach (second century BC) we read, "Wisdom praises herself and tells of her glory in the midst of her people . . . whoever obeys me will not be put to shame, and those who work with me will not sin. All this is the book of the covenant of the most high God, the law that Moses commanded us as an inheritance for the congregations of Jacob" (24:1, 22–23 NRSV).

We are also prone to overlook wisdom in the New Testament because Christian theology tends to focus more on Jesus' king*ship* than his king*dom*.[58] As king, Jesus' mission is to bring the reality of his kingdom to bear, reconciling the orders of the heavens and the earth and bringing about the work of a new creation. Wisdom is the genre of the orders of creation and its restoration in Jesus' resurrection.

Wisdom shows up in four distinct ways in the New Testament and we discuss each of these throughout the commentary and in the following Live the Story sections. First, we find Jesus depicted before his parents as wise in his words and deeds, (Luke 2:40, 52), the model son of Proverbs 1:8 and 6:20. Only here Jesus' parents, the people, and the teachers marvel as the son arrives to become the true teacher of wisdom. For Greeks who seek wisdom and Jews who demand signs, Jesus is a "stumbling block," but to believers he is "the power of God and wisdom of God" (1 Cor 1:23, 25). (See Live the Story in Prov 30; pp. 414–16)

Second, Jesus' wisdom is evident in his great teaching and mighty works (Matt 8:27; Mark 1:22, 27). (See further discussion in the commentary in 1:20–33.)

Third, the New Testament reveals Jesus through a wisdom Christology. The most obvious example of this Christology is found in John 1:1–18 and Hebrews 1:1–3 where we see Jesus depicted as a manifestation of Woman Wisdom in Proverbs 8:22–36. Paul makes a similar wisdom claim about Jesus

58. See Bartholomew and O'Dowd, *Old Testament Wisdom*, 290–92.

in Colossians 1:15–20. Just as Wisdom was present in the creation of the world, so Jesus was in the beginning with God. We will see that there are also differences between Jesus and Woman Wisdom. A wisdom Christology is also evident in the parallel between the wisdom feasts in Proverbs 9 and Jesus' meals and parables (Matt 25:1–13; Luke 14:7–24; John 2:1–12) as well the teaching about a house built on wisdom (Matt 7:24–27). (See commentary in 8:1–36 and 9:1–18.)

Finally, wisdom is a virtue for Christians to know God's mysteries in Christ and to live accordingly (Col 4:5). Paul repeatedly prays for the church to be given "wisdom," "knowledge," "understanding," and "revelation" (Eph 1:8, 17; 3:10; Phil 1:9; Col 1:9, 28; 2:23; 3:16; Phlm 6). "In [Jesus] are hidden all the treasures of wisdom and knowledge" (Col 2:3). Consider Proverbs 15:1–33. James similarly appeals to the church to live according to the "wisdom that comes from heaven" (3:17); see Proverbs 18:1–24.

Reading from the Perspective of the Twenty-First Century

> If you want to build a ship, don't drum up people to collect wood and don't assign them tasks and work, but rather teach them to long for the endless immensity of the sea.[59]

Wisdom is God's gift to us, not merely to get by in life, but to bring about the flourishing of the whole creation. And so, as we will see in Proverbs 1–9, wisdom naturally begins by orienting us to its deep, inspiring vision of God's design and intentions for our world. Despite the presence of sin, suffering, injustice, and inequality, Proverbs reaffirms the goodness of the creation and God's commitment to see his work through to perfection. Only then does the book turn to specific guidance for lives of obedience (chs. 10–29).

Of course in seeking solutions to problems in life, Proverbs primarily looks back to creation rather than to some eschatological renewal. In the New Testament we see Proverbs' affirmation of creation now looking forward to what God is doing in Christ. Here Paul testifies that in his prayers.

> [17] I keep asking that the God of our Lord Jesus Christ, the glorious Father, may give you the Spirit of wisdom and revelation, so that you may know him better. [18] I pray that the eyes of your heart may be enlightened in order that you may know the hope to which he has called you, the riches of his glorious inheritance in his holy people. (Eph 1:17–18)

---

59. From Antoine de Saint-Exupéry, *The Little Prince*, cited in James K. A. Smith, *Imagining the Kingdom: How Worship Works*, CL 2 (Grand Rapids: Baker Academic, 2013), 7.

Within this view of the world and its redemption, we find that "we are God's handiwork, created in Christ Jesus to do good works, which God prepared in advance for us to do" (Eph 2:10). The story of the world sets that context for human action.

It could be argued that wisdom has the broadest applicability of the genres in the Bible. It is concerned with everything. The diagram on pages 47–48 lists all of the Live the Story topics that are found at the end of each chapter. Each of these sections serves as a spark for reflection, a sermon or class, or an expanded study.

How to Read this Commentary

I have tried to serve pastors and scholars without weighing down the text with footnotes. I have been particularly careful to leave a trail where further research is required or where I assert my own opinions about debatable matters. I have also tried to give credit to the innumerable insights I have drawn from other scholars. The citations include sources from a broad range of historical eras and a range of religious and non-religious backgrounds: evangelical, Catholic, Orthodox, Jewish, agnostic, and atheist. Sadly, neither Calvin nor Luther, nor many of our go-to giants of the past, wrote commentaries on Proverbs, so references to Christian commentaries prior to 1800 will be extremely limited.[60]

Furthermore, as I explained in Genre under *Literary Analysis* (pp. 23–29), Proverbs is a book uniquely challenging for its short lines, ambiguity, and play on words. As Robert Alter warns us, "The poets in Proverbs constantly exploit this compactness to which Hebrew lends itself, and the effect is often blunted or destroyed in the wordiness of translations . . . [which] frequently flatten a pointed thrust into a clumsy ruler swat."[61] For this reason, I provide a fair amount of transliterated Hebrew and notes that allow, and even force, the reader to wrestle with the difficulties among the sayings. So while chapters 1–9 and 30–31 provide lengthier reflections in the Live the Story sections, chapters 10–29 spend more time unpacking the complexity of individual sayings. I end this introduction by providing a table summarizing all of the Live the Story discussions. This table makes for a helpful topical reference for the commentary and can be used for selecting teaching and preaching topics on Proverbs.

---

60. A rare exception is Philipp Melanchthon's *Explicatio Proverbiorum Salomonis Philippi Melanthonis,* Witebergae: Per Iohannem Lufft, 1552, DLCPT (Alexandria, VA: Alexander Street Press, 2007).
61. Alter, *Art of Biblical Poetry*, 165–66.

Live the Story Topics

1:1–7	Wisdom: A Comprehensive Approach to Life and Learning	Ethical Wisdom	The Fear of the Lord and Beginning of Wisdom	
1:8–19	The Story of Wisdom	The Thresholds of Adulthood and New Life	The Struggle to Tame Human Desire	
1:20–33	Wisdom, Jesus, Rhetoric			
2:1–22	A Comprehensive Education: Anthropology and Cosmology	An Upward Spiral of Learning	Discerning the Structure of Things	
3:1–12	Wisdom and Law	Metaphors for Memory	Prosperity and Despair	
3:13–20	Jesus' Blessings	A Father's Commendation of Desire	God Made the World by Wisdom	
3:21–35	Wisdom, Desire, Jesus			
4:1–27	Tradition	The Way, the Truth, and the Life		
5:1–23	Marriage	Sex	Pedagogy and Anthropology	
6:1–19	Wisdom, Business, and Economics	Is This Anyone I Know?		
6:20–7:27	A Homiletical Theology of the Adulteress	Sex, Rationalization, Deception	Is the World of Proverbs Patriarchal?	
8:1–36	Wisdom, Discernment, and the Created Order	Wisdom in Jewish and Christian Theology	Jesus is Wisdom—the Power and Limits of Poetry	
9:1–18	Houses, Feasts, and Faith	Competing Worldviews	Community and Family	Desire (Again) / Keep Growing in Wisdom
10:1–32	Don't Trust Your Intuitions	Wisdom Goes Beyond the Mind	Wisdom and Love	
11:1–31	City, Community, Poverty	The Righteous and the Wicked		
12:28	Animal Rights?	Public Opinion and Shame	The Healing Power of Words	
13:1–25	Authority and the Desires of the Heart	Hope and Waiting	Corporal Discipline	
14:1–35	Kindness and contempt	Liberation of the Heart		

15:1–33	God's Searching Wisdom		Wisdom, Worship, and Prayer		
16:1–33	Human Limits		Gods, Kings, and Subjects	Human Oglers	
17:1–28	The Power of a Bribe		Judas's Bribe and Kiss		
18:1–24	Jesus, James, and Wisdom		Friends, Enemies, and Community		
19:1–29	Hermeneutics and wisdom		Man's Desire is His Unfailing Love: Poetry and Wisdom	Christological Prefiguring in Proverbs	
20:1–30	Wine is a Mocker		Blameless and Innocent? Who's Afraid of Romans?		
21:1–31	Victory Through Technology				
22:1–29	Discernment and Danger		Poor Pressure		
23:1–35	To Stand Before Kings		Envy, Vice, and Virtue: Part I		
24:1–34	House-Building and the Stars		Envy, Vice, and Virtue: Part II		
25:1–28	Shock, Surprise, and Moral Shaping		Water, Life, Fertility, and the Ordered Society		
26:1–28	Fittingness and Wisdom	Fittingness and Speech	Fittingness and Vocation	Fittingness and Ethics	
27:1–27	Good Friends and Good Family		Good Shepherds, Good Kings		
28:1–28	Kings, Power, Justice, and the Ordinary Citizen	A Praying Wisdom		Proverbial Families in the Gospels	
29:1–29	Wisdom, the Prophetic Vision, and Discipleship		Brief Interviews with Wicked and Righteous Men		
30:1–33	A Forgotten Side of Wisdom	Recovering the "Primary" Work of Art	Instilling a Worldview of Wonder	A Realistic View of Political Power	Agur, Jesus, and the Foolishness of Wisdom
31:1–31	For the Life of the World and Not Just for Women	Education, Craftsmanship, and Social Hierarchy	Works and Good Works: Secular and Sacred	Do What You Love	

Resources for Teaching and Preaching

Most of the footnotes in the commentary are provided to aid the teaching and preaching of Proverbs. Indiviudally, the commentaries by Van Leeuwen, Waltke, Longman, and Clifford are excellent resources. Together, these sources address virtually every question and practical concern one might imagine. The following resources are also highly recommended for understanding wisdom literature and Proverbs.

Alter. R. *The World of Biblical Literature*. London: SPCK, 1992.

Bartholomew C. G. and O'Dowd, R. P. *Old Testament Wisdom Literature: A Theological Introduction*. Downers Grove, IL: InterVarsity Press, 2011.

Brueggemann, W. *In Man We Trust: The Neglected Side of Biblical Faith*. Atlanta: John Knox, 1972.

O'Donovan, O. *Resurrection and Moral Order: An Outline for Evangelical Ethics*. Grand Rapids: Eerdmans, 1986.

Wolters, A. *The Song of the Valiant Woman: Studies in the Interpretation of Proverbs 31:10–31*. Carlisle: Paternoster, 2001.

Van Leeuwen, R. "Liminality and Worldview in Proverbs 1-9." *Semeia* 50 (1990): 111–44.

_____. "Wealth and Poverty: System and Contradiction in Proverbs." *Hebrew Studies* 33 (1992): 25–36.

Von Rad, G. *Wisdom in Israel*. Trans. James D. Martin. London: SCM, 1970.

¹ The proverbs of Solomon son of David, king of Israel:

> ² for gaining wisdom and instruction;
>   for understanding words of insight;
> ³ for receiving instruction in prudent behavior,
>   doing what is right and just and fair;
> ⁴ for giving prudence to those who are simple,
>   knowledge and discretion to the young—
> ⁵ let the wise listen and add to their learning,
>   and let the discerning get guidance—
> ⁶ for understanding proverbs and parables,
>   the sayings and riddles of the wise.
> ⁷ The fear of the LORD is the beginning of knowledge,
>   but fools despise wisdom and instruction.

Listening to the Text in the Story: Genesis 2–4; Deuteronomy 10:12–22;
1 Kings 3–10; Psalm 119; Ecclesiastes; Daniel 1; Amenemope 1:1–12

As discussed in Wisdom and Law in the Introduction, Franz Delitzsch argued 150 years ago that the language and theology of Deuteronomy were reflected in the book of Proverbs. Delitzsch's ideas were largely rejected at first. In recent decades, however, many scholars have begun to return to the idea that Proverbs is interested in, indeed sympathetic to, the theology in other books in the Old Testament. Surely the debate of Proverbs' relationship to the Old Testament will continue, but Christian readers should be confident that Proverbs makes sophisticated use of the Hebrew canon—Law, Prophets, and Writings.

The superscription in verse 1 resembles other superscriptions in the Law (Deut 1:1), Prophets (Jer 1:1), and later Writings (Eccl 1:1), which shed light on Solomon's role in the formation of Proverbs. For instance, the openings to Proverbs and Ecclesiastes are almost identical, although Solomon's name is not mentioned in Ecclesiastes. This absence of Solomon's name in Ecclesiastes is not incidental: it plays a significant role in the type of wisdom embraced by "the Preacher" (see Authorship and Date in the Introduction). Just as the type of wisdom portrayed in Ecclesiastes is selective, the sayings collected in Proverbs are not an exhaustive listing of Solomon's sayings. The writer of 1 Kings remembered Solomon for his great wisdom (ch. 3–10) and records him as having written over 3,000 proverbs (4:32). But there are less than 1,000 sayings in Proverbs, so Proverbs can only be a selection of Solomon's work. Additionally, other authors' collections of proverbs were included in the book (Prov 22:17; 24:23; 30:1; 31:1). Thus, Solomon's name in the title functions less as a statement of verse-by-verse authorship and more as a way of ascribing the book of Proverbs to Solomon's reputation as known from elsewhere in the Old Testament. In this view, Solomon stands as Israel's king of wisdom and wisdom literature, just as Moses serves as the honorific giver of Israel's lawgiver and David for the whole book of Psalms. David's example especially stands out, as many songs were written by musicians other than David.

In the next chapter we will study the father's introductory address to the son (Prov 1:8), which is similar to ancient Egyptian and Mesopotamian wisdom sayings that also frequently begin with a superscription, often by a king, and frequently directed to children or a son. Proverbs' closest noted parallel is in the prologue to Amenemope:

> Beginning of the teaching for life,
> The instructions for well-being,
> Every rule for relations with elders,
> For conduct towards magistrates;
> Knowing how to answer one who speaks . . .
> Steering clear of Evil;
> To save him from the mouth of strangers,
> To let (him) be praised in the mouth of people . . .
> Amenemope, the son of Kanakht,
> The justified in Ta-wer.
> <For> his son, the youngest of his children,
> The smallest of his family. (Amenemope 1.1–5, 10–12, 2.11–15)[1]

Proverbs 1:2–6 offers a similar list of the contents and purposes of the book: to teach "wisdom," "instruction," "words of insight," "instruction in prudent behavior," "just," "right," "fair," "knowledge," and insight into the words and riddles of the wise. As noted under "Genre" in the Introduction,

---

1. "Instruction of Amenemope" trans. Miriam Lichtheim, *COS* 1.47:116.

wisdom literature is a modern concept and we have little indication that the biblical authors thought in this way. That does not make the distinction false or unhelpful. Aside from the ethical vocabulary in 1:3, which we will address shortly, these wisdom terms appear far more often in Job, Proverbs, and Ecclesiastes than anywhere else in the Old Testament. The Song of Songs, which is sometimes grouped with wisdom books, does not share the vocabulary or focus in wisdom literature on growing in knowledge and ethical understanding. Singling out wisdom literature as a distinct genre helps us appreciate the ancient Israelite way of thinking about practical living and learning as intended by the God of the law, Psalms, and the prophets.

Translated literally, the second half of verse 3 promises instruction in "righteousness, justice, and equity" (cf. Prov 2:9). These three terms are found throughout the Old Testament, though they fit more naturally among the books of law, psalms, and prophecy than among wisdom literature (cf. Gen 18:19; Pss 9:9; 58:2; 90:9; Isa 11:4; 33:15; 45:19). So why does this prophetic and legal triad appear in these two places in Proverbs and nowhere else in the wisdom literature?

An answer may be found in Moshe Weinfeld's study of this judicial vocabulary in the Bible and the surrounding Near Eastern culture of Israel's ancient world.[2] While we often think of justice and righteousness in merely political or judicial terms, Weinfeld argues that when these terms appear in pairs and triadic chains, as they do in Proverbs 1:3 and 2:9, they point to a common vision of judicial, political, social, and interpersonal harmony—a vision that not only exists in Mesopotamian and Egyptian literature but lies behind Jesus' kingship in the New Testament as well. Justice and righteousness imply order in the human world that is grounded in God's own cosmic wholeness and order.[3]

In this light, the appearance of these terms in Proverbs is not surprising. As Weinfeld points out, the prophets themselves considered wisdom essential for a king's ability to establish the wholeness of justice and righteousness.[4] The Psalms and Isaiah recognized that God's ordering of the creation provides the foundation for kings to bring order to their kingdoms (Pss 33:5–6; 93:5; 99:4–7; Isa 45:18–25; 48:13–16).[5]

The link between wisdom and justice is probably most explicit in the story of the Queen of Sheba who came to see Solomon after hearing of the *wisdom* in his extraordinary sense of natural beauty and craftsmanship, but particularly in his administration of justice. As the queen departed, she offered

---

2. Moshe Weinfeld, *Social Justice in Ancient Israel and in the Ancient Near East* (Minneapolis: Fortress, 1995). See especially pp. 25–44.

3. Van Leeuwen, "Liminality," 120–22.

4. Weinfeld, *Social Justice*, 45–56.

5. Ibid., 198–208.

Solomon a tribute and these words of praise: "Praise be to the LORD your God . . . Because of the LORD's eternal love for Israel, he has made you king to maintain *justice* and *righteousness*" (1 Kgs 10:9, emphasis added). As we will see below, this holistic way of viewing creation, wisdom, and righteousness pervades wisdom literature, even if the legal terms are not always present.

The commentary in Proverbs 3:18–20 and 8:1–36 shows that wisdom literature relies heavily on the account of the creation and the fall in Genesis 3. In this light, we pause to recognize the distinct parallels between the vocabulary in Proverbs 1:3–4 and Genesis 2–4, specifically the way that the terms *daat* "knowledge," *ormah* "crafty/prudence/wisdom," and *sakal* "wise dealing" appear in Genesis *only* in these first four chapters.[6]

Genesis		Proverbs
2:9, 17; 4:1	"knowledge" (*daat*)	1:4, 7
3:1	"crafty/prudence/wisdom" (*ormah*)	1:4
2:25; 3:1, 7, 10, 11	"nakedness" (*arom*)	
3:6	"wise dealing" (*sakal*)	1:3

The source of eventual rebellion in Genesis, and thus the primary object of our intrigue, is in the "tree of the *knowledge* of good and evil" (Gen 2:9, emphasis added)—a feature of the garden that offers both physical pleasure and a means to bypass the divinely established limits of human knowledge. Furthermore, physical pleasure, sexual desire, and the acquisition of wisdom and knowledge are interwoven throughout Genesis and Proverbs. The word for "knowledge" in the tree in Genesis doubles as a euphemism for sexual relations in Genesis 4:1 and elsewhere throughout the Old Testament. The forbidden fruit, which is itself a symbol of sexual pleasure, when it is eaten by Adam and Eve reveals the shame of nakedness, i.e., exposes their sexual identity. There are strong acoustic parallels in Adam and Eve's "nakedness," *arom* and *erom* (Gen 2:25; 3:7, 10, 11, 21), and the "craftiness," *arum* (3:1) that the serpent used to draw Eve's attention to the tree.[7]

Proverbs gathers all of these terms and images from the account of the fall and reframes them in a redeemed light. Whereas the savory appeal of the fruit for Eve was tied to her desire for *sakal*, or a wisdom of rebellion (Gen 3:6), Proverbs offers *sakal*, "wisdom," of righteousness, justice, and equity (Prov 1: 3).[8]

---

6. See *NIDOTTE* 3:539–40.

7. See Gordon Wenham, *Genesis 1–15*, WBC (Waco, TX: Word Books, 1987), 72, and Victor P. Hamilton, *The Book of Genesis 1–17*, NICOT (Grand Rapids: Eerdmans, 1990), 187.

8. Cf. the NIV, "right, just, and fair," which slightly obscures the legal or judicial weight of these terms.

Proverbs 1:5 and 7 depart from the meter and chain of infinitive verbs in verses 2–4 and 6. The effect in verse 7 brings the prologue to its climactic conclusion: "the fear of the LORD [Yahweh] is the beginning of knowledge" (7a). We will discuss the translation and meaning of this phrase in the interpretation section below. For now, note that wisdom in Proverbs is tied to submission to Yahweh, the God of Israel's covenant history (2:5; 9:10, etc.; cf. Deut 6:4–9; Jer 31:31–34; Isa 11:2).

Proverbs emphasizes this theological presupposition by its preference for the name Yahweh, using it eighty-seven times to only five uses of Elohim, a more generic title for God in the Old Testament.[9] Further still, while religious "fear" and "fearing God [Elohim]" are not uncommon in the Old Testament, the phrase "the fear of the LORD," is quite specific and only occurs about twenty times in the Old Testament, fourteen of those in Proverbs. In its other locations the fear of Yahweh is used to capture the appropriate response to God's self-revelation and giving of the laws and commandments at Sinai (Exod 20:20; Deut 10:12–22; cf. Deut 5:29; 6:2; Josh 24:14; Ps 111:10).

EXPLAIN the Story

1:1 Resembling the modern hardcover book jacket, verse 1 introduces the author, his credentials, and the contents and purpose of his book. As we discussed in "Authorship and Date" in the Introduction, there are at least four authors for this book, but the final editors of Proverbs likely added this verse because they wanted all of the material to stand under Solomon's name and his reputation as Israel's king of wisdom.

"Proverb," *mashal,* is used throughout the Old Testament to refer to several different forms of speech, such as ballads, oracles, maxims, and bywords (Num 23:7; 1 Kgs 4:32; Job 13:12; 29:1; Pss 44:15; 49:4; Eccl 9:17). Although most of Proverbs consists of comparison sayings, the book's superscription is less concerned with a specific form of speech than with the fact that these sayings have a cultured history, or a time-tested currency, among the folk. The first verse authenticates these sayings both by appealing to Solomon's reputation and also by highlighting the fact that these sayings have a tradition among previous generations.

1:2–6 These verses pile up seven verbs and fourteen nouns that are virtual synonyms for wisdom,[10] which is impressive, both because of the symbolic repetition of units of seven and also because of the sheer volume of nearly

---

9. See Waltke, *Proverbs 1–15,* 66–67.
10. Clifford, *Proverbs,* 34.

synonymous terms. Fox's commentary helpfully delineates the important distinctions between each of these words for wisdom and how they help us understand the nuances of learning, ethics, and knowledge. But Fox also concedes that this collection of terms in the introduction is focused less on verbal distinctions than in boasting of Proverbs' breadth of wisdom.[11]

With the exception of verses 5 and 7, all of the aims listed in the prologue are presented with infinitive verbs: "*to know . . . to give* instruction . . . *to give* prudence." The jussive forms in verse 5, which we translate with the word "let," alter the tone slightly to offer an exhortation in the midst of straightforward statements.[12] This rhetorical combination of pleading and exhortation continues throughout Proverbs 1–9.

Scholars have suggested several outlines for the content in verses 2–7, and most of them are valid.[13] To my mind, Clifford's structure best captures the vision of this prologue to present three types of wisdom that operate simultaneously in the growth to maturity: sapiential (vv. 2a, 4–6), ethical (v. 3), and theological (v. 7).[14]

1. Sapiential learning encompasses the range of study found in the modern humanities, from philosophy and epistemology (knowledge) to language and literature. Proverbs certainly doesn't engage philosophy in a theoretical way, but it does deal with basic metaphysical questions like the nature and sovereignty of God, human purpose, suffering, and the scope of relationships between God, humans, and nature. Epistemologically, Proverbs guides us to a particular way of getting knowledge and being assured that our knowledge is valid.

Too often wisdom is assumed to be a matter of living conscientiously or with basic common sense. The problem, as Proverbs warns us, is that sometimes our best thinking turns out to be totally wrong: "A person may think their own ways are right, but the LORD weighs the heart" (21:2, cf. 16:2). Wisdom must be studied to be obtained. Providing understanding for all ages and all types of people, both those simple and those already wise (vv. 4–5), it is not a destination or status, or terminal degree, but involves a life-long journey of submitting our minds, hearts, and values to those of the creator of our world.

Furthermore, this sapiential form of wisdom is not just knowledge in the abstract, but what Proverbs labels *musar*, "discipline" or "instruction" (vv. 2, 3, 7). The use of this term assumes a social or communal context for wisdom, since at least two people are involved. This social or communal aspect is noticeable in the shift from student-oriented verbs of *getting* wisdom and

11. Fox, *Proverbs 1–9*, 58–67.
12. Ibid., 62.
13. See the helpful outline in Longman, *Proverbs*, 95.
14. Clifford, *Proverbs*, 36.

insight in verses 2–3 to teacher-oriented verbs of *giving* wisdom in verse 4. With this combination of perspectives, wisdom stands in marked contrast to the image of an isolated scholar in an ivory tower or a lone student on a computer taking an online class. Wise people live in communities of fellow learners, where some teach and all learn.[15]

Finally, sapiential wisdom includes the study of language and literature, or as verse 6 puts it "proverbs and parables, the sayings and riddles of the wise." Scholars often pause at this point, finding it difficult to translate the rare words in this verse. We do not find anything fitting with the technical definition of a riddle in the book except perhaps in Proverbs 30. Even if these sayings are riddles, we cannot be sure that this is the figure of speech that the authors had in mind. There is no reason to get bogged down here. As discussed in "Genre" in the Introduction, the very thing that gives a proverb its staying power over time is the nature of its catchy wording—a common truth captured by a memorable form and sound. Unpacking these sayings, whatever their literary form and however great their difficulty, is at the center of this wisdom book.

The book of Daniel offers an enlightening parallel in this regard. The story begins with Nebuchadnezzer's request to find "young men without any physical defect, handsome, showing aptitude for *every kind of learning*, well informed, quick to understand, and qualified to serve in the king's palace. He was to teach them the *language and literature* of the Babylonians" (1:4, emphasis added). Those chosen men of Judah included Daniel, Hananiah, Mishael, and Azariah, to whom "God gave knowledge and understanding of *all kinds of literature* and *wisdom*. And Daniel could understand visions and dreams of all kinds" (1:17, emphasis added).[16] Joseph, too, was "a discerning and wise man" who was able to interpret Pharoah's otherwise impenetrable dreams (Gen 41:33, 39). Among the great riches of godly wisdom are its power to open up literature and language and to yield access to riddles, mysteries, and dreams.

2. The specifically intellectual learning in Proverbs is interwoven with the ethical or upright life. History teaches us again and again that great learning can, and often does, coexist alongside corruption, evil, and senseless violence. Biblical wisdom responds to this, channeling our learning into ways of discipline, justice, mercy, and righteousness (v. 3). When Paul says that, "knowledge puffs up while love builds up" (1 Cor 8:1), he captures the Hellenistic tendency to divorce learning from a sense of ethical accountability and social responsibility. Like Paul, Proverbs holds these two together.

---

15. See McKane, *Proverbs: A New Approach*, OTL (Philadelphia: Westminster, 1970), 263–64.

16. The NIV has been amended here, replacing "learning" with "wisdom" to capture the presence of the Hebrew word *hokmah*.

Furthermore, as we observed above, wisdom is not limited to personal conduct. Righteousness and justice apply equally to the order of society, family, nature, and government; political leaders, parents, children, laborers, business owners, caregivers, and inventors all need wisdom to live peaceably together, to share their resources properly, to protect the weak, and to restrain the powerful.

3. At the climax of the prologue, Proverbs submits all wisdom to a single starting point: "The fear of the LORD is the beginning of knowledge" (v. 7; cf. 9:10). The word "beginning" has two possible senses, first in time and first in importance, and both are in view here; the fear of the Lord begins our path to wisdom and sets the conditions for the journey as a whole.

The decision to render God's covenant name "Yahweh" with the generic title "LORD," has been one of the more unfortunate decisions in the history of English translations. As with "God" (Elohim), the title "Lord" can be applied to many kinds of deities in a variety of religions. Yahweh, by contrast, is a specific name belonging to the one and only creator God who covenanted Abraham, Moses, David, and Israel to bring redemption and blessing to the whole world. To submit wisdom to Yahweh does more than make wisdom merely religious, it requires those wanting to be wise to stake a belief in the story of God's work of creating and redeeming our world. It means finding the core of our faith and the meaning of our lives in the revelation given to Moses and the prophets.

Proverbs describes people who reject "the fear of the LORD" as "fools" who "despise wisdom and instruction." Fox points out that the word for "fools" implies moral perversity, and thus, "[d]eep-seated attitudes, rather than lack of raw intelligence, prevent them from gaining wisdom."[17] In this light, we can see that the fear of the Lord is the very thing that Eve, Adam, and the serpent lacked in their pursuit of the forbidden pleasures of knowledge in Genesis 3. It was only after their rebellion and the exposure of their nakedness that Adam and Eve became aware of their need to fear God (3:10). Proverbs reverses the flow of the Genesis story, emphatically making the fear of God a prerequisite to acquiring knowledge and pleasure.

LIVE the Story

This carefully crafted prologue of just seven verses lays out an inspiring and appealing introduction to the study of wisdom. Wisdom provides our point of entry and our guide for the good life. Beneath these extravagant claims we can identify several indications as to what biblical wisdom entails.

---

17. Fox, *Proverbs 1–9*, 68. See also von Rad, *Wisdom*, 64.

Wisdom: A Comprehensive Approach to Life and Learning

It is one thing to say that wisdom relates to *everything*, but something entirely different to claim that wisdom speaks to the *whole of things*. Consider the modern superstore and online sales outlets, which net billions of dollars in annual revenues and occupy the major force of the western pursuit of "the good life." These retailers are popular because they offer something for *everyone*. And yet these companies contribute little to the health of the world as a whole, inter-dependent system.

In few places is the lack of the whole more evident than in modern universities, which function more and more like superstores.[18] As these institutions have become increasingly diversified, they have excelled in offering instruction in every topic or profession in the world, but almost nothing altogether or as a unity. One's study of chemistry, literature, engineering, ethics, or finance provides little or no sense of the inherent interrelationships between them: e.g., structural engineers who are not required to integrate their studies with classes in environmental studies or social and health impacts of urban design and bankers who do not have to combine their learning with research in psychology and ethics. Such a lack of wholeness in education comes at a cost to family and society.

The fragmentation of the educational system is especially disconcerting considering the age of students at universities. Adolescence, apart from the first years of life, is the most pivotal time for our moral and social formation. We will discuss this in detail in Proverbs 1:8–19. For now, suffice it to say that the modern education system is drastically unsuited to transform adolescents into ethically, socially, and intellectually mature members of society.

We are also witnessing the increasingly popular decision to abandon traditional humanities in favor of professional and technical training centers. This has made it virtually impossible for universities to continue to offer disciplined study of ideas, morals, values, and the big questions of life.[19] Students go to college to learn practical hows but not ethical hows; personal whys but not ultimate whys. Morality, meaning, and purpose, it is hoped, will be addressed somewhere else. But where? And how?

Sadly, modern education is increasingly driven by economic and industrial ends rather than cultural formation. Ecologist and cultural critic David Orr has argued in recent decades that the problems *in* education—methods, funding,

---

18. See Bill Readings, *The University in Ruins* (Cambridge: Harvard University Press, 1997), especially pp. 27–28 and 51–52.

19. See Julie Reuben's study of the transformation of the American university system in the last two centuries, *The Making of the Modern University: Intellectual Transformation and the Marginalization of Morality* (Chicago: University of Chicago, 1996).

and content—are a secondary concern to this problem *of* education—that our public schools and universities have wedded themselves to the ethos and power of the marketplace, from its deceitful advertising culture and its emphasis on jobs, labor production, and profitability to its numbers-based approach to measuring success.[20] Universities now look like modern corporations that sell a product to optimize capital. Corporate power and individual desire reign supreme in such a world.

Proverbs speaks definitively to an education in the whole of things—one of unity, responsibility, and community. As we discussed in the section on interpretation above, proverbial wisdom is learning that is *simultaneously* sapiential (philosophical, artistic, and literary), ethical, and theological. Lacking any of these three, learning becomes uprooted from serving God's design and desire for an orderly world and becomes a tool for humans to use to pursue personal comfort, power, or opportunity. Proverbial wisdom equips us for success in life, but it does so with an abiding concern for how the skills we acquire relate to God's desire to redeem and build a just, generous, good world.

Ethical Wisdom

Childhood education today is frequently captured by the three Rs of Reading, [w]Riting, and [a]Rithmetic. Missing here are two key elements in proverbial education: Religion and Righteousness. Surely today's students learn values like mutual respect, honesty, and fairness. But in the competitive climate of high schools and post-secondary education the value that is most carefully measured and most highly rewarded is individual success.

When I started my undergraduate education, students at our college took an oath to uphold an honor code that forbade lying, stealing, and cheating. Many other colleges and universities have similar codes. And yet my college is among countless others where cheating scandals on tests and websites that sell term papers are rampant. David Orr rightly says, "education is no guarantee of decency, prudence, or wisdom."[21] More than that, education's competitive culture often exacerbates dishonestly, indecency, and selfishness.

The approach to education in Proverbs involves more than just ethical and moral *content* in the curriculum. By giving young men and women training in "justice, righteousness, and equity," Proverbs embeds itself in a specifically religious approach to ethical learning. As we will see below, Proverbs' ethical teachings continually echo the thematic language of compassion, social

---

20. David W. Orr. *Hope Is an Imperative: The Essential David Orr* (Washington, DC: Island Press, 2011), Kindle edition.

21. David W. Orr. *Earth in Mind: On Education, Environment, and the Human Prospect* (Washington, DC: Island Press), Kindle edition.

justice, and moral order resident in Israel's ancient law, prophets, and history (cf. 2:9; 3:3).

The study of Israel's laws was rooted in Yahweh—his person and his works. The first words memorized by an ancient Israelite child were from Deuteronomy: "Yahweh our God, Yahweh is one. Love Yahweh your God with all your heart with all your soul and with all your strength" (6:4b-5; cf. Matt 22:34–40, author's translation). From this first lesson a child moved on to study Israel's laws and stories. Justice and righteousness in the law, therefore, were not abstract ideals but covenant responses to the God who first loved and rescued Israel, the God who answered promises, who forgave the nation's disobedience, and who provided a good land, rich crops, and overflowing population. Before learning about how to live life in the land with the issues natural to families and society, a child learned that ethics are grounded in a responsive love to God (cf. Jas 1:5–6).

Proverbs, like the laws in Deuteronomy, grounds its ethical teaching in a deep, transcendent, and ultimate reality: the one and only Yahweh, creator and designer of the heavens and the earth, has saved a people, blessed them, and called them to love him by working to the health, redemption, peace, and fruitfulness of his world. Ethics is a wisdom that arises out of a covenant response to the one who first loved us (1 John 4:19).

The Fear of the Lord and Beginning of Wisdom

Old Testament wisdom has us begin with the fear of the Lord. As we have discussed above and under "Theology of the Book" in the Introduction, this culturally rich phrase imagines the world of the law and the prophets, where Israel is called to remain faithful to her creator and redeemer. And yet it is a fairly common assumption in modern evangelical Christianity that "fear" is for the God of the Old Testament while New Testament believers live under a God of "love." But this idea does not arise from a study of the New Testament, where we find faith and religion equated with fearing God (Rom 11:20; Phil 2:12; 1 Pet 2:17; 2 Cor 7:1; Rev 19:5). After all, Father, Son, and Spirit all participate in the revelation of wisdom after the resurrection (Eph 1:11–23; Col 1:1–23). What difference might this make for a Christian pursuing wisdom today?

1. Ordering the world from the outside. Few book titles provide a better insight into the world of Proverbs than Alasdair MacIntyre's *Whose Justice? Which Rationality?* The well-recognized problem among philosophers and cultural theorists is that the West is pluralistic, having countless views of good, right, moral, and rational. The approach of

MacIntyre and many others is that we should work to find a compromise that best fits the makeup of our surrounding communities—a kind of democratic and utilitarian process of resorting to what most people believe and what makes sense for most people's interests. This compromise recognizes that appeals to religion, history, or philosophical systems, which do provide a kind of view from above, are the root sources of disagreement and so cannot provide a point of appeal if we are going to get along in this world. Christians have good reasons to participate in this process of compromise as opposed to railing against moral relativism; many sayings in Proverbs will lead us to find the right balance, even in the presence of fools (e.g., 26:1–12).

But Proverbs nevertheless remains aware that the fundamental questions matter because that is the only way to prevent the drift to relativism that begins to rationalize immorality and injustice. We need a point from outside our world to speak to the order we need within it. "The fear of the LORD" affirms that Israel's story of God and the world provide the sole starting point for answering the hard questions of ethics.

This is largely why Augustine, the fourth century bishop of Hippo, rejected the dominant Greek conceptions of the moral life. Whether Plato's belief that "justice" stood as the ordering principle of the world or Aristotle's notion of eudemonia or happiness as the objective of human action, Augustine argued that love alone is able to provide that point of ethical and rational order; and not just love, but that love embodied in the greatest commands of the Old and New Testaments (Deut 6:5; Lev 19:18; Matt 22:37–39).[22] In Augustine's framing of the biblical teaching we find an appeal not to abstract ideas (justice or happiness) but to the actions and words of a divine person within human history. In this light, how significant it is that the Old Testament love commands in Deuteronomy 6 and Leviticus 19 are both motivated by Israel's memory of God's deliverance in Egypt. So too does our Christian ethic act out of the repeated memory of the body and blood of the one who delivers us.

2. Values and intentions matter. Granting the distinction Proverbs makes between the benefits of wisdom and folly, all sorts of people with different belief systems all manage to get along in things like exchanging money, running local, state, and federal governments, managing youth sports leagues, and producing research in universities. Painful as our

---

22. See Nicholas Wolterstorff, *Justice: Rights and Wrongs* (Princeton: Princeton University Press, 2008), 180–84; 188–206.

deeper disagreements may be, we're able to come together on most practical things. So what difference does it make in our daily lives for us to have our knowledge grounded in the fear of the Lord?

Above all, the fear of the Lord reinforces that knowledge is more than a means to an end; it is a journey to full maturity in our thought, desires, and actions. Even Jesus had to grow in wisdom to assume the role assigned to him by the father (Luke 2:52). As we look on the mature Christ child growing in wisdom, we discover the limitations of our own humanity against the backdrop of God's fuller designs for each of his creatures.

Two people may come to agree on financial, scientific, social, or even philosophical ideas, but they may have radically *different reasons* for doing so. In the same way, two people may perform equally in their chosen profession and yet do so with very different *motivations* and different *sets of values*. The appeal to the fear of the Lord—i.e., faith in and obedience to God—requires the submission of our passions in order that our intellects and actions may follow (cf. Luke 22:42). In the believer's life in this world, our values, intentions, and the purposes for which we believe the world exists all matter ultimately.

3. Purpose and values ultimately matter because wisdom embodies a vision for human flourishing. In a world where so many believe that religion is oppressive and naïve, it bears emphasizing that the gift of wisdom is the first installment in God's plan for us to be really and truly happy for all eternity.

Flourishing in Proverbs is depicted like the utopia and peace of the garden of Eden spread into a world of many lands, families, nations, and cultures. For the most part, the modern university trains students for a kind of flourishing that imagines employment, promotion, physical comforts, and financial well-being. This does not mean that many people don't think about issues of compassion and justice but that our culture and educational systems do very little to nurture this. Biblical wisdom, particularly in Paul's prayers, is depicted as our insight into the ultimate benefits that await God's children, benefits of love that "surpasses knowledge—that you may be filled to the measure of all the fullness of God" (Eph 3:19).

LISTEN to the Story

⁸ Listen, my son, to your father's instruction
   and do not forsake your mother's teaching.
⁹ They are a garland to grace your head
   and a chain to adorn your neck.
¹⁰ My son, if sinful men entice you,
   do not give in to them.
¹¹ If they say, "Come along with us;
   let's lie in wait for innocent blood,
   let's ambush some harmless soul;
¹² let's swallow them alive, like the grave, and whole,
   like those who go down to the pit;
¹³ we will get all sorts of valuable things
   and fill our houses with plunder;
¹⁴ cast lots with us;
   we will all share the loot"—
¹⁵ my son, do not go along with them,
   do not set foot on their paths;
¹⁶ for their feet rush into evil,
   they are swift to shed blood.
¹⁷ How useless to spread a net
   where every bird can see it!
¹⁸ These men lie in wait for their own blood;
   they ambush only themselves!
¹⁹ Such are the paths of all who go after ill-gotten gain;
   it takes away the life of those who get it.

Listening to the Text in the Story: Numbers 16:30–33; Deuteronomy
6:1–25; Job 31:9; Isaiah 5:14; 59:1–8.

Throughout Proverbs 1–9 we hear many echoes of the teaching material in Deuteronomy, which has been recognized among the books of the Pentateuch as standing apart for its teaching and learning rhetoric.[1] In this light it is possible that Proverbs 1–9 has some relationship to the laws of the cities of refuge in Deuteronomy 19, specifically the language of "innocent blood," and "lying in wait" (cf. also Job 31:9).

The image of one being "swallowed" by "the pit," or Sheol, in Proverbs 1:12 resembles both the story of Korah and his followers in Numbers 16:30–33 (cf. Deut 11:6) as well as the metaphorical image of Sheol devouring sinners in Isaiah 5:14. Isaiah 59:1–8 also bears a striking resemblance to the sinners depicted here in Proverbs, and most believe 1:16 has been adapted from Isaiah 59:7. Still, most scholars shy away from attributing direct influence between wisdom books and other texts in the Old Testament. Yet it makes sense that the authors of Proverbs, in a culture known for deeply respecting their oral and written traditions, would draw upon familiar passages in the Law and Prophets to provide natural examples for instruction.

EXPLAIN the Story

1:8 The pervasive image of fathers and mothers teaching their children in Proverbs (1:8; 2:1; 3:1, 11, 21; 4:1, 10, 20; 5:1, 7; 6:1, 3, 20; 7:1, 24; 8:32; 31:2) mirrors the expectation in Deuteronomy that both parents will teach their children the laws and stories of Israel (6:6 and 11:19).

Yet parents and teachers know how difficult it can be to convince children, let alone adolescents, to pay attention to important instructions. Throughout these chapters Proverbs employs a number of tools to deal with this age-old problem. The predominant strategy Proverbs uses to get boys' attention is to illustrate the urgency of the threshold of entering into adult life. "Two roads diverged in a yellow wood," wrote Robert Frost, portraying the sense of possibility, risk, and inevitability in the choices that life throws at us. Genesis, too, depicts life as a choice between two trees—of life and of the knowledge of good and evil. Deuteronomy 28 portrays the future of the Israelites along two lines— obedience to Yahweh and his blessing versus disobedience to Yahweh and his curse. Likewise Psalms 1–2 introduce the book with a presentation of two ways. First, in Psalm 1 the way of the "blessed," whose delight is in the law of the Lord, contrasts the way of the "wicked," who will perish (1:1–6). In Psalm 2 the anointed stand to receive God's blessing (2:2, 12) while the kings and nations who conspire against God doom themselves to destruction (2:9, 12).

---

1. O'Dowd, *Wisdom of Torah*, 20–52.

Proverbs calls upon these same images at many points, expressing them in all or nothing categories: wisdom vs. folly, righteousness vs. sin, life vs. death. Verse 7 already introduced us to the stark opposition of the wise and the foolish, and now verses 8–19 construct a vivid picture of the young man's two ways and the two sources of temptation: enticing sinners and the temptations of the woman (1:10–19; 2:16–19). You must choose!

1:9 Another way Proverbs interests the young man is by provoking vivid images of life and blessings that will come to those who choose the path of wisdom. Verse 9 compares the parents' teaching to jewelry adorning the head, heart, fingers, and neck. We may not be able to recover the full cultural significance of jewelry in the ancient world, but it is clear that the image exists in both legal (Exod 13:9; Deut 6:6–9; 11:18–21) and wisdom texts (Prov 3:3, 22; 4:9; 7:3), and in both contexts the jewelry is metaphorical. Symbolic locations on the body, in the house, and in family property are to be surrendered to Yahweh's command and act as benefactors of his protection and blessing.

1:10–14 Proverbs also vividly animates the fate of the foolish. The fool, first introduced in verse 7, is shown amongst a community of reckless young men who seek to recruit the naïve into their ranks (1:10–14). This young cohort "lie[s] in wait for innocent blood" to "ambush" the innocent and "swallow" them alive like Sheol. After ambushing and devouring the innocent, they promise to divide their loot amongst the whole gang (1:13–14). But in the end they only end up trapping themselves (vv. 18–19).

The behavior in these verses closely resembles the situation with Joseph and his brothers in Genesis 37–47. The brothers unquestionably lie in wait for "blood" (37:18–19). Furthermore, the word "pit" in Genesis 37:20 and 22 is only used three times in Proverbs and one is for the "pit" that acts as a metaphor for wicked men in 1:12. Finally, the brothers also end up committing an act that only ends up backfiring on them—a point the brothers recognize themselves (Gen 42:21). In the Jewish Midrash on Proverbs (Tanhuma) we find the rabbis making these same connections between the language and situations in Proverbs 1 and Genesis 37–45.[2]

1:15–19 After his condemning description of the deceitful young men, the father appeals emphatically again to "my son" (v. 15), giving him this memorable saying, "How useless to spread a net where every bird can see it!" (v.16). Who is the bird here? Given the ambiguity in the poetry, Fox seems right to suggest that the bird likely has dual significance: first as standing for

---

2. *The Midrash on Proverbs*, Yale Judaica XXVII, trans. ed. Burton L. Visotzky (New Haven: Yale University, 1992), 23–25.

the simple and vulnerable son who has had a trap laid for him but then also as the band of thieves and murderers who will end up caught in their own plots.[3]

The trapper's net provides a transition to the closing assurance that justice awaits the wicked; the young men will end up "ambushing" their own lives and suffer the fate they intended for others. As Clifford puts it, "Paradoxically, the wealth that is possessed kills its possessor (10:2; 11:4)."[4] This language and paradox of the sinners here closely parallels the laws in Deuteronomy: first, of those who would seek to prevent wrongful revenge of "innocent blood," (19:1–10) and second, of those who conspire "in wait" to kill the innocent (19:11–13). Both suffer the penalty of death they first wished upon others. The young men in Proverbs are like Korah and his followers in Numbers 16:30–33, who jealously seek to displace Aaron and Moses and end up swallowed into Sheol. A similar image appears yet again with the sinners in Isaiah 5:8–14 who store up wealth and oppress the weak only to suffer hunger and be swallowed alive into Sheol.

At several points the appeals of these young men parallel the seductions of the adulterous woman in Proverbs 7. She also "lurks" (7:12) for the innocent, appealing for the young man to freely partake of sexual treasures that are not his own (7:18). Like the fate of those who follow deceitful men, the young man who heeds this woman's charms will have his fate reversed and suffer the death of "Sheol" (7:23–27).

LIVE the Story

The Story of Wisdom

Proverbs is not a story. But the book does present countless smaller story-pictures alongside root metaphors (ways, paths, houses) that guide us to imagine the shape and order in the world and the natural consequences for living outside of that order. Sitting at the center of these storied sayings and metaphors are sons and daughters who are entering into a world of work, responsibility, opportunity, and risk, as well as temptation, evil, injustice, and suffering. Proverb by proverb Christians enter into these sayings through the perspectives of these adolescents, finding ourselves likewise trained and urged to walk in this world with wisdom.

But it is also true that, as the young man or woman emerges from childhood into maturity, Christians emerge from lives of death into new life in Christ. Paul exhorts us, "count yourselves dead to sin but alive to God in

---

3. Fox, *Proverbs 1–9*, 89.
4. Clifford, *Proverbs*, 39.

Christ Jesus. Therefore do not let sin reign in your mortal body so that you obey its evil desires . . . but rather offer yourselves to God as those who have been brought from death to life; and offer every part of yourself to him as an instrument of righteousness" (Rom 6:11–13). In other words, for the Christian, the rhetoric of the father in Proverbs is expanded from merely growing in maturity into a larger picture of embodying a risen life in obedience to Christ.

The Thresholds of Adulthood and New Life

Reading Proverbs "in Christ," however, should not be mistaken as a reason to invalidate its concrete lessons for daily life in this world. As we discussed in the introduction, all of us live on thresholds every day, thresholds of friendship, work, morality, meals, leisure, etc.

It remains true today that adolescents encounter some of the most momentous thresholds of life within a short amount of time, such as decisions about education, vocation, marriage, and family. At this point a person's self-identity and worldview are often decided, as Steven Garber has rightly stated: "The years between adolescence and adulthood are a crucible in which moral meaning is formed, and central to that formation is a vision of integrity which coherently connects belief to behavior."[5] Similarly, in his appeals for us to give renewed attention to our approach to education, David Orr quotes E. Cobb who says, "Childhood is the 'point of intersection between biology and cosmology, where the structuring of our worldviews and our philosophies of human purpose takes place.'"[6]

Yet as Orr and others point out, our secondary schools, colleges, and universities are losing their place in nurturing citizens of ethics, values, and purpose with a united comprehensive sense of knowledge.[7] So what do we do?

First we must recognize that most schools today are so dependent on these economic and corporate structures that there is little they can do to change on their own. Nor should we hold them solely responsible for the situation they are in. The well-being of our adolescents must be a national, community, church, and family concern. Rather than simply critiquing education, we need to get involved in understanding our youth and the changing world

---

5. Steven Garber, *The Fabric of Faithfulness: Weaving Together Belief and Behavior* (Downers Grove, IL: InterVarsity Press, 2007), 34.

6. E. Cobb, *The Ecology of Imagination in Childhood* (Dallas: Spring Publications, 1993) in David Orr, "Loving Children: A Design Problem" in *Hope Is an Imperative: The Essential David Orr*, Kindle edition.

7. See, e.g. Robert P. George, *Conscience and its Enemies: Confronting the Dogmas of Liberal Secularism* (Wilmington, DE: ISI Books, 2013), 27–41 and Bradley G. Green, *The Gospel and the Mind: Recovering and Shaping the Intellectual Life* (Wheaton IL: Crossway, 2010).

that faces them. More participation, creativity, and constructive involvement are needed in order to advance young men and women into responsible and meaningful adulthood.

The Struggle to Tame Human Desire

Today's youth, especially young men, are often caricatured as drifting through their education without taking serious interests in the urgent questions of life. Frats are more popular than libraries! This problem is not new. At the turn of the last century, schools like Harvard, Johns Hopkins, Yale, and Columbia were trying to understand the failure to attract young students to moral and religious programs. After the Noble lectures at Harvard in 1906, President Eliot's secretary reported that, "the audiences have been large and good, but you would be disappointed in the relatively small number of the younger undergraduates. It is not that they have been crowded out, but simply that the form of successful appeal to the religious instinct of boys that age seems yet to be discovered."[8] The temptations of alternative voices at that age are strong, symbolized in Proverbs by young enterprising men and seductive women (1:11–33). Proverbs captures the attention of young men and women by exposing the deceitful and destructive nature of these competing voices.

A central argument in this commentary is that wisdom is not simply a program of improving intellect by accumulating knowledge. Instead, wisdom recognizes that our affections and desires can warp and distort what we take to be "knowledge." The first step in wisdom is to discipline the wandering desires of our hearts (cf. 3:5–7). In Proverbs' world, our thoughts flow out of the desire of our hearts (4:23). Jesus also tells his disciples, "But the things that come out of a person's mouth come from the heart, and these defile them. For out of the heart come evil thoughts—murder, adultery, sexual immorality, theft, false testimony, slander" (Matt 15:18–19).

In Proverbs 1:7 above we saw that the word used for the "fools," or those who are opposed to wisdom, describes people characterized by moral perversity and not intellectual inability. In Proverbs, wisdom and foolishness originate in the intentions and passions of the heart. It should therefore be easy for us to imagine why the emphasis on temptations is so important: knowing the right thing to do is altogether different (and easier) than doing it.

---

8. In Reuben, *Making of the Modern University*, 128.

Proverbs 1:20–33

 LISTEN to the Story

²⁰ Out in the open wisdom calls aloud,
 she raises her voice in the public square;
²¹ on top of the wall she cries out,
 at the city gate she makes her speech:
²² "How long will you who are simple love your simple ways?
 How long will mockers delight in mockery
 and fools hate knowledge?
²³ Repent at my rebuke!
 Then I will pour out my thoughts to you,
 I will make known to you my teachings.
²⁴ But since you refuse to listen when I call
 and no one pays attention when I stretch out my hand,
²⁵ since you disregard all my advice
 and do not accept my rebuke,
²⁶ I in turn will laugh when disaster strikes you;
 I will mock when calamity overtakes you—
²⁷ when calamity overtakes you like a storm,
 when disaster sweeps over you like a whirlwind,
 when distress and trouble overwhelm you.
²⁸ "Then they will call to me but I will not answer;
 they will look for me but will not find me,
²⁹ since they hated knowledge
 and did not choose to fear the LORD.
³⁰ Since they would not accept my advice
 and spurned my rebuke,
³¹ they will eat the fruit of their ways
 and be filled with the fruit of their schemes.
³² For the waywardness of the simple will kill them,
 and the complacency of fools will destroy them;

³³ but whoever listens to me will live in safety
and be at ease, without fear of harm."

This is Woman Wisdom's first of three speeches in Proverbs 1–9 (cf. 8:4–36; 9:4–12), each of which takes place in a similar scene—a crowded city, a woman's voice, an appeal to young men to hear, and a promise of safety and life. The speeches stand alongside the wife (5:15–19) and opposed to Dame Folly (9:13–18) and the strange woman (5:3–6, 15–20; 7:5–27). Similarly, both the father's warnings about the young men (Prov 1:10–19) and Wisdom's warning about the fate of fools (1:26–27, 31–32) present readers with images of violent ends for folly, both symbolic and literal.

One example of a woman calling out for safety and life can be found in 2 Samuel 20. As Joab's forces pursue Sheba, we hear echoes of Woman Wisdom in the "wise woman" who called out to Joab. Sheba had denounced David's leadership and called Israel to abandon their king, and when Joab trapped Sheba in Abel Beth Maakah, a "wise woman" called out to Joab, warning him not to invade the city and "swallow up the Lord's inheritance" (20:19). Like Woman Wisdom, this woman is concerned with the welfare of the city and its people. When this woman learned of Sheba's treachery, she appealed to the citizens of the city with "wise advice" to behead Sheba and deliver him to Joab, thus saving the city from Sheba's folly and their own violent destruction (2 Sam 20:15–20).

Specific parallels with Psalms are also evident in Wisdom's speech. Psalm 1 addresses three types of fools or sinners (1:22), parallels to the three types of people to be avoided by the godly man or woman in Psalm 1:1—"wicked," "sinners," and "mockers." See further discussion in 1:22–27 below.

EXPLAIN the Story

1:20–21 Woman Wisdom's voice follows seamlessly from the teachings of the father in 1:8–19, reinforcing his teaching with a voice from the cosmic realm. The son or reader should conclude that the personal, moral, social, and political structures in this world are grounded in the order of God's creation. This assurance is strengthened again in 3:18–20 and 8:1–36. The point of Wisdom's first speech, like the father's, is to provide an urgent warning about the consequences of rejecting her counsel.

As noted above, Woman Wisdom in Proverbs is consistently portrayed in the most public of places in the busiest times of the day (8:3; 9:3). Dame Folly and the strange woman likewise offer invitations in public places (7:12; 9:14), probably because prostitutes used central places to entice customers. Their true character, however, is revealed in their actions in their homes—in secret—when their husbands are gone and it is dark (5:8; 6:29; 7:9, 19). By comparison, wisdom has no secretive ploy or seduction.

The apocryphal book of Sirach presents a similar picture of Wisdom calling out in the streets and inviting the young man to a feast. Paralleling this chapter of Proverbs, Sirach emphasizes both the benefits for listening to her and the consequences for those who do not obey (Sir 24:19–23). Sirach is distinct from other Old Testament wisdom literature in the way it speaks of the covenant with Jacob and Israel and equates wisdom with the torah of Moses.

1:22–23 Wisdom's speech begins with an address to three classes of people who have rejected her counsel—the "simple," "mockers," and "fools" (cf. Pss 1–2). The image of rejected counsel appears often in the Pentateuch (Exod 10:3–6; Num 14:2–4, 11, 27; Deut 1:26, 43) and in prophetic literature (e.g. Isa 65:12; Mic 3:4; cf. Prov 29:1–27). Many scholars here rightly highlight the powerful role that affections or emotions have in the rejection of wisdom and counsel. The simple "*love* . . . simple ways," mockers "*delight* in mockery," and fools "*hate* knowledge."[1] Wisdom's second and third speeches also juxtapose the mutual love that she shares with the "wise" and the love and hatred that motivate fools (8:17, 21, 36; 9:8).

As we have already noted in Proverbs 1:7 and 1:10–14, wisdom is founded on the proper orientation of our human "*eros,*" our deep-seated loves and desires.[2] The Shema in Deuteronomy urges us to "Love the LORD your God" first and foremost (Deut 6:5) the same way that the torah Psalms (1, 19, 119) describe the "blessed" as those whose "delight is in the law of the LORD" (1:2) and who "love your law" (119:97). Wisdom upholds and reinforces the Old Testament view of the ideal human life as one that sets its heart on God and his wisdom, teaching, and law.

1:24–27 In these verses Wisdom spells out the consequences of rejecting her counsel. The father addresses the son directly in 1:1–22, but these words speak to an imaginary audience. Think of the way a child within earshot of a sibling being disciplined or corrected immediately snaps into a posture of obedience and respect, even if it's only short-lived. Watching or overhearing the rebuke given to fictional characters in Proverbs appeals to the readers

---

1. See Longman, *Proverbs*, 120.

2. See again Van Leeuwen's important words on liminality, worldview, and eros in "Liminality and Worldview," and the discussion of "Theology" in the Introduction.

through this same phenomenon; we'd rather learn from the failure of others than be confronted ourselves.[3]

Wisdom warns the fools of pending calamity, violence, chaos, and death. Such language in the Bible needs to be read in light of its genre and context. For example, the word for "calamity" (*ed*) in 1:26 and 27 is used twenty-four times in the Old Testament, all of them in poetry.[4] Thus, like Wisdom herself and the fictional characters she addresses, these interludes in Proverbs create a symbolic and metaphorical world that accentuates the cosmic opposition between wisdom and folly. The New Testament applies the same apocalyptic language in Jesus' Olivet discourse (Matt 13; Mark 24; Luke 21) and John's Revelation. In all of these contexts, the language aims more at shaping present behavior and belief than predicting future events.

Perhaps the strongest image in this section is Wisdom's laughter at the fate of the fool. Yahweh too laughs at conspiring and rebellious kings and nations in Psalm 2:4. In both Psalms and Proverbs, these images are not those of thoughtless or unsympathetic *schadenfreude*. Rather, the laughter in these poetic surroundings emphasizes the ultimate triumph of wisdom over folly while illuminating the deep spirit of defiance, indifference, and antiauthoritarianism that pervades the hearts of the wicked. It is ludicrous to believe their aims will succeed.

1:28–31 Wisdom's address shifts from second to third person ("you" to "they") here, making us an audience to her personal reflections and sorrow over the fate of the foolish. Ultimately, to choose folly is to reject the fear of the Lord—the entry point and key to wisdom (v. 29; cf. 1:7; 2:5). Indeed, such rebellion in this verse is marked by a hatred of knowledge. Wisdom also laments that fools have rejected her "advice" or "counsel" (v. 30).

Modern readers should avoid interpreting her counsel as a kind of mere suggestion. The word for "counsel" here is the same one used for God's "decrees" and "commands" throughout the Old Testament, including twenty times in Exodus and sixteen times in law-loving Psalm 119. The counsel of wisdom, like that of law, is grounded in Yahweh's wisdom and the cosmic order of our world.

LIVE the Story

Wisdom, Jesus, Rhetoric

Wisdom's cosmic speeches resemble Jesus' public teachings in the New Testament. His public discourses like those in the Sermon on the Mount make

---

3. See Fox, *Proverbs 1–9*, 98.
4. Waltke, *Proverbs 1–15*, 207.

a public appeal to Israel to turn to lives of true faith and righteousness (Matt 5–6). Like Woman Wisdom, Jesus uses parables, rhetoric, and hyperbole to provoke our imaginations to reckon with the cosmic realities that lie behind our personal and private behavior (Matt 7). The parable of the wise man who built his house on the rock (Matt 7:24–27) is a particularly striking echo of the speeches of Woman Wisdom in Proverbs 1–9 in the way that it not only affirms wise behavior in the world but even more in the way that it describes the wise person as one who has faith in the creator of the world. In this way Jesus assumes the role of Wisdom in Proverbs 1–9, calling the world to hear a new and urgent message about his work to redeem the whole creation.

While the poetic images in Woman Wisdom's next two speeches (8:4–36; 9:4–11) entice us with the benefits of wisdom—safety, happiness, life, and intimacy with God—this first speech corners us with its stern warnings about the consequences of folly.

As noted above, Jesus takes on this role in his own preaching: (1) The promises and warnings are the same, e.g., "The thief comes only to steal and kill and destroy; I have come that they may have life, and have it to the full" (John 10:10); and (2) The source of help and salvation is the same, i.e., embrace Yahweh/Jesus.[5]

Proverbs directs its poetry to a present sense of urgency about folly, specifically in the way it originates out of deep *hatred* for wisdom and God and a corresponding *love* for wickedness. Whereas popular, modern ideas of ethics are motived by emotions or often vague ideas of personal "conscience," wisdom scorns those who will not critically evaluate and discipline their loves and desires.

The urgency and rhetoric that Jesus and Wisdom share can also be seen in Paul's words to Timothy who faced a church full of conflict, false teachers, and immorality: "Keep reminding God's people of these things. Warn them before God against quarreling about words; it is of no value, and only ruins those who listen" (2 Tim 2:14–15); and "Flee the evil desires of youth and pursue righteousness, faith, love, and peace, along with those who call on the Lord out of a pure heart. Don't have anything to do with foolish and stupid arguments . . ." (vv. 22–23). And as the book concludes, Paul tells Timothy, "Preach the word . . . For the time will come when people will not put up with sound doctrine. Instead, to suit their own desires, they will gather around them a great number of teachers to say what their itching ears want to hear. They will turn their ears away from the truth and turn aside to myths" (4:2, 3–4).

---

5. Thanks to Scott Brodie for alerting me to this connection.

¹ My son, if you accept my words
    and store up my commands within you,
² turning your ear to wisdom
    and applying your heart to understanding—
³ indeed, if you call out for insight
    and cry aloud for understanding,
⁴ and if you look for it as for silver
    and search for it as for hidden treasure,
⁵ then you will understand the fear of the LORD
    and find the knowledge of God.
⁶ For the LORD gives wisdom;
    from his mouth come knowledge and understanding.
⁷ He holds success in store for the upright,
    he is a shield to those whose walk is blameless,
⁸ for he guards the course of the just
    and protects the way of his faithful ones.
⁹ Then you will understand what is right and just
    and fair—every good path.
¹⁰ For wisdom will enter your heart,
    and knowledge will be pleasant to your soul.
¹¹ Discretion will protect you,
    and understanding will guard you.
¹² Wisdom will save you from the ways of wicked men,
    from men whose words are perverse,
¹³ who have left the straight paths
    to walk in dark ways,
¹⁴ who delight in doing wrong
    and rejoice in the perverseness of evil,
¹⁵ whose paths are crooked

and who are devious in their ways.
¹⁶ Wisdom will save you also from the adulterous woman,
    from the wayward woman with her seductive words,
¹⁷ who has left the partner of her youth
    and ignored the covenant she made before God.
¹⁸ Surely her house leads down to death
    and her paths to the spirits of the dead.
¹⁹ None who go to her return
    or attain the paths of life.
²⁰ Thus you will walk in the ways of the good
    and keep to the paths of the righteous.
²¹ For the upright will live in the land,
    and the blameless will remain in it;
²² but the wicked will be cut off from the land,
    and the unfaithful will be torn from it.

Listening to the Text in the Story: Deuteronomy 4–11; 28; 30; Proverbs 1–9; Isaiah 11:1–9; Hosea 4:1–6; 6:1–6

Many scholars have rightly noticed that Proverbs 2 serves as a summary or overview of the contents in chapters 1–9. It also appears to resemble much of the material in the book of Deuteronomy, which is the book most explicitly concerned with the "teaching" of the five books in the Pentateuch.

We first make note of the significant correspondences between Proverbs 2 and 1–9, especially the beginnings of each of the parental instructions.

2	1–9	Parental Instructions
2:1		My son, if you accept my words and store up my commands within you
	7:1	My son, keep my words and store up my commands within you
2:2		turning your ear to wisdom and applying your heart to understanding
	5:1	My son, pay attention to my wisdom; turn your ear to my words of insight,
2:3		Indeed, if you call out for insight and cry aloud for understanding

2	1–9	**Parental Instructions**
	8:1	Does not wisdom call out? Does not understanding raise her voice?
2:4		and if you look for it as for silver and search for it as for hidden treasure
	3:14	for she is more profitable than silver and yields better returns than gold.
2:9		Then you will understand what is right and just and fair—every good path
	1:3	for receiving instruction in prudent behavior, doing what is right and just and fair;

How likely is it that chapter 2 was written as a summary of these first nine chapters? In answering this, several points deserve consideration. First, the vocabulary shared in these parallels is quite precise. Second, chapter 2 is also highly stylized in its own right, written in acrostic form, which suggests attentive crafting and editing. Third, the fact that chapter 2 is the only section in these chapters lacking imperatives or explicit commands suggests that this material gathers sample contents from the first nine chapters while inspiring the student to pursue them with utmost diligence. Fourth, in addition to the allusions internal to Proverbs, chapter 2 also shares similarities with the language and rhetoric in Deuteronomy and Isaiah. A brief comparison between Proverbs 2 and Deuteronomy 6 and 9 reveals parallels like the "fear of the LORD" (Deut 6:2; Prov 2:4–5), hearing the laws and sayings (Deut 6:3; Prov 2:2), laying up these teachings in the "heart" (Deut 6:5; 11:18; Prov 2:2, 10; 11:18), speaking laws and sayings (Deut 6:7; 11:19; Prov 2:3), and promises of future protection (Deut 11:23; Prov 2:7–22). These types of parallels are also explicit in Proverbs 3, 6, and 7 (see commentary below).

Among the prophets a similar connection exists between "knowing" God and doing works of justice, righteousness, and mercy (Isa 11:1–9; Jer 22:13–17). The parallel in Isaiah goes even further, tying the righteous works that will be done by a future king (11:4–5) to wisdom and the fear of the Lord: "The Spirit of the LORD will rest on him—the Spirit of wisdom and of understanding, the Spirit of counsel and of might, the Spirit of the knowledge and fear of the LORD" (11:2).

Proverbs 1–9 was probably written in the postexilic period, when Israel's confidence in the law and covenants was seriously strained.[1] Many scholars

---

1. See Murphy, *Proverbs*, xx–xxi.

even argue that Israel's later writings reveal a desire to abandon the cultic and nationalistic focus of law in favor of a more secular and international approach to wisdom. It would be naïve to claim that Proverbs does not engage its readers' doubts about the covenants after the exile. But it would be equally short-sighted to assume that the evidence of these questions, or even two rhetorical ways of describing wisdom and law in Proverbs or elsewhere in the Old Testament, means that Proverbs endorses wisdom over law—much less that the two should even be opposed in an either/or way. Such views inevitably reduce law to a strict legal code rather than—as in the Pentateuch—instructions interwoven with narratives that provoke discussion and reflection. We will address these issues throughout chapters 2–9, and 30 below.

EXPLAIN the Story

Proverbs 2 is a self-contained poem; some scholars even translate it as a single sentence. The poem's twenty-two paired lines match the twenty-two letters in the Hebrew alphabet[2] and the verses divide equally between two halves, 1–11 and 12–22, each having three stanzas. This two-part structure corresponds to two levels of argument. The first three stanzas (1–4; 5–8; 9–11) all begin with *aleph*—the first letter in the Hebrew alphabet—and appeal to the son to acquire wisdom, whether by studying, hearing, or receiving it from God. The stanzas in the second half (12–15, 16–19, 20–22) begin with the Hebrew letter *lamed*, and their content as a whole contrasts the "paths" or "ways" of deceitful men and those of the adulterous woman with the paths and ways of righteousness, life, and uprightness.

Fox comments that the sophisticated symmetry in the poem allows its message to come across as one extended thought: "If you do what I say, you will learn wisdom, which will bring you to the fear of God and righteousness, which will protect you and keep you away from wicked men and women and thereby ensure you a long life."[3]

As already noted, a comparison of this speech to the rest of the material in Proverbs 1–9 reveals that there is no explicit advice or command. The teacher does not give specific lessons in what we must do but arranges his teachings pedagogically to suit the way we learn: teachers, parents, and God have a role to play in this project of getting wisdom, but it will never happen if the student does not seek and work diligently for it.

---

2. This poem does not flow from a-z like the poem in Chapter 31:10–31 or the twenty-two stanzas in Psalm 119, which are true alphabetic acrostics. Lamentations has five acrostic poems of twenty-two lines or sections. The last poem in chapter 5 is not in a-z order either.

3. Michael V. Fox, "The Pedagogy of Proverbs 2," *JBL* 113 (1994), 235–36.

2:1–4 This first stanza sets up the protasis, or conditional "if" statements, in the father's long speech. In this stanza the conditions appeal across the whole range of the son's human identity, make-up, and sensory nature: desires (v. 1), heart and ears (v. 2), voice (v. 3), and eyes (v 4). Elsewhere in Proverbs we find tasting as an element of sensory pursuit of wisdom and folly (cf. 1:31; 13:2; 24:13). Wisdom appears as pursuit of physical engagement with our bodies in the world, which should be pursued with the fervency of one in search of treasure (v. 4).[4]

2:5–8 These verses begin a long list of benefits that result from seeking wisdom. Above all, wisdom provides understanding of the fear of the Lord and discloses the knowledge of God (v. 4). Taken together with the motto in Proverbs 1:7, the path of wisdom is an upward spiral: we begin the search for wisdom with the fear of the Lord (1:7), which leads to greater understanding of God, who then increases our wisdom (2:6).

In 2:7–8 God promises that he will provide a shield of protection and "guard" the path of the blameless. This is not a command to be righteous, though that might be implicit; nor is this a guarantee that the son will be secured from all future unrighteousness and harm (cf. 3:11–12). Rather, this is the father's experienced observation that wise, God-fearing people are also always righteous, just, and blameless people. Just as God gives wisdom to those who seek it, so he helps the wise apply their learning to obedience. This accentuates the image of an upward spiral of learning in this chapter. To pursue wisdom is to enter into a life-long journey of higher and higher levels of knowledge, piety, divine intimacy, and faith.

2:9–11 Echoing chapter 1, chapter 2 now promises that the wisdom-seeker will come to know righteousness, justice, and equity (1:3; 2:9). In our discussion of 1:3 in the first chapter, I commented that this is the only other place in the wisdom literature that uses all three of these terms together. They appear frequently in the books of law, psalms, and prophets. We have here strong evidence that wisdom, rather than offering an alternative to the law, works in a complementary way, providing the deliberative powers we need to act obediently in the novel situations that face us in day-to-day life.

Verse 10 promises that studying wisdom creates an increasing desire for wisdom in our hearts, or deepest cognitive and emotional centers, and it satisfies our "appetites." Like most English translations, the NIV here translates the Hebrew *nephesh* as "soul" rather than "appetite." But in most cases in the Old Testament, *nephesh* signifies our physical body and its accompanying

---

4. Cf. Clifford, *Proverbs*, 47.

desires.[5] Verse 11 promises that "discretion" and "understanding" will protect and watch over the wisdom-seeker, paralleling images where "wisdom" and God guard us from the ways of the wicked, of evil, and of death (vv. 7, 12, 16, 20–21).

2:12–15 We have seen that God, "knowledge," and "discretion" all protect the wise. In these verses wisdom promises to "save" or deliver young men from the two principal evils that threaten the young man in chapters 1–9: "wicked men" (12–15) and the "adulterous" or "wayward woman" (vv. 16–19).

The wicked men in these verses pick up on the father's first warning against the ways of sinful men in 1:10–14. These men are singled out for "perverse" speech, paths that walk in "darkness," and hearts that "delight" and rejoice in rebellious and evil behavior (2:12–13). Just as wisdom is elsewhere expressed as a matter of desire—love and hatred (see 1:22 above)—here Proverbs exposes the heinousness of the desires and passions of the wicked. Proverbs 12:26 echoes the father's exhortation for the son to choose his friends carefully. We are impressionable beings whose paths are inevitably influenced by the company we keep.

Michael Fox rightly discourages us from viewing the "two ways" in Proverbs as two simply defined highways in life.[6] Proverbs indeed warns that there is a sharp, unambiguous line between good and evil and wisdom and folly. But owing to the infinite variety evident with individual humans and the creation in which we live, there are countless paths of wisdom and countless paths of folly. This invitation comes with a sense of urgency for the individual to pursue the path to wisdom.

2:16–19 This is the first explicit reference to the woman "stranger" or "outsider" in Proverbs.[7] It is likely that this description alludes to some kind of legal or social status, or both. As we will summarize in chapter 9 below, the feminine characters of the adulterous woman and Dame Folly gradually merge throughout chapters 2–8 before coming together in Folly's final erotic appeal to the young man in 9:13–18. Still, some scholars doubt that these two figures are in play throughout these chapters, arguing instead that they represent two different threats to the young man. Clearly, the fact that the seductions of the adulterous women and cosmic Folly consistently lead to the literal and cosmic ends of "death" and "Sheol" (2:18; 5:5, 23; 7:26–27; 9:18) is a strong sign that the feminine imagery is designed to reside simultaneously in literal and metaphorical worlds in these chapters.

2:20–22 The father's lecture concludes with a final assurance and a

5. See Waltke, *Proverbs 1–15*, 227.
6. Fox, *Proverbs 1–9*, 130.
7. See Murphy, *Proverbs*, 16.

warning. On the one hand, seeking wisdom and avoiding sinners and the adulterous woman will take the son along paths and ways of goodness and righteousness to a long life in the land. On the other hand, those who walk in folly will suffer the consequences of being "cut off" and "torn" from the land. Van Leeuwen notes that the specific language in these threats about the land in verse 22 makes it unlikely that these are only a coincidental parallel to Israel's historical narratives about the promised land, but rather that they are designed intentionally to align the benefits of wisdom with God's covenant promises of future real estate (cf. Deut 8:1; 28:1–14; Ps 37; Zech 31:1: Isa 40–55).[8] This concrete image of dwelling forever in the land juxtaposed sitting alongside the adulterous woman and her connection to death serve to tie all the mundane activities of daily life to the structure of the cosmic architecture built into our world.

LIVE the Story

A Comprehensive Education: Anthropology and Cosmology

The father's instruction in Proverbs 2 can be boiled down to two basic precepts—seek wisdom and avoid the paths of unscrupulous men and adulterous women which lead to folly and death. As we saw above, this speech actually does not give any explicit commands but instead uses the framework of behavior and consequences to paint an overall portrait of education.

We noted in the commentary on chapters 1–2 that higher education in the West over the last century has departed from a comprehensive approach to learning. Because of the increasing diversity of areas of study and the loss of a center or organizing principle for knowledge, academic subjects are now studied in isolation; learning is now like pouring sand into an array of buckets of various sizes and shapes.

Furthermore, a student's health, well-being, and sense of vocation—once a major part of the teacher's responsibility—have gradually been delegated to student services, which includes functions like advising, mental health, religious programs, and career counseling, to name but a few.

Christians are not going to change this model, at least not to any significant degree. But we can and should think critically about how education is shaping students' sense of knowledge and wholeness and fill in the gaps when we find them. Proverbs 2 provides two significant insights that assist us in this process.

---

8. Van Leeuwen, *Proverbs*, 47.

An Upward Spiral of Learning

The first half of the chapter (2:1–11) leads the reader to view learning as a journey on an upward spiral. Seeking and calling out for wisdom promises to reveal knowledge of God, who gives more wisdom and knowledge and understanding of righteousness and justice. Learning, moreover, coincides with a shaping by and of our sensory human identity: mouths, tastes, eyes, ears, hearts, and desires. When we desire wisdom and seek it diligently (vv. 2–4), God promises to fill our hearts with wisdom and increase our delight in learning (vv. 6–10). In the book of James the Lord Jesus Christ takes the place as the source and giver of wisdom. It is the Lord in whom we trust and whom we seek to fill our lack of wisdom (Jas 1:1; 2:1).

Seeking wisdom gives way to learning and a corresponding increase in our desire for God and for wisdom. The love of God might not be mentioned in this chapter, but it's certainly implicit. Read alongside the rest of Proverbs 1–9, we find a kind of circle of love shared between wisdom, God, and humans (cf. 3:12; 7:4; 8:30). While it's almost automatic for us to think of learning, pleasure, devotion, and worship as distinct activities, Proverbs imagines them as an integrated part of us coming to full maturity.

Relying on the teachings of Proverbs, Ecclesiastes, and Song of Songs, the monastic culture derived a way of learning that was characterized by a pursuit of knowledge, wisdom, and desire of God and heaven.[9] To grow in the love and desire of God required study of literature and natural science. Such a view of learning is only possible if God is the source of creation and wisdom.

Discerning the Structure of Things

Our lives in the public arena subject us to an assault of competing discourses that seek to lure us with their enticing rhetoric of power, greed, sexuality, violence, and injustice. The upward spiral of faith and learning—of knowledge of God and increase in wisdom—leads to a sharpened understanding of the world that God has made. In the process, we come to view the world through God's eyes, which equips us to resist the competing discourses or worldviews we meet in the public arena of life.

And yet in the Old Testament, our intimacy with God is limited, mediated through the sacrificial and cultic laws and rituals. The fact that the high priest alone is permitted to enter the holy of holies is a reminder of our alienation from God.

Things change drastically in the New Testament. Jesus gives us access to the very person and personality of God (Heb 10:19–22), and through this

---

9. See Jean Leclercq, *The Love of Learning and the Desire for God: A Study of Monastic Culture* (New York: Fordham University Press, 1982), 71–88.

union with the Father through the Son, the Spirit gives us access to the very mind of God (1 Cor 2:8–16). Pope Francis describes our new experience this way:

> Faith does not merely gaze at Jesus, but sees things as Jesus himself sees them, with his own eyes: it is a participation in his way of seeing. In many areas in our lives we trust others who know more than we do. We trust the architect who builds our home, the pharmacist who gives us medicine for healing, the lawyer who defends us in court. We also need someone trustworthy and knowledgeable where God is concerned. Jesus, the Son of God, is the one who makes God known to us (cf. John 1:18). Christ's life, his way of knowing the Father and living in complete and constant relationship with him, opens up new and inviting vistas for human experience . . . . Far from divorcing us from reality, our faith in the Son of God made man in Jesus of Nazareth enables us to grasp reality's deepest meaning and to see how much God loves this world and is constantly guiding it towards himself.[10]

This does not mean that we become God or come to know all things. It does, however, signal a grand transformation of our human nature so that we come to love the world as God has loved it (John 3:16). Francis says again, "Here we see the Holy Spirit at work. The Christian can see with the eyes of Jesus and share in his mind, his filial disposition, because he or she shares in his love, which is the Spirit. In the love of Jesus, we receive in a certain way his vision."[11]

---

10. Pope Francis, Encyclical Letter *Lumen Fidei*, 18, (29 June 13).
11. Ibid., 21.

Proverbs 3:1–12

 LISTEN to the Story

¹ My son, do not forget my teaching,
   but keep my commands in your heart,
² for they will prolong your life many years
   and bring you peace and prosperity.
³ Let love and faithfulness never leave you;
   bind them around your neck,
   write them on the tablet of your heart.
⁴ Then you will win favor and a good name
   in the sight of God and man.
⁵ Trust in the LORD with all your heart
   and lean not on your own understanding;
⁶ in all your ways submit to him,
   and he will make your paths straight.
⁷ Do not be wise in your own eyes;
   fear the LORD and shun evil.
⁸ This will bring health to your body
   and nourishment to your bones.
⁹ Honor the LORD with your wealth,
   with the firstfruits of all your crops;
¹⁰ then your barns will be filled to overflowing,
   and your vats will brim over with new wine.
¹¹ My son, do not despise the LORD's discipline,
   and do not resent his rebuke,
¹² because the LORD disciplines those he loves,
   as a father the son he delights in.

Listening to the Text in the Story: Deuteronomy 6:6–9; 8:1–20; 11:18–20;
Judges 2:17; 17:6; 21:5; Jeremiah 31

Scholars dispute the best way to outline Proverbs 3 and how many independent poems exist. Nevertheless, we can identify two sets of admonitions from a father (vv. 1–12 and 21–35) that surround his central digression about Woman Wisdom (vv. 13–20). We will consider each of these three sections of chapter 3 in three consecutive chapters.

Scholars also express a wide range of opinions as to whether Proverbs intentionally alludes to, or is even aware of, other Old Testament contexts. This commentary has argued that the most natural source of material for a Hebrew writer in thinking practically about teaching wisdom to an audience would be the Old Testament. The Old Testament narratives are what their audience would have been steeped in from generation to generation.

Notice in this context (Prov 3:1–12) that we find strong parallels between the father's injunction in verse 1, "do not forget my teaching, but keep my commandments in your heart," and the classic passage on memory and forgetting in Deuteronomy 8, which warns Israel that God will test the content of Israel's "heart" (8:2) by whether they will "remember" and "not forget" (8:11, 14, 17–19) what God has done. This "not forgetting" in Deuteronomy would be evidenced by Israel keeping and doing his "commands" (8:1, 2, 6, 11). Keeping commands in Proverbs is also equated with "ways" and "paths" that are obedient, as well as people "fearing [God]," just as Deuteronomy enjoins Israel for "walking in obedience to him and revering him" (8:6). Of course long life (in the land) is what is at stake in both Deuteronomy 8 and Proverbs 3:1–12. Both passages, while using different Hebrew words, correspond in their intent for readers to accept the "discipline" of the Lord (Deut 8:5) and the "discipline" of the father (3:11–12). In sum, the father in Proverbs appears to take on the characteristics and teachings of God in Deuteronomy.

The language and images in Proverbs 3 and Deuteronomy also appear throughout Judges, which expresses God's design to use hardship to "test Israel" (2:22) to see if they would "obey the LORD's commands, which he had given their ancestors by the hand of Moses" (3:4). Israel did not "listen" and turned away from the "way of their fathers who had listened to the commandments of Yahweh" (2:17, author's translation).

All three books also appropriate the same visual anthropology. Yael Avrahami has helpfully highlighted the fact that sight is the only sense in the Bible that is used as a metaphor for personal knowledge or opinions.[1] She comments that the phrases "in his eyes" and "in your eyes," which express such personal knowledge, are unique in the way they imply "not

---

1. Yael Avrahami, *The Senses of Scripture: Sensory Perception in the Hebrew Bible* (New York: T&T Clark, 2011), 258–62.

just thought but judgment."[2] In this light we find Proverbs warning consistently against foolish personal judgment: "do not be wise in your own eyes" (3:7; cf. 12:15; 26:12); instead "trust in the LORD" (3:5). The book of Judges too equates doing "evil in the eyes of the LORD" (3:7,12) with each person doing what was right is his own eyes (17:6; 21:25; cf. Deut 12:8; Isa 5:21; Jer 9:23).[3] It should be added that personal knowledge is not always portrayed negatively, as when Jacob served seven years for Rachael and it seemed ("in his eyes") to be "only a few days to him" (Gen 29:20). Similarly, Job's friends cease their debate with him because Job was "righteous in his own eyes" (32:1). Still, both of these cases make clear that visual perception represents individual opinions. Proverbs, like Deuteronomy and Judges, consistently warns that we should not depart from the commands of God as taught by our ancestors.

Proverbs also makes use of "memory metaphors" that appear particularly in Deuteronomy.[4] The images of adorning ourselves with teachings and "writing," or "binding" commands on our "hearts," signify a deep and permanent state of apprehension that is evidenced in consistent behavior, not simply from rote learning (Prov 3:3; cf. 1:9; 6:22; 7:3; Deut 6:8; 11:18; Jer 17:1).

There is no mistaking the fact that the book of Jeremiah provides a particularly pessimistic perspective on our ability to do what Deuteronomy and Proverbs command. The new covenant that God promises in Jeremiah 31 comes with the promise that God himself will have to "put [the law] in their minds and write it on their hearts" (Jer 31:33). Such a reading, however, makes it seem as if Proverbs and Deuteronomy are somehow naïve and less worthy of our reading than the Prophets and especially the New Testament. This would be an inattentive reading of these two books, a point we will examine more closely in Live the Story below.

EXPLAIN the Story

Just as chapter 2 proceeded from a set of conditions (vv. 1–4) to a long list of outcomes or consequences (vv. 5–22), so 3:1–12 involves a poetic alternation of conditions and consequences. Except here the alternation occurs in pairs of verses where the odd verses list the condition and the even verses the outcome:

---

2. Ibid., 258.
3. Cf. the NIV "everyone did as they saw fit." The loose paraphrasing of the NIV here and elsewhere obscures the important anthropological use of senses throughout Proverbs.
4. See Fox, *Proverbs 1–9*, 146–147.

Condition	Consequence
3:1 Keep commands	3:2 Life of peace and prosperity
3:3 Bind love and faithfulness	3:4 Win favor before God and others
etc.	

Looking more closely at the poetic composition, we find that the conditions usually appear with two commands and two consequences. Verses 3 and 5 stand apart in that they both offer three conditions and one consequence. We will discuss these below.

3:1–4 As noted in the section above, Proverbs employs language typical of Deuteronomy, exhorting the son not to "forget" but to keep his torah and "commands," and to "bind" them on his neck and heart. The result in both Deuteronomy and Proverbs is long life in the land. As we will see throughout this whole admonition, the son's attitude, effort, and piety are more in focus than the intellectual achievements of wisdom.

Verse 1 demands that we treasure the teachings and commands in our heart—the existential center of our human nature—while verse 3 warns us not to let "love and faithfulness" depart from us (cf. 20:28). "Love and faithfulness" occurs several times in the Old Testament, perhaps most significantly in the book of Exodus where God reveals himself as abounding in "love and faithfulness." And, not coincidentally, these two actions appear in Hosea 4:1–3 as a summary of the ethical behavior that God required but found lacking in Israel.

Together, verses 1–4 continue Proverbs' emphasis on wisdom as a quality that grows out of and is sustained by submissive and loving relationships with parents and others. Paul depicts our life in Christ with similar language about the community and children in Ephesians 5–6, the same hope promised in Proverbs: "that it may go well with you and that you may enjoy long life on the earth" (6:3; cf. Prov 3:2). As Waltke notices, this command to keep "love and faithfulness" joined with the promise of the Lord's protection in vv. 3–4 is expanded by the commands and assurances at the end of this speech from the father (3:27–35).[5]

3:5–8 This quatrain of sayings (four verses) is among the most popular and memorized verses in the book of Proverbs, if not the Old Testament. The attraction is likely due to its simple yet all-encompassing vision for human life. Simple as the metaphors and figures of speech are, they are rich sources for reflection. Though they present some challenges for translation and interpretation, viewing these verses aligned in their parallel structure and positive and negative commands and consequences helps us to better decipher these issues.

---

5. Waltke, *Proverbs 1–15*, 365–66.

Commands	Consequences	
+ trust in God (5a)		
- do not rely on self (5b)		
+ know God in everything (6a)	life of straight paths (6b)	
- do not be self-reliant (7a)		
+ fear the Lord and turn from evil (7b)	health to your body (8a)	life to your bones (8b)

Seen in this light, these four verses call for submitting the whole life and self to God and his wisdom rather than our own. Interestingly, the word "wisdom" appears nowhere in 3:1–12, but the blessing of wisdom is inferred by the son embracing the behaviors and attitudes commanded by the father.

Two interpretive challenges emerge in these verses. First, there is some disagreement on how best to translate verse 6a, literally, "in all your ways, know him." The NIV renders it "in all your ways submit to him," though most other translations choose to retain a sense of the Hebrew verb *yada* "to know." Something else is lost in the NIV translation besides verbal equivalence and the repetition of key words. The verb *yada* has a remarkably wide range of connotations in the Old Testament that go far beyond submission. Knowledge can mean everything from the intuitive understanding a bird has in knowing how to fly to the aesthetic sense received from seeing a magnificent natural scene to sexual intercourse. With this understanding we cannot help but notice how the benefits in verses 6b and 8 imagine the fullness of a physically blessed life. This implies that knowing God is not just obeying or submitting to him, but a calling to discover fellowship with and understanding of God in and through every single thing we do, say, and think (cf. 2:5). Perhaps it is little coincidence that David's final fatherly appeal to Solomon is to "know the God of your father and serve him with a whole heart and with a delighting mind, for Yahweh searches all hearts and understands every plan and thought" (1 Chron 28:9, author's translation). Knowing God equates to serving God wholly and fully in every area of life.

A second difficulty arises from what it means for God to "make your paths straight" (6b). Similar wording appears in Isaiah's messianic vision, "in the wilderness prepare the way for the LORD; make straight in the desert a highway for our God" (40:3), a promise that Mark cites as being fulfilled at the beginning of his Gospel (1:3). Christians have been known to use this verse, along with verses 9–10, in support of a "health and wealth" gospel: if you obey God, your life will flourish and all your desires will be met. Notice, however, that on the "straight" path to accomplishing his mission, Jesus suffered misunderstanding and opposition, was rejected by his followers, forsaken by the Father, and eventually murdered. We must conclude that, as in the story of Job, proverbial wisdom seeks to hold together the idea of a life guided and protected by God in the midst of God's discipline alongside the reality of unexpected injustice and suffering. In fact, in his own defense Job makes a long speech about the reality of the wicked prospering in the world (Job 21).

3:9–10 These verses promise the young man that if he "honor[s] the Lord" with his "wealth" and his "firstfruits," then God will fill his barns with food and vats with wine. Beneath these promises are a host of issues that demand thoughtful interpretation. First, the terms "wealth" and "firstfruits" belong to Israel's laws for liturgical and festival offerings (Num 15:21; Deut 14:28; 16:15; 26:1–12). While this is the only place that Proverbs alludes to Israel's liturgical life, we do find other examples where cult and wisdom are combined both in the Old Testament (Job 2–3; Eccl 5:1–2) and other ancient Near Eastern wisdom writings, such as Merikare, Ani (Any), and the Babylonian Counsels of Wisdom.[6] Contrary to the popular view in the eighteenth and nineteenth centuries that the temple and cult were considered outdated by the wisdom writers, these verses encourage us to instead see the sages working to connect God's desire to bless and fill the creation (Gen 1:27–31) with the requirements in the priestly laws.

Second, we have to deal with wisdom apparently promising that obedience to the law will automatically result in financial and material blessing; and not just blessings, but full barns and vats of wine. Imagine the most luxurious level possible in ancient lifestyles. Yet all of us know life does not work this way. Is Proverbs that naïve? A person could think so from a cursory and careless reading with little sense for the mechanics of poetry. Surely Proverbs wants us to see that an obedient life will lead to fewer obstacles and God's favor, even in a fallen world. But as the next two verses (11–12), and many more in Proverbs, Job, and Ecclesiastes caution, this is not all there is to wisdom's worldview. While we pursue obedience to God with hope for a better life, we recognize that the powers of sin and evil, the wildness of the created world, and God's hand in our affairs forbid a name-it-and-claim-it approach to life.

3:11–12 The young man or woman who hears remarkable optimism in the promises of verses 5–10 must immediately balance it with God's promise to discipline us throughout our lives. We find here, as in chapters 1–2,

6. Fox, *Proverbs 1–9*, 152.

3:10–12, and in similar passages in Deuteronomy 4–11, that God's discipline is always a model for fatherly discipline. The writer of Hebrews encourages Christians to persevere with this same assurance of the Lord's loving discipline (12:5–6).

LIVE the Story

Wisdom and Law

A literal translation of Proverbs 3:1 calls us to keep the father's torah and obey his "commandments." As we've discussed various places above (1:8; 2:1, 9) the language in Proverbs 1–9, 28, and 30 sounds remarkably similar to Deuteronomy 4–11.

Yet most readers see little, if any, connection between law and wisdom. Most scholarly socio-historical readings of the Old Testament want to find strong distinctions between the historical settings and worldviews held respectively by wisdom writers, law writers, prophets, etc. More conservative readers, meanwhile, tend to see the law only in in its moral dimension, convicting people of sin. This reading tends to view wisdom as little more than an afterthought and thus show little appreciation for the common way law and wisdom make a connection between the cosmic order of creation and daily life.

The primary issue that motivates both of these groups is the fact that the wisdom literature makes almost no explicit mention of the cultic law, Israel's history, or its covenantal theology apart from the frequent use of God's covenant name, Yahweh. A second issue is the apparent tension with the law, prophets, and poetry about Israel's ability to obtain wisdom and uphold the law. The law writers and early wisdom writers held a more optimistic view while the prophetic and late wisdom writers held to a much more pessimistic view.

It must first be pointed out that we have no documentary evidence that wisdom and legal writings arose within different communities or during different social eras. Nor does history demonstrate that wisdom or legal communities felt compelled to distance themselves from one another. This does not mean that there were not different communities or perspectives on the state of Israel's well-being, only that the strong lines between them are a matter of speculation rather than fact.

It is also necessary to point out that both socio-historical and traditional readings often suffer from a modern desire to reduce the poetry of the Old Testament to merely analytical categories or theological doctrines.

Social-historical misreadings overlook places like Proverbs 3:1–12, for example, in wisdom and legal writings. This is where we find a poetic or rhetorical movement between two seemingly contradictory views of the world where the writer, on one hand, promises blessings for obedience and yet on the other hand, clouds those promises with assurance of discipline in the form of unexplained hardship in life (cf. Deut 28–31). Modern, Western culture longs for a precision that poetry and narratives do not provide. In fact, a person can very reasonably see that modern, social-historical research is just that—a modern approach to reading biblical texts that is predisposed to diminish the literary and authoritative nature of the Bible.

Such views do not give credit to the many exceptions of the character-consequence view of human behavior, especially. As a literary whole, Proverbs admits to the fact that obedience and wisdom can escape our grasp (30:3) while refusing to let us abdicate our responsibility to seek out and obey God's created design for the world.

Traditionalist doctrinal misreadings often seek to center interpretation of the Old Testament around Israel's covenant history and the outdated "covenant law" that is superseded by the New Testament gospel. As Frank Crüsemann rightly notes, the legal material in the Pentateuch contains both law and gospel—God's righteous demands and judgments sit alongside promises of grace, forgiveness, and restoration.[7] Paul contrasts law and gospel in his letters, but his language is carefully nuanced to address particular social problems that arise from misuses of the law. On the whole, the New Testament provides an approving attitude to the law and the wisdom it provides for moral living.

This commentary shows that law and proverbs provide various kinds of commentary on daily situations that prompt reflections on life as a whole. Putting it differently, most laws and proverbs serve more of a *contemplative* function than a *legislative* one. As Oliver O'Donovan has pointed out, God's creation is not a random world of unrelated things, but a "pluriformity" in which the great diversity we find in the world exists within "a total framework of intelligibility."[8] Moral learning, therefore, is not "a matter of accumulating new information about the moral code, but of discovering in closer detail that which we already know in broad outline."[9] God's laws do not give way to legal lists but to "knowledge of the created order" expressed in "our ordering

---

7. Frank Crüsemann, *The Torah: Theology and Social History of Old Testament Law*, trans. Allan H. Mahnke (Edinburgh: T&T Clark, 1996), 1–12.

8. Oliver O'Donovan, *Resurrection and Moral Order: An Outline for Evangelical Ethics* (Grand Rapids: Eerdmans, 1986), 189.

9. Ibid., 195.

principles," which are "something rather more significant than mere proce-
dural rules-for-applying-rules. They will provide insight into what the rules
are really about."[10]

Metaphors for Memory

Here we pause to reflect on the use of memory or learning metaphors in this
section of Proverbs.[11] We should first notice that these metaphors are not
abstract—at least not sophisticated abstractions—nor are they drawn ran-
domly from nature. Instead they involve associating knowledge with familiar
actions of the body: keeping teachings in the "tablet of the heart" (3:3, cf. 7:3;
Jer 17:1; 31:33) and writing on and adorning body parts. Paul Ricoeur has
discussed the role that metaphors have in instilling memory and, more particularly, their unique power with language in requiring us to imagine human
action (writing, binding, setting, walking, etc.).[12]

Recent work by scholars in other fields helps us to appreciate why this is
so important. For example, folklorists and anthropologists have shown that
our modern Western culture places overwhelming emphasis on knowing as
a matter of "sight" and "reading texts" over hearing, feeling, experiencing,
and other bodily ways of knowing.[13] Neuroscientists and psychologists reveal
the narrow way we have understood concepts of "body," "mind," "brain,"
and "soul."[14] Proverbs, as we have repeatedly shown, places its emphasis for
knowledge on the heart—the seat of desire—and the act of hearing.[15]

It should be further noted that Proverbs and Deuteronomy both employ
these same memory metaphors. In his work dealing specifically with metaphor, Ricoeur observes that Hebrew language and literature relied upon "root
metaphors," which provided foundational ways for a society to relate to the
world.[16] It becomes clear that not only do wisdom and law constitute the

---

10. Ibid., 203.

11. On this topic see also Fox, *Proverbs 1–9*, 146–47.

12. Paul Ricoeur, *Memory, History, Forgetting*, trans. Kathleen Blamey and David Pellauer (Chicago: University of Chicago Press, 2004), 262–63.

13. See Alan Dundes, "Seeing is Believing," 8–92, and Avrahami, *Senses of Scripture*, 223–76.

14. See Malcolm A. Jeeves and Warren S. Brown, *Neuroscience, Psychology, and Religion: Illusions,
Delusions, and Realities about Human Nature* (West Conshohocken, PA: Templeton Foundation
Press, 2009).

15. In my opinion, Avrahami, *Senses of Scripture*, 250–51, totally overlooks the use of sensory
metaphors in Proverbs, which are distinctly *not* visual. And it is the visual way of knowing that is the
most problematic for Qohelet. See Ryan P. O'Dowd, "Epistemology in Ecclesiastes: Remembering
What It Means to be Human" in *The Words of the Wise are like Goads: Engaging Qohelet in the 21st
Century*, ed. Mark Boda, Tremper Longman III, and Cristian Rata (Winona Lake, IN: Eisenbrauns,
2013), 195–217.

16. Paul Ricoeur, *Interpretation Theory: Discourse and the Surplus of Meaning* (Fort Worth, TX:
Texas Christian University Press, 1976), 64.

essential building blocks of Israel's national identity—as well as the individual identity of each member—but also that the biblical pattern of identify formation makes use of sophisticated language and rhetoric as well as a full range of embodied sensory metaphors.

How does this bear out practically? One could easily question not just the degree to which our dominant modes of education today make use of the power of language and metaphor but also what message those metaphors and language relay about our human identity. How, in other words, might children develop differently when asked to imagine "coming to see things," and "filling their heads" with information versus "hearing," "crying out," "impressing on our hearts," and "adorning ourselves" with the jewelry of wisdom? Which metaphors are more inviting? Which create a greater degree of appreciation for the role of the heart and desire in the learning process and the value and goodness of the human body? And which, as we will discuss in the section below, will actually have a greater impact on influencing our moral behavior? Debates in modern education ought to give serious attention not only to questions of curriculum but also to its preferences for language, symbols, and metaphors in pedagogy.

Prosperity and Despair

In the "Theological Message" section of the Introduction we introduced the relationship between character and consequence in Proverbs—how it is that wisdom and folly lead respectively to blessing and judgment and death. But it is easy to misread that emphasis in Proverbs. Ironically, this section of Proverbs 3 provides some of the most frequently misinterpreted promises and the verses that most strongly correct such misinterpretations.

Make no mistake, Proverbs is a highly optimistic and idealistic piece of writing. While there are many places we hear a sense of realism (cf. 30:1–33), by and large Proverbs promises us protection, life, pleasure, and blessings if we seek wisdom and righteousness. This is not unlike much of what we read in portions of the law and prophets, though they are more serious in their threat. Yet our experiences in life fail to reveal the promise of the righteous being blessed and the wicked being cursed. In fact, the visionary promises in Proverbs 3:2–10 are followed by verses 11–12, which show a clear warning of God's future discipline. So why does God or the human authors of the Bible make such extravagant claims that they know will not come true?

This question is really only pressing if we collapse the language of poetry into a narrow, literal application to the immediate circumstances of daily life without regard for how the literature of the Bible works. Consider that, in addition to the inflated promises of blessings, the biblical threats to fools and the unrighteous are likewise daunting. Those who claim a health and wealth gospel in the Bible would do well to wonder why they have not suffered utter ruin for their foolish behavior. Why, we should ask, would the promises only work in the positive direction?

It also helps to recognize the close affinity and inseparability that exist between desire, reward, and learning.[17] If wisdom were only a matter of knowing and applying ethical and principled facts, there would be little point to the portrayals in chapters 1–9 of Woman Wisdom and Dame Folly. Proverbs works with rich and powerful metaphors to shape the orientation of the desire of our hearts. What we envision as the purpose and outcome of our actions and beliefs plays a major role in what we *do*, so by shaping our sense of reward, pleasure, and motivation, the poetry of Proverbs inclines us to wise behavior.

Said another way, the pervasive presence of eschatology in the Bible serves the function of promising an eternal reward that trains us to live faithfully in the present. In his commentary on Job, Gregory the Great describes this effect:

> . . . [the judgments of God] are more mysterious when things go well with good people here, and ill with bad people . . . since the human mind is hemmed by the thick fog of its uncertainty among the divine judgments, when holy people see the prosperity of the world coming to them, they are troubled with a frightening suspicion. For they are afraid that they might receive the fruits of their labors here; they are afraid that divine justice detects a secret wound in them and, heaping external rewards on them, drives them away from internal ones . . . . Consequently, holy people are more fearful of prosperity in this world than of adversity.[18]

Gregory goes on to say, "Their mind endures all the prosperity of this world grudgingly because it is wounded by the love of heavenly happiness. The more they see how the sweetness of the present life treacherously entices them to turn away from eternal glory, the more they choose to spurn the present instead."[19]

---

17. See "Theology of the Book" in the Commentary introduction and Timothy Schroeder, *Three Faces of Desire* (Oxford: Oxford University Press, 2004).

18. *Moralia in Job*, Book 5, in Stump, *Wandering in Darkness*, 15.

19. See http://www9.georgetown.edu/faculty/jod/texts/moralia5.

¹³ Blessed are those who find wisdom,
   those who gain understanding,
¹⁴ for she is more profitable than silver
   and yields better returns than gold.
¹⁵ She is more precious than rubies;
   nothing you desire can compare with her.
¹⁶ Long life is in her right hand;
   in her left hand are riches and honor.
¹⁷ Her ways are pleasant ways,
   and all her paths are peace.
¹⁸ She is a tree of life to those who take hold of her;
   those who hold her fast will be blessed.
¹⁹ By wisdom the LORD laid the earth's foundations,
   by understanding he set the heavens in place;
²⁰ by his knowledge the watery depths were divided,
   and the clouds let drop the dew.

Listening to the Text in the Story: Genesis 1–3; Psalm 104; Job 38–41; Psalm 1–2; Proverbs 8:1–36; 24:3–4

Scholars of Psalms often make note of the fact that Psalms 1–2, which might have once been a single unit, begin and end with the word "blessing" (Pss 1:1, 2:12). So too the short poem in Proverbs 3:13–18 begins and ends with "blessing." Furthermore, the "delight" the son should have for wisdom in Proverbs (3:15) is also held out to the addressee in Psalm 1 who should "delight" in the "torah of Yahweh" (1:2, author's translation). Added to this, whereas Psalm 1 promises to make the reader a "tree planted by streams of water" (1:3), so wisdom is to the son a "tree of life" (3:18). John Goldingay in fact suggests that Psalm 1 fits more naturally with the content in Proverbs 1–9 than it does with the rest of the Psalter.[1]

---

1. John Goldingay, *Psalms, Volume 1: Psalms 1–41*, BCOTWP (Grand Rapids: Baker Academic, 2006), 80.

These images in Proverbs, of course, resonate both with the creation scene in Genesis 1–3 and related passages that speak of God making the world with wisdom (Pss 104:24; 136:5–9; Prov 8:22–31; cf. 24:3–4).

Sacred or life-giving trees were common in the ancient Near East. In Egypt the sycamore was particularly known for its nourishing qualities, and the goddess of the sycamore is often found engraved in tombs.[2]

EXPLAIN the Story

Aside from a distinct unity in 3:1–12, scholars remain divided as to the structure of the rest of chapter 3. Nevertheless, we can identify several largely independent units that may have once existed as separate poems: 13–18, 19–20, 21–26, and 27–35. That said, the creation imagery overlaps in verses 18 and 19–20, and, as such, we will consider verses 13–20 together here and 21–35 in the next chapter.

3:13–18 Fox designates these verses as one of the five interludes in chapters 1–9 that describe Woman Wisdom and Dame Folly.[3] Other scholars, however, notice that it is the father speaking here and not one of the cosmic women as in the other interludes. I suggest that this mixture of the cosmic speeches with the instructions of the father demonstrates that Proverbs poetically overlaps the images of the women in these chapters: the good wife and the adulterous woman put flesh on the transcendent powers of cosmic Wisdom and Folly.

Verse 13 delivers the first of two promises that wisdom will be a "blessing" to the man who gets it (cf. v. 18). Verses 14–15 then repeat a common motif, that wisdom, in this case her profits, are greater than treasures like silver, gold, or jewels (cf. 2:4; 8:10–11, 19; Job 28:12–19).

The Hebrew term used for "rubies" is rare, and, with only one exception, appears in four contexts that all elevate the value of wisdom over earthly treasures (Prov 3:15; 20:15; 31:10; and Job 28:18).[4] David Daube observes that this unusual term uses the same Hebrew root (*peniyyim*) as Elkanah's wife Peninnah (1 Sam 1). The coincidence could be regarded as coincidental, but as Daube goes on to argue, the story of Hannah and Peninnah has several other distinct parallels with wisdom sayings. Peninnah fits the proverbial caricature of the "unloved woman"—one of the four things under which "the earth trembles" and cannot "bear up" (30:21–23). Peninnah also emphatically "irritates" Hannah (1 Sam 1:6–7), paralleling the vexation of the fool (27:3)

---

2. Fox, *Proverbs 1–9*, 158.

3. Ibid., 155–61.

4. The sole exception is Lam 4:7, which states that the "bodies [of Israel's princes] were more ruddy than corals."

and the unbearable woman of vexation (21:19; cf. also 12:16). And finally, Hannah's name, which is a derivative of "grace," exemplifies her way of life just as it corresponds to the affinity between wisdom and grace in Proverbs (1:9; 3:4, 22, etc.).[5]

These parallels between Proverbs and Samuel suggest that the worldview and language of wisdom informed most of the writings of the Old Testament, or, at the very least, that there are elements of culture, worldview, and figures of speech that pop up through the full range of genres in the Old Testament. More significant in this regard, such parallels allow us to put flesh on otherwise abstract teachings. As wisdom and folly play a central and palpable role in lives and origins of Israel's religious and political leaders, readers grow in their appreciation for the urgency in the father's teaching.[6]

Proverbs 3:16–17 continue to describe the benefits that wisdom offers in this chapter: life, health, prosperity, and peace (cf. vv. 1–10). The verses thus provide a natural transition to the climactic refrain that wisdom is a blessing (v. 18). She is a "tree of life" to those who "take hold" of her and "hold her fast." Longman comments that the imagery is once again sexual in nature, prompting the young man to orient his natural passionate desires toward this figure.[7]

We noted above that this section is set apart in the way it begins and ends with this word "blessing." And yet the image of the "tree of life" in verse 18 overlaps with the language of creation in verses 19–20, softening the seams between the two sections.

We should also observe that this is the only place in the Old Testament where the "tree of life" appears outside of Genesis 2–3. We find similar images of life-giving trees in Psalm 1 and Ezekiel 47:12, and I do not think it is coincidental that Revelation also creates a sense of urgency for the reader with images of cosmic women and a tree of life (cf. Rev 12:1–17; 13:12; 15:4; 17:1–18:24; 21:9; 22:2).

God's use of wisdom to make the world appears elsewhere explicitly and implicitly throughout the Old Testament (cf. Job 28; 38–41; Ps 104:24; Prov 8:22–31). Raymond Van Leeuwen has observed a common pattern in Mesopotamian and biblical writings of what he calls "royal-building

---

5. See these and other parallels in David Daube, "Wine in the Bible," in *Biblical Law and Literature: Collected Works of David Daube*, vol. 3, ed. Calum Carmichael (Berkeley: University of California at Berkeley Press, 2003), 501–12.

6. Daube illustrates similar striking uses of wisdom language and themes in the story of David, Nabal, and Abigail in 1 Samuel 25, "Wine in the Bible," 510–12.

7. Longman, *Proverbs*, 137. Cf. Fox, *Proverbs 1–9*, 59, who appeals to figures in Egyptian iconography holding on to a tree to suggest that this is the image depicted in Prov 3. This, however, overlooks the fact that the woman is the object grasped here, not a tree.

inscriptions."[8] In this pattern of building, the human house serves as a metaphor both for the divine work of creation but also consequently for the ultimate realities in the cosmos. More specifically, the creation is depicted in two stages in which the god or gods first "build" and then "provision," or fill, the houses of the world. This pattern clearly informs the passage in Genesis 1 where God built the skies, waters, and earth on days 1–3 and then filled them with appropriate forms of life on days 4–6. The creation pattern leads to humans viewing the world as ultimately an ordered place: fish don't fill the skies and birds don't live under water.

Following this pattern, Proverbs 3:19 says that God first built creation—he "laid the earth's foundations . . . [and] . . . set the heavens in place"—and then in the next verse that he provisioned it, "the watery deeps were divided and the clouds let drop the dew." The divine creating and filling pattern in Genesis gives way to God's first command for humanity to imitate his pattern of provisioning: "be fruitful . . . and fill the earth" (1:28). As we will see in the commentary on chapter 24:3–4, Proverbs mirrors this pattern, instructing humans to build houses "by wisdom" (v. 3) and to use "knowledge" to fill its rooms (.v 4). Of course house-filling, or life-building, is not an ethically neutral activity. The first band of young men who tempt the son in Proverbs 1:13 conspire to "fill our houses with plunder."

LIVE the Story

Jesus' Blessings

In the New Testament, Jesus makes use of the wisdom blessings or "macarisms" in his sayings in the Beatitudes (Matt 5:3–12). On this occasion Jesus encourages those in suffering on account of the gospel to remain committed to their cause. It is striking how many of his sayings parallel admonitions in this chapter of Proverbs:

Humility and meekness	Matt 5:3, 5; Prov 3:7, 34
Righteousness	Matt 5:6; Prov 3:33
Mercy	Matt 5:7; 3:27–30
Non-violence	Matt 5:8; 3:17, 31

It also bears repeating how pervasive wisdom language and memorable sayings are in Jesus' teachings. Another example can be found in Jesus'

---

8. Van Leeuwen, "Cosmos, Temple, House," 67–90.

admonition not to take the seat of honor at a wedding feast but to wait to be elevated by the host when he comes (Luke 14:7–11). This most likely draws on the same advice in Proverbs 25:7. In his life and his teaching Jesus continually embodies the images of humility, patience, and simplicity. This serves as a judgment for Israel just as it provides a positive model for the church: "Better a little with righteousness than much gain with injustice" (Prov 16:8).

A Father's Commendation of Desire

These verses depict the only time in Proverbs that the father speaks explicitly about Woman Wisdom; in all of her other appearances it is her own voice we hear. In a way, this passage mirrors the song of the valiant woman in Proverbs 31:10–31, where a second-person voice describes a concrete woman and her remarkable accomplishments in order to motivate the son to seek wisdom.

But this passage is about a cosmic woman and it employs sexual imagery that is not found in the valiant woman's song. It often goes unnoticed or unmentioned that the father seeks to stir up his son's desires—including sexual ones. In other words, in order to help the son avoid the destructive paths of violent men and seductive women, Proverbs does not call us to the monasteries of sensual neglect. Rather, it offers its own vision of wise ways, prosperous homes, and alluring women (9:1–12 and 31:10–31). In this context, the father seeks to discipline the power of sexual desire to the confines of the wisdom worldview, encouraging the son to engage in a passionate pursuit of the wise life (cf. 13:12). Such a life will find its delight in hard work, honest speech, social justice, and fulfilling sexual relationships (cf. 5:15). Desires are a good and natural part of our humanity and wisdom is our aid in directing them properly.

God Made the World by Wisdom

It is also worth reflecting for a moment on the fact that both God's making the world by wisdom (3:19) and wisdom becoming to us a tree of life (3:18) appear in this context. On the one hand, the making of the world with wisdom, specifically in the pattern of building and provisioning that we discussed above, leads us to view the world as a physically and logically ordered place. Moreover, the fact that God's activity of filling is always life giving and life affirming allows us to see that God's physical ordering of the world is also moral ordering. And so, just as humans are called to be fruitful and fill the earth, so God's affirming and giving ways establish the foundations for human moral action. Destructive handling of the creation disorders God's work and is, therefore, immoral. This issue will be taken up again in the commentary on Proverbs 24:3–4.

A related implication of God's making the world with wisdom is the fact that God left an imprint of himself and an imprint of the moral life in the grooves and patterns of the natural world he has set in motion. And yet our access to these imprints is clouded through the working of sin in our lives and the world. We will return to this issue in the commentary on chapter 8.

One final issue we will address here is that, apart from the account of creation and fall in Genesis 2–3, Proverbs is the only book in the Old Testament that speaks of the "tree of life." Besides this occurrence (3:18), we find three other references in the main body of sayings in chapters 10–29 (11:30; 13:12; 15:4). None of these latter passages is accompanied by accounts of creation or cosmic wisdom, so the symbolism of the tree is more limited in those cases.

What is most interesting in this case in 3:18–20, and yet seldom noted, is that the promise of the tree of life to those who seek wisdom manifests a strong and clear theme of redemption in the book of Proverbs. That is, the tree from which Adam, Eve, and their progeny were barred from eating (Gen 3:24) God has made available again. Wisdom offers a way to access the blessings lost by the first human couple (cf. Ezek 47:12).

In the New Testament, it is Jesus who is wisdom and who offers this path to life. Jesus also completes the renewal of the creation foreshadowed by the work of wisdom in Proverbs (cf. 1 Pet 1:3), most vividly portrayed in the scene in Revelation 21–22. Fittingly, our access to the revelation of creation's renewal in Jesus also comes to us through wisdom (i.e., Eph 1:7–10, 17–18; Col 1:9–14). Jesus is the wise one in his life and the one who restores the wise order of all that exists in his death and resurrection. The consequence for a Christian reading Proverbs is that wisdom is a paradigmatic insight into the redemptive work God was doing in Israel and would finally do in Christ for the whole world. Christians should confidently read Proverbs expecting to see designs for reconciling and renewing a fallen world.

²¹ My son, do not let wisdom and understanding out of your sight,
 preserve sound judgment and discretion;
²² they will be life for you,
 an ornament to grace your neck.
²³ Then you will go on your way in safety,
 and your foot will not stumble.
²⁴ When you lie down, you will not be afraid;
 when you lie down, your sleep will be sweet.
²⁵ Have no fear of sudden disaster
 or of the ruin that overtakes the wicked,
²⁶ for the LORD will be at your side
 and will keep your foot from being snared.
²⁷ Do not withhold good from those to whom it is due,
 when it is in your power to act.
²⁸ Do not say to your neighbor,
 "Come back tomorrow and I'll give it to you"—
 when you already have it with you.
²⁹ Do not plot harm against your neighbor,
 who lives trustfully near you.
³⁰ Do not accuse anyone for no reason—
 when they have done you no harm.
³¹ Do not envy the violent
 or choose any of their ways.
³² For the LORD detests the perverse
 but takes the upright into his confidence.
³³ The LORD's curse is on the house of the wicked,
 but he blesses the home of the righteous.
³⁴ He mocks proud mockers
 but shows favor to the humble and oppressed.

> [35] The wise inherit honor,
>   but fools get only shame.

Listening to the Text in the Story: Genesis 37–43; 34:25; 37–43; Leviticus 19:11–18; Deuteronomy 24

On the whole, the admonitions in chapters 1–9 tend to extol the benefits of wisdom and provide generalized commands to gain wisdom or act righteously and justly. But in a few places, including 3:25–32 and 6:1–19, the father gives specific commands that are more like legal material in that they are focused on a common topic, the treatment of others. These are joined by the motivation clauses of the Lord's blessing and protection. Their content is similar to the legal texts in Exodus 23:1–9, Leviticus 19, and Deuteronomy 24.

We saw earlier that the imagery of adorning the body with wisdom (3:21–22; cf. 1:9; 3:3; 6:21–23; 7:23) manifests the familiar language of Deuteronomy 4–11, where Moses enjoins Israel to write laws and commands on parts of the body, house, and city. In these cases the metaphorical injunctions emphasize that wisdom and law must be pursued with the full breadth of our human, bodily makeup and in every fiber of our individual, familial, and social lives.

Meanwhile, the commands in verses 25–35, which are interspersed with motivations and assurances, focus on interpersonal relationships and prompt us to imagine a number of applicable situations in the lives of the Patriarchs and the monarchy. I will draw on these other passages in the Explain the Story section below.

EXPLAIN the Story

After the enticing description of Woman Wisdom and her promise that the lost benefits of Eden could be recovered through wisdom (3:13–20), the father now delivers eight commands that are interspersed with motivations and assurances of the Lord's blessing and protection (3:21–25). These commands and promises sustain the persuasive building in the chapter that wisdom is something to pursue with a sense of incomparable urgency, not only so that life may go well but also that the son may be found faithful to the covenant Lord of wisdom.

The father's words can be divided into three parts:

3:21–26, two commands "do not . . ." followed by reasons "for . . ."

3:27–31, five commands with no reasons "do not . . ."

3:32–35, a closing collection of reasons or assurances "for . . ."

3:21–26 The first admonition in verses 21–22 echoes language through-out chapters 1–9, which encourages the son to adorn his body with wisdom (1:9; 6:21; 7:3). Wisdom in Proverbs is more than a shallow memorization of ethical rules. It is a comprehensive shaping of character and desires.

The material in verses 23–26 is enclosed with two references to the "foot" that will not "stumble" (v. 23a) or be snared (v. 26b), paralleling the list of dangers in between—foolish behavior of the son and the actions of the wicked. Elsewhere in Proverbs and the Old Testament the feet symbolize the way of life as a whole and the fate of wise/righteous and the fool/wicked (Pss 1:1; 37:24; 121:3; Prov 1:1; 4:12; 6:18).

Given this broader perspective, the father's promises or assurances in verses 23–26 address a series of progressively intense situations where wisdom will accompany or guard the son: (1) safety (23a); (2) not stumbling (23b); (3) a defenseless state (24a); (4) the dream state (24b); (5) "sudden disaster" (25a), and; (6) the "ruin that overtakes the wicked" (25b).

Similar to the metaphor of walking, the otherwise mundane activity of sleep, in this case sound or "sweet" sleep, here depicts safety in our most defenseless and vulnerable state. In Judges 16:19 Samson is foolishly lured into the defenselessness of sleep. Unsound sleep is often accompanied by dreams: Job is tormented in his dreams (Job 7:13–15), and the dreams of Pharaoh and Nebuchadnezzar bring both of them fear (Gen 41:8; Dan 2:1; 4:5). God, however, gives restful sleep to his people even in the danger of the wilderness (Ezek 34; cf. Jer 31:26; Pss 3:5; 4:8).

The wise and diligent sleep soundly (cf. Eccl 5:12); work that seems futile can just as easily rob us of sleep (Eccl 2:23). Elsewhere in Proverbs deep sleep is a metaphor for the neglect of work (19:15; 24:33). In this context, wisdom is a discipline of finding goodness and value in work such that it leads to rest.

The summary in verse 26 promises that the Lord will be a "confidence" for the young man. Fox suggests that the word *kesil*, "fool," is likely derived from *kesel*, which can be translated "confidence." In such a case the fool is really one who has confidence of a false or "pernicious sort" (cf. Ps 49:14; Job 8:14; 31:24).[1] This would create an intentional play on the false trust of the "fool" at the end of the poem (3:35).

3:27–30 The commands in these verses (and verse 31) have been carefully arranged, moving from sins of omission (vv. 27–28) to sins of commission

---

1. Fox, *Proverbs 1–9*, 164.

(vv. 29–30) to a sin of sheer desire (v. 31), and moving from good done to family or neighbors (*rea*) to that done to broader humanity (*adam*). There is also an increase intensity of the harm that is to be avoided from the first to the last. Israel's historical narratives provide a fruitful background for unpacking the relevancy and need for such commands.

The first two commands direct the son not to withhold the good "due," which is due the needy, and not to hold back something belonging to "your neighbor" overnight (cf. Lev 19:13; Deut 24:17). Withholding something due to another is an injustice but also an act of cruelty that is ultimately destructive (cf. Luke 18:1–8). Jacob serves as a prime example. His withholding stew from his brother Esau was mean. In turn, Jacob was fittingly punished by having both his promised wife and his earned wages withheld by Laban (Gen 26:30–34; 29:2; 31:7). The result in all of these relationships is a loss of trust, estrangement, and a breakdown of family and community life.

After condemning two sins of omission, the father forbids three sins of commission (vv. 29–30). The first (v. 29) involves plotting evil against a defenseless or unsuspecting neighbor, an offense repeated throughout the Old Testament. Simeon and Levi arrange a ruse and lead their brothers to slaughter and plunder the men of Hamor (Gen 34:25–29), and David plots the betrayal and murder of Uriah who sleeps peacefully in David's own house (2 Sam 11:6–21). The tribe of Dan also acts ruthlessly in falling upon the unsuspecting people of Laish (Judg 18:7–10, 27–28). In the last century we've witnessed the violation of this proverb played out on a global scale, with the Germans attacking Poland in WWII, Iraq invading Kuwait in 1990, and the sudden and extreme violence of the Rwandan genocide in the 1990s.

Verse 30 warns the son not "to contend with anyone for no reason when they have done you no harm."[2] As with the proverbs above, Israel's history is rife with examples to the contrary. For "no reason" Cain contends with Abel (Gen 4:8), Sarai with Hagar (Gen 16:6), Laban with Jacob (Genesis 28–31), David with Uriah (2 Sam 11:6–25), and so on (cf. Prov 25:8–10).

3:31–35 The final rule from the father warns the son not to "envy the violent" person, (v. 31), which is followed by a stark comparison of the fates of the wise/righteous and foolish/wicked (vv. 32–35). Psalm 37 voices this same tension in the form of a prayer and portrays an extended reflection on the fate of the righteous and the wicked: "Do not fret because of those who are evil or be envious of those who do wrong" (37:1; cf. Ps 73:3). We can point to several other parallels between these two texts: wisdom or commands on the "heart" (3:3; 37:31); the foot or feet saved from slipping (3:23, 26; 37:31); a call for

---

2. NIV reads "accuse anyone . . . ."

"trust" in the Lord (3:5; 37:3, 5); and an admonishment to the reader to seek wisdom, justice, and generosity (3:13–20, 27–30; 37:26–28, 30).

It ought further to be emphasized that, unlike the four offenses in 3:27–30, this rule addresses only the desire of the heart (cf. Ps 37:4). The many parallels between this conclusion in verses 31–35 and Psalms 37 and 73, in this light, are all the more significant, since the psalms are extended meditations of a righteous follower of the Lord, working in prayer to guard his covetous and envious desires. The righteous actions in these passages are objects to be desired rather than commands to be obeyed. In the New Testament, the book of James contains an extended set of instructions that echo these same themes of avoiding envy and coveting, doing good, and trusting the Lord (4:1–17).

 LIVE the Story

Wisdom, Desire, Jesus
In the larger scope of Proverbs 3, the address in verses 13–35 moves in four waves; from desiring cosmic wisdom (13–18), to a wisely ordered world (19–20), to desiring wisdom for daily life (21–26), to wisely ordered relationships with others (26–35). In this light, our ordering of our public and private worlds can be imagined as living consistently within the grooves of the created world.

As Roland Murphy notes in this context, Proverbs 1–9 consistently assures us that wise behavior will result in God's material blessing.[3] But Murphy rightly goes on to guard against the conclusion that the promise of blessings and curses here and in places like Deuteronomy 28–30 somehow narrowly encourages human greed and selfishness, as if wisdom is a matter of seeking our own ends. Rather, the fact that the constant appeal to the order and health of the creation in these contexts allows us to speak of "a sacramental view of the universe; the goods of this world are a sign of divine pleasure, a sign that the covenant relationship is in good order."[4]

We might then say that Proverbs 3:21–35 calls us to consider our passions and treatment of others with sacred devotion. As noted above, the only relational prohibition from the father in this context is against envy (3:31). And yet all of the other prohibitions arise out of a common concern to nurture a desire for our neighbor's flourishing, even at our own cost. Verse 31, in effect, names the base desire that must be disciplined if the other commands are to be obeyed.

---

3. Murphy, *Proverbs*, 24.
4. Ibid.

James 4 weaves together a similar combination of warnings about passions and admonitions concerning social responsibility toward others. In fact, many scholars believe that James is citing Proverbs 3 in his references to envy and humility (Jas 4:2, 6). And while James lacks the cosmic imagery of Woman Wisdom in Proverbs, he is more emphatic than Proverbs in stating that the passions of the heart are at the root of public and private sins (4:1). Taking these two passages together, we can speak confidently about the biblical approach to our ethical behavior. Conduct, in this sense, is always an expression of desire, whether for righteousness and wisdom or wickedness and folly.

This portion of Proverbs 3 opens a surprising window into Jesus' temptation in the wilderness. Both in Matthew and Luke, Jesus' ultimate aim during his temptation is to persevere in his mission to love the world and redeem it from judgment and death (cf. John 3:15–17). His obedience in the face of temptation can thus be understood as discipline of his passions in order to bring flourishing to the lives of others. And at the center of his temptation, the devil is careful to lure him with the envy of power over the nations. Surely this power rightly belongs to Jesus in principal. But in the context of his earthly ministry and mission, it was a privilege that had to be denied. Just as the serpent and Adam and Eve assumed power and privilege that was not theirs, so the work of redemption took the opposite shape of giving up power that was otherwise rightly possessed. And thus in humility and weakness did we see true power and wisdom (1 Cor 1:18–31).

LISTEN to the Story

¹ Listen, my sons, to a father's instruction;
　　pay attention and gain understanding.
² I give you sound learning,
　　so do not forsake my teaching.
³ For I too was a son to my father,
　　still tender, and cherished by my mother.
⁴ Then he taught me, and he said to me,
　　"Take hold of my words with all your heart;
　　keep my commands, and you will live.
⁵ Get wisdom, get understanding;
　　do not forget my words or turn away from them.
⁶ Do not forsake wisdom, and she will protect you;
　　love her, and she will watch over you.
⁷ The beginning of wisdom is this: Get wisdom.
　　Though it cost all you have, get understanding.
⁸ Cherish her, and she will exalt you;
　　embrace her, and she will honor you.
⁹ She will give you a garland to grace your head
　　and present you with a glorious crown."
¹⁰ Listen, my son, accept what I say,
　　and the years of your life will be many.
¹¹ I instruct you in the way of wisdom
　　and lead you along straight paths.
¹² When you walk, your steps will not be hampered;
　　when you run, you will not stumble.
¹³ Hold on to instruction, do not let it go;
　　guard it well, for it is your life.
¹⁴ Do not set foot on the path of the wicked
　　or walk in the way of evildoers.

[15] Avoid it, do not travel on it;
　　turn from it and go on your way.
[16] For they cannot rest until they do evil;
　　they are robbed of sleep till they make someone stumble.
[17] They eat the bread of wickedness
　　and drink the wine of violence.
[18] The path of the righteous is like the morning sun,
　　shining ever brighter till the full light of day.
[19] But the way of the wicked is like deep darkness;
　　they do not know what makes them stumble.
[20] My son, pay attention to what I say;
　　turn your ear to my words.
[21] Do not let them out of your sight,
　　keep them within your heart;
[22] for they are life to those who find them
　　and health to one's whole body.
[23] Above all else, guard your heart,
　　for everything you do flows from it.
[24] Keep your mouth free of perversity;
　　keep corrupt talk far from your lips.
[25] Let your eyes look straight ahead;
　　fix your gaze directly before you.
[26] Give careful thought to the paths for your feet
　　and be steadfast in all your ways.
[27] Do not turn to the right or the left;
　　keep your foot from evil.

Listening to the Text in the Story: Deuteronomy 6:23; 26:3, 7, 15; Psalms 1:1; 44:1; 78:3–4; 139:23; Proverbs 1:10–19; 17:6; Ecclesiastes 2; 1 Kings 8; The Instruction Addressed to Kagemeni (Kagemni)[1]

While Proverbs consistently imagines instruction passing from a father and mother to a son, this is one of a few places where "sons," plural, are mentioned (cf. 5:7; 7:24; 8:32; 17:6). Such references are rare in ancient wisdom literature in general, but the intertestamental book of Sirach twice mentions "sons" (39:13; 43:30), and the epilogue to the Egyptian instruction to Kagemeni also addresses children.[2]

---

1. *AEL*, trans. Miriam Lichtheim, 1:59–161.
2. See Fox, *Proverbs 1–9*, 172–73.

Proverbs 4:1–8 is also one of only two places in the book where Proverbs explicitly mentions grandparents (cf. 17:6). As we have repeated often in this commentary, Deuteronomy offers many close parallels to the language of Proverbs, and in this case we find significant resemblance in the way that Deuteronomy describes promises made to Israel's fathers and passed on to children and children's children (4:9; cf. 6:23, etc.). Scholars often also rightly highlight the explicit legal vocabulary in these verses, which strengthens the connection between these two books, for example, "precepts," "discipline" (4:1), "teaching (torah)" (4:2, 11), and "commandments" (4:4). Proverbs sustains the sense that Deuteronomy and its pedagogical appeals lie not far in the background of the teachings in Proverbs, adding authority to the father's teachings.[3]

One notable example of this can be found in 1 Kings when David, who just before his death pleads with Solomon ". . . observe what the LORD your God requires: Walk in obedience to him, and keep his decrees and commands, his laws and regulations, as written in the Law of Moses" (1 Kgs 2:3). Of course the fact that Solomon failed in this very task (11:4) invites our attention, not only because Solomon turned away from God's commands—the laws for the king in Deuteronomy 17:14–20 in particular—but also because we find that the major causes for Solomon's failures appear throughout the rhetoric of Proverbs 1–9. First, Solomon clearly fails to listen to David's advice, which is at least implicit in 4:4. Second, Solomon amasses "silver" and "gold" (1 Kgs 10:25), which are inferior to and even in competition with acquiring wisdom (3:14–15; 8:10, 19). Third, whereas women are blamed for turning Solomon's heart away from God (1 Kgs 11:4), so the strange woman, the adulteress, and Dame Folly are imagined as competitors and opponents of wisdom and Woman wisdom (2:16–19; 5:1–23; 6:20–35; 7:6–27; 9:1–18). In fact, the love Solomon feels toward his wives (1 Kgs 11:1–2) belongs to wisdom and one's own wife (4:6; 5:15–19).

Psalms 44, 78, and 1 Kings 8 take up this same language of promises and commands in the context of a national history that is passed on from one generation to the next. We will discuss "Tradition" in more detail in the Live the Story section below.

Deuteronomy and Psalm 139 also share obvious parallels with Proverbs' emphasis on the heart and the body as sources of obedience and objects of blessing (4:21–27). In particular, Deuteronomy's foremost command to love Yahweh with "all your heart" (6:5) complements the command in Proverbs, "Above all else, guard your heart . . ." (4:23).

---

3. See the introduction to Proverbs 2 above as well as Longman, *Proverbs*, 119, 149.

Finally, Proverbs 4:10–19 emphasizes the two ways of righteousness/wisdom/life and wickedness/folly/death that we saw in Proverbs 1:10–19 (cf. also Ps 1). The father's words are confident and clear, but in Ecclesiastes Qohelet muses long over the way these two paths can often appear obscure and confounding. As we will see below, Proverbs 4:10–19 echoes Ecclesiastes at several other points: the fate of the wise and foolish, (2:12–16), the problem of finding "rest" (2:23), light and darkness (2:13), and eating and drinking (2:24).

EXPLAIN the Story

Typical of the material in Proverbs 1–9, this chapter has been creatively and carefully arranged. Like chapter 3, this material has three divisions distinguished by clear shifts in vocabulary:

4:1–9	A father and grandfather's appeal to get wisdom
4:10–19	Wisdom and ways, paths, and feet
4:20–27	Wisdom and the human body

This structure helps us appreciate the many means of appeal in this chapter, including the tradition in society and family, erotic desire, the urgency of choosing between two paths, and the appetites of the body.

4:1–4a These verses repeat a common appeal from the father to get wisdom and insight, only in this case it is to his "sons" (plural). The use of the plural, possibly also "children," could be a way of showing that the sayings are universal, applying to all young men and women.

In verses 3–4a the father introduces his own father's teachings, which he will quote in verses 4b–10. The father's appeal to tradition employs a proverb known as a wellerism, where an ancestor or popular figure is cited as a source: "as Jesus said" or "as Shakespeare once said . . ." A wellerism gives a saying the added authority of a respected source, and so the father here shows the son that his teachings are grounded in a running tradition and not just his opinions about the world.

The word used for "sound learning" (*leqah*), as Van Leeuwen notices, retains something of the word for "to receive," reinforcing the setting of passing down a tradition to their children (cf. 1:5; 9:9; 16:2).[4]

4:4b-9 The grandfather's first command is to "get wisdom." This appeal resembles the "if statements" in Proverbs 2:1–10, where the young man is motivated by commands and the positive consequences that come from

---

4. Van Leeuwen, *Proverbs*, 58.

keeping them. Just as in chapter 2, the student's obligation to be active in listening and learning is emphatic; the student of wisdom must labor for wisdom (cf. Prov 8:32–35).

Moreover, the grandfather's speech issues a total of nine commands in only five verses; commands are phrased in a combination of positive and negative tones, e.g., "cherish her" and "do not forsake wisdom." Not only is this speech impassioned in its intensity, it enchants the son, personifying wisdom in a feminine guise that erotically lures him to "love," "cherish," and "embrace" her.[5]

4:10–19 Buttressed by the tradition of the elders, the father's teaching now resumes with a familiar promise that wisdom offers health, prosperity, and long life to the son. The father's vocabulary in these verses draws on the language of the "feet," "ways," and "paths" of wisdom and of folly. Unlike the grandfather's sayings, which only list positive consequences, the father's words include warnings about the fate of walking with the "wicked" and "evildoers" (14–17, 19).

Verses 10–12 introduce the section of 4:10–19 as a whole and verses 19–20 bring the section to a conclusion, while the heart of this lesson consists of warnings about the evildoer (cf. 1:10–19; 2:9, 12–22). The warnings bring to light the root desires that motivate wicked behavior, desires that are to be avoided at all costs (1:15; cf. 7:25). Such evildoers are unable to "rest until they do evil" or "sleep until the make someone stumble" (v. 16). Both "rest" and "sleep" come from the same Hebrew word. The emphasis on sleep creates a marked antithesis to the sleep given to the wise in 3:24. Here the hearts of the wicked have been so malformed that they can only rest when injury has been done to another.

The wicked are motivated by their desires: they "eat the bread of wickedness and drink the wine of violence" (v. 17; cf. 1:31; 20:1, 17; 21:17). As we will see later in chapter 9, the final appeals of Woman Wisdom and Dame Folly revolve around these metaphors of food and mixed wine, which are combined with sexual innuendos. Proverbs continually makes clear that wisdom is a moral, intellectual, aesthetic, and practical way of life that *sets its desire on love of God and love of wisdom.*

The father's exhortations and promises do not offer much new in the way of content. Yet, by emphatically speaking to *ways* and *paths*, the teaching in chapter 4 undergirds what we have called the "liminal" tone in Proverbs 1–9 as a whole, where the son is confronted with the dilemma of choosing between two ways, two women, two houses, and two ultimate fates. This is not to imply that every decision we make or every course of life has only two options but rather that every human life can, on the whole, be measured by its orientation, whether it aims at wisdom and righteousness or at wickedness and folly.

---

5. See Murphy, "Wisdom and Eros in Proverbs 1–9," *CBQ* 50 (1988), 600–603.

4:20–27 In the final section of this chapter the father entreats the son to bring the whole of his being into submission to wisdom. The sequence of body parts runs from the hearing ear to eyes, heart, flesh, heart, mouth, lips, eyes, eyelids, and feet (2x). These organs, the heart in particular, are elsewhere aligned with the "way" and "right paths" (4:10–19; 3:3–6, 23; 4:26–27).

Among all of the bodily metaphors, the heart sits at the center of the human anatomy in Proverbs. The NIV's translation of verse 23, "Above all else, guard your heart, for everything you do flows from it," obscures the Hebrew and the broader meaning it communicates. For one, the first half of the verse is literally "More than all your guarding, watch your heart," which pictures a more concrete and open-ended image of a busy person guarding essential things like property, animals, crops, city borders, and family members. More than all this naturally important care for our livelihood, we must watch over the course of our thoughts and desires. The second half of the verse in the NIV, "flows from it," flattens the poetic image of life symbolized by springs of water. The full metaphor in the Hebrew shows that the most essential things flow abundantly from the center of our being—our desires, emotions, and attitudes.[6] A guarded heart is absolutely essential to being wise in speech and discerning one's way.

 LIVE the Story

Tradition

Modern western culture worships at the feet of progress. Our reliance on and respect for education, technology, and political empires feeds our underlying faith that a better world lies only slightly beyond our grasp.[7] In this modern world, "tradition" has a rustiness or, at best, a quaintness to it; but "tradition" is rarely thought of as something to be respected. The fading of tradition from our cultural consciousness developed over many centuries, fueled by philosophical, scientific, and religious ideas.[8]

Speaking at a time when tradition was under intense cultural scrutiny, G. K. Chesterton wryly noted, "Tradition means giving votes to the most obscure of all classes, our ancestors. It is the democracy of the dead. Tradition refuses to submit to the small and arrogant oligarchy of those who merely

---

6. Murphy, *Proverbs*, 28.

7. See Richard Bauckham, *Bible and Mission* (Grand Rapids: Baker Academic, 2003).

8. For a recent historical treatment of the fading of tradition and the rise of subjectivism and individualism, see Brad S. Gregory, *The Unintended Reformation* (Cambridge: Belknap Oxford, 2012), 74–128.

happen to be walking about . . . tradition asks us not to neglect a good man's opinion, even if he is our father."[9]

Only decades later, Hans-Georg Gadamer issued a philosophical critique of the essential bias that lies behind the rejection of tradition. As he traces the history of ideas, Gadamer shows that tradition was rejected in the modern age because it was considered "prejudiced," tainting pure *reason* with the poison of prior commitments. But Gadamer demonstrated that this judgment was simply another prejudice—one with questionable assumptions—which was stated as if it were neutral.[10]

Said another way, modern "progressivism" is as embedded in tradition as "liberalism" and "conservatism." Each of these ideologies assumes a body of beliefs held between groups of people over time. We learn our trades by profession and we find our place in the world by retelling traditional stories we find meaningful—even if those stories are about progress and the bias of tradition. Humans, in other words, are inescapably traditioning creatures.

Like Proverbs, the point Chesterton is making is not simply about becoming "pro-tradition" in the abstract. In fact, as the novelty of scientific progress sets in for so many in the West, it's not uncommon for us to find people looking for *traditional* trades or moving away from the city to discover "older" and "simpler" ways of life. Those are all good and well in their own way. But for Chesterton and Proverbs, "tradition" is a source of *authority*—an affirmation that in the records and voices of the past abide stories and teachings concerning meaning, value, purpose, ethics, and vocation.

Because of their inherent authority, traditions inevitably come into conflict. And, while there may be fads of adopting older, traditional *ways of living*, science and progress still have the upper hand when it comes to trusted sources of tradition for what is *true*, whether ethically or ontologically. For example, we can point to an age of pluralism that is increasingly tolerant of a diversity of religious practices, and yet also recognize that these religions are under constant pressure to conform to the traditions of modernity. Whether it is the nature of marriage and family or a stance on abortion, promiscuity, or divorce, "traditional" religions are assumed to be de facto out of step.

The anti-authoritarian spirit of our age has naturally worked its way into religious communities and cultures. We find a growing trend among Gen X Christians who view pastors and elders as peers or sources of advice, rather than those who have God-given authority. Skipping church or coming late is considered perfectly acceptable. Consumer-oriented shopping for acceptable

9. Chesterton, *Orthodoxy* (San Francisco: Ignatius Press, 1908), 53. Van Leeuwen, *Proverbs*, 62, brought this passage to my attention.
10. Gadamar, *Truth and Method*, 235–74.

doctrines, good preaching, and music is par for the course. Children are increasingly free to address adults by their first names; no doubt the intention is for children to feel welcome and equal, but then those same children lack any structure for responding to authority when it is present at work, at home, or at school.

The voice of the fathers and grandfathers in books like Exodus, Deuteronomy, and Proverbs speak from the dead with a message to heed the lessons of the past spoken through authorities in the present. In fact, the failure of Solomon, Rehoboam, and the kings of Israel amount to a pattern of a son's refusal to heed dad's advice. It is incumbent on religious believers to measure our lives by the structure and truths that God has laid down in the writings and stories of our forebearers—the Bible most especially; but we are equally responsible to pass those stories, values, structures, and accounts of truth on to another generation as well.

On another level we can say that we are obliged to raise the children around us—in our families, neighborhoods, and churches—to guide them along the paths of time-tested faith and respect for authority. But in the larger scope the tradition in Proverbs makes us responsible agents for the health and well-being of the human race as a whole.

The Way, the Truth, and the Life

"Where do you want to go today?" went a popular question posed by Microsoft Inc. in a 1990s ad campaign. While that campaign was running, Microsoft CEO and founder Bill Gates wrote a book entitled *The Road Ahead*. In both cases the journey metaphor tells a story, whether about personal desires or the history of a company.

These examples from Microsoft sit in the middle of several decades when there was a sharp rise in the personal memoir—a genre of writing that summarizes some part of a person's life journey. Writing just as this movement began to take off, Frederick Buechner wrote a short memoir entitled *The Alphabet of Grace*, where he begins with the claim that theology, like poetry and fiction writing, is always an act of autobiography—of personal discovery through storytelling. And then, recounting a single day of his life as a summary of who he (Buechner) is as a person, he says, "if you want to know who you are, watch your feet. Because where your feet take you, that is who you are."[11] A little later he observes, "Writing novels, I got into the habit of looking for plots. After a while I began to suspect that my own life had a plot. And after a while more, I began to suspect that life itself has a plot."[12]

11. Buechner, *The Alphabet of Grace* (New York: Harper Collins, 1927), 25.
12. Ibid., 51.

The metaphor of the "way" or "path," of course, actually speaks to the unfolding of life events over time and not so much a series of physical destinations. In "Theological Message" in the Introduction, we described this use of the way, the road, and the path as being liminal—the crossing of thresholds or rights of passage on the way to new stages in life. These journeys are highly concentrated in Proverbs 1–9 and especially 2–4, and they only reappear with any consistency in Proverbs 16, which we'll see in the commentary on that chapter.

The overwhelming thrust of this imagery in Proverbs teaches the son to see life as a journey. What is interesting in Proverbs, and in most of the Old Testament as well, is that the final destination in this journey is not altogether clear. It is a journey toward life, toward God, toward flourishing and—in times of exile—back to the promised land. But that's about all we can gather. The New Testament is far more clear about the fact that we are all on a journey to a place that Jesus has gone and prepared for us. It is a place of a new creation where death, evil, and suffering are finally vanquished.

By contrast, the focus of the journey in Proverbs is a matter of developing the skills to wisely and and faithfully walk before the Lord. Take note of the fact that the "way" in Proverbs 4:10–19 sits between the grandfather's impassioned and even erotic invitations to get wisdom (4:1–9) and the father's final words that encourage the son to orient his whole body, heart, and being to wisdom (4:20–27): the path is bookended by images of stark desire. And so the wise path of life is one that orients the deepest passions of the heart so that the rest of life will *go well* (4:23).

In its earliest years, Christianity was known simply as "the way." The pastoral writings in the letters of the New Testament continually invite believers to "walk" in the Christ-like way of love, obedience, purity, life, and, of course, wisdom.

More than that, Proverbs' depiction of the "way" resembles the language in Jesus' apocalyptic discourses. Matthew 24:36–51 in particular has several close parallels to the material in Proverbs 4:10–19. Above all, both passages present an urgent demand to choose between two ways that result in an eternal or cosmic sense of life and death, respectively. "Eating and drinking" also appears in both passages as a representation of the way of wickedness and evil, and in both passages those who love evil are characterized by their predilection to violence.

The depiction of the way in Proverbs thus helps us to understand what it means to believe in Jesus as the Son of God and to follow him. It is a commitment that commands faithfulness in the deepest core of our being and obedience that is evident in our thoughts, desires, words, and actions.

LISTEN to the Story

1 My son, pay attention to my wisdom,
  turn your ear to my words of insight,
2 that you may maintain discretion
  and your lips may preserve knowledge.
3 For the lips of the adulterous woman drip honey,
  and her speech is smoother than oil;
4 but in the end she is bitter as gall,
  sharp as a double-edged sword.
5 Her feet go down to death;
  her steps lead straight to the grave.
6 She gives no thought to the way of life;
  her paths wander aimlessly, but she does not know it.
7 Now then, my sons, listen to me;
  do not turn aside from what I say.
8 Keep to a path far from her,
  do not go near the door of her house,
9 lest you lose your honor to others
  and your dignity to one who is cruel,
10 lest strangers feast on your wealth
  and your toil enrich the house of another.
11 At the end of your life you will groan,
  when your flesh and body are spent.
12 You will say, "How I hated discipline!
  How my heart spurned correction!
13 I would not obey my teachers
  or turn my ear to my instructors.
14 And I was soon in serious trouble
  in the assembly of God's people."
15 Drink water from your own cistern,

running water from your own well.
¹⁶ Should your springs overflow in the streets,
    your streams of water in the public squares?
¹⁷ Let them be yours alone,
    never to be shared with strangers.
¹⁸ May your fountain be blessed,
    and may you rejoice in the wife of your youth.
¹⁹ A loving doe, a graceful deer—
    may her breasts satisfy you always,
    may you ever be intoxicated with her love.
²⁰ Why, my son, be intoxicated with another man's wife?
    Why embrace the bosom of a wayward woman?
²¹ For your ways are in full view of the LORD,
    and he examines all your paths.
²² The evil deeds of the wicked ensnare them;
    the cords of their sins hold them fast.
²³ For lack of discipline they will die,
    led astray by their own great folly.

Listening to the Text in the Story: Exodus 20:14; Ecclesiastes 7:23–29;
    Song of Songs 4–5

This chapter begins a series of extended warnings about the dangers of the adulterous or promiscuous woman (2:16–19; 6:20–35; 7:1–27). Some commentators take this woman to be a harlot or prostitute rather than an adulteress. The difference, according to biblical law, is that adultery attracts the death penalty while sexual relations with a prostitute does not (cf. Lev 20:10; Deut 22:22; 23:18).

The tone of the chapter would be familiar to any young man raised under the stories and poetry of the Old Testament, which repeatedly emphasize God's condemning disapproval of marital infidelity.[1] In the Pentateuch, adultery appears in the Ten Commandments (Exod. 20:14; Deut 5:18) as well as several laws, many of which recommend a penalty of death. There are also many stories that speak to adultery's socially destructive power (Gen 12:19; 20:1–18; Lev 20:10–14; Deut 22:13–30; 24:1–4; 2 Sam 11). And yet these passages reveal the human inclination to cross this forbidden line again and again.

---

1. The warnings about adultery and the encouragement to enjoy one's own wife could indicate that the son is married or of marriageable age. In other words, we do not need to imagine adolescents as the target audience.

Ecclesiastes contains an unusual passage in which Qohelet speaks of *finding* a "woman" at the end of his unsuccessful *search* for "wisdom." Scholars of Ecclesiastes hold various opinions about who this woman might be, including women in general, a woman Qohelet knows, or an adulteress. Most of these views fail to read this verse in the light of the rest of Ecclesiastes specifically and wisdom literature more broadly. C. L. Seow highlights the many parallels between this part of Qohelet's monologue and the women featured in the book of Proverbs, which may shed light on the end of Qohelet's search.[2]

Ecclesiastes 7	Proverbs
[23] All this I tested by wisdom and I said, "I am determined to be wise"— but this was beyond me.	
[24] Whatever exists is far off (*rahoq*) and most profound—who can discover (*matsa*) it?	[31:10] A wife of noble character who can find (*matsa*)? She is worth far more (*rahoq*) than rubies.
[25] So I turned my mind to understand, to investigate and to search out wisdom and the scheme of things and to understand the stupidity of wickedness and the madness of folly.	
[26] I find more bitter (*mar*) than death (*mawet*) the woman who is a snare, whose heart is a trap and whose hands are chains. The man who pleases God will escape her, but the sinner she will ensnare.	[5:4] but in the end she is bitter (*mar*) as wormwood, sharp as a two-edged sword. [5] Her feet go down to death (*mawet*); her steps follow the path to Sheol;
[27] "Look," says the Teacher, "this is what I have discovered: Adding one thing to another to discover the scheme of things—	
[28] while I was still searching but not finding—I found one upright man among a thousand, but not one upright woman *ishah*) among them all.	[2:16] Wisdom will save you also from the adulterous woman (*ishah*), from the wayward woman with her seductive words, (cf. 5:18; 6:24, etc.)

---

2. C. L. Seow, *Ecclesiastes*, AB 18C (New York: Doubleday, 2007), 259–64.

Ecclesiastes 7	Proverbs
[29] This only have I found: God created mankind upright, but they have gone in search of many schemes."	

Seow here summarizes the implications of these parallels:

> But the recognition of this feminine figure comes not only from the reference to folly in v 25, but also from the depiction of this *femme fatale* in language reminiscent of the personification of folly in conventional wisdom (see especially Proverbs 1–9); she is deadly, she lays a trap, one must escape her . . . [These] are images used to describe anyone who represents folly, anyone who seduces people away from wisdom.[3]

Combining the imagery in Proverbs and Song of Songs, Qohelet is on a "lover's pursuit" (Song 3:1–6; 5:6:1; Hos 2:7; cf. Prov 1:28; 18:22).[4] In this light, we find many resonances between Song of Songs and the descriptive, even erotic, language of the father. The metaphor of lips dripping honey in Proverbs 5:3 appears in a positive light in Song of Songs 4:11 and 5:1. And the erotic metaphors of fluids in Proverbs 5:15–18 appear even more descriptively in Song of Songs 5:1–5.

EXPLAIN the Story

Chapter 5 can be outlined as having four lines of development:

5:1–6	Introduction to the adulteress
5:7–14	Consequences for consorting with her
5:15–19	Exhortation to enjoy one's own wife
5:20–22	Concluding motivation and warning

5:1–6 Verses 1–2 repeat common admonitions for the son to get "wisdom," "understanding," "discretion," and "knowledge." Here we encounter the only time the father tells the son to "pay attention to *my* wisdom" (5:1); elsewhere wisdom comes from, or belongs to, God. This need not pose a problem, as if the father claims to be the origin or source of this wisdom. Chapter 4 has just depicted the father getting wisdom from his own parents,

---

3. Ibid., 262–63.
4. Ibid., 264.

who, by implication, got wisdom from their parents. The possessive suffix thus most likely expresses the father's commitment to, and stewardship of, God's wisdom—an attitude he wants his son to embrace, especially in the face of a temptress whose sweet attraction will test the son's deepest moral fibers.

The reference in 5:2 to the son's lips that "preserve knowledge" puzzles some scholars. Fox comments that while verses 1–6 have some unusual qualities, intellectual and spoken wisdom are aligned elsewhere in 4:23–24.[5] The context in chapter 4 comes amidst a string of allusions to the human body figuratively doing things with wisdom. Furthermore, the image of lips that "preserve" wisdom is unique to Proverbs here, but it does occur elsewhere in Malachi 2:7.[6] So while the saying is unexpected, it appears to fit with other metaphors of the body doing things with wisdom.

It is also important to recognize that the reference to lips in this context sets up the adulterous woman's lips that "drip honey" in verse 3. As Waltke notes, speech is closely tied to sexual relations. Waltke also highlights the dangerous exchange of words between Joseph and Potiphar's wife, where Joseph's answer (his lips) *preserve knowledge*, to paraphrase Proverbs 5:2, in that his words represent a wise response to sexual temptation uttered through another's mouth.[7]

The abrupt turn to the adulterous woman in 5:3–6 begins the central theme of chapters 5–7 and 9—the folly of adultery and the danger of the words of the strange woman. That her lips "drip honey, and her speech (mouth) is smoother than oil," again signifies the interplay between speech and sexual intercourse with its exchange of bodily fluids (cf. 5:15–18). Tempting as she might be, she is "bitter as gall, sharp as a double-edged sword"—in the end "her feet go down to death" (5:4–5).

As alluded to above, this deadly or, at the least, tragic image could have very likely been the inspiration for the "bitter" woman that Qohelet "finds" in his unsuccessful search for wisdom in Ecclesiastes 7:23–26. To be in a place where you cannot find wisdom is akin to looking for your wife and finding a harlot.

Of all the possible ways the father could illustrate or apply wisdom for his son—wealth, fame, speech, power, etc.—why single out sexual purity and faithfulness as the primary example?[8] In light of what we have seen here,

---

5. Fox, *Proverbs 1–9*, 191.

6. Crawford H. Toy, *Proverbs*, ICC (Edinburgh: T&T Clark, 1988), 102, says of these verses that "lips utter, but do not keep . . ." But Toy overlooks the reference to priest's lips that "preserve knowledge," using the same Hebrew root in Mal 2:7.

7. Waltke, *Proverbs 1–15,* 308, who cites Newsome, "Woman and the Discourse of Patriarchal Wisdom," 153.

8. Consider similar questions raised by Murphy, *Proverbs*, 31.

it cannot simply be because young men (and increasingly young women) yearn to explore their sexual identity as they pass through adolescence. Far more than that, the desire, lure, and ultimately ruinous consequences for folly are the most apt characterization of the challenges of the wisdom journey as a whole.

5:7–20 After a sobering introduction to the lure of adultery in verses 1–6, the father now presents two opposing paths: giving in to adultery (5:7–14) and enjoying one's own wife (5:15–20).

As in the last chapter, the father addresses his sons, plural, perhaps to reinforce the universal application of this teaching beyond one young man (5:7; see commentary on 4:1). This concentrated warning about the harlot can be further divided into two halves. In verses 7–10 the father looks forward to the social, financial, and physical consequences of giving in to temptation. While translations render the terms for these consequences differently, the essential point is that the sons' wealth, social position, and reputation will be forfeited to others, often those who are least deserving. The ambiguity of these "others" is probably intentional as it leaves readers to imagine people in their own circles who might benefit from their folly.

In verses 11–14, the father depicts an autobiographical speech of his future grown son amidst the guilt he would feel for giving in to folly. It is no coincidence that the son will deeply regret that he has shunned his "teachers" and "instructors" (v. 13), as the father is among them. And yet the most salient image depicts the son's guilt exposed before "the assembly of God's people," with all of his family and friends looking on (5:14; cf. 6:26, 30–35). The term for "assembly" (*qahal*) may well signify a legal gathering or court, perhaps even prepared to execute civil capital punishment (cf. 26:26; Sir 7:7).[9]

The second central panel in this lecture (5:15–20) turns from the forbidden fruit of the strange woman to the goodness of sexuality within marriage. Marital intimacy in this context is conveyed through the metaphor of water, which appears in six different terms: "cistern," "running water," "well," "springs," "streams of water," and "fountain." The fact that these terms allude not just to marriage but to sexuality can be seen in the parallel use of the terms used for "spring," "fountain," and "well" in Song of Songs 4:12, 15.

In ancient Palestine water was a scarce and precious resource, and so the father's instruction carries an implicit urgency as it encourages the son to value and protect the treasure of intimacy with his wife. Some commentators believe that such instruction about "your own cistern" (v. 15) and "the wife of your youth" (v. 18) implies that the son must be married. But, as in 5:12–14

---

9. Cf. Waltke, *Proverbs 1–15*, 316. But see Fox, *Proverbs 1–9*, 198–99, who does not believe a court is necessarily imagined here.

and elsewhere in Proverbs 1–9, the father's rhetoric often imagines the future adult life as a whole, just as any parent today raises a child with future health and flourishing in mind; the teaching applies with equal force to the married and the yet-to-be married. This set of commands works on yet another level as well. Just as the father wants the son to guard "my wisdom," so the son's treasuring of his own wife coincides with his jealously treasuring wisdom.

Notice too, as Van Leeuwen comments in this context, that quality of water sources in 15–16 and 18 increases in value, from a cistern, that would have held runoff and rainwater, to a rare spring of fresh or living water. He says, "The images continue to grow in clarity and desirability . . . These sequential, parallel images do not stand in contrast with one another, as if several wives were portrayed. Rather, they cumulatively picture one's wife as a personal source of life, sexual delight, blessing, and fecundity."[10]

In verses 17–20 the father places his lesson to the son in the broader context of social order and, by implication, the moral and created order. Just as the son would not want a "stranger" to be intimate with his wife (v. 10), so it would violate God's moral order for him to give in to the adulteress, perhaps another's wife (v. 20). Meanwhile, the wife who is loved *within* the created order is an excellent thing; her "breasts" are a delight and her love "intoxicates" (v.19). In contrast, the foreign woman "intoxicates" in a disordered way. In the Live the Story section below we will reflect more closely on God's taking pleasure in the pleasure we enjoy *within his created limits*.

5:21–23 The father ends this lesson with a reminder that God sees us even when we are in secret and will reward and punish accordingly (Matt 6:4, 6, 18). This conclusion creatively broadens the perspective of his teaching from the family (vv. 15–16), to the community (17–20), to humanity in general as it exists within God's cosmic order (21–23). What is good for the son in his particular life and marriage is true for human sexuality and the creation as a whole.

Furthermore, the cosmic perspective is evident not just in God's all-seeing eye but also in the fact that the fool's ultimate fate is death. As we discuss below (9:13–18), the temptation in the garden of Eden in Genesis should inform our understanding of the father's instruction here; that is, to "take" and "eat" and "knowledge" that exposes human "nakedness" in Genesis, together comprise a creative intermixing of wisdom and sexual themes that we find in Proverbs, especially in chapters 5–9. In the garden there was eating that was good and led to life, and eating that opened the door for death. So too in Proverbs.

---

10. Van Leeuwen, *Proverbs*, 69. But cf. Fox, *Proverbs 1–9*, 201–2, who believes the terms are synonymous in this context.

LIVE the Story

The dominant presence of women in chapters 5–9 offer us three important points for reflection on the way we interpret and respond to the culture in which we live.

Marriage

Human marriage has a central place in the biblical story and worldview. Marriage, it should be noted, includes an exhaustive range of theological principals such as faithfulness, desire, satisfaction, boundaries, love, devotion, mutual commitment, pleasure, a source of ongoing life, and a place of refuge and safety. And so unfaithfulness and the violation of marriage stand as a sign for everything that brings division, suffering, and ruin to people, societies, and cultures (Prov 2:21–23).

In this light we must not overlook the fact that the Bible begins with the foundational narrative that brings Adam and Eve together in the garden of Eden. In the last scene before the fall, we read: "That is why a man leaves his father and mother and is united to his wife, and they become one flesh" (Gen 2:24). This sexual union of the first man and woman becomes the source for all societies in human history, and Abram/Abraham and his "seed" become the locus of God's blessing upon those families (Gen 12:1–3). Christopher Wright comments, "the household was seen to be of primary importance as the locus of the individual's experience of the privileges and obligations of national relationship with God and, to a large degree also, as the basis on which his membership of the privileged community was founded."[11]

As we have noted at several points, Proverbs and Song of Songs contain the most concentrated focus on human marriage and sexuality, affirming sexuality as good *within the bonds of marriage*. When we come to the New Testament the family household takes on even greater significance. Marriage and sex continue to be affirmed and adultery condemned (1 Cor 7:1–7; Heb 13:4), but marriage also points to the union of Christ and the church (Eph 5:21–33). In his first public act in the Gospel of John, Jesus blesses a marriage ceremony by turning water into wine. John records this as the "first," or literally, "beginning," of the signs Jesus performed, using the same Greek word for the "beginning" in the Septuagint version of Genesis 1:1. John also places the miracle at Cana on the "third day," which corresponds to the dividing of water to bring forth land and fruit on the third day of creation in Genesis 1:9–13. For these

---

11. Christopher Wright, *God's People in God's Land: Family, Land, and Property in the Old Testament* (Grand Rapids: Eerdmans, 1990), 97.

and other reasons, many scholars have argued that John's portrayal of Jesus at Cana echoes the first creation and this dramatically captures the nature of his own purpose in coming into the world[12]—to bring flourishing to our human institutions and give himself as a bridegroom for the world. In this way, human marriage is also in some way "subsumed" by the eschatological marriage between the church and the heavenly bridegroom (Isa 54:5; 62:4–5; Jer 2:2; Ezek 16:8; Hos 2:19–20; Matt 22:1–14; John 3:29; 2 Cor 11:2; Eph 5:27–32; and Rev 19:7–9; 21:1–9).[13]

We will say more below about the way our sexual human nature should inform our understanding of pedagogy in Proverbs. It suffices for now to recognize that Proverbs' pedagogy assumes the centrality of marriage in the biblical worldview and the inseparable relationship between the concrete and cosmic women in these chapters—wives and harlots, Wisdom and Folly.[14]

Sex

These chapters also reaffirm the goodness of sex. As musician Butch Hancock once noted, Christian attitudes on sex are typically confused, "Life in Lubbock, Texas, taught me . . . that sex is the most awful, filthy thing on earth and you should save it for someone you love."[15] But God's perspective on love, heard through the voice of the father, delights in the intimacy of a husband and a wife. He created marriage for enjoyment: "rejoice in the wife of your youth . . . may her breasts satisfy you always, may you ever be intoxicated with her love" (5:18–19). All of the abuses of sexuality that have arisen among human cultures—adultery, rape, incest, and abortion—are evil for the very reason that they take sex out of its proper place within marriage where there is love, mutual consent, and a welcoming place for children.

Putting this another way, when God declares that man and woman will become "one flesh," (Gen 2:24) he does so in the context of the whole created order (Gen 1:31).[16] God blesses, not commands, the man and woman to "be fruitful and increase in number" (Gen 1:28) as an expression of the goodness of sexuality. The first human marriage and family, in turn, become a symbol for the expansion of life and order for the whole developing world.

---

12. See Calum M. Carmichael, *The Story of Creation: Its Origin and Its Interpretation in Philo and the Fourth Gospel* (Ithaca, NY: Cornell University Press, 1996), 67–78.

13. See Robert A. J. Gagnon, "Sexuality" in *Dictionary for Theological Interpretation of the Bible*, ed. Kevin Vanhoozer, et al. (Grand Rapids: Baker Academic, 2005), 739–48.

14. See Murphy, *Proverbs*, 31.

15. Cited in James Moore, "The Lies of Texas are Upon You," *Huffington Post* (Sept 4 2009), http://www.huffingtonpost.com/jim-moore/the-lies-of-texas-are-upo_b_277749.html.

16. And so also sexual sin as a sign of the corruption of the created order. Cf. Calum Carmichael, *Sex and Religion in the Bible* (New Haven: Yale University Press, 2010), 99–102.

Recognizing the organic link in creation between human marriage and the relationship of humanity with God, Lauren Winner says,

> Marriage serves as the biblical analogy par excellence to the relationship between God and his people. Over and over in sacred scripture, that relationship is described as a marriage. When the people of Israel are faithful to God, Israel is described as a bride; when she turns away from God, she is called a harlot. Similarly the writers of the New Testament found that one way to capture the relationship between Christ and the church was to draw an analogy to husband and wife. Through these analogies, marriage is substantially linked to community. Marriage—because of what marriage is, the analogue to God and his relationship to his people—precedes sex. The order of marriage to sex . . . implies a resonance between sex and community.[17]

Having made this link between sex and community, Winner continues, "Marriages, in other words, are not meant to be simply pairs of people in love; they are institutions out of which cultures and societies are formed. Households are the foundations of communities."[18] So, contrary to the embarrassment Christians often have in talking about sexuality, God places the pleasure of sex at the center of all society, calls it good, and adds his divine blessing.

Pedagogy and Anthropology

One final point should be made about the relationship between the father's pedagogy and human anthropology. The father's rhetoric, themes, and language can be used as a lens into how Proverbs views our psychological, social, and spiritual makeup.

In his study of ancient Israel's education, James Crenshaw attempts to do something like this. He observes several types of learning in the wisdom literature, including observation, human tradition, divine revelation, and direct encounter with God. These in turn are channeled through three major forms of teaching or pedagogy: "ethos"—the appeal to the character of the speaker, "pathos"—the appeal to the emotions of the student, and "logos"—an appeal to argument.[19]

Daniel Estes represents another common way of describing the pedagogy, in this case only of Proverbs 1–9. He uses language like "values," "goals," "curriculum," and "process."[20] Notably, according to Estes, one primary

---

17. Lauren Winner, *Real Sex: The Naked Truth about Chastity* (Grand Rapids: Brazos, 2005), 50.

18. Ibid., 57.

19. James Crenshaw, *Education in Ancient Israel*, 115–38.

20. Daniel Estes, *Hear My Son: Teaching and Learning in Proverbs 1–9* (Grand Rapids: Eerdmans, 1997).

responsibility of the student is to "value" wisdom by "demonstrating a positive appreciation for it."[21] We will return to his notion of value below.

Crenshaw and Estes stand in the majority as they represent biblical epistemology and pedagogy, and it should be said that it is true that one can find all of these modern pedagogical methods and themes in Proverbs. However, this descriptive approach for all its clarity also suffers from two faults. First, it seeks to organize and put into propositions what has been left intentionally unarranged and poetically expressed. Proverbs frequently uses wisdom terms in different ways, resisting any sense that there is systematic language being applied to the instruction. The second major fault is that these methods tend to overlook or misrepresent the role of the four female personae in speaking to human learning and human nature.[22]

Michael Fox, meanwhile, recognizes a more holistic quality in the pedagogy and anthropology in Proverbs.[23] Wisdom does not begin as a rational or intellectual exercise that leads us to be good people. Rather, wisdom addresses our very desire and inclination to prefer folly. Here Fox observes that the predominant concern in the father's instructions is "seduction," whether by men, women, riches, pride, or what have you. He goes on to conclude that "Such wisdom is the ability to discern right from wrong and also the desire to pursue the right, because inert wisdom would not provide protection . . . That is why the son is urged not only to learn wisdom but to love and desire it (4:6–8)."[24] Putting these chapters of Proverbs in the perspective of sexuality and whoredom in the Old Testament, Calvin Seerveld says, "The 'strange woman' or 'exotic foreign woman' (7:5) of Proverbs is not a sermonette against chance fornication, but is a vivid, deep-going injunction against the sons of God from mingling their holy seed with what is profane . . . 'the strange woman' of Proverbs 7 has the dimensions of the whore of Revelation 17:1–19:10, namely, Babylonic culture."[25]

It should be noted also that Jesus addresses adultery many times, condemning not only the practice but also the manipulative way people—almost always men—maneuver their way around the letter of the law (Matt 5:27–28, 31–32; 19:1–11; John 8:1–11). The motivating role of desire in almost all of these contexts helps us appreciate the parallel between Jesus' admonitions

---

21. Ibid., 144.
22. Actually, Estes, Ibid., 52–57, argues that the four women in Prov 1–9 work together to interweave the literal and figurative desire for women. But this has little to no bearing on his overall approach to Proverbs' pedagogy.
23. Michael Fox, "Ideas of Wisdom in Proverbs 1–9" *SBL* 116/4 (1997): 613–33.
24. Ibid., 620.
25. Calvin Seerveld, *Rainbows for the Fallen World: Aesthetic Life and Artistic Task* (Toronto: Tuppence Press, 2005), 98.

and the father's choice of adultery as the central theme for his commands in Proverbs 1–9.

For help appreciating the strength of this perspective, we can turn to philosophers and psychologists who study human desire. Significantly, for them desire is one of many "pro-attitudes" toward wisdom such as valuing, appreciating, and liking, without wanting or wishing for it.[26] For desire to be present, there must be some motivation to do something to realize the state of affairs in question.

The basic difference is this: We could describe Proverbs' pedagogy by saying that it teaches many types of learning, one of which is coping with sexual temptation and desire, and another of which is valuing wisdom and intelligence. But another way of describing this pedagogy, one more in tune with the dominant rhetoric that shapes the book, is to say that *learning at its very essence is a discipline of shaping desires that allow for growth in virtuous action and intellectual discretion.* Paraphrasing Augustine, James K. Smith has said, "we love *in order to* know"—education is more about "formation" than "information."[27]

Our worldviews, or "perceptual frameworks" as they are sometimes called, always involve the deep impulses of the heart (Prov 4:23). And so, echoing Michael Fox again, wisdom is a "power" that orients our human will and nature. That power, I would add, is motivated by and expressed in human and divine mutual love.

---

26. See Schroeder, *Three Faces of Desire.*

27. Smith, *Desiring the Kingdom: Worship, Worldview, and Cultural Formation* (Grand Rapids: Baker Academic, 2009) 18, 26.

CHAPTER 10

Proverbs 6:1–19

 LISTEN to the Story

¹ My son, if you have put up security for your neighbor,
    if you have shaken hands in pledge for a stranger,
² you have been trapped by what you said,
    ensnared by the words of your mouth.
³ So do this, my son, to free yourself,
    since you have fallen into your neighbor's hands:
Go—to the point of exhaustion—
    and give your neighbor no rest!
⁴ Allow no sleep to your eyes,
    no slumber to your eyelids.
⁵ Free yourself, like a gazelle from the hand of the hunter,
    like a bird from the snare of the fowler.
⁶ Go to the ant, you sluggard;
    consider its ways and be wise!
⁷ It has no commander,
    no overseer or ruler,
⁸ yet it stores its provisions in summer
    and gathers its food at harvest.
⁹ How long will you lie there, you sluggard?
    When will you get up from your sleep?
¹⁰ A little sleep, a little slumber,
    a little folding of the hands to rest—
¹¹ and poverty will come on you like a thief
    and scarcity like an armed man.
¹² A troublemaker and a villain,
    who goes about with a corrupt mouth,
¹³ who winks maliciously with his eye,
    signals with his feet
    and motions with his fingers,

¹⁴ who plots evil with deceit in his heart—
  he always stirs up conflict.
¹⁵ Therefore disaster will overtake him in an instant;
  he will suddenly be destroyed—without remedy.
¹⁶ There are six things the LORD hates,
  seven that are detestable to him:
¹⁷ haughty eyes,
  a lying tongue,
  hands that shed innocent blood,
¹⁸ a heart that devises wicked schemes,
  feet that are quick to rush into evil,
¹⁹ a false witness who pours out lies
  and a person who stirs up conflict in the community.

Listening to the Text in the Story: Genesis 44:32; Exodus 22:25–26;
  Deuteronomy; 15:1–7; Proverbs 17:14; 20:16; 30:18–31

Proverbs 6:19 builds upon previous warnings against evil and foolish types of men (1:10–14; 2:12–15; 3:27–35). The chapter begins with a warning not to put up "security" (or surety) for a neighbor or take a "pledge" for a stranger (6:1–5).

The language of surety and pledges occurs elsewhere in Proverbs (17:18; 20:16, 22:26–27), but the full import of these terms becomes clear in light of their use elsewhere in the Old Testament. The law in the Pentateuch is well aware of the practice of giving loans to neighbors and the poor (Exod 22:25–26; Deut 24:10–13), and it also commends generosity to the most needy of social classes (Lev 25:35–36; Deut 15:1–7; 24:19–22; cf. Pss 3:21, 26; 112:5, 9). However, these are loans, gifts, or pledges designed to cover one's own debts, not that of a neighbor or stranger as imagined in Proverbs 6. The concern in Proverbs is that promises made on behalf of another person open one up to future debts, which could escalate and exceed that person's ability to repay (cf. 2 Kgs 4:1–7).[1]

One interesting example of putting up surety can be found in Judah's offering of himself as a future pledge against the life of his brother Benjamin (Gen 44:33). Judah had every reason to believe that, should his brothers be prevented or delayed in returning from Canaan to Egypt, he would be killed or severely punished. After all, Benjamin stands accused for stealing Joseph's sacred silver cup. However, Judah's pledge has a twist: Benjamin was set up

---

1. See David Daube, *Law and Wisdom in the Bible: David Daube's Gifford Lectures, Vol II*, ed. Calum Carmichael (West Conshohocken, PA: Templeton Press, 2010), 96.

by Joseph and is actually innocent. In the narrative it is actually Judah who still bears the primary guilt for spreading "strife among brothers" (Prov 6:19, author's translation) by proposing that the brothers sell Joseph to Midianite merchants (Gen 37:26–28). In the perspective in Genesis, Judah's pledge is not really one of generosity, but an attempt at restitution.

Proverbs 6:6–11 advises the sluggard to consider the virtues of the ant and warns against the consequences of laziness and excessive sleep, common themes elsewhere in Proverbs and the Old Testament (cf. 10:26; 13:4; 19:4; 20:4; 24:33; Eccl 4:5).

Finally, Proverbs 30:24–31 points to several examples of wisdom among the animals, including the ant (see commentary below). Proverbs 30 also provides the only parallel in Proverbs to the numerical sayings in 6:16–19 (see commentary below).

EXPLAIN the Story

Structurally, Proverbs 6 sits between two passages that warn against the temptations of the strange or adulterous woman (5:1–25; 6:20–27). It also interrupts five running chapters that focus on cosmic or literal women (5–9). Many scholars have thus argued that this material is out of place or awkwardly inserted, but unpredictability and surprises are a sign of skill in a poet.

Putting this differently, the father's teachings are rhetorically suited to fit the boy's age and interests, making provocative comparisons between sex with an adulteress and with one's own wife and *then* turn that energy upon other kinds of temptations in the world.

The first 19 verses divide neatly into four sections:

6:1–5	Warning on security and the pledge
6:6–11	Warning to the sluggard
6:12–15	Warning about the wicked man
6:16–19	Seven abominable sinners

Together, these sections offer a sampler plate of the sins of foolish and evil men pictured throughout chapters 1–9—and Proverbs as a whole.

Waltke has shown that this section has been carefully connected to the warnings in chapter 5: the Hebrew root for "stranger" in 5:10 and 6:1 parallels the catchword "caught," *laqad*, in 5:22 and 6:2. Waltke comments, "the fatal consequences of wickedness with the Lord as the final Agent of judgment" appears in both contexts (5:22–23; 6:15–19).[2]

2. Waltke, *Proverbs 1–15*, 329.

The first two stanzas (vv. 1–5, 6–11) have been artistically linked together as well: the doubling addresses to the son (6:1, 3) and the sluggard (6:6, 9); the catchword "go" (6:3, 6); "sleep" and "slumber" (6:4, 9, 10); and the examples of wisdom among animals (6:5, 6).[3]

6:1–5 Unlike the father's other instructions in chapters 1–9, this one omits the command to "keep his words" or "commands." The instruction instead moves directly from "My son, pay attention" to addressing the danger of becoming a security or a pledge (6:1). As discussed in the Listen to the Story section above, Proverbs, like most of the Old Testament, commends acts of generosity and compassion. And yet the Old Testament also realizes that debts can be ruinous for the debtor. Whereas the law makes a distinction between the freedom to charge interest to a foreigner (or stranger) and the prohibition against doing so with a fellow Israelite (a neighbor), Proverbs here is concerned with risky financial dealings with either type of person as is clear in other proverbs on this same subject (11:15; 17:18; 22:26–27; 27:13). The book of Sirach commends generosity (17:22) while warning against the risks of putting up future security for another (28:14, 18). This parallels Proverbs, which values compassion (3:27–30; 11:25) but also remains aware of the obvious risks associated with uncertain social and economic ventures.

The material surrounding this warning (5:1–23; 6:20–7:27) is concerned with avoiding sexual temptations. It may be that the father sees this as an opportunity to address the topic of avoiding similar impulsivity in the financial realm. It is not hard to imagine social settings that combine loose sexual practices and gambling. On their own, the financial sayings resemble Jesus' teachings in Luke 14:28–33: as a king considers his resources before building a tower or going to war, so too should Jesus' disciples consider whether they have counted the cost of following him.

Because unsound ventures are such a risk to the son, the father warns him to exhaust every effort to be relieved of his obligation (6:3–5). Clifford highlights the emphasis and repetition in these verses that the father uses to communicate his urgency: "free yourself" is mentioned twice (3, 5); the imagery of bodily organs in the transaction and the effort to be free—hand (twice), lip, eye, and pupil; the metaphor of hunting as an image of the trap; finally, the son is pictured as if he has already made such a rash pledge, luring the son to imagine living with such a predicament.[4]

6:6–11 This is the first of several warnings in Proverbs against excessive sleep, idle living, and laziness; verses 10–11 here are identical to 24:33, where "poverty" is personified as a "thief" and "scarcity" as an "armed man." This imagery parallels

---

3. Ibid., 328–29.
4. Clifford, *Proverbs*, 75.

the language in verse 5 above where the son is imagined as a gazelle or bird escaping a hunter. Putting up a surety and becoming a sluggard are deadly traps.

The father's shift in topics seems smooth, even natural. It is almost as if his command for the son to "allow no sleep" to his eyes in order to be free of surety in verse 4 and the animal reference in verse 5 leads him to the diligence and wisdom of the ant (v. 6), which he expands on in the following verses.

The two-fold structure in this stanza proceeds from a fable about the wise ant (vv. 6–8) to a counter-example of foolishness in the life of a sluggard (vv. 9–11). Agur provides a shorter example of the ant in Proverbs 30:25, highlighting the ant's ability to overcome, "not weakness, but the want of anyone to organize its task. Wisdom enables it, despite this deficiency, to rise to a collective effort."[5] Meanwhile the sluggard, with no one to wake him, submerges himself in neglect and inactivity.

6:12–15 The father now turns to expose what Fox calls "The Good-for-Nothing" man[6] (cf. NIV's, "a troublemaker and a villain"). The "trouble-maker" or "son of belial" is a familiar character in the Old Testament: rapists (Judg 19:22), those who despise justice (1 Kgs 21:10, 13; Prov 19:28); perjurers (Deut 13:14), drunks (1 Sam 1:16), gluttons, and womanizers (1 Sam 2:12–15, 22–25).[7] This passage in Proverbs lays out his outward behavior (6:12–13), his inner disposition (6:14), and his ultimate fate (6:15). Clifford points out that the explicit references to his "mouth," "eye," "foot," "finger" and "heart" demonstrate that he is wholly devoted to evil.[8] Such evil men bring lasting harm to themselves and to society. The son should therefore do everything in his power to avoid consorting with such men or becoming one himself.

6:16–19 "There are six things . . . and seven . . ." This is the only graded numerical saying in Proverbs outside of chapter 30, which includes several of them. These sayings may be unique to wisdom literature, as they demonstrate the innate human need to count and number to find order in the world. The form of the sayings also facilitates memorization. See "Genre" in the Introduction and the commentary on chapter 30 below for a description of this type of proverbial saying.

This graded saying delves into things that are an "abomination" (*toebah*, cf. NIV "detestable") to the Lord. Commenting on the use of this term in Proverbs 3:22, Fox notes that the term *toebah* in Proverbs does not necessarily designate something ethically, legally, or religiously forbidden, but rather

---

5. David Daube, "A Quartet of Beasties in the Book of Proverbs," *Journal of Theological Studies* 36, (1985): 380–86 (381).
6. Fox, *Proverbs 1–9*, 219.
7. Cf. Ibid.
8. Clifford, *Proverbs*, 76.

"[condemns] offenses in situations where discovery is unlikely or redress is difficult to obtain, as well as to rebuke antisocial . . . attitudes and deeds."[9]

The first five condemned acts move downward from the "eyes" and "tongue," to the "hands" (or arms), "heart," and "feet." The sayings illustrate sin's power in every part of our human nature. Added to that, the heart sits at the center of this list, signifying its place at the center of our human nature and desires; it must be controlled above all else (cf. 4:23). The last two actions depart from themes related to the body to emphasize the destructive results upon other people in the community.

LIVE the Story

Wisdom, Business, and Economics

My wife once worked with a Christian woman whose husband was a car salesman. This woman casually described how auto manufacturers deceptively create a sense of urgency that "all cars must go" and "prices good now through Sunday only." But instead of being bothered by the practice, she said, "this is just how the business works." Indeed, and it does this well.

The difficult passage at the beginning of this chapter concerning a security and a pledge is one of the many proverbs that speak to the ethics and practices in the world of business and economics.[10] Virtues of integrity, such as honest weights and just scales, are fairly obvious (11:1; 16:11; 20:10, 23), as God warns those who sell in the marketplace against taking advantage of customers.

Besides warning merchants, Proverbs also cautions buyers to be on the lookout for schemes aimed at them. In 2013 auto dealers first decided to get in on the energy of "Black Friday" and the tidal wave of impulse buying that happens in a one-to-two day period after Thanksgiving, selling cars just because people are in the buying mood. Some dealers increased sales by 20 percent or 30 percent, and most sales happened solely as the result of increased advertising, since prices were seldom actually reduced.[11] Surely the schemes of auto dealers and many stores take advantage of addictions and the complex psychological factors that fuel our desire to purchase goods we do not *need*. In a day where the advertising industry recruits its spin-masters from prestigious

---

9. Fox, *Proverbs 1–9*, 167.

10. See Longman, *Proverbs*, 553.

11. See Jaclyn Trop, "Out of the Doldrums: Automakers Post Strong U.S. Sales," *NY Times* (Dec 3, 2013), http://www.nytimes.com/2013/12/04/business/out-of-a-lull-automakers-post-strong -us-sales-in-november.html?_r=0. See also, Sonari Glinton, "Advertising Push Helps Last Month's Car Sales" *National Public Radio*, (Dec 4, 2013), http://www.npr.org/2013/12/04/248718298/ advertising-push-helps-last-months-car-sales.

universities, we are greatly in need of wisdom among the masses. A sale does not mean a sale and a new smartphone will not equate to long-term happiness.

The sayings on the security and pledge clearly aim to discourage overly risky and naïve investments (cf. 17:18; 22:26–27). Proverbs also warns against the spirit of quick profit, instead encouraging wealth that comes from care and diligence over the long run (13:11; cf. 14:23; 16:8).

In the recession of 2007–2009 the US witnessed a collapse of housing loans and major investment banks. In many cases the loans were not secured or were offered at high interest rates to at-risk borrowers, a practice clearly forbidden in Proverbs (14:31; 20:17; 21:6; 22:16). There are good indications that the wealth of the upper "1 percent" will continue to grow in the years ahead of us. This will certainly mean that the middle and working classes will be dependent on the wealthy at the top of the capital economic food chain to care for those at lower levels of the system.

With all the risks, deceptions, defaults, and recessions in the economic world, it can be tempting to reject capitalism altogether (e.g., 16:16; 22:1). But it should be remembered that, while Proverbs warns against abuses, it also imagines a world where wisdom both takes advantage of wise practices in investments *and* uses those resources and profits for the expansion of markets in the interest of the common good (see commentary at 24:3–4 and 31:10–31).

Is This Anyone I Know?

It can be easy to read Proverbs superficially and feel that the sayings are like distant vague advice with no connection to the world where we live. To break through this distance we need to read slowly, asking questions about the themes and structure in the passages in a way that makes them come to life in our own lives. Why, for example, would the author(s) of Proverbs 6:1–19 string together these sayings, themes, and metaphors about wicked men as they have? The same can be seen in the characters in Proverb 29 (see "Brief Interviews with Wicked and Righteous Men" in Live the Story in that chapter). Were there people like this in their community? It may be that personal experiences or stories led to particular ways of imagining such wicked men. It's also possible that the proverbs arose from circumstances in the narratives of the Old Testament.

We rarely know the origin of a proverb with certainty. But the very fact that stories and poetry cannot emerge in a vacuum devoid of lived experiences leads us to imagine the settings that inspired these writings. As we imagine these original settings, we often come to see new windows into our own circumstances. This commentary has taken several opportunities to model a reflective hearing of the Proverbs in order to help us learn how to read the sayings with an imaginative interest in making them applicable (cf. 3:13–18, 27–30; 5:2–3; 7:6–23; 30:1–9).

The wicked characters in Proverbs 6:16–19 become far more concrete when we read them in the light of actual lives and stories. Consider the sayings against the backdrop of Jacob and his children and the otherwise heroic characters of Joseph and Judah. The list of seven abominable acts begins with a condemnation of "haughty eyes," literally, "eyes that are exalted" (Prov 6:16). Several types of pride could be in view, but this image fits almost perfectly with the beginning of Genesis 37 with the story of Joseph and his dreams. Joseph's dreams are especially questionable in the way they imagine his older brothers, parents, and the moon and stars (perhaps God?) bowing down to him. Of course, since people cannot control what they dream, Joseph's sin is not what he imagines but in the prideful naiveté of reporting the dreams to his father and his already jealous brothers (Gen 37:7, 9–10).[12]

Joseph's naïve haughtiness only serves to turn his brothers more firmly against him, leading them to "devise" in their hearts to kill Joseph (Gen 37:18; cf. Prov 6:18). The brothers explicitly recognize that their plans amount to spilling "innocent blood" (Prov 6:17; cf. Gen 37:22, 26). Then, after selling Joseph into slavery, the brother's return to Jacob with a "lying tongue" (Prov 6:17) to report that Joseph had been killed by a wild creature (Gen 37:20, 32).

The one who "bears false witness" (Prov 6:19) is a specific type of lying that involves a false accusation of guilt, often in a legal hearing. The chief priests and the Sanhedrin gathered false witnesses to accuse Jesus, though none were found who could offer a convincing case (Matt 26:59–60). In the Jacob story, Joseph conspires to hide his silver cup of divination in Benjamin's sack of grain in order to frame him for theft (Gen 44:1–15). This injustice mirrors the brother's injustice in taking money for Joseph's life. The actions tear the family apart. In the words of Proverbs, they sow "conflict in the community" (6:19), leaving each of the brothers accusing one another and fearing for their lives (Gen 42:22, 37). Yet Joseph does not follow through in the vengeful path he begins. In this way he becomes a model of wisdom in the midst of wickedness. By forgiving and receiving his brothers, he essentially reversed the damage wrought by all the sins listed in Proverbs 6:16–19.

In 6:20–35 and 7:4–27, we will again find that the sexual temptations of Judah and Joseph in Genesis 38 and 39 provide a perfect backdrop for hearing the warnings against the strange woman and the adulteress.

---

12. It is common to believe that these dreams are from God as most dreams in the Old Testament seem to be. And yet Joseph's dreams are the only incidence where God does not give an interpreter. At the very least, it makes these dreams more ambiguous and in need of greater scrutiny.

LISTEN to the Story

6:20 My son, keep your father's command
    and do not forsake your mother's teaching.
21 Bind them always on your heart;
    fasten them around your neck.
22 When you walk, they will guide you;
    when you sleep, they will watch over you;
    when you awake, they will speak to you.
23 For this command is a lamp,
    this teaching is a light,
and correction and instruction
    are the way to life,
24 keeping you from your neighbor's wife,
    from the smooth talk of a wayward woman.
25 Do not lust in your heart after her beauty
    or let her captivate you with her eyes.
26 For a prostitute can be had for a loaf of bread,
    but another man's wife preys on your very life.
27 Can a man scoop fire into his lap
    without his clothes being burned?
28 Can a man walk on hot coals
    without his feet being scorched?
29 So is he who sleeps with another man's wife;
    no one who touches her will go unpunished.
30 People do not despise a thief if he steals
    to satisfy his hunger when he is starving.
31 Yet if he is caught, he must pay sevenfold,
    though it costs him all the wealth of his house.
32 But a man who commits adultery has no sense;
    whoever does so destroys himself.

³³ Blows and disgrace are his lot,
  and his shame will never be wiped away.
³⁴ For jealousy arouses a husband's fury,
  and he will show no mercy when he takes revenge.
³⁵ He will not accept any compensation;
  he will refuse a bribe, however great it is.

* * *

^{7:1} My son, keep my words
  and store up my commands within you.
² Keep my commands and you will live;
  guard my teachings as the apple of your eye.
³ Bind them on your fingers;
  write them on the tablet of your heart.
⁴ Say to wisdom, "You are my sister,"
  and to insight, "You are my relative."
⁵ They will keep you from the adulterous woman,
  from the wayward woman with her seductive words.
⁶ At the window of my house
  I looked down through the lattice.
⁷ I saw among the simple,
  I noticed among the young men,
  a youth who had no sense.
⁸ He was going down the street near her corner,
  walking along in the direction of her house
⁹ at twilight, as the day was fading,
  as the dark of night set in.
¹⁰ Then out came a woman to meet him,
  dressed like a prostitute and with crafty intent.
¹¹ (She is unruly and defiant,
  her feet never stay at home;
¹² now in the street, now in the squares,
  at every corner she lurks.)
¹³ She took hold of him and kissed him
  and with a brazen face she said:
¹⁴ "Today I fulfilled my vows,
  and I have food from my fellowship offering at home.
¹⁵ So I came out to meet you;

I looked for you and have found you!
¹⁶ I have covered my bed
    with colored linens from Egypt.
¹⁷ I have perfumed my bed
    with myrrh, aloes and cinnamon.
¹⁸ Come, let's drink deeply of love till morning;
    let's enjoy ourselves with love!
¹⁹ My husband is not at home;
    he has gone on a long journey.
²⁰ He took his purse filled with money
    and will not be home till full moon."
²¹ With persuasive words she led him astray;
    she seduced him with her smooth talk.
²² All at once he followed her
    like an ox going to the slaughter,
    like a deer stepping into a noose
²³ till an arrow pierces his liver,
    like a bird darting into a snare,
    little knowing it will cost him his life.
²⁴ Now then, my sons, listen to me;
    pay attention to what I say.
²⁵ Do not let your heart turn to her ways
    or stray into her paths.
²⁶ Many are the victims she has brought down;
    her slain are a mighty throng.
²⁷ Her house is a highway to the grave,
    leading down to the chambers of death.

Listening to the Text in the Story: Genesis 38–39; Deuteronomy 6, 8, 11; Proverbs 2:16–19; 3:1–5; 5:1–23; 9:1–18; Song of Songs

I have chosen to comment on Proverbs 6:20–35 and 7:1–27 together for several reasons. First, both groups of sayings share a similar structure: they both open with Deuteronomic exhortations for the son to hear the parents' "commands" and "teaching" (Deut 6:7; 20; 11:19; cf. Prov 6:20–23; 7:1–4), then move to a statement of purpose (6:24; 7:5), and close with exhortations about the "wayward woman" (6:26–35; 7:6–27). Second, both passages poetically imagine this woman as a prostitute and an adulteress. Third, the passages mirror one another. 6:24–35 focus on the actions of a man, while 7:5–27 focuses on those of a woman. Furthermore, we must remember that our chapter and verse divisions were not added to the Bible until the Middle Ages. The material in chapters 5, 6, and 7 all carries along a common set of images and ideas that are finally concluded in the father's final address of 7:24–27.

In the commentary on Proverbs 2–7 above we have already considered the many connections between Proverbs and Deuteronomy 1–11. The most significant connections are between the "teaching" (torah), "commands," and "words" of the father, which echo the words of Moses (Prov 6:20; 7:1–2). The warning not to "forget" from Deuteronomy 8 appears in Proverbs 6:20, and the familiar memory metaphors of "writing" and "binding" words and commands on the fingers and heart appear in both books (see commentary at 6:21; 7:2–3). Proverbs 6:22 also mirrors the three positions of lying down, rising up, and walking by the way from Deuteronomy 6:7. It is also significant that the rare use of the "apple" or "pupil" of the eye in Proverbs 7:2 occurs elsewhere only in Deuteronomy 32:10.

These two chapters also share parallels with Israel's patriarchal stories about Abraham, Isaac, and Jacob. Of course this leads us to ask what it would look like for a poet of proverbs to make reference to these ancient stories. Though this is a difficult and seldom-raised question, it bears asking, for, as we will see here, we have many reasons to wonder whether the writer of Proverbs 6–7 didn't have in mind some kind of parody or poetic allusion to Genesis 38–39 when he wrote about the young man, the adulteress, and the prostitute in these chapters.[1] In this section we will only observe a few of the overall structural and thematic patterns found in both Genesis 38–39 and Proverbs 6–7 and then speak to more specific echoes and parallels in the Explain the Story section below.

Taken as a whole, Proverbs 6:24–7:27 presents sayings about the seductive woman, interweaving and overlapping descriptions of her as an adulteress and a prostitute. Genesis 38–39 also presents two juxtaposed narratives that describe temptations from seductive women, like Judah with Tamar in chapter 38 and Joseph with Potiphar's wife in chapter 39. Potiphar's wife is a seductive adulteress (cf. Prov 6:26) with "smooth talk" (Prov 6:24), while Tamar appears both as an adulteress and, in the act of covering her head, as a prostitute (Gen 38:14–15; Prov 7:10). Also note that the allusion to the prostitute is vague in both Genesis 38 and Proverbs 6–7.

Furthermore, the four main characters in Genesis 38–39 all play the role

---

1. Or, as could be argued, that the influence runs from Proverbs to Genesis or, as Murphy, *Proverbs*, 42, suggests, the "example story" in chapter 7 could have come from a real life experience or expanded from the scene in Song 3:1–5.

of wise and foolish characters depicted in Proverbs. Tamar's motive for deceiving Judah is her desire to fulfill the levirate custom of carrying on the name of her dead husband, Er (cf. Deut 25:6). In this way Tamar is wiser than Judah, who is a fool having been caught in a trap and dishonored publicly in the end (Prov 6:33). Potiphar's wife is a striking embodiment of the adulteress and a boisterous woman of Proverbs. Finally, viewing Joseph through the lens of Proverbs, Gordon Wenham says,

> Joseph is here portrayed as a model, the wise man who fears God (Prov 1:7), who is totally loyal and dependable, and who thus enjoys "favor and good repute in the eyes of God and man" (Prov 3:3–4) and is not seduced by "the lips of the loose woman" (Prov 5:3), the "adulteress [who] stalks a man's very life" (Prov 6:26).[2]

The two narratives also portray two sides of wisdom—one brother (Joseph) wisely resists temptation and the other (Judah) who thoughtlessly succumbs.

A final point should be made about the parallels between Proverbs 6–7 and the Song of Songs. In Song of Songs the loved woman is often called a "sister" who goes about at night to seek her lover (3:1–4; 5:2–8) in the "streets" and "squares" (Song 3:2; Prov 7:12). This woman also boldly desires to kiss her love publicly (Song 8:1; cf. Prov 7:13). Reading Proverbs and Songs of Songs together, we must conclude that darkness, public kisses, city squares, and the like—while often associated with forbidden sexual acts—can also be seen in a redeemed light. The scene in Proverbs singles out the sexual boundaries that must not be crossed while Song of Song celebrates the love within those bounds.

EXPLAIN the Story

6:20–24; 7:1–4 As the mother's and father's sayings come to a close we hear two final echoes from Moses's sermons in Deuteronomy 1–11. By drawing on Moses in this way, the parents' teachings are infused with unique authority: these words, too, are from God and promise life to those who hear and obey.

The commands to "bind," "fasten," "store up," and "write" are all memory metaphors that imagine a deep engagement, not just with our intellect, but with our desires as well (cf. Exod 28:29; Song 8:6). So too the image of calling wisdom our "sister" and "relative" (7:4) characterizes the learning in this book as a relational and loving commitment to ideals like truth, life, goodness, honesty, diligence, and purity.

---

2. Ibid., 377–8.

The legal themes in Deuteronomy also intersect with wisdom, for when Israel obeys the words and torah of Moses they become "wisdom and understanding to the nations," who will look on the life of Israel as a nation and say "Surely this great nation is a wise and understanding people" (Deut 4:6).

6:25 This verse introduces the argument in 6:26–33. The woman's "beauty" and the "eyes," or eyelids, appeal to the man visually, but at a deeper level they capture his "heart." The heart plays several roles in these two chapters, first representing the place where commands are sealed or written to protect the son (6:21; 7:3, cf. v. 25). The word "heart" is also used for a foolish man who "has no sense," or, literally, "lacks heart" (6:32; 7:7), and the deceptive woman who is "wily of heart" (7:10). Tamar and Potiphar's wife are both peculiarly wily of heart—Tamar in her deception of Jacob and Potiphar's wife in her deception of her husband.

6:26–33 This extended argument focuses exclusively on the behavior and motives of a young man facing the temptation of a wayward woman. As we will see in a moment, in the argument of chapter 7:10–21, the verbs and reported speech are all of a woman.

The argument begins with a salient comparison: a "prostitute can be had for a loaf bread, but another man's wife preys on your very life" (6:26). The phrase about bread in the first line seems to be a unique Hebrew idiom, which surpasses our interpretive reach. Surely a prostitute costs more than just bread (cf. the goat that Judah pays for Tamar's service in Gen 38). Some commentators often translate the saying as "a prostitute will leave you with but a loaf of bread," in other words, deprive you of your wealth and belongings. However we translate it, the obvious point is that the adulteress is far more dangerous as she will cost the man his "very life" (cf. 2 Kgs 1:14). A similar lesser-to-greater argument is made in verses 30–33.

Meanwhile, verses 27–28 express the same message as our modern proverb "play with fire and you may get burned." The image of burning returns again in verse 34 in the description of the wronged husband's "fury," literally "heat," or "burning" jealousy. To play with another man's wife is the same as starting a fire that will consume the fool; in essence, he "destroys himself" (6:32).

Notice that despite all the good that Joseph brought to Potiphar's house (Gen 39:2–6; cf. Prov 6:35), Potiphar "burned with anger" at the thought of Joseph lying with his (Potiphar's) wife (Gen 32:19).

Proverbs 6:27–28 leads us to another interesting connection with Genesis 38. When Judah heard the report that Tamar was pregnant, he ordered her to be burned (Gen 38:24). Perhaps Judah had in mind the kind of law in Leviticus 20:14 that prescribed burning for a man who was involved with two generations of women. In any case, as in Proverbs, should Judah have actually carried out the penalty, Judah would have wrongly taken the life of a pregnant woman and her two children, and this would have incurred the same sentence on himself in the act: "eye for eye, tooth for tooth, hand for hand, foot for foot, *burn for burn*, wound for wound, bruise for bruise" (Exod 21:24–25). So, too, the young man in Proverbs 6 will suffer a fate commensurate with the folly of his sexual burning for the woman.[3]

7:6–23 This long description of the foreign or wayward woman is the only narrative depiction of its kind in the book of Proverbs. The passage begins with a witness, perhaps the father, watching through his window of an unfolding dramatic encounter between the son and the wayward woman.

Verses 6–9 describe the careless sexual wandering of "a youth who had no sense." Everything in this scene highlights the hiddenness and secret nature of his behavior. The obvious implication is that the lines of sexual morality in that day—like most sins that involve desire—were well known. The young man only "has no sense" with respect to the ultimate consequences that will face him, not the maneuvering needed to satisfy his sexual curiosity.

The group of sayings in 7:10–21 focuses entirely on the actions and motives of the wayward woman. The opening verse imagines her "dressed like a prostitute and with crafty intent" (v. 10). Other translations describe her as "wily of heart," which retains the important role of the heart in sexual motives specifically and the pursuit of wisdom in general.

It is commonly recognized that her use of the garment to pose as a prostitute closely parallels Tamar's actions when she left her home and disguised herself to fool Judah to lay with her (Gen 38:14–15).

Verses 11–13 highlight her total disregard for self-restraint and social discretion: she squanders her own reputation and that of her home; she is sexually devious; and she assumes the role of the man in her initiation of sexual intimacy. Voice, hands, feet, lips, and heart all work together to ensnare the simpleton.

Verse 14 may be the most perplexing saying in the chapter: "Today I fulfilled my vows, and I have food from my fellowship offering at home." The NIV changes the order and adds the phrase "I have food from my fellowship offering at home." A more literal translation is, "I had to make my offerings; today I have paid my vows."

What are we to make of these sacrifices, vows, and offerings? More importantly, how are they meant to persuade the son? Karel Van der Toorn examines a number of arguments and concludes that the woman in question has offered sacred vows (cf. Num 30:1–16) but is unable to pay for the vow because her

---

3. See Calum Carmichael, *Law, Legend, and Incest in the Bible: Leviticus 18–20* (New Haven: Yale University Press, 1997), 163.

husband, who holds the family money, is not at hand.[4] Fox, however, agrees with the paraphrase in the NIV and believes that the woman is referring to the type of fellowship offering described in Leviticus 7:15–16 because this would mean that she has meat that she plans to offer in a feast before having sex with the young man.[5] Fox's theory does better at explaining why the information would matter to the young man in Proverbs 7, but it does require us to read information and motives into the passage that are not there. Murphy speaks for many in his conclusion that "The implications of this verse escape us."[6]

Given the absence of obvious meanings, it is plausible that the vows and sacrifices are an allusion to Tamar, who in Genesis 38 met Judah at the cult shrine in Timnah where drinking and prostitution were common. The vow could be a subtle way of commenting on Tamar's motives, which are to fulfill the sacred vow she made to her husband Er, a commitment that Judah has neglected in withholding Shelah from his daughter-in-law. Upon conception of a child, Tamar will have technically fulfilled a woman's obligation of the Levirate custom of having a child to uphold the name of her dead husband.

In verses 16–17 the woman describes the extravagant preparation she has made for her tryst. The list of spices like cinnamon and aloe and foreign linens on the bed are all indications of a luxurious setting, similar to the bed prepared by the Shulammite in Song of Songs 4:14, but with licentious intent.

Her final argument seeks to persuade the young man that her husband is not at home, making her home a safe place to meet (vv. 18–20). Having taken "his purse filled with money," he is unlikely to return soon. Notice that in verse 19 the woman does not say that her *husband* is gone (as many English translations take it) but "the man of the house" is gone. Franz Delitzsch comments that by withholding the word "husband," she "ignores the relation of love and duty in which she is placed to him" (cf. 2:17).[7] In the same way, Potiphar's wife intentionally avoids referring to "her husband," instead calling him "the man of the house," whom she then blames for bringing this Hebrew slave into their house.

The father's voice returns in verses 21–23. Like an "ox" goes to "slaughter" or a "deer" in a "noose," so the son has not only been trapped but will be slain and consumed by death. These hunting metaphors echo similar metaphors from the beginning of these two speeches (6:5) and their force makes the wise path more than just a matter of avoiding obstacles beneath our feet, so

4. Karel Van der Toorn, "Female Prostitution in Payment of Vows in Ancient Israel, *JBI* 108/2 (1989): 193–205.

5. Fox, *Proverbs 1–9*, 245–46.

6. Murphy, *Proverbs*, 44.

7. Franz Delitzsch, *Biblical Commentary on the Proverbs of Solomon*, vol 1. (Ann Arbor: University of Michigan Press), Kindle edition.

to speak, but being cognizant of the way evil and folly are intent on seeking us out as prey. Genesis 4:7 similarly portrays sin as a predator. The ox and slaughter may also be allusions to the vows and sacrifices in verse 14.

7:25–27 The final verses appeal again to "my son" and bring the father's instructions to a close. Recalling the imagery of "ways" and "paths" (v. 25) that dominate these first nine chapters, he speaks of the adulterous as a fully personified cosmic warrior, boasting in her triumph and spoils. Those who go into her will end their journey in the "grave" (Sheol) and "death" (v. 27).

LIVE the Story

A Homiletical Theology of the Adulteress

The connections described above between Proverbs 6:20–7:27 and Genesis 38–39 deserve more comment. As we saw above, the links between these passages are sometimes uncanny and yet other times remote. There is no simple answer for how the reader can find the right balance between seeing too much and too little.

Most academic commentary typically steers clear of connections or echoes that seem too loose or uncertain. This is largely because academic biblical interpretation works within the general belief that the meaning in the Bible can be reached through the most objective method in vogue at any one time.

But these methods of interpretation and their human application can never be fully free from individual and cultural biases.[8] On the one hand, despite the many weaknesses and naïve assumptions within the scholarly method, we cannot do without its insights of social and historical research and the fruits of scholarly dialogue and critique that sharpen the academic field as a whole.

On the other hand, pastoral and theological commentary work with different assumptions about the Bible, namely that the text before us is the mysterious result of human intention and divine inspiration. Christians should thus read the Bible with the expectation that God, who supervened the gathering of these books into a canon, speaks beyond what the human authors intended or understood. In recent decades many Christian scholars have pursued a form of "theological interpretation" that holds together a critical reading of the Bible and a belief in divine inspiration. Simply because reading is done out of faith does not mean that it cannot be scholarly too!

It is in within this frame of reading that I have approached Proverbs, and chapters 6–7 in particular. On the one hand we have been able to encounter

---

8. Merold Westphal, *Whose Community? Which Interpretation? Philosophical Hermeneutics for the Church* (Grand Rapids: Baker, 2009), 77–78.

the metaphors and rhetorical hyperbole in these chapters with a sense for the moral framework in view of the writers of wisdom literature. Proverbs teaches that jealousy, laziness, pride, resentment, and lack of sexual restraint all abide on the path of folly. At the same time we expect to find these ethical categories evidenced within the familiar and more realistic stories of the Old Testament. Immoral and foolish behaviors threaten to tear apart the families of Abraham, Isaac, and Jacob, not to mention the period of the judges and kings of Israel.

Any experienced preacher knows the benefit of putting these passages alongside one another. The poetry of cosmic wisdom with its two women, two ways, and two houses catches one side of the imagination—of things eternal, divinely instituted, fixed in the creation. And yet that slightly abstract or distant vision infuses itself in our minds when we see it come to life in stories like those of Judah and Tamar and Joseph and Potiphar's wife. These narratives also allow us to see that a character like Judah, who was essentially feasting in Sheol with Dame Folly in Genesis 38, was able to turn and honor the family again by offering himself as a ransom for Benjamin (see commentary on Prov 6:1–5). Joseph provides something of the opposite lesson, having been a good steward in Potiphar's house and resisting the temptation of his master's wife, he still ended up wrongly accused in prison in a foreign land. Any sense of blessings and life promised by Woman Wisdom were delayed indefinitely. This is surely a valuable wisdom lesson that the immediate consequences are never the motive in moral choices concerning promiscuity and infidelity.

Sex, Rationalization, and Deception

Proverbs uses sexual immorality as the window into human depravity as a whole. Few other temptations, it seems, can equal the desire for sex, and just as few have the same degree of consequences.

Furthermore, education, intelligence, and professional success are little help when it comes to the impulses of desire. Presidents, senior military officials, and business leaders have all succumbed to the temptations that come with positions of power and opportunity. The "smooth talk" and "seductive words" of the wayward woman in Proverbs (6:24; 7:5) reveal how intelligence can actually be a detriment to avoiding evil. The smarter we are the easier it is too draw others into immorality and rationalize it for ourselves.

At times, seduction is deceptive. People talk about how "everyone is doing it," "we love each other," and abstinence "is a generational thing." These types of attitudes resemble others that use the Bible's ancient setting and social customs to provide a means for modern readers to ignore their unambiguous moral teachings. But, as we will see in the commentary on 9:17, there is a part of us that is seduced by the truth that we sometimes revel in the thought that we're defying God, authority, and social mores.

The passage of the woman caught in adultery in John 7:53–8:11 is not in the earliest Greek manuscripts and is considered an addition to John. The story nevertheless highlights common themes of sexuality and adultery in the world where Jesus taught. In keeping with Mosaic law, which provides for punishment of a woman by a jealous husband, a group of men have brought a woman to Jesus whom they have caught in the act of sexual sin. There is no husband to accuse the woman, and yet the multitude of male witnesses is legally sufficient to punish the woman. Jesus uses her guilt to expose the guilt of those in the crowd, "Let any one of you who is without sin be the first to throw a stone at her" (John 8:7). It is unlikely that the crowds disperse simply because Jesus appealed to their conscience, since it is clear that the Pharisees and teachers of the law are looking to catch Jesus in violation of the law. Rather, it is likely that he points to their own sexual guilt as a legal matter that disqualifies them as witnesses.[9] Here Jesus' superior wisdom in matters of the law are signs of his deity and his unique standing as one without sin.

Is the World of Proverbs Patriarchal?

This is a difficult question. On the one hand, the Bible is "androcentric" in the sense that it was largely written by, or through, a man's eyes. Israel was also patrilineal in the sense the inheritance belonged to male sons. And the Bible tends to emphasize the role of men in political positions who accumulate wives with minimal repercussions. Women are also less frequently shown in political and economic positions of power. These things that were typical of nations that surrounded Israel and the Bible do not always critique or improve upon social customs we view as inappropriate today (though they certainly do at many points).

Additionally, this female in Proverbs plays the deplorable role of the prostitute and the wayward woman. Just as Eve in some ways bears the burden for first to be deceived by the serpent, so the forbidden women in Proverbs lead the way into forbidden sexual pleasures.

This sense of female "inferiority" calls for a response. First, in the context of Proverbs, woman has the privilege of being the first of God's works of old and an architect in the work of creation (8:22–31). While her sexual appeals to the man may sound sexist to modern ears, they are complimentary in this context. Sex within its proper limits is a good thing and, in the world of Proverbs, it is Woman Wisdom, not a man, who sits in the position of

9. See Carmichael, *Sex and Religion in the Bible*, 102–13.

power and control of sexual relations. She is also the man's teacher for all of life (cf. 9:9) and stands to deliver judgment both to the wise and the foolish.

Second, as observed in a recent study of Israel's social relationships, Carol Meyers has argued persuasively that the term "patriarchy" is a modern invention of Western anthropology that has been inaccurately and inconsistently applied to ancient cultures.[10] In reality, women held notable economic, family, cultural, religious, and political roles in ancient Israel. These were positions with significant power at many levels of society. Meyers also shows that there were hierarchies where men had superiority, but there were also hierarchies within male and female groups as well as those of an ethnic, religious, and political nature.[11] The "patriarchal" model tends to oversimplify power structures and oppression into gender categories alone.

As we will see in Proverbs 31, the image of woman puts the glorious and beautiful exclamation point on the teachings of wisdom in this book.

---

10. Carol Meyers, "Was Ancient Israel a Patriarchal Society?" *JBL* 133/1 (2014): 8–27.
11. Ibid., 20–23.

LISTEN to the Story

¹ Does not wisdom call out?
  Does not understanding raise her voice?
² At the highest point along the way,
  where the paths meet, she takes her stand;
³ beside the gate leading into the city,
  at the entrance, she cries aloud:
⁴ "To you, O people, I call out;
  I raise my voice to all mankind.
⁵ You who are simple, gain prudence;
  you who are foolish, set your hearts on it.
⁶ Listen, for I have trustworthy things to say;
  I open my lips to speak what is right.
⁷ My mouth speaks what is true,
  for my lips detest wickedness.
⁸ All the words of my mouth are just;
  none of them is crooked or perverse.
⁹ To the discerning all of them are right;
  they are upright to those who have found knowledge.
¹⁰ Choose my instruction instead of silver,
  knowledge rather than choice gold,
¹¹ for wisdom is more precious than rubies,
  and nothing you desire can compare with her.
¹² "I, wisdom, dwell together with prudence;
  I possess knowledge and discretion.
¹³ To fear the LORD is to hate evil;
  I hate pride and arrogance,
  evil behavior and perverse speech.
¹⁴ Counsel and sound judgment are mine;
  I have insight, I have power.

¹⁵ By me kings reign
and rulers issue decrees that are just;
¹⁶ by me princes govern,
and nobles—all who rule on earth.
¹⁷ I love those who love me,
and those who seek me find me.
¹⁸ With me are riches and honor,
enduring wealth and prosperity.
¹⁹ My fruit is better than fine gold;
what I yield surpasses choice silver.
²⁰ I walk in the way of righteousness,
along the paths of justice,
²¹ bestowing a rich inheritance on those who love me
and making their treasuries full.
²² "The LORD brought me forth as the first of his works,
before his deeds of old;
²³ I was formed long ages ago,
at the very beginning, when the world came to be.
²⁴ When there were no watery depths, I was given birth,
when there were no springs overflowing with water;
²⁵ before the mountains were settled in place,
before the hills, I was given birth,
²⁶ before he made the world or its fields
or any of the dust of the earth.
²⁷ I was there when he set the heavens in place,
when he marked out the horizon on the face of the deep,
²⁸ when he established the clouds above
and fixed securely the fountains of the deep,
²⁹ when he gave the sea its boundary
so the waters would not overstep his command,
and when he marked out the foundations of the earth.
³⁰ Then I was constantly at his side.
I was filled with delight day after day,
rejoicing always in his presence,
³¹ rejoicing in his whole world
and delighting in mankind.
³² "Now then, my children, listen to me;
blessed are those who keep my ways.

³³ Listen to my instruction and be wise;
    do not disregard it.
³⁴ Blessed are those who listen to me,
    watching daily at my doors,
    waiting at my doorway.
³⁵ For those who find me find life
    and receive favor from the LORD.
³⁶ But those who fail to find me harm themselves;
    all who hate me love death."

Listening to the Text in the Story: Genesis 1–2; Psalm 104; Sirach 24

We come now to the longest poem in Proverbs. The public invitations in 8:1–5 sound nearly identical to Proverbs 1:20–23. But where the speech in chapter 1 turns into a scolding for rejecting wisdom (1:24–33), chapter 8 goes to great lengths to boast of wisdom's promises (8:6–21). In this way Proverbs 8 is an expansion and closure to the introductory speech in chapter 1.

Chapter 8:22 begins an obvious turn to focus entirely on wisdom's origin and experience of God's work in creation. The details of God's work resemble language in Genesis 1–2, Psalm 104, and Job 38, all of which emphasize a unique perspective on the creation and created order—the origins of the order, the goodness of the order, and the mystery of suffering in God's order.

The image of wisdom with God at creation also appears in the book of Sirach:

> Then the Creator of all things gave me a command, and my Creator chose the place for my tent. He said, "Make your dwelling in Jacob, and in Israel receive your inheritance." Before the ages, in the beginning, he created me, and for all the ages I shall not cease to be. In the holy tent I ministered before him, and so I was established in Zion. (Sir 24:8–10 NRSV)

While Sirach sounds a lot like Proverbs 8, it is distinct in its explicit references to Israel and the covenants. In fact, whereas the early church cited Proverbs 8:22 in favor of Jesus' work in creation, his deity, and his place in the Trinity, Sirach was foundational for Judaism to equate wisdom with torah. See the discussion in "Jesus is Wisdom—the Power and Limits of Poetry" in Live the Story below.

EXPLAIN the Story

In chapter 8 wisdom presents her exceptional résumé. This chapter is the fourth and longest in the sequence of five poems featuring Woman Wisdom (cf. 1:20–33; 2:1:22; 7:6–20; 9:4–6, 11–12).

Most scholars outline this chapter in four sections:

8:1–11	Treasures and expertise in Wisdom's words
8:12–21	Benefits and riches of Wisdom's teachings
8:22–31	Wisdom's origins and in the creation of the world
8:32–36	Wisdom's final appeal to humanity

8:1–11 After the speech of the wayward or "foreign" woman in Proverbs 7:6–27, wisdom takes center stage. In contrast to the foreign woman, who addresses the passerby, wisdom calls out to all humanity. Wisdom is like the forbidden woman (7:12) in the way she (wisdom) stands at the high points, crossroads, and marketplace (8:2–3), the most visible and public places. But the forbidden woman also lurks in hidden places (7:8–9).

Wisdom's opening invitation assures the young man that her words are "right," "upright," "just," and "true." In juxtaposition to chapter 7, Clifford says that "[Wisdom issues] an implied rebuke to the other woman's twisted and lethal words."[1] Her words also repeat similar descriptions of wisdom in 1:3 and 2:9, where we explored the many parallels between wisdom and law. Both wisdom and law affirm the same moral and physical order built into the world at creation, an order that is central to verses 22–31 below.

Like 8:13, verse 7 is in the third person and some scholars believe it is an addition to the poem, though we cannot be sure. What we do know is that the comparison to gold, silver, and rubies (vv. 10–11) matches 3:14–15. Furthermore, the word for "rubies" only appears again in 31:10, showing evidence of a careful and strategic hand in writing or editing the whole of Proverbs. This shapes our understanding of the valiant woman and her application to living *for men and women* in chapter 31.

8:12–21 These verses stands apart for their emphasis on what wisdom loves and hates (8:13, 17, 21). As in all of chapters 1–9, properly oriented desire is the doorway to wisdom. The benefits of wisdom in these verses extend to statecraft and civic order: "By me kings reign" and "by me princes govern" (8:15, 16). David (2 Sam 14:20) and Solomon (1 Kgs 3–5) are examples of wisdom applied to rule.

Solomon's wisdom in 1 Kings 3:16–28 is the most memorable. The passage

---

1. Clifford, *Proverbs*, 95.

features two harlots who share a home with each woman nursing a young baby. In the night one mother rolled over on her own baby and it died. She then swapped her dead child for the living one. When both women came to Solomon claiming to be the mother of the living child, he decided that they kill the living child and divide it between the mothers.

Some scholars believe Solomon's method was rash, as if Solomon would have carried out the threat. But David Daube has persuasively demonstrated that Solomon's judgment demonstrates true wisdom.[2] The judgment involves a bluff, a ploy that naturally belongs to battlefields and statecraft. Solomon discerns its usefulness in a new context.

But Solomon also discerns the peculiar role of a human life in deciding this case. A judgment about land, food, or even an animal could be brought to a compromise or a truce by dividing the property between the parties, even if it means killing the animal (cf. Exod 21:35). So, at first, Solomon's wisdom appears to appeal to this common practice, luring the women in with what is an absurd application in the case of human beings. This is no threat to the false claimant for she has nothing to lose—her child is already dead. Only the living woman truly recognizes the injustice and impropriety of applying the Exodus law in this way. In other words, Solomon had that sense of the modern proverb, "it takes a thief to catch a thief," intuiting the inclinations of the heart and motives of these two opponents in court.

Solomon draws out the response of the true mother and thus arrives not at a compromise, but at true justice. Rightly do the people affirm in conclusion to the judgment scene: "When all Israel heard the verdict the king had given, they held the king in awe, because they saw that he had wisdom from God to administer justice" (3:28)

Solomon's judgment demonstrates precisely how law and wisdom are meant to work together. The laws represent particular judgments or values about right and wrong, life and death, purity and impurity, etc. They exist at a point in time and speak to limited circumstances. To apply such laws and principles in new situations, one needs wisdom.

Verses 17–21 close this section, echoing sayings and promises from earlier in Proverbs 1–9. If the son "loves" and "seeks" Wisdom, she will yield help on the paths of righteousness and justice, and grant him great riches.

8:22–29 Together with verses 30–31 and chapter 31, this may be the most well-known passage in Proverbs.[3] As we discussed in the opening section of this chapter, this may also be the most significant passage in the book from the perspective of Jewish and Christian theology. The passage can be divided

---

2. Daube, "The Wise Judge" in *Law and Wisdom*, 105–26.

3. See the "Theological Message" in the Introduction above.

between wisdom's origins before creation (vv. 22–26) and wisdom as witness and participant in the work of creation (vv. 27–31).

The verb in 8:22 for "brought forth" (NIV) is from the Hebrew verb *qanah* and could also be translated "acquired," "possessed," "created," or "begot." Translators must decide whether *qanah* describes wisdom as an eternal entity, perhaps existing alongside God, or wisdom as God created as he began to make the world.

Here it helps to look to verses 24–25, where we find metaphors for bearing or giving birth, which together suggest that wisdom has its origin in God, her metaphorical mother. Furthermore, other Jewish sources written close to the time Proverbs reached its final form, such as Sirach 24 and Wisdom of Solomon 9:9, also make the interpretation more likely that wisdom was created in time than that she was an eternal being. We will address the implications this has for Jesus as wisdom below.

Because wisdom was created first she is witness to all God created and, more importantly, how and why he created it all. Verses 24–26 paint God taming the waters to make space for land and life. Such images of the primordial waters in the ancient world signified the cosmic powers and chaos. God is the conqueror of chaos who brings order and life, and, with them, the possibility of love and beauty.

Chapter 8:27–29 then describe God making foundations and boundaries for the heavens and the deep. Creation is no accident of chance and chaos; it is the work of a visionary mastermind.

8:30–31 But is wisdom no more than a *witness* to creation? Scholars typically point out that wisdom does not appear to *do* anything in Proverbs 8:22–31. This leads to the difficult question about how we translate the rare Hebrew word *amon* in 8:30. There are four main possibilities:

1. "Constantly" as a particle, as in the NIV: "Then I was constantly at his side . . ." As Waltke notes, this lacks strong historical support and depends on questionable grammatical analysis. It also adds nothing to the argument.[4] The main motive for this translation is avoiding the implication that God had a non-divine helper in creation, a conclusion that can be addressed in other ways.
2. "Faithfully," or "constantly," derived from the Hebrew qal infinitive absolute of I *mn*.[5]
3. "Pedagogue," or "nursling," as the passive participle *amun*. Or, appealing to the same Hebrew stem, *amon* as an infinitive absolute, meaning

---

4. Waltke, *Proverbs 1–15*, 419.
5. Ibid., 420. Cf. Fox, *Proverbs 1–9*, 286–87.

"growing up with."[6] The idea of a nursling, contrary to Watlke's objections, does in fact add persuasive force to wisdom's argument.[7] Indeed, according to such a translation, wisdom portrays herself learning from God during his act of creating, thus gaining the expertise she offers now to humanity (8:32–36). Because she was a close and loving student of God, she is fit to be a good teacher of God's creatures.

4. "Artisan," "craftsman," "sage," or "architect's plan," based on the Akkadian cognate *ummamu*. This is the predominant meaning chosen by modern English translations (e.g., NASB, ESV, NRSV). Van Leeuwen argues for this meaning based upon similar images of a master artisan or sage of creation in Sumerian wisdom.

This translation also fits with images of God who, at times, works in a heavenly court (Gen 1:26; Deut 32:6–9; 1 Kgs 22:19–22; Job 1–2; Isa 6:1–9).[8] Contrary to Fox's objections about wisdom as an architect, the metaphor makes perfect sense in light of the context of 8:22–29 where it is the very craftsmanship and design of the creation that are explicitly in question.[9] Fox supports his position by appealing to the fact that wisdom in Proverbs 3:19 is an *instrument* in creation and not an *active agent*: "*By wisdom* the LORD laid the earth's foundations."[10] This claim overlooks the obvious fact that wisdom is not explicitly personified in chapter 3 as it is in chapter 8, nor is she described in terms of the learning or expertise gained from the boundaries and limits laid down in the creation in chapter 8; the contexts differ too greatly to use them against one another in this way. The architecture and structure of creation provide the context of her expertise in chapter 8, which allows her to speak persuasively to human living in this same created world. It is such "boundaries" and "limits" that make wisdom possible at all.

Anyone interested in certainty on this issue of translation is certain to be disappointed. Options three and four have the greatest lexical, contextual, and historical support. In any case, the more important focus of this section is that of the order of creation. Wisdom is an expert of this structure and order and is uniquely qualified to guide us obediently and safely through life.

8:30b–31 Wisdom's active presence with God during the creation leads to great delight, literally, "I am delights," where the plural indicates a superlative

---

6. Fox, *Proverbs 1–9*, 287.

7. Cf. Waltke, *Proverbs 1–15*, 420.

8. Van Leeuwen, *Proverbs*, 94–95.

9. See Fox, *Proverbs 1–9*, 286 and Van Leeuwen's arguments cited above.

10. Why can't something be an instrument and active at the same time? Are not mules used to plow a field active agents?

(v. 30b). But whose delight is this? Most translations imagine God as the subject of delight, whereby God's delight in wisdom in verse 30 sits symmetrically balanced to wisdom's delight in humanity in verse 31.[11] Van Leeuwen, meanwhile, is among those who rely on a parallel in Psalm 119 to argue that, just as God's commandments bring delight to the psalmist (119:24)—providing valued counsel—so wisdom as a counselor brings delight to God in the creation (cf. also Isa 5:7).[12] According to this interpretation, wisdom is imagined delighting in two directions—upward to God the creator and outward to humanity and all creation. Not wanting to press the metaphor too far, we can say that wisdom and God both derive pleasure from their relationship and the way it has been a part of the making of the world.

In the midst of, and no doubt in tandem with delight, wisdom plays or dances before God with *sahaq*, "rejoicing" (v. 30b). Samuel uses *sahaq* to describe David and the people of Israel "dancing" or "celebrating" before the ark of the Lord as it is brought back to Jerusalem (2 Sam 6:5, 21). The word *sahaq* also appears in Psalm 104 where the scene portrays God creating Leviathan to "play" or "frolic" in the ocean. The psalm also concludes with a statement of God's own delight in the creation (104:31). Wisdom dances and plays in the deep and rich goodness God has designed for humans to experience, which leads to her delight in the humans who will inhabit these elements.

Delight is also central to the account of creation in Genesis 1 and God's seven judgments that the creation was "good" and "very good." In addition to the confidence wisdom wants to give us about her expertise in the order of created things, she models for us God's joy and his desire of us to have joy and delight in his world. It is fair to say that the original creation was in many ways made as a place for play. The world also contained dangers and evil, but it was certainly not a place of chaos for punishment by an angry God. Whatever joy is lacking in this world results from human folly and sin, the mysterious force of evil, and the innate wildness and danger of the natural world.[13]

8:32–36 Having recited her credentials, wisdom turns to teach her "children" in the ways of wisdom. As in 3:12–18, this conclusion offers two macarisms or blessing proverbs for those who will "keep" and "listen" to wisdom's ways (vv. 32, 34; cf. 3:13, 20). Wisdom addresses her children as they sit at her "doors" or "doorway." In this way she opposes the door of the wayward woman (7:8) and of Dame Folly (9:14). Wisdom's house and teaching offer "life" (8:35), whereas both of these women lead to the way of death (7:27; 9:18; cf. 8:36).

---

11. See Clifford, *Proverbs*, 97 and Longman, *Proverbs*, 227.

12. Van Leeuwen, *Proverbs*, 95.

13. See Christopher Wright, *The God I Don't Understand* (Grand Rapids: Zondervan, 2008).

LIVE the Story

Wisdom, Discernment, and the Created Order

One might only come away from Proverbs 8 with a sense of wisdom's expertise and yet recognize the connection of this expertise to the *order* or *structure* of the world. This seems to be Fox's position, who holds that "the description of *creation*... adds no new information."[14] If Fox is right, wisdom can be trusted because of her antiquity, not because the many references to foundations, limits, and borders in this chapter might imply something about the content of that wisdom.

But in the larger scope of the Old Testament, wisdom is that gift from God that rightly orders the various spheres of life, whether architecture, politics, textiles, parenting, teaching, or dream interpretation. This is true of Proverbs 8 as well, which unambiguously confirms for us that the world is ordered both in relation to stars, planets, elements, plant, and animal life (8:22–31; cf. Ps 104), as well as ethics and practices such as justice, right and wrong, and basic sense in living (8:6–21, 32–36).

The moral structure is particularly important, for wisdom allows us to affirm and to discern a permanent order while remaining aware of the destructive effects of the fall on the inclinations of our desire and the limitations of our discernment. Dame Folly constantly reminds us that our desires inevitably work to distort our perception and thus our sense of order, right, and wrong. It is worth belaboring this point amidst the spread of ethical pluralism and moral relativism today where the church increasingly finds itself at odds with the ethical practices of the surrounding world.

This has led to more and more efforts to reach a best case scenario in our laws and public policies—a kind of "proximate justice" that recognizes that only God can bring about permanent and lasting justice. Whether we affirm this approach to cultural compromise or not, it is hard to deny that compromise can also lead to a softening of moral stances *within* the church on the Bible's moral teachings. While the Bible is full of wise compromises in politics, economics, and other negotiations, it never undermines the moral scaffolding carved into the creation.

Still, the idea of "proximate" or partial justice does help us think about areas where right and wrong are not clear choices and where we have to choose between good and better and bad and worse. Such deeper moral discernment surely lies behind the decisions of the Hebrew midwives to hide Moses from the Egyptians and so also Rahab's hiding the Israelite spies (Exod 1:15–21;

---

14. Fox, *Proverbs 1–9*, 293, italics added.

Josh 2:1–24). Jesus' teachings likewise allow for the Sabbath to be broken for reasons of compassion and justice (Mark 2:24–26; Luke 14:5).

All these examples assist us in the everyday decisions we have to make on matters in determining a scale of value and a priority among alternative options: if and when should we share confessions made in confidence with others and how truthful we should be when asked by a host whether we enjoyed a poorly cooked dinner. These situations are all played out on larger scales as well: Can a soldier disobey orders in the interest of a greater good? Is a contractor ethical in revealing state secrets? Is a larger government worth its high financial costs and loss of efficiency? Do immigrants have a right to medical care? As Oliver O'Donovan argues, these kinds of questions require wisdom to discern the texture and hierarchies in God's moral ordering of the world.

> We have to formulate our basic commitments somehow; but equally we cannot be content merely to repeat them, or even to add to them, as though we could, by mere accumulation of moral demands, express the whole content of the moral law. The items in a code stand to the moral law as bricks to a building. Wisdom must involve some comprehension of how the bricks are meant to be put together . . . We look within [the Bible] not only for moral bricks, but for the order in which the bricks belong together.[15]

It is in this light that we understand how the "love command" stands as the organizing principle for all other rules (Deut 6:5; Lev 19:18; Matt 22:37–40) as well as how God desires justice, mercy, thanksgiving, and contrition more than sacrifice (Mic 6:6–8; Pss 50:8–15; 51:16–17). Jesus as wisdom incarnate renews this life and restores all of the ordered interactions and operations that lead to its ultimate good. In appealing to these "greatest commandments," Jesus affirms moral order from top to bottom.

Wisdom in Jewish and Christian Theology

The focus on wisdom and creation in Proverbs 8:22–31 has played a central role in Jewish and Christian theology. Within Judaism, wisdom's origin and role in the creation first provided a way to understand the revelation of knowledge from an infinite God to finite creatures. The passage eventually provided a way to situate the origin of the law of Moses in the six days of creation. Similar passages can be found in the pseudepigraphical book of Jubilees (first or second century BC), which depicts God speaking the law to Adam and Eve on the sixth and seventh days of creation (Jub. 1:25–28 and chapters 2–3).

Elsewhere, in Baruch, God's wisdom is directly equated to the law of Moses

---

15. O'Donovan, *Resurrection*, 200.

and the revelation and commands given to the patriarchs (Bar 3:9–4:4). As noted above, the book of Sirach provides yet another place where the law is identified with wisdom: "All this is the book of the covenant of the Most High God, the law that Moses commanded us as an inheritance for the congregations of Jacob" (Sir 24:23 NRSV; cf. 1:9; 17:11–12).

The scene of the world's creation also naturally appealed to the church as a way of understanding both Jesus' deity and his origins in eternity. The early Christian church fathers sometimes equated wisdom with the Holy Spirit for similar reasons, but the parallel with Jesus remained stronger, primarily because of the need for a means to peer into the mystery of the incarnation of an eternal and spiritual being. As we saw in the discussion of verses 22 and 30 above, the translation of a few key words made the difference between Jesus as created being and subordinate to the Father (Arianism) and Jesus as eternally begotten and one with the Father and the Spirit (orthodox Trinitarianism). In his defense of the Trinity against Arianism, Athanasius quotes Proverbs 8:25:

> "Before all the mountains He begat me" and goes on to say, "All these passages proscribe in every light the Arian heresy, and signify the eternity of the Word, and that He is not foreign but proper to the Father's Essence . . . [I]t becomes superfluous, or rather it is very mad to dispute about it, or to ask in an heretical way, How can the Son be from eternity? or how can He be from the Father's Essence, yet not a part? since what is said to be of another, is a part of him; and what is divided, is not whole."[16]

The fact that Christ comes from creation and yet exists with God before creation indicates for Athanasius that the Word in flesh must also be one with God. While we should judge that Athanasius and the anti-Arians were right to insist on Jesus' being one with God—as is clear in John 1:1, 18; 8:58; and 20:28—they were on less firm ground arguing that Proverbs 8:25 and the surrounding context in Proverbs 8 support the idea that wisdom and Jesus were one and the same. We will say more about this in in the context of John's gospel below.

Proverbs 8:22–31 clearly lies in the background of several of Paul's epistles and perhaps at the center of his presentation of Christian discipleship. In 1 Corinthians 1:30 Paul identifies Jesus as wisdom: "It is because of him that you are in Christ Jesus, who has become for us wisdom from God." The connections to Jesus as creator and source of wisdom are more explicit in Ephesians and Colossians. As we will see below, Paul draws on the language of Proverbs 8 to describe Jesus, and yet he also goes beyond this chapter in important ways.

---

16. St. Athanasius, "Selected Works and Letters," XXIII.32, http://www.ccel.org/ccel/schaff/npnf204.xxi.ii.iii.v.html?highlight=all,these,passages,proscribe,in,every,light,the,arian,heresy,and,signify,eternity,of,word,that,he,is,not,foreign,b#highlight.

Jesus is Wisdom—the Power and Limits of Poetry

Above all, Proverbs 8 draws our attention to God's use of wisdom in making the natural world. Von Rad comments, "What is objectified here, then, is not an attribute of God but an attribute of the world, namely that mysterious attribute, by virtue of which she turns towards men to give order to their lives." [17]

Von Rad observes that wisdom also presented Israel with "the same phenomenon, which more or less fascinated all ancient religions . . . namely that of the religious provocation of man by the world."[18] In other words, the ordered nature of the world leads us not to worship wisdom as an ideal or virtue, as in Greek philosophy, but to marvel at the Creator and his wisdom. So it is that Paul claims, "since the creation of the world God's invisible qualities—his eternal power and divine nature—have been clearly seen, being understood from what has been made" (Rom 1:20).

Whereas explicit reflection on God is limited in Proverbs 8, the New Testament by contrast uses creation and wisdom as a basis to marvel at God's power, rule, and work of redemption. We will look at this more closely at the end of this section. First we pause to ask how or to what degree Proverbs 8 and Woman Wisdom herself anticipate or "foretell" a coming messiah of wisdom. James Dunn, for example, observes that:

> When Christ is accorded a role in creation at or as the beginning of all things (as in 1 Cor 8:6; Col 1:15–17; Heb 1:1–3), the clear implication is that Christ is being accorded the role previously ascribed to Wisdom. In which case, the question cannot be ignored, Who is this wisdom?[19]

To answer this we turn to John's gospel, which seems to draw on wisdom as described in Proverbs 8:22 and Sirach 24:8–9: "In the beginning was the Word, and the Word was with God, and the Word was God" (John 1:1). And yet John never uses the Greek word for wisdom, *sophia*, and instead equates Jesus with the *logos*—a Greek term that is far more expansive than wisdom. This leads Waltke and others to believe that John is not appealing to Proverbs, Baruch, or Sirach at all.[20] But this is far too narrow a reading given the fact that Jewish wisdom literature (cited above), which was at its height in popularity in Jesus' day, clearly united the ideas of wisdom, law, and creation. This overlaps conspicuously with John's own interest in creation, *logos*, and the Mosaic law (cf. 1:1, 17–18). In particular, John aims to show that the *logos* was both the

17. von Rad, *Wisdom*, 156.

18. Ibid.,156.

19. James Dunn, "Jesus: 'Teacher of Wisdom or Wisdom Incarnate?'" in *Where Shall Wisdom Be Found: Wisdom In the Bible and the Contemporary Church*, ed. Stephen C. Barton (Edinburgh: T&T Clark, 1999), 80.

20. Waltke, *Proverbs 1–15*, 129–30.

source of creation and humbled to become part of the creation itself—an idea that was essentially blasphemous in the Greek wisdom tradition. Here Keener is closer to the mark when he states that, "John's choice of the Logos (embracing also Wisdom and Torah) to articulate his Christology is brilliant: no concept better articulated an entity that was both divine yet distinct from the father."[21] And no concept showed the superiority of Christian wisdom in the incarnate Christ to the gnostic view of wisdom among the Greeks.

That said, we only see this relationship between Jesus and wisdom in retrospect through the reading of the New Testament and not within Proverbs 8 in its setting in the Old Testament. Longman rightly warns, "Prov. 8 is not a prophecy of Jesus or any kind of literal description of him. We must remember that the text is poetry and is using metaphor to make important points about the nature of God's wisdom."[22] And we should add, the nature of God's wisdom is *in the world*, which is really the major point to take away from this chapter as it speaks to the relationship of Jesus and wisdom. It is this world of ordered stuff, in which Woman Wisdom has her delight, that Jesus as the successor to wisdom not only created but also claimed for full redemption.

In sum, whereas Woman Wisdom provides expert guidance for daily living while pointing to the creator, she does nothing to eliminate or suggest a solution to the problems of evil, sin, and death. The doctrine of the "two ways" in Proverbs merely accepts sin and folly as realities. By contrast, when we set Colossians 1 alongside Proverbs 8 we see clearly how Jesus holds together both mundane life in Old Testament wisdom and redemption from the powers of evil by wisdom incarnate.[23]

[16] For in him all things were created: things in heaven and on earth, visible and invisible, whether thrones or powers or rulers or authorities; all things have been created through him and for him. [17] He is before all things, and in him all things hold together. [18] And he is the head of the body, the church; he is the beginning and the firstborn from among the dead, so that in everything he might have the supremacy. [19] For God was pleased to have all his fullness dwell in him, [20] and through him to reconcile to himself all things, whether things on earth or things in heaven, by making peace through his blood, shed on the cross. (Col 1:16–20)	[15]By me kings reign and rulers issue decrees that are just; [16]by me princes govern, and nobles—all who rule on earth. (Prov 8:15–16)

21. Craig S. Keener, *The Gospel of John*, vol 1 (Peabody, MA: Hendrikson, 2003), 363.
22. Longman, *Proverbs*, 212.
23. See Longman, *Proverbs*, 210–13.

Before Jesus, the best hope for humanity was to be helped along the way, or even rescued *from* this world. Jesus, however, embodies all that wisdom promises in order that he might redeem the whole reality of daily life here on earth. In redeeming earthly life, he reaffirms and restores the wise patterns we need to carry out our days.

Once again, Jesus is both like wisdom in Proverbs and yet far more than her as well. Like wisdom, Jesus' human life is characterized by learning and growing in wisdom (Luke 2:40–52). Like wisdom, he knows, and is a reflection of, the created order. But unlike wisdom in Proverbs 8, Jesus is not created and does not have a beginning. He is not separate from God, but rather fully God. And he was not only delighting in the creation but also the unambiguous source of creation and the savior of creation in his resurrected body (John 1:3; 1 Cor 15:20–58; Col 1:15; Heb 1:1–4).

Furthermore, the resurrection of Jesus' body in the flesh is a reaffirmation of matter or "stuff" of creation: human flesh, social structures, culture, and the whole natural environment that is celebrated so exuberantly by Woman Wisdom in Proverbs 8:1–36. This is perhaps nowhere as apparent as in the epistle of 1 Peter. After Peter blesses God for the "living hope [we have] through the resurrection of Jesus Christ from the dead" (1 Pet 1:3), he gives instruction for living out that hope in every area of life: moral purity, religion, public witness, government, labor, social relations, marriage, suffering, and church administration. In Christ, everything that was dead, dying, and broken in our world has been reordered for new life in the resurrection. In the end Woman Wisdom is a glimmer of light in the mirror reflected by the Son of God in the fullness of his glory, as we draw out in Proverbs 9 and 31 below.

CHAPTER 13

Proverbs 9:1–18

 LISTEN to the Story

¹ Wisdom has built her house;
  she has set up its seven pillars.
² She has prepared her meat and mixed her wine;
  she has also set her table.
³ She has sent out her servants, and she calls
  from the highest point of the city,
⁴ "Let all who are simple come to my house!"
  To those who have no sense she says,
⁵ "Come, eat my food
  and drink the wine I have mixed.
⁶ Leave your simple ways and you will live;
  walk in the way of insight."
⁷ Whoever corrects a mocker invites insults;
  whoever rebukes the wicked incurs abuse.
⁸ Do not rebuke mockers or they will hate you;
  rebuke the wise and they will love you.
⁹ Instruct the wise and they will be wiser still;
  teach the righteous and they will add to their learning.
¹⁰ The fear of the LORD is the beginning of wisdom,
  and knowledge of the Holy One is understanding.
¹¹ For through wisdom your days will be many,
  and years will be added to your life.
¹² If you are wise, your wisdom will reward you;
  if you are a mocker, you alone will suffer.
¹³ Folly is an unruly woman;
  she is simple and knows nothing.
¹⁴ She sits at the door of her house,
  on a seat at the highest point of the city,
¹⁵ calling out to those who pass by,

who go straight on their way,
¹⁶ "Let all who are simple come to my house!"
To those who have no sense she says,
¹⁷ "Stolen water is sweet;
food eaten in secret is delicious!"
¹⁸ But little do they know that the dead are there,
that her guests are deep in the realm of the dead.

Listening to the Text in the Story: Ruth 4:11; Esther; Ugaritic Epic of Keret; Enuma Elish, The Akkadian Myth of Nergal and Ereshkigal, and The Hittite Myth of Illuyankas

In chapters 1–8, Proverbs frequently returns to the contrast between wisdom and folly, accentuating their conflict through pairs of two ways, two houses, and two women. These metaphors for wisdom and folly lead us to reflect on the power our desires have in influencing the way we learn and understand. Beginning in chapter 7, the two women become personified forms of wisdom and folly, appealing to young men with the carefully crafted words and sexual allure to take their paths and to dwell in their houses. This contest culminates in chapter 9 in two sets of banquets that draw the women, their houses, and their ways together in one grand vision of wisdom and folly.

The Banquet of Lady Hurriya in the Ugaritic legend of King Keret provides one example of many ancient texts that share the banquet imagery in Proverbs. Written sometime between 2000 and 1500 BC, Lady Hurriya mirrors Woman Wisdom and Dame Folly in Proverbs 9 in the way they carefully prepare a banquet: "She prepares the fattest of her [stall-fed-ones]; She opens a jar of wine." Like Wisdom and Folly, she also issues a formal invitation to her guests to come and partake: ". . . to eat and drink have I summoned you."[1]

The tradition of public feasts exists in most ancient cultures in the centuries after Hurriya, but the developments in the Greek symposia in the fourth century BC are the most significant for our understanding Proverbs. While these symposia were originally just luxurious feasts, they evolved to provide a context for learning, poetry, and the study of wisdom. Such feasts were well-known in Jewish cultures in the centuries around Jesus' earthly ministry

---

1. Translation Murray Lichtenstein, "The Banquet Motifs in Keret and in Proverbs 9," *JANES* 1 (1968/69): 19–31. This is also an excellent introduction to the Enuma Elish, the Akkadian Myth of Nergal and Ereshkigal, and the Hittite Myth of Illuyankas.

and probably also at the time of the final editing of the book of Proverbs (cf. Sir 32:1–13; Luke 14:7–24; John 2:1–12).[2]

The book of Esther also has five sets of paired banquets. Each pair of banquets is creatively structured around the ultimate fate of some individual or group in the story: Queen Vashti, Esther, Mordecai, Haman the Agagite, and the Jewish people. The heart of the book (chapters 5–7) narrates two feasts that Esther holds for king Xerxes (Ahasuerus), hoping to convince him to retract his edict that calls for the destruction of all the Jews in the land. The survival of the Jewish people out of a moment of sure destruction provides the reason to inaugurate the feast of Purim (9:17–19). While Esther is not a wisdom book (see "Genre" in the Introduction), it clearly illustrates the role that feasts played in Israel's sense of national and cultural identity.[3]

Much like banquets, houses and house building are two other common metaphors that symbolize the life of wisdom. We saw this already in our discussion of Proverbs 3:18–20 and will return to it in Proverbs 24 and 31 below. While actual house building is manual labor that the biblical authors usually attribute to men, we find several important examples where women are figuratively portrayed as house builders, like Leah in Genesis and Ruth (4:11–12). We will visit the parallels between Proverbs and Ruth in more detail in Proverbs 31 below.

EXPLAIN the Story

Chapter 9 ends the prologue to the book. As mentioned above, it constructs a series of oppositions that set up the liminal tension of the "two ways." Proverbs uses the contest between Woman Wisdom and Dame Folly to tie these opposing pairs together and intensify the choice between them. By choosing the company of Woman Wisdom, we set our lives on the path of obedience, goodness, and life; when we follow Folly, we go in the opposite direction.

In the commentary in chapters 2–8 we visited the many appeals to the feminine metaphors: "look for it" (2:4), "love her," "embrace her" (4:6, 8), call her our "sister" (7:4). Chapter 5 extends the feminine motif to a warning to avoid the wiles of the harlot, or the adulterous woman, and the admonition to enjoy the wife of one's youth (5:15–19).

In chapter 7 the father calls wisdom our "sister" and understanding our "woman friend" (NIV "relative"), both of whom desire to help us avoid the dangers of the harlot introduced in chapter 5. By personifying wisdom and

---

2. Fox, *Proverbs 1–9*, 306.
3. See Fox, *Character and Ideology*, 156–58.

understanding in these feminine roles, the father unites the cosmic and eternal Wisdom with the practical issues and temptations of daily life. As these eight chapters progress, the imagery of two women and two ways makes us increasingly aware of the powerful role that our desires play in the pursuit of wisdom. We are torn between good and evil, wisdom and folly, and a good wife and the adulterous woman (1:22; 4:6; 5:3, 19; 6:25; 7:18; 8:17, 21, 34–35).

With a final flourish, chapter 9 presents two speeches that close the prologue and draw all of the images and themes together in one place. The speeches are in fact invitations to two feasts, which imagine two kinds of sexual allure, two kinds of pleasure, and two kinds of wealth and happiness.

The chapter presents these speeches in the following chiastic structure:

A 9:1–6: Woman Wisdom's final speech: 9:1–6
B 9:7–12: Narrator's interlude
A' 9:13–18: Dame Folly's final speech

This structure strengthens the contrast between the women's houses, meals, and invitations, and that serves to reinforce the mutual exclusivity of their two offers.

9:1–6 Wisdom's speech is introduced by an elaborate description of her building her house and preparing a feast (vv. 1–3). As in her speech in chapter 8, where wisdom is at "the highest point along the way, where the paths meet" (8:2), here she is at the "highest point of the city" (9:3)—public front and center. Wisdom's speech alludes to the sacred temple, which returns to our discussion in chapter 3 where we observed that God's building of the house of the sacred cosmos (3:19) mimics the building of the First Temple (Exod 31:3; 35:31).[4]

As we will see below, the intricacy of the details in wisdom's speech stands out at many points because of its contrasts to Dame Folly's offerings. Wisdom begins by building a house with seven pillars (v. 1). We know from archaeological studies that seven-pillared houses existed in the ancient world. But this emphasis on seven is almost certainly a sign of life and perfection. The number seven also bridges her wise house building to God's seven days of building the creation in Genesis 1, which strengthens the connection between wisdom and creation that we find in Proverbs 3:18–20 and 8:1–36. The number seven, in fact, may play a major role in shaping chapters 8 and 9.[5]

As we saw in the Keret Epic, ancient stories of house building are traditionally followed by the preparation of food and an invitation. Wisdom's preparation appears in verses 4–6. Throughout Proverbs, food and wine symbolize

---

4. See Van Leeuwen, *Proverbs*, 101–02.
5. Ibid., 102.

wickedness, violence, and immorality (4:17; 23:6) but also the goodness of creation and the rewards of diligent labor (6:8; 12:11; 20:13; 28:19; 30:25; 31:14, 27). Wisdom's banquet fits more closely with this latter context, where her mixed wine and meat emphasize the rich rewards that come from a life of wisdom (vv. 2, 4). As a final sign of perfection and wholeness, wisdom's speech ends where it began, with an appeal for the "simple" person to heed her invitation and choose the way of life (vv. 4, 6).

9:7–12 Some scholars regard this cluster as an awkward or misplaced insertion between the two banquet speeches in this chapter; there is no way to know for sure how this material reached its final order, but in its current place the interlude plays an important role between the two speeches.[6]

First, by returning to the practical language of the father in chapters 1–7, the interlude reinforces the connection between his practical advice about life in this world and the ultimate cosmic structures of the world that lie hidden from our sight. Second, the interlude echoes the motto of the book of Proverbs first stated in Solomon's opening words: "The fear of the LORD is the beginning of wisdom and knowledge of the Holy One is understanding" (9:10; cf. 1:7). Solomon and the father echo Woman Wisdom's call to wisdom, giving the first nine chapters a sense of unity. Third, the cosmic rebuke sets the stage for future sayings about correcting the wise and the foolish (15:12; 19:25; 24:25; 25:12; 28:23; 30:6).

Finally, this interlude offers the son a final invitation to reflect on the consequences of his choice before hearing the last appeal of Dame Folly. The interlude gives three warnings against being a "scoffer" (7, 8, and 11), sometimes translated "mocker" or "imprudent man." To turn away from wisdom means embodying a stance of pride and skepticism that will pay a price in the end.

9:13–18 Dame Folly's speech concludes the chapter in verses 13–18. In a way, folly has been discredited by the interlude and speech by Woman Wisdom, but—and this is a lesson to the reader—folly refuses to surrender.

Like wisdom, folly's house sits at the heights of the city, probably near a central marketplace where crowds gather daily (3, 14). She also issues her invitation to the "simple" or naïve. Both women thus target the vulnerability of youth that has not seen enough of life to know the ultimate consequences of decisions like this.

Compared with the exquisiteness of wisdom's character, house, and the meal she prepares, folly appears to be idle, lazy, and offering a pitiful incentive to listen to her. Folly also lacks the powerful association of cosmological

---

6. See the essay on this passage by Mark Boda, "The Delight of Wisdom" *Themelios* 30/1 (2004), 4–11. Boda discusses the interlude in verses 7–11 on page 7.

roots that wisdom has in creation. And, unlike wisdom who built her own house, folly simply sits in a doorway as an "unruly" or "restless woman"—a troublemaker. The word for "restless" (*hama*) is the same term used to describe the adulterous woman in Proverbs 7:11, possibly serving as an additional link to cosmic Dame Folly. Furthermore, unlike the luxurious meal prepared by wisdom, folly offers stolen water and bread eaten in secret (9:17). These bespeak a life of haste, dishonesty, and shame.

But her weakness is also her strength. Her relaxed style makes her easy to approach, and her choice of language, which mimics the invitations of the ancient prostitute, creatively invigorates the son to let his private erotic imagination wander.

Yet, like the naïve people she hails, she too is shortsighted, not knowing that her suitors are guests of the dead (v. 18). Fox aptly summarizes this final scene in the prologue: "Folly has no counterpart to Wisdom's building her house before her feast, because building one's house is an act of wisdom, whereas folly destroys it (14:1)."[7]

Woman Wisdom is also an echo of the personification of wisdom in chapters 1, 3, and 8. The "tree of life" in 3:18 recalls Adam's and Eve's decisive choice between the two trees and two ways of life in the garden of Eden. Chapter 8 expands on these two paths with its emphasis on humans discerning the proper boundaries, limits, and thresholds that God built into the creation. In chapter 9 these thresholds are symbolized by the houses, food, and the sexual allure of these women. Just as the doorways to the houses symbolize sexual thresholds and paths of wisdom and life, so also do the liquids of wine, water, and honey. Similarly Numbers 25:1–18 portrays the women of Moab who invite Israel to a cultic temple feast, a scene laden with sexual immorality. So too it is that the women in Proverbs 9 call these men to cross sacred thresholds, one into pure and wholesome pleasure, and the other into forbidden realms of lust, adultery, and folly.[8]

We must be careful here not to separate the father's instructions on adultery in chapters 1–9 from the sexual allusions in the speeches of Woman Wisdom and Dame Folly that are nestled between them (see "Structure" in the Introduction). As Van Leeuwen rightly notes, "If the short poems [of the father] are isolated, they serve as warning against marital infidelity. But in the larger context of Proverbs 1–9, they serve as powerful metaphors to reinforce the primary message of the collection. In this world there are two contrary loves: for Wisdom, Good, and Life or for Folly, Pseudo-good, and Death."[9]

---

7. Fox, *Proverbs 1–9*, 301.
8. See Longman, *Proverbs*, 222.
9. Van Leeuwen, "Liminality and Worldview," 130.

LIVE the Story

Houses, Feasts, and Faith

Placing Woman Wisdom and Dame Folly in the streets and byways and at feasts in houses, Proverbs emphasizes the public nature of the contest between wisdom and folly. Furthermore, whereas chapter 8 emphasized wisdom's cosmic home and the expertise she gained as God's assistant in the work of creation, this chapter places her in the middle of the daily life of the average Israelite. Wisdom thus gives our lives a sacramental nature, in which our daily life flows out of our worship and our faith.

In chapter 8 we saw that the Gospel of John makes use of the imagery of wisdom's origins in Proverbs to introduce Jesus as God's helper in the work of creating the world (John 1:1–4). Just like the transition from cosmic origins to public voice in Proverbs 8–9, Jesus leaves his cosmic throne to take on flesh and plant himself in the mundane and even crude fabric of Israel's first-century world, starting his ministry at a wedding feast at Cana (2:1–11). The gospel does not promise to take us out of the world but sounds good news of salvation *for* the world (John 3:16).

In the parable of the ten bridesmaids in Matthew 25:1–13, Matthew uses the banquet as a backdrop for a lesson on wisdom and lordship. The parable presents ten virgins—five wise and five foolish—all of them waiting for the master to return and open the doors to his feast. The five wise women prepare for a long night by taking extra flasks of oil. The foolish women are away in search of oil when the master returns and are locked out of the feast with no hope of becoming the master's bride. The message here isn't so much "be wise and plan ahead" as it is "don't do anything that will jeopardize your entry into the feast of this King." Folly trivializes the unparalleled privilege of dining as a guest in his kingdom. And Jesus is the fullness of the expression of the feast portrayed by Woman Wisdom. He recognizes that our fallen human nature will inevitably keep us from this feast, and so he secures our way to it by dying to death and folly for us.

Finally, Jesus' short parable of the two houses in Matthew 7:24–27 revolves around the connection between house building and wisdom. The one who hears Jesus' sayings and "puts them into practice" is like a wise man who builds his house on a rock, which withstands the storms and winds. Meanwhile, the one who rejects Jesus' sayings is like a foolish man who builds his house on the sand and finds it washed away in the storms. As in Proverbs, the house is a metaphor for our whole way of life.

Competing Worldviews

Above all, this chapter reinforces the reality that every human life sits amidst a field of competing stories that seek to explain the meaning and purpose of our lives. Proverbs is not a narrative, but it does have the general qualities we find in most stories: character development among the protagonists and antagonists, the call to a choice, and a climax and resolution. These last two are the focus of chapter 9, which catches the reader in the horns of a dilemma, something like Hamlet's famous soliloquy "To be or not to be," where he contemplates whether he will take his own life or go on living.

The cosmic overtones in Proverbs present a more urgent dilemma than Shakespeare, setting up a choice that applies to every human life. And yet, unlike Hamlet's case, the final consequences for our choices are known from the outset. Surprisingly, perhaps, that does not mean that the promises wisdom makes are easy to believe; on the contrary, the constitution of our fallen human nature makes it extremely difficult to choose the way we know to be right. Like God's testing of Adam and Eve in the garden, the narrative tension between a good wife and Woman Wisdom on the one hand, and an adulterous woman and Dame Folly on the other, remind us that it is a part of our created human nature to walk through life struggling daily to control our desires.

Furthermore, as we saw in the Introduction above, Proverbs is composed of two kinds of material: individual sayings that shape our character in particular circumstances in life and cosmic or teleological visions that plant those activities in a grand story that gives purpose to our world and our lives. This storied or narrative focus is what we called a *telos* or goal that keeps us focused as we develop the wisdom of godly character.[10] James K. A. Smith captures this well in his description of our natural "passional orientation to the world." He says,

> What we do is driven by who we are, by the kind of person we have become. And that shaping of our character is, to a great extent, the effect of stories that have captivated us, that have sunk into our bones—stories that "picture" what we think life is about, what constitutes "the good life." We live *into* the stories we've absorbed; we become characters in the drama that has captivated us. Thus, much of our action is acting out a kind of script that has unconsciously captured our imaginations.[11]

The dominant approaches to teaching and learning in our modern, Western world fail to attend adequately to the passionate roots of our human

---

10. See N. T. Wright, *After you Believe: Why Christian Character Matters* (New York: HarperOne, 2012), 27–71.

11. *Imagining the Kingdom: How Worship Works* (Grand Rapids: Baker Academic, 2013), 32.

nature and that the *information* and *formation* of education go hand in hand. Our concept of a "worldview" tends be reduced to the world of ideas, obscuring its affective and pastoral dimensions. By speaking so provocatively about the power of desire in our path to wisdom, Proverbs 1–9 makes the heart the point of entry for the mind—not vice versa.

It is rarely noticed that the feasts in Proverbs share many parallels with Israel's festival life, especially the instruction from fathers to sons. The sons ask their fathers for the meaning of the memorial stones at the Jordan (Josh 4:6), the meaning of the ritualized lamb meal at Passover (Exod 13:14), and the significance of booth-living in the Sinai (Lev 23:41–43; cf. Deut 6:20; Jer 6:16).[12] Proverbs is also the book that precedes the fives books of the *megillot* (scrolls) that were read at Israel's feasts. Festival, ritual, pilgrimage (ways and paths), and instruction have been carefully interwoven into Proverbs and the biblical poetry that surrounds it.

In this way Proverbs 9 enriches our understanding of Jesus' parables of the building of two houses and the banquet feast for the ten virgins. Jesus has come to offer an abundant and eternal life to all who are devoted to him in love. The foolish turn their hearts to take pleasure in the forbidden pleasures in our world. Jesus' miracle at a feast (John 2:1–11) embodies the promises of wisdom as "the way and the truth and the life" (14:6). He brings us to a point where we must decide between the "wisdom of God" and "the wisdom that comes from heaven" and the wisdom of the world (1 Cor 1:21; Jas 3:17). And, as the parable of the wedding feast also makes clear, we are either his guests or else are shut out from his presence forever.

Religion has some measure of popularity in this day of cultural pluralism. Many of us meet people who welcome religious people; they like Jesus as a teacher and model of goodness, justice, and mercy. But most of these people have little patience for Jesus as King of the world, the way to eternal life, or the source of ultimate "Truth."

To preach and popularize a Jesus that is palatable to these masses means denying the central thesis in the biblical story: there is one true God, one source of truth, one key to justice and righteousness, and one way of salvation and life. The sense of urgency placed on the reader of Proverbs 9 is consistent with what the Bible says about all of life. Every person who lives in this world comes to the same crossroads in life: what will you decide to love more, God or yourself, his kingdom and his righteousness, or pleasure and folly? For those who choose him, he has prepared an eternal cosmic feast.

---

12. See Dru Johnson, *Knowledge by Ritual: A Biblical Prolegomenon to Sacramental Theology* (Winona Lake, IN: Eisenbrauns, 2016), 33–56.

Community and Family

Proverbs 9 also invites us to reimagine the earthly family, which sits at the heart of wisdom instruction. Most of chapters 1–29 and 31 are attributed to parents or to Solomon imploring children to heed their parents' teaching. And yet, throughout these teachings we're constantly reconnected with cosmic Woman Wisdom. By the end of chapter 9 the two are inseparably intertwined in our minds. This reassures parents that their efforts to train their children are far from trivial. God has given them the privileged opportunity of guiding their little ones along the paths of life that were carved into God's design for the world.

The union between parents and wisdom also reminds adolescents that their parents teach with an authority that has divine, eternal foundations. Parents instruct, yes, but Woman Wisdom is the real teacher and the real thing taught. She embodies all that we saw in chapter 8, mediating wisdom and knowledge of the created order from God to us, and yet she also appeals to us with the intimacy and familiarity of instructions in the home. Little acts of discipline, reflection, kindness, prudence, honesty, and generosity that we do in our daily lives are anything but trivial. They are acts that obey the deep cosmic rhythms God built into this world.

It's important not to overlook the increasing numbers of children being raised in this world with only one or no parents at all, particularly in developing countries and the urban centers in North America and Europe. In America, these single parent families add momentum to the growing opportunity gap between the upper and middle classes as it becomes increasingly difficult to escape the patterns of poverty and poor education.

We could simply lift children out of their broken surroundings and enroll them in successful private and charter schools. Or we could invest our resources into improving public educational programs, increasing teacher pay, and providing better access to technology.

Proverbs resists any simple or one-sided answer to these problems. By locating wisdom's origins in God's creation of the world (chapter 8) and by continually acknowledging our fallen predisposition to folly and sin, Proverbs presents a comprehensive vision for addressing interrelated brokenness in families, communities, tribes, cities, and governments. Conservationist David Orr recognizes the way our problems with society, government, and education intersect with the plight of children in our world today:

> No society that loved its children would consign nearly one in five to poverty and leave them without adequate health care. No society that loved its children would put them in front of a television four hours or more

every day . . . No society that loved its children would create places like the typical suburb or shopping mall. . . . No society that loved its children would build so many glitzy sports stadiums and shopping malls while its public schools fall apart.[13]

Orr's point is not that we do these things intentionally or because we consciously choose not to love our children. On the contrary, our failure to think comprehensively about our world stands to blame for these and thousands of other unwanted destructive patterns in our society. The presence of Woman Wisdom and Dame Folly at the heights of the city (Prov 9) places learning not in a secluded schoolroom but in the center of our civic and global way of life. If we do not think intentionally about the comprehensive nature of our world, we will continue this pattern, not only leaving our children increasingly in need, but training their generation that there is no other way to exist in this world. The problem is not with our children, but with us.

Desire (Again)

The cosmic imagery in this chapter again illumines the complex inner workings of human desire. We can discern at least three kinds of desire in this chapter.

First, our immediate interest in folly's sexual appeal exposes how instinctively we are drawn to evil and unrighteousness. Sights and sounds can stir up our desire in an instant.

And yet, second, the whole picture surrounding Dame Folly serves to capture the way we are often lured into sin and folly by seductive and seemingly harmless trains of thought. We begin by rationalizing the attention we give to folly's public appeals, and from there it is an easy step to approach her house and cross her threshold, as if only for a minute. Each step in her direction feels only slightly unsettling, until we are tucked away in the bowels of her home with stolen water and bread eaten in secret.

And then there is a third and even more rebellious way that we seek out the pleasures of folly. Commenting on folly's statement "stolen water is sweet" (9:17), Michael Fox remarks how often Dame Folly and the seductive women in Proverbs 1–9 actually tell the truth about our desires: we enjoy casting off authority, reason, and morality and delighting in our rebellion.[14] There is a sweetness in satisfying our base desire, and another sweetness—a "special tang"—in "relishing" the defiance of authority and having what we know we should not.[15]

---

13. David Orr, "Loving Children: A Design Problem" in *Hope is an Imperative: The Essential David Orr* (Washington, DC: Island Press, 2011), Kindle edition.

14. See Fox, *Proverbs 1–9*, 302.

15. Ibid.

This picture of folly also illumines the tendency of believers in every age to deny the God-given goodness in pleasure. The tree of life in Proverbs 3:18–20, echoing Genesis 1–3, imagines a life full of good pleasures found in communion with God. Meanwhile, Woman Wisdom's banquet feast offers much better pleasures than folly's, whether in the rich meat and wine or the deeper sexual pleasures symbolized by her invitation to come to her house. Just as the father exhorts his son to "drink water from [his] own cistern" (5:15), enjoying intimacy with his wife, so too does wisdom's invitation affirm the goodness of human pleasures, *so long as they are constrained by God's designs for us.*

As we head into the main sayings in Proverbs 10–29, we have been prepared to engage its teaching with our whole heart, body, and strength—to begin with faith (1:7; 9:10) and learn out of our love for God and his world, seeking to conform our pleasures and desires into the contours he has designed for his world.

Keep Growing in Wisdom

It is appropriate to close our study of the prologue by emphasizing the cumulative approach to learning described in verse 9, "Instruct the wise and they will be wiser still; teach the righteous and they will add to their learning." Echoing the exhortation in 1:5, wisdom is imagined here as a life-long journey. (See "An Upward Spiral of Learning" in 2:1–22.)

In his study of the transformation of the modern university, Bill Readings states that education has become a parking place where students abide inconvenience for a short time to get the qualifications to get on with life. Readings describes this model of twelve years of primary education followed by four years of secondary college or university time as one of "strange temporality" where "Time to Completion" is the primary aim of educators.[16] This comes with the unfortunate consequence of thinking of learning as a closed period of time that's done when we have our diploma or first job. It also makes the mistake of assuming that everyone needs the same amount of time to learn.

Proverbs encourages us to preserve the idea of education and learning as a journey shared by all humans, young and old. As one friend is fond of saying, a biblical view of wisdom discourages us from calling ourselves Masters or Doctors of some subject of study. We are all moving along a path toward the fullness of knowledge in eternity, when we see God face to face. The longing that Woman Wisdom has for growing in wisdom comes to life as Jesus grows into full manhood, "And Jesus grew in wisdom and stature, and in favor with God and man" (Luke 2:52). Here we meet yet another important distinction

---

16. Readings, *University*, 148, 128.

between Jesus and Woman Wisdom. Woman Wisdom is never more than a metaphor for wisdom in the cosmic design of the world. But Jesus embodies that wisdom in his own flesh as he learns the gritty nature of life familiar to us. He then embraces this whole natural world, redeems it, and brings it to the full potential that Woman Wisdom seems to anticipate as she danced before the Lord in delight (Prov 8:30–31).

Proverbs 1–9 presents us with a chain of extended proverb-poems that imagine the pursuit of wisdom as a path marked by urgency and erotic desire. Chapters 30–31, meanwhile, gather three final poems that accentuate the wonder of wisdom on one side (Prov 30) and the beauty and practicality of wisdom on the other (Prov 31). We turn now to chapters 10–29, which introduce us to almost five hundred individual sayings that stand apart from the material before and after it. This interlude between chapters 9 and 10 is meant to prepare us for this transition.

The Individual Sayings in Proverbs 10:1–29:27

Many scholars believe that these sayings were gathered with little thought for organization, apart from a few clusters in places like 16:1–15 and chapters 25–27. Other scholars believe that careful thought has been given to pairs and groups of proverbs in addition to the general design in the overall flow of material in these nineteen chapters of sayings.[1] As argued in "Structure" in the Introduction, this issue must be answered in the light of Proverbs status as poetry.

There is an undeniable sense of randomness and almost senseless repetition in chapters 10–29. Michael Fox admiringly refers to this material as "a heap of jewels" arranged in "sweet disorder."[2] Indeed, in the Introduction to the commentary we likened these sayings to countless stones on a rocky shore whose primary merits are in their quantity and variety rather than in their organization. The randomness among the sayings matches our experiences in daily life, where new situations constantly arise and beg for our judgment, discernment, and response.

But the randomness also has a distinct educational advantage to the reader. Rather than piling up all of the sayings about righteousness, hard work,

---

1. See especially Knut M. Heim, *Like Grapes of Gold Set in Silver: An Interpretation of Proverbial Clusters in Proverbs 10:1–22:16*, BZAW 273 (Berlin: de Gruyter, 2001).
2. Fox, *Proverbs 10–31*, 481, 477.

humility, honesty, and self-control into neat lists and eliminating the many duplicates, the sayings constantly move between familiar subjects, creating a sense of repetition, rhythm, and constancy amidst endless change. This rhythm makes the sayings more memorable as lessons. The rhythm also presents an endless series of familiar principles recombined in new contexts, which facilitates growth in discernment. The end result of this arrangement is mastery or a sense of the whole that allows the reader to make sense of particulars.

This educational feature overlaps with the many places where proverbs have been gathered in pairs or smaller groups, usually around common sounds or common themes. The editing style appears light-handed, so to speak, like the work of a careful and mature artist. We will see many of these signs of artistry in the section below.

Home and School

In the Introduction we considered the various possible provenances for these sayings. Joseph Blenkinsopp argues that the sayings of two lines in chapters 10:1–22:16 and 25:1–29:27 "show few signs of having originated in popular usage and little, if any, overlap with proverbial sayings occurring here and there in biblical narrative."[3] Norman Whybray, meanwhile, highlights the utter practicality of most of the sayings, stating that they are true to the "lore, or wisdom, of ordinary people."[4] Whybray is probably right that many of these sayings originated in ordinary settings, but his research also supports Perdue's contention that the use of parallel lines, repetition, and the precision evident in collecting thirty-one chapters of sayings are all evidence of sages in a royal court.[5] Also, they may have originated in schools where the sayings would have been memorized, discussed, and even debated.

In popular readings of Proverbs today, there is little appreciation for the variety and artistic ordering of the material that we have outlined here. As a result, we benefit less than we should from the educational, theological, and aesthetic richness of Proverbs as a collection. The material below summarizes the various sections and notable patterns in chapters 10–29.

Solomon's First Collection: Proverbs 10:1–22:16

Many ancient cultures did not have number systems and had to use letters in their place. Proverbs 10:1–22:16 is composed of 375 sayings, which is

---

3. Joseph Blenkinsopp, *Sage, Priest, Prophet: Religious and Intellectual Leadership in Ancient Israel* (Louisville, KY: Westminster John Knox, 1995), 41.

4. Norman Whybray, *The Composition of the Book of Proverbs*, JSOTSup 168 (Sheffield: JSOT Press, 1994), 62.

5. Leo Perdue, *Proverbs*, Interpretation: A Bible Commentary for Teaching and Preaching (Atlanta: John Knox, 2000).

the number value of the Hebrew letters in Solomon's name, *šlmh* (*š*, 300 + *l*, 30 + *m*, 40 + *h*, 5 = 375), thus emphasizing his royal influence in the collection.

10:1–15:32[6] Of 184 sayings in this section only about fifteen are not antithetical sayings, e.g., "The prudent keep their knowledge to themselves, *but* a fool's heart blurts out folly" (12:23, emphasis added). Pivoting on the conjunction "but," these sayings invite a constant contrast between two opposite paths or states of affairs (cf. 10:18).

All six chapters also maintain a focus on four major themes. A careful analysis reveals that chapters 10–12 place a greater emphasis on the contrast between the "righteous" and the "wicked," and chapters 13–15 emphasize the contrast between the "wise" and "foolish."[7] These are the principal themes of opposition in chapters 10–29 as a whole, so this fairly rudimentary material provides an introduction to the more diverse types of sayings in chapters 16–29.

Van Leeuwen speaks to the important relationship between wisdom and righteousness and wickedness and folly, observing that, although wisdom and righteousness speak to a similar set of ideas and situations, wisdom is the larger of the two concepts. Righteousness addresses "social-spiritual-moral-legal right and wrong."[8] A person can do what is righteous by caring for the poor, yet do it in an unwise manner. But a person cannot be wise without also being righteous, since wisdom encompasses those aspects that have no explicit moral value.

15:33–16:11 The break from antithetical sayings at the end of chapter 15 is accompanied by the presence of the divine name "Yahweh" in every verse between 15:33 and 16:11. The name appears nowhere in chapter 13, so the reader can appreciate the shift that occurs as follows:

Passage	Appearances of "Yahweh"
12:1–28	2
13:1–25	0
14:1–35	3
15:1–32	8
15:33–16:11	12
16:12–33	2

The pattern of only two to four uses of "Yahweh" per chapter continues through chapter 29, so while the transition may not be sharp, the conspicuous

---

6. Much of the discussion that follows relies on the outline in Whybray cited above.

7. See the commentary on these chapters below for a more detailed analysis of these terms.

8. Van Leeuwen, *Proverbs* 105.

rise to twelve sequential appearances of Yahweh catches the reader's attention and reinforces the theological emphasis on wisdom in Proverbs so clearly laid out in chapters 1–9. As Van Leeuwen notes, the string of references to Yahweh in this short stretch also illuminates the proper balance between divine sovereignty and human freedom.[9]

16:12–33 Just as the twelve references to Yahweh seem to fade away, the sayings also turn to focus on wisdom for kings, a pattern that emerges again in 20:26–21:4 and 25:1–6.

17:1–20:1 Meinhold describes the divisions here as a failed education (17), human stability and security (18), and compassion as the goal of education.[10] 19:1–20 also includes a number of proverbs concerned with instruction and the behavior of children in addition to a smaller group of sayings about the "friend" (vv. 4–7).

20:1—21:31 In these last two chapters, two sections stand out: proverbs concerned with the "heart" and the mystery of discerning our deep thoughts and intentions (20:5-12), and proverbs dealing in some way with the king (20:26-21:4).

Final Divisions in Proverbs 22:17–29:27

22:17–24:34 These verses are set off by two distinct references to the "sayings of the wise" in 22:17 and 24:23. The form of the sayings is more like the lessons in 1–9 or what McKane calls "Instruction" with teachings followed by motive clauses.[11]

The majority of scholars believe that 22:17–23:11 was adapted from the Egyptian sayings of Amenemope or another source available to Egyptian and Israelite wisdom writers, but the similarities between these writings and Proverbs are not certain and need more attention. We will address this in the commentary beginning at 22:17. The final sayings in 23:12–24:34 depart from the sayings of Amenemope and only have one or two parallels in Ahiqar and Ani (Any).[12]

25:1–29:27 This final section falls under the heading of proverbs of Solomon gathered by the men of Hezekiah. Whybray notices the distinct scarcity of references to Yahweh. Three further points deserve mentioning here.[13]

First, some scholars have argued that 25:2–27 and 26:1–12 represent two independent proverb-poems. Van Leeuwen's detailed analysis of chapters

---

9. Ibid., 159.

10. Arndt Meinhold, *Die Sprüche: Teil 1: Sprüche Kapitel 1–15* (Zurich: Theologischer Verlag Zurich, 1991), 161.

11. McKane, *Proverbs*, 269–70.

12. On the Egyptian parallels, see Fox, *Proverbs 10–31*, 705–69.

13. Whybray, *Composition*, 64–65.

25–27 further demonstrates poetic structures that hold together poems in 26:13–16, 17–28; 27:1–22; and 23–27.[14]

Second, these chapters also contain the highest number of visceral and grossly violent proverbs in the book. These sayings are even more striking because of the way they reverse the normal topic-comment to comment-topic, or what Alter calls a riddle form.[15] See "Literary Analysis" in the Introduction.

Third, the final two chapters have a conspicuous number of sayings about "oppressive rule."[16] More will be said on these points in the commentary below (see 23:29–30; 25:16–22; 26:3, 8, 11, 17, 18, 22).

In summary, chapters 10–29 exhibit two distinct traits. One, the chapters contain a breadth and variety of sayings that seems random at the same time that the chapters show numerous signs of artistry, careful editing, and repetition.

Two, the chapters also progressively move from orderly sayings focused on wisdom and folly and righteousness and wickedness (10:1–15:33), to a breadth of new forms and topics (16:1–22:16),[17] to a final section marked by scarce references to Yahweh and violent, gross, and unsettling proverbs (22:17–29:27). As we will see in the commentary below, the movement to more challenging and less explicitly theological sayings creates a tension that prepares us for the unique material of Agur's oracle in 30:1–33.

---

14. See Van Leeuwen, *Context and Meaning*, 57–143.

15. Alter, *Art of Biblical Poetry*, 175–77.

16. See Jerry Allen Gladson, *Retributive Paradoxes in Proverbs 10–29* (Ann Arbor: University Microfilms International, 1980), 175.

17. Three types of sayings in particular are concentrated in chapters 16–29: "not fitting" (17:7; 19:10; 26:1); "not good" (17:26; 18:5; 19:2; 20:23; 25:27; 28:21); and "better than" (3:14; 8:11, 19; 12:9; 15:16–17; 16:8, 16, 19, 32; 17:1; 19:1, 22; 21:9, 19; 22:9; 25:7, 2; 27:5, 10; 28:6). See commentary for Prov 19 and 26.

LISTEN to the Story

¹ The proverbs of Solomon:

A wise son brings joy to his father,
    but a foolish son brings grief to his mother.
² Ill-gotten treasures have no lasting value,
    but righteousness delivers from death.
³ The LORD does not let the righteous go hungry,
    but he thwarts the craving of the wicked.
⁴ Lazy hands make for poverty,
    but diligent hands bring wealth.
⁵ He who gathers crops in summer is a prudent son,
    but he who sleeps during harvest is a disgraceful son.
⁶ Blessings crown the head of the righteous,
    but violence overwhelms the mouth of the wicked.
⁷ The name of the righteous is used in blessings,
    but the name of the wicked will rot.
⁸ The wise in heart accept commands,
    but a chattering fool comes to ruin.
⁹ Whoever walks in integrity walks securely,
    but whoever takes crooked paths will be found out.
¹⁰ Whoever winks maliciously causes grief,
    and a chattering fool comes to ruin.
¹¹ The mouth of the righteous is a fountain of life,
    but the mouth of the wicked conceals violence.
¹² Hatred stirs up conflict,
    but love covers over all wrongs.
¹³ Wisdom is found on the lips of the discerning,
    but a rod is for the back of one who has no sense.
¹⁴ The wise store up knowledge,
    but the mouth of a fool invites ruin.

¹⁵ The wealth of the rich is their fortified city,
  but poverty is the ruin of the poor.
¹⁶ The wages of the righteous is life,
  but the earnings of the wicked are sin and death.
¹⁷ Whoever heeds discipline shows the way to life,
  but whoever ignores correction leads others astray.
¹⁸ Whoever conceals hatred with lying lips
  and spreads slander is a fool.
¹⁹ Sin is not ended by multiplying words,
  but the prudent hold their tongues.
²⁰ The tongue of the righteous is choice silver,
  but the heart of the wicked is of little value.
²¹ The lips of the righteous nourish many,
  but fools die for lack of sense.
²² The blessing of the LORD brings wealth,
  without painful toil for it.
²³ A fool finds pleasure in wicked schemes,
  but a person of understanding delights in wisdom.
²⁴ What the wicked dread will overtake them;
  what the righteous desire will be granted.
²⁵ When the storm has swept by, the wicked are gone,
  but the righteous stand firm forever.
²⁶ As vinegar to the teeth and smoke to the eyes,
  so are sluggards to those who send them.
²⁷ The fear of the LORD adds length to life,
  but the years of the wicked are cut short.
²⁸ The prospect of the righteous is joy,
  but the hopes of the wicked come to nothing.
²⁹ The way of the LORD is a refuge for the blameless,
  but it is the ruin of those who do evil.
³⁰ The righteous will never be uprooted,
  but the wicked will not remain in the land.
³¹ From the mouth of the righteous comes the fruit of wisdom,
  but a perverse tongue will be silenced.
³² The lips of the righteous know what finds favor,
  but the mouth of the wicked only what is perverse.

Listening to the Text in the Story: Deuteronomy 28:2; Psalms 1; 36; 37; 73;
Proverbs 13:14; Ecclesiastes 1:11; 2:16; 7:15–18; 9:5, 15; 7:15–18

Chapters 10–15 contain a long list of antithetical sayings that contrast the wise/righteous to the foolish/wicked. The sayings vary widely in their content, ranging from the nature of work, ethics, and speech to prudence, desire, emotion, and fear. These topics parallel numerous passages of the Old Testament.

For example, the pronouncement of blessings and curses in Deuteronomy 27–28, as in this section of Proverbs, emphasizes not just God's establishment of moral order in the world but also the overall design of a world that rewards the just and punishes the wicked. As we will see below, Proverbs acknowledges the exceptions to this cosmic order, where the wicked appear to be blessed while the righteous endure suffering. Yet the exceptions are just that—occasional deviations from the order that is otherwise essential to human life.

Furthermore, we have mentioned at various points in this commentary the way Psalms 1–2 establish a contrast between the righteous and the wicked and the blessings and curses that come to each. Several other psalms put into prayer the groans a righteous follower of God experiences in the face of the wicked life and the unsettling experiences of watching the wicked escape the consequences of sin (e.g., Pss 37; 73). In Psalms 36–37 David reassures himself that God loves the righteous, even making special mention of the wicked who "fail to act wisely" (36:3).

Similarly, much, if not most, of Ecclesiastes revolves around Qohelet's (Solomon's) observations as he considers the outcomes of righteous and wicked people in the world. Echoing portions of Proverbs 10–29, Qohelet affirms his obligation to do good and avoid evil (3:17; 11:9; 12:13–14); but he also returns again and again to the nagging sense that the righteous, for all their virtuosity, don't fare any better than the wicked (7:15–18; 8:14; 9:1–3). He comes to the same conclusions about wisdom and folly (1:11; 2:16; 9:15), echoing the language of the benefits of the righteous and the wicked.

EXPLAIN the Story

Clifford succinctly captures several literary and linguistic features that give unity to this chapter: numerous sets of proverb pairs (2–3, 4–5, 6–7, 8–9, 11–12, etc.), opposition of the righteous and the wicked, and the many references to organs or other body parts as a basis of opposition.[1] We will expand this observation in the Live the Story section below.

[1] The proverbs of Solomon:
   A wise son brings joy to his father,

---

1. Clifford, *Proverbs*, 111.

but a foolish son brings grief to his mother.
  ² Ill-gotten treasures have no lasting value,
    but righteousness delivers from death.
  ³ The LORD does not let the righteous go hungry,
    but he thwarts the craving of the wicked.

10:1–3 These verses provide an introduction to the chapter, singling out educational (v. 1), ethical (v. 2), and theological (v. 3) teachings. The section begins with the superscription, "The proverbs of Solomon." Solomon was already listed as the author or collector in 1:1, so why insert his name again here? The LXX omits this reference. In a book as carefully edited as Proverbs, Solomon's repeated name should not be read as a mistake but rather as a thematic way of tying the sayings of chapters 1–9 with the authority of Israel's token king of wisdom.

Likewise, the mention of the mother and father in the second half of this verse links the wisdom in these chapters to the sayings in chapters 1–9 (see especially 4:1–9). At face value, the lesson teaches that parents are affected by their children's behavior (cf. 15:20; 17:21, 25; 19:23, 26; 23:22–26). But such an obvious point is overshadowed by the deeper fact that wisdom is traditional. Each generation stands as a link between the blessing or grief they will receive from their forbearers, and the responsibility they have toward their own children (see the commentary at 4:1–9).

Verse two reinforces the ethical order undergirding the wisdom tradition. Much like the material in chapters 10–15, verses 2–3 portray a strict relationship between acts and consequences (see also 3:15–16; 9:11; 11:4; 28:16). These two verses also parallel many others in the chapter that confirm the divine and material rewards that come from wisdom and righteousness (cf. 4, 7, 15, 16, 17, 22, 24, 25, 27, 29–30).

The Hebrew verb *hawwah*, "craving," in 10:3 is a homonym for "destruction" and is used elsewhere of the fool's fate (17:4; 19:13).[2]

  ⁴ Lazy hands make for poverty,
    but diligent hands bring wealth.
  ⁵ He who gathers crops in summer is a prudent son,
    but he who sleeps during harvest is a disgraceful son.

10:4–5 This verse pair reinforces the benefits of diligent labor and making wise use of time (cf. 6:6–11; 12:24, 27; 13:14; 15:19). In an agrarian culture harvest time is critical to a society's economic vitality, but the larger principle of timeliness naturally applies to the wisdom of starting early,

---

2. See Van Leeuwen, *Proverbs*, 107.

seizing opportunities, and avoiding procrastination (Ps 90:12; Eph 5:16). The confidence or predictability of this view is balanced by realism expressed in Proverbs 13:23 and elsewhere. Also notice the placement of the son in verses 1–5, possibly meant to depict five types of sons in the introductory verses.[3]

Chapter 10:6–14, 18–21, and 31–32 all address the patterns and consequences of wise and foolish speech.

> [6] Blessings crown the head of the righteous,
>   but violence overwhelms the mouth of the wicked.
> [7] The name of the righteous is used in blessings,
>   but the name of the wicked will rot.

10:6–7 These verses consider two types of blessing that come to the "righteous." The NIV in verse 6 takes some liberties to try and eliminate ambiguity. The NRSV stays closer to the Hebrew and resembles most modern translations, "Blessings are on the head of the righteous, but the mouth of the wicked conceals violence."

The pairs in these sayings are also disjointed: "blessings" is not the opposite of "violence," nor is "on the head" the opposite of "conceal." In a gap between the pairs one can often assume the unspoken opposite cases: "blessings *do not* fall on the heads of the wicked" and "the righteous *expose* violence." (See "Genre" in the Introduction.)

> [8] The wise in heart accept commands,
>   but a chattering fool comes to ruin.
> [9] Whoever walks in integrity walks securely,
>   but whoever takes crooked paths will be found out.

10:8–9 Waltke observes a syntactical and thematic link between these verses: "Their A versets represent the lifestyle of the wise, and the B versets the perishing of the wicked."[4] Verse 8 imagines two sides to Proverbs 1:7. The wise receive the instruction of the elders whereas the fool rejects instruction and only babbles foolishly. In Hebrew the antithesis is even clearer, setting a listening "heart" against "babbling lips" (cf. 10:10 below).

Verse 9 returns to the language of paths and ways from chapters 1–9 and the specific image of "crooked paths" in 2:15. Psalm 26 provides an extended meditation on images of walking faithfully before Yahweh (cf. Ps 1:1). Those whose "path" is "crooked" will be publicly "exposed" (Prov 26:26). The path goes beyond individual actions to imagine righteousness as a whole way of life. Such language is typically used to describe the kings of Israel and Judah

---

3. See Murphy, *Proverbs*, 72.
4. Waltke, *Proverbs 1–15*, 458.

and whether they walked in the ways of the Lord and did "what was right" or not (cf. 2 Kings 10:31; 13:2, 6, 11, 16:3; 17:8; 17:19, etc.).

¹⁰ Whoever winks maliciously causes grief,
    and a chattering fool comes to ruin.

10:10 This verse may be one of the few synonymous parallels in chapters 10–15. The NRSV, following the LXX, suspects a copyist's error and retains the antithetical meaning by eliminating line B, "but a babbling fool . . .", and replacing it with, "but one who rebukes boldly makes peace." "Wink the eye" is always linked with dishonest and evil intent (6:13; 16:30). Assuming the NIV is correct in following the original Hebrew, the comment on the "babbling fool" repeats the sentiment in verse 8 that such people are insolent and bent on violence.

¹¹ The mouth of the righteous is a fountain of life,
    but the mouth of the wicked conceals violence.
¹² Hatred stirs up conflict,
    but love covers over all wrongs.

10:11–12 These verses form another loose pair linked by the repetition of Hebrew *kasah*, translated in the NIV as "conceals" (v. 11) and "covers" (v. 12). The proverb imagines the upright "mouth," or speech, as a "spring of life." Elsewhere, "teaching," "the fear of the Lord," and "prudence" are equated with a "fountain of life" (13:14; 14:27; 16:22). Readers in modern, developed countries can easily overlook benefits associated with the life-giving power of water and the opposing power of dry wells, droughts, and desert lands—not only to weigh down the heart but to kill. In this way righteous words have the power to animate and restore life (cf. Ps 1:3; Jer 17:8; Rev 22:1).

Verse 12 contrasts the powers of hatred and love. The emotional/ethical nature of love and hatred in chapters 1–9 serve to reinforce the *eros* or role of ultimate desires in the pursuit of wisdom. (See commentary at 1:22 and the Live the Story below.)

¹³ Wisdom is found on the lips of the discerning,
    but a rod is for the back of one who has no sense.
¹⁴ The wise store up knowledge,
    but the mouth of a fool invites ruin.

10:13–14 Verses 13 and 14 present another pair of proverbs that oppose wise and foolish speech and their effects. Wisdom on the lips of fools is a frequent image (v. 31; 14:3). Furthermore, the rod and violence appear frequently as deterrents to folly and foolish speech (13:24; 22:8, 15; 23:13, 14;

29:15; cf. Deut 25:3). Verse 14 also contrasts the placidness of wisdom and knowledge to the violence and destruction that comes from foolish speech.

> [15] The wealth of the rich is their fortified city,
>   but poverty is the ruin of the poor.
> [16] The wages of the righteous is life,
>   but the earnings of the wicked are sin and death.

10:15–16 These verses appear to be linked to 13–14 by the use of "ruin" in 14 and 15 and the fact that wisdom and wealth can both be stored up or else be absent because of neglect. Verses 15–16 admonish the son to cherish wealth. Waltke comments that of the ten references to "wealth" in Solomon's sayings half take an optimistic stance, while the other half caution "not to trust it" (cf. 10:22; 11:18; 13:11; 21:6).[5] Verse 16 also contrasts wages as matters of "life" and "death" (cf. Rom. 6:23), which is reminiscent of the rhetoric in chapters 1–9 and the anticipation of the benefits of "life" in verse 17.

> [17] Whoever heeds discipline shows the way to life,
>   but whoever ignores correction leads others astray.

10:17 Verse 17 speaks reflectively on receiving "discipline" that leads to the "way of life." "Discipline" is a gift offered by Solomon, one's parents, and Woman Wisdom (1:2, 8; 8:33), while the "way of life" (path) echoes the liminal vision of crossing thresholds or rights of passage that we find throughout the book of Proverbs (see v. 9 above).

> [18] Whoever conceals hatred with lying lips
>   and spreads slander is a fool.
> [19] Sin is not ended by multiplying words,
>   but the prudent hold their tongues.
> [20] The tongue of the righteous is choice silver,
>   but the heart of the wicked is of little value.
> [21] The lips of the righteous nourish many,
>   but fools die for lack of sense.

10:18–21 These verses are the last major section of sayings on speech until the conclusion to the chapter in verses 31–32. Verse 18 returns to the image of the fool "cover[ing]" or "conceal[ing]" (vv. 11, 12). Truth brings sin to light, and "honest conflict is better than hidden love (Prov 27:5–6; Lev 19:17–18)."[6] Joseph brought this same "slander" or "bad report" to his father (Gen 37:2) only to have his brothers return with lying lips to their father (Gen 32:32).

---

5. Ibid., 463.
6. Van Leeuwen, *Proverbs*, 111.

In 10:19, restraining one's words is always a mark of prudence (cf. 17:27).

The verse pair in 10:20–21 contrasts the treasure and fruits of a "righteous" "tongue" and "lips" against the worthless "heart" of the fool and the "lack of [heart]" (cf. NIV "sense") of the fool that leads to death (cf. 16:23; 26:23–26; 3:1).

[22] The blessing of the LORD brings wealth,
without painful toil for it.

10:22 In the first line we hear an oft-repeated message that "wealth" is the result of God's blessing (cf. 3:9–10, 15–16; 10:15–16; 14:23–24). The second line is less clear. Like most translations, the NIV assumes Yahweh is the subject of "blessing," and that it is "without painful toil for it." But it is preferable instead to take "toil" as the subject and translate it as, "And toil adds nothing to it." This shows that Proverbs doesn't deny the benefit of toil (14:23) but that it prizes wisdom over wealth and assigns God as the ultimate source of prosperity (15:16–17; 16:8, 16; 17:1; 22:1; Ps 127:1–2).

[23] A fool finds pleasure in wicked schemes,
but a person of understanding delights in wisdom.
[24] What the wicked dread will overtake them;
what the righteous desire will be granted.

10:23–24 These verses compare two human affections. The fool finds pleasure in wickedness (see 9:17) while the righteous person finds pleasure in obtaining wisdom (23). Meanwhile, the fears of the wicked will eventually befall them, though as in Job's case, righteousness doesn't always protect us from this curse (Job 3:25–26). In the end, the righteous will find their desires fulfilled. Psalm 37 presents an extended prayer on the battle of desires and affections within the believer (cf. 28; Isa 66:4).

[25] When the storm has swept by, the wicked are gone,
but the righteous stand firm forever.

10:25 Verse 25 extends the notion of the fate of the righteous and the wicked from verse 24 (cf. 12:7). Jesus' parable in Matthew 7:24–27 unpacks this same lesson on the righteous/wicked but in the language of the "wise man"/"foolish man" who built their houses on two types of foundations. Van Leeuwen comments that the combination of "storm" in 25a and the ability to "stand firm" in 25b "corresponds to declarations concerning the stable foundations of creation itself (Ps 78:69; 104:5; cf. Job 38:4; Ps 24:2; Prov 3:19)."[7]

---

7. Ibid., 112.

> [26] As vinegar to the teeth and smoke to the eyes,
> so are sluggards to those who send them.

10:26 Verse 26 presents another of the very few verses in chapters 10–15 that are not in antithetical form (cf. 10). Instead the saying is a tricola with two sayings in 10:26ab, which provoke a palpable sense of the bite of vinegar on teeth and sting of smoke in the eyes, as apt comparisons for the "sluggards to those who send them" in 10:26c.

> [27] The fear of the LORD adds length to life,
> but the years of the wicked are cut short.
> [28] The prospect of the righteous is joy,
> but the hopes of the wicked come to nothing.
> [29] The way of the LORD is a refuge for the blameless,
> but it is the ruin of those who do evil.
> [30] The righteous will never be uprooted,
> but the wicked will not remain in the land.

10:27–30 These verses list several more comparisons between the righteous and the wicked. The "righteous" are not explicitly mentioned but are implied as those who fear Yahweh in verse 27. The righteous have "long life" in contrast to the years of the wicked that are "cut short" (cf. 1:7; 14:26–27; 15:16, 33: 16:6; 19:23; 22:4). Further comparisons include "joy" versus "hopes . . . that come to nothing" (v. 28; cf. 24), "refuge" versus "ruin" (v. 29), and—in inverse wording—the righteous who "will never be uprooted" and "the wicked [who] will not remain in the land" (v. 30). These last two images call to mind language from elsewhere in the Old Testament: (1) the "refuge" and the person or city who "will never be uprooted" (Pss 10:6; 11:1; 14:6; 37:1–40; 46:5; 62:3, 7; 91:1; 93:1; 125:1; cf. Prov 12:3) and (2) the covenant promise that obedience will result in long life in the "land" (Deut. 4:1; 8:1; 25:15; 28:36–37; Jer. 7:7).

> [31] From the mouth of the righteous comes the fruit of wisdom,
> but a perverse tongue will be silenced.
> [32] The lips of the righteous know what finds favor,
> but the mouth of the wicked only what is perverse.

10:31–32 The end of the chapter returns to the dominant theme of speech in this chapter with each half verse pointing to the mouth, tongue, lips, and mouth respectively. The sayings also emphasize the fruits of both righteous and wicked speech as well as their consequences (cf. 2:12, 14; 15:2; 21:23; 26:28; 31:26).

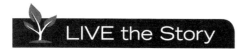
LIVE the Story

Don't Trust your Intuitions

The "Theology of the Book" in the Introduction describes the overall frame-work of character-consequence or retribution patterns in the book of Prov-erbs. The majority of sayings depict a consistent picture of retribution where the good are rewarded and the evil are punished. But a considerable number of sayings challenge this view, either by reversing these expected outcomes, or by using better-than sayings that assign limited value to morally gray areas.

Here we reflect on how this should influence the way we live. Chapters 10–15 contain the largest number of sayings that support the traditional view. In a school context where students might study these proverbs closely, the curriculum inculcates the traditional worldview through repetition. The other parts of Proverbs and especially Ecclesiastes will help us think critically about the exceptions we encounter in life. The exercise of extensive repetition serves to ground us when the exceptions seem to challenge order in the world or the existence of a sovereign God.

For example, anyone learning to drive a car learns something of the teach-ing style of Proverbs by the way to right a car that is skidding or sliding on the road. A person should always, against all intuitions, "turn against the skid" or against the "slide" of the back of the car. This lesson is even more emphasized in the world of flying where pilots memorize "bold face" instructions for flying an airplane safely through clouds and darkness. Human intuition about which way is up inevitably proves unreliable. The pilot must obey the bold face instructions and trust the instruments.

It is common to encounter ethical people in the world who experience suf-fering and others who are self-interested and power-hungry that seem to float along in life. Intuition tells us to be pragmatic and follow the path of least resistance. But the repetitive training of Proverbs tells us to trust the instru-ments and obey the memorized bold face instructions God has provided. Beyond our abilities of discernment, the moral order of this world holds fast.

Wisdom Goes Beyond the Mind

Fourteen verses, almost half of Proverbs 10, address our physical organs of perception, expression, and activity: heart, eyes, head, tongue, mouth, lips, and hand.[8] The theological study of human nature is prone to make distinc-tions between the mind, body, soul, and spirit. This inevitably leads us to

---

8. See Clifford, *Proverbs*, 111.

tolerate the body but place all intellectual and religious emphasis on the mind and spirit. Throughout this commentary we have persisted in the argument that the Bible teaches a cohesive view of humanity—whatever divisions we might make for technical beings, we are only truly human when body (or soul) and spirit are together. In fact, many scholars now argue that all learning is embodied—that the mind is a physical thing interwoven with every other part of our body.[9]

This helps us to understand why biblical wisdom, in contrast to Greek wisdom, always addresses our thoughts, desires, and actions as a whole. What we think and what we most want cannot help but flow from, and be manifested in, the actions of our eyes, lips, hands, and feet. This is illuminated in Jesus's words when he said to the Pharisees, "For the mouth speaks what the heart is full of" (Matt 12:34).

Wisdom and Love

In the Bible love is *the* supreme virtue and the root of all virtue—both the love of God and the love of his creatures. But what is love? Many mistakenly oppose love to God's law where the former is an expression of freedom and the latter one of compulsion. But it is in the *law* of Moses that God reveals the double command to love God and neighbor (Deut 6:5; Lev 19:18). Jesus actually rarely speaks of love in the Gospels, but when he does it is memorable. He combines the two Mosaic laws above as the answer to the two greatest *commandments* upon which all of the others hang (cf. Matt 22:36–40). The turning point of John's Gospel, furthermore, takes place at the Last Supper with Jesus washing the disciples' feet and giving them "a new command"—to "love one another. As I have loved you . . ." (John 13:34–35). Indeed, love keeps the commands (Rom 13:8–10). Proverbs also grounds wisdom in law and love. In language that echoes Deuteronomy 6, Proverbs commands us to "bind" "love and kindness" around our neck and imprint them on "the tablet of our heart" (3:3). As we saw in Proverbs 10:12 above, love covers sins (also 17:9). 1 Peter 4:8 appears to borrow or at least be aware of these proverbs when he says: "Above all, love each other deeply, because love covers over a multitude of sins." Love benefits the one who loves (11:17; 21:21). It is the key to a good home (15:17). Below we will see that "unfailing love" is the virtue most desired of a man or woman (19:22).

---

9. George Lakoff and Mark Johnson, *Philosophy in the Flesh: The Embodied Mind and its Challenge to Western Thought* (New York: Basic Books, 1999).

LISTEN to the Story

1 The LORD detests dishonest scales,
  but accurate weights find favor with him.
2 When pride comes, then comes disgrace,
  but with humility comes wisdom.
3 The integrity of the upright guides them,
  but the unfaithful are destroyed by their duplicity.
4 Wealth is worthless in the day of wrath,
  but righteousness delivers from death.
5 The righteousness of the blameless makes their paths straight,
  but the wicked are brought down by their own wickedness.
6 The righteousness of the upright delivers them,
  but the unfaithful are trapped by evil desires.
7 Hopes placed in mortals die with them;
  all the promise of their power comes to nothing.
8 The righteous person is rescued from trouble,
  and it falls on the wicked instead.
9 With their mouths the godless destroy their neighbors,
  but through knowledge the righteous escape.
10 When the righteous prosper, the city rejoices;
  when the wicked perish, there are shouts of joy.
11 Through the blessing of the upright a city is exalted,
  but by the mouth of the wicked it is destroyed.
12 Whoever derides their neighbor has no sense,
  but the one who has understanding holds their tongue.
13 A gossip betrays a confidence,
  but a trustworthy person keeps a secret.
14 For lack of guidance a nation falls,
  but victory is won through many advisers.
15 Whoever puts up security for a stranger will surely suffer,

but whoever refuses to shake hands in pledge is safe.

¹⁶ A kindhearted woman gains honor,
    but ruthless men gain only wealth.

¹⁷ Those who are kind benefit themselves,
    but the cruel bring ruin on themselves.

¹⁸ A wicked person earns deceptive wages,
    but the one who sows righteousness reaps a sure reward.

¹⁹ Truly the righteous attain life,
    but whoever pursues evil finds death.

²⁰ The LORD detests those whose hearts are perverse,
    but he delights in those whose ways are blameless.

²¹ Be sure of this: The wicked will not go unpunished,
    but those who are righteous will go free.

²² Like a gold ring in a pig's snout
    is a beautiful woman who shows no discretion.

²³ The desire of the righteous ends only in good,
    but the hope of the wicked only in wrath.

²⁴ One person gives freely, yet gains even more;
    another withholds unduly, but comes to poverty.

²⁵ A generous person will prosper;
    whoever refreshes others will be refreshed.

²⁶ People curse the one who hoards grain,
    but they pray God's blessing on the one who is willing to sell.

²⁷ Whoever seeks good finds favor,
    but evil comes to one who searches for it.

²⁸ Those who trust in their riches will fall,
    but the righteous will thrive like a green leaf.

²⁹ Whoever brings ruin on their family will inherit only wind,
    and the fool will be servant to the wise.

³⁰ The fruit of the righteous is a tree of life,
    and the one who is wise saves lives.

³¹ If the righteous receive their due on earth,
    how much more the ungodly and the sinner!

Listening to the Text in the Story: Exodus 8:22; Leviticus 19:15, 35;
Deuteronomy 25:15; Esther; Amos 8; Micah 6; Amenemope 16–17

As we have discussed at various points above, every saying in chapters 10–29 depicts a mini-narrative that invites us to play out a scene, imagining the setting, the motives of the actors, and the consequences of their actions. Many of these scenes have striking parallels with laws, narratives, and prophecies of the Old Testament.

So, for example, the saying that "dishonest scales are an abomination to Yahweh" (11:1, my translation) calls to mind legal provisions for scales in the marketplace (Lev 19:35–37; Deut 25:13–16) and the idolatrous actions of unjust scales that the prophets call an "abomination" (Mic 6:11; Amos 8:5, etc.). Much of the background for these scenes comes from the laws of the Old Testament. Other ancient Near Eastern literature also sheds light on these stories.

Additionally, verses 5–10 resemble lessons that arise from situations in the Esther narrative. Of special note, the reversal in 11:5 and 8, where the wicked man becomes the victim of his own schemes, has a clear parallel with Mordecai and Haman. This affirms the desire many scholars have to list Esther among the wisdom books. Countless other Old Testament narratives have this same quality of teaching wisdom or affirming popular wisdom aphorisms.

The Egyptian Instruction of Amenemope devotes two whole chapters (16–17) to this concern with just scales and weights in the marketplace. For example:

> Do not move the scales nor alter the weights,
> Nor diminish the fractions of the measure;
> Do not desire a measurer of the fields,
> Nor neglect those of the treasury.
> The Ape sits on the balance . . . [1]

As maintained throughout this commentary, the likelihood that Proverbs influenced other ancient writings, or vice versa, is simply impossible to discern with the evidence we have. It is, however, clear that many common ethical, agricultural, and social sayings worked their way into all of these writings.

EXPLAIN the Story

[1] The LORD detests dishonest scales,
   but accurate weights find favor with him.

11:1 The Hebrew term *toebah*, "abomination," is translated by the NIV as "the LORD detests," which imaginatively draws out God's emotional and active

---

1. M. Lichtheim, *AEL*, 2:156 in Tremper Longman III, *Proverbs*, *Zondervan Illustrated Bible Backgrounds Commentary*, vol. 5, ed. John H. Walton (Grand Rapids: Zondervan, 2009), 483.

response to human deception (see 3:32; 6:16). "Abomination" simultaneously depicts the abhorrent and evil practices of Israel's pagan neighbors in their immoral actions and Yahweh's response to those (Lev 18:22–30) and their idolatrous worship of false gods (Deut 7:25–26). Yahweh's visceral reaction towards dishonest dealings in the marketplace in verse 1 anticipates "those whose hearts are perverse" in 11:20.

The practice condemned involves the use of scales for transactions in which a seller shaves or chisels a weight in order to make small profits in each sale. The specific mention of "differing weights" addresses the same practice in Proverbs 20:23. This moral principle set in sales, of course, applies equally to everything from dishonest clocking of timesheet and falsifying travel claims to petty manipulation of household responsibilities among spouses and children.

> ² When pride comes, then comes disgrace,
>   but with humility comes wisdom.

11:2 This verse presents a contrast between pride and humility. The Hebrew of this verse is even more succinct than the English, which, in effect, leaves it to the reader to imagine how pride goes with dishonor and humility with wisdom. In one way the proverb is played out in the story of Naaman, King of Assyria in 2 Kings 5. Although Naaman experiences great success and favor from Yahweh, he is beset with leprosy. In the course of the story, Elisha the prophet sends a messenger to Naaman to tell him to wash in the river Jordan that he might be healed from his disease. Naaman is too proud to bathe, however, and it takes the pleading of his servants to convince him to humble himself, wash, and be healed. Wisdom and humility go hand in hand and surely Naaman was in a place of dishonor when his servants confronted his pride.

> ³ The integrity of the upright guides them,
>   but the unfaithful are destroyed by their duplicity.
> ⁴ Wealth is worthless in the day of wrath,
>   but righteousness delivers from death.
> ⁵ The righteousness of the blameless makes their paths straight,
>   but the wicked are brought down by their own wickedness.
> ⁶ The righteousness of the upright delivers them,
>   but the unfaithful are trapped by evil desires.
> ⁷ Hopes placed in mortals die with them;
>   all the promise of their power comes to nothing.
> ⁸ The righteous person is rescued from trouble,
>   and it falls on the wicked instead.

11:3–8 These verses repeat several themes and terms, such as "integrity," "upright," "die" "destroy," and "deliver." Meinhold is right to read these together.[2] The emphasis in these verses falls on the fate of the wicked or treacherous ones: they die, perish, are trapped, lack profit, are destroyed, etc. (cf. Prov 11:18, 27, 29; Ps 73:18–19). The righteous, by contrast, have "straight paths" or are "delivered." The juxtaposition of the hopes and desires of the righteous and wicked resembles 11:23 (see below).

Some scholars notice a close parallel between 11:5–6 and 8, and the lives of Mordecai and Haman in the book of Esther, which, as noted in the commentary previously, shares many parallels with the banquet imagery in chapter 9. In the story, after Mordecai makes a report to save King Xerxes from a murderous plot, the king honors him. Haman, in turn, having no equivalent valor in his favor, exalts himself and demands homage from the people. Mordecai refuses to bow, and Haman viciously and jealousy seeks to put him to death along with all of the Jews. In the end Mordecai and Esther again gain the king's favor and are rewarded with deliverance from the king they honored and protected. Haman meanwhile is trapped in his evil desires and dies the very death he planned for Mordecai the righteous (cf. Prov 1:19). Similar narratives can be found in Daniel and in the story of Lazarus and the rich man (Luke 16:25).

[9] With their mouths the godless destroy their neighbors,
    but through knowledge the righteous escape.
[10] When the righteous prosper, the city rejoices;
    when the wicked perish, there are shouts of joy.
[11] Through the blessing of the upright a city is exalted,
    but by the mouth of the wicked it is destroyed.
[12] Whoever derides their neighbor has no sense,
    but the one who has understanding holds their tongue.
[13] A gossip betrays a confidence,
    but a trustworthy person keeps a secret.

11:9–13 These verses present five types of human speech and their personal and social outcomes. Clifford notices that all of the lines except 11:12b begin with the Hebrew letter *bet* (b).[3] I include 11:13 in this group both because it sustains the pattern of types of speech but also because verses 9, 11, 12, and 13 all speak to holding one's tongue.

The comparisons in verses 9 and 11 imagine two indirect contrasts, one between the speech ("mouths") of the godless and the "knowledge" of the righteous, and the other between derisive speech and the "understanding"

---

2. Meinhold, *Sprüche*, 187.
3. Clifford, *Proverbs*, 123.

that restrains speech. In one way these proverbs commend silence, as many words are always prone to sin (cf. 10:19). Meanwhile, knowledge, or wisdom, keeps the righteous out of trouble, a lesson spelled out at length in 2:11–15.

Verses 10–11 speak to the relationship between speech and the city. Our speech has more than just relational value or consequences; it influences the shape and health of the place where we live (cf. 28:12, 28; 29:2, 16). Verse 11 closely resembles the prayer in Psalm 125:3–5.

Verses 12–13 not only reinforce the lesson in 9 about limiting one's speech, but they also depict the damage done by careless words. Similarly, James admonishes his readers, "be quick to listen, slow to speak" (Jas 1:19).

¹⁴ For lack of guidance a nation falls,
but victory is won through many advisers.

11:14 Verse 14 cautions against acting without the help of outside counsel, particularly in the spheres of war-making and statecraft (cf. 15:22; 20:18; 24:6). Of course, counsel itself is never a guarantee on its own. When Rehoboam assumed leadership of the kingdom from his father Solomon, he rejected the counsel of the wise older men in favor of the young men (1 Kgs 12:7–10). Counsel must also be discerned with wisdom.

¹⁵ Whoever puts up security for a stranger will surely suffer,
but whoever refuses to shake hands in pledge is safe.

11:15 Proverbs frequently warns against taking a pledge or security for a stranger just as it expresses concern about financial risky dealings on the whole. See commentary on 6:1–5.

¹⁶ A kindhearted woman gains honor,
but ruthless men gain only wealth.
¹⁷ Those who are kind benefit themselves,
but the cruel bring ruin on themselves.

11:16–17 These verses offer pictures of kindness in a man and a woman. The NIV's "kindhearted" (Hebrew *hen*) probably signals physical beauty here.[4] However, the overemphasis on beauty in modern culture probably makes most of us wince at the thought that Proverbs encourages or celebrates physical beauty in a woman. McKane proposes that the word *hen* here suggests a woman of "depth" rather than just outward beauty.[5] His point is confirmed by the second line, which emphasizes the importance of pursuing wholeness. Single-minded ambitions of wealth, fame, or beauty distort God's

---

4. See Van Leeuwen, *Proverbs*, 117–18.
5. McKane, *Proverbs*, 430.

image bearers. Wisdom and kindness go hand in hand elsewhere in Proverbs. Also, feminine beauty is a matter of wholeness that touches every part of a woman's identity (11:22; 31:30). The New Testament celebrates the beauty of women in their godliness and good works, because beauty is a matter of the entire person. Inward wisdom is a manifestation of true beauty (1 Pet 3:3–4; 1 Tim 2:9–10).

Verse 17 echoes verses 5–8 and complements the saying of the woman of depth; the retributive orders of our world tend to reward those who favor goodness and kindness.

> [18] A wicked person earns deceptive wages,
>   but the one who sows righteousness reaps a sure reward.
> [19] Truly the righteous attain life,
>   but whoever pursues evil finds death.

11:18–19 Following the tone in verse 17, these two sayings reinforce the moral order of creation: righteousness leads to rewards beyond immediate comfort or material possessions. But the sayings also provide a subtle recognition of retributive paradoxes: life presents circumstances that appear to contradict this order (the wicked who have wealth). At those times, these sayings admonish the reader to trust in a final or ultimate reckoning of consequences.

> [20] The LORD detests those whose hearts are perverse,
>   but he delights in those whose ways are blameless.
> [21] Be sure of this: The wicked will not go unpunished,
>   but those who are righteous will go free.

11:20–21 This verse pair seems to go together. In the first verse Yahweh's approval or disapproval is mentioned explicitly, whereas the second verse promises judgment from some sovereign source—perhaps fate or God. Some of the themes and vocabulary here echo 11:1 and 3–8—notably Yahweh's "hatred" of evil [literally, ". . . an abomination to Yahweh"] and the assurance that the "blameless" will be delivered from judgment.

> [22] Like a gold ring in a pig's snout
>   is a beautiful woman who shows no discretion.

11:22 As noted above, this verse balances the praise of physical beauty in verse 16 in its insistence that physical beauty is scarred by folly. Scholars debate many possible meanings of this unique image, but the basic point is that gold is not fitting for a pig and so neither is folly for a beautiful woman. The saying echoes modern proverbs such as "A pig in the parlor is still a pig" and "A pig used to dirt turns up its nose at rice boiled in milk." Pigs have generally carried this negative association in folklore, whatever contrary evidence we may have about pigs and cleanliness today. The saying concerning "apples of gold in settings of silver" presents a contrasting use of this kind of visual imagery (Prov 25:11).

> [23] The desire of the righteous ends only in good,
> but the hope of the wicked only in wrath.

11:23 Like verse 7, this proverb adds a degree of complexity to those sayings that speak to the fates of the righteous and the wicked. Our conduct in life cannot be detached from the things we most desire. The final line is succinct in Hebrew and could be translated, "the hope of the wicked is wrath." See verse 27 below.

> [24] One person gives freely, yet gains even more;
> another withholds unduly, but comes to poverty.
> [25] A generous person will prosper;
> whoever refreshes others will be refreshed.
> [26] People curse the one who hoards grain,
> but they pray God's blessing on the one who is willing to sell.

11:24–26 All three of these sayings contrast generosity and greed. Indeed, while many proverbs merely commend "righteousness" and "wisdom" in the abstract, many others provide specific examples of these ideals. Sitting in the middle of these sayings, verse 25 presents one of the few proverbs in chapters 10–15 that are not antithetical. The surprising exception was likely intended to emphasize how cheered and helped we are by generosity.

The NIV generously expands on the Hebrew of 11:26. In the first line, the NIV "hoard" is stronger than the Hebrew "withhold." In the second line the Hebrew states only that "a blessing" is on the one who sells, but the NIV emends line B to "they [the people] pray God's blessing" to make the line sit in a stricter parallel with line A. This is certainly possible, but, as discussed in the Introduction, many proverbs present incomplete parallels—a technique that typically adds richness to the sayings. Suffice it to say that there is ambiguity in the original text.

> [27] Whoever seeks good finds favor,
> but evil comes to one who searches for it.

11:27 Waltke observes that 11:23 and 27 are alike in their use of "good" and their "generalizations about the topic of desires and their fulfillment."[6]

---

6. Waltke, *Proverbs 1–15*, 505.

This passage is a reminder that desire lies at the root of wisdom in Proverbs. That is, wisdom is gained less by a study of ethical rules and skills than by developing the virtue of controlling and directing our deepest passions. Favor and blessing, in turn, come not to those who desire them but to those who desire righteousness and truth.

> [28] Those who trust in their riches will fall,
>   but the righteous will thrive like a green leaf.
> [29] Whoever brings ruin on their family will inherit only wind,
>   and the fool will be servant to the wise.
> [30] The fruit of the righteous is a tree of life,
>   and the one who is wise saves lives.
> [31] If the righteous receive their due on earth,
>   how much more the ungodly and the sinner!

11:28–31 These verses continue working in the pattern of the "two ways" in life and the two ends or consequences that will come to us. Verse 28 uses the horticultural imagery of a flourishing leaf as a contrast to those who trust in riches and fall (cf. v 30). The Hebrew word *prh*, "thrive" or "flourish," occurs only one other time in Proverbs, speaking of the "tent of the upright" (14:11). The term is used elsewhere to describe the flourishing of the righteous, of Israel, and even of the wicked (Pss 72:7; 92:8, 13–14; Isa 27:6; 66:14).

Verse 29 reinforces the social and communal nature of wisdom that emerges throughout this chapter (vv. 9–14, 25). Those who bring "ruin on their family will inherit only wind" (cf. Job 15:2; Eccl. 1:14; Isa. 26:18). In 1 Samuel 25, Nabal, whose name literally means "fool," impetuously invites ruin on his family, threatening the large inheritance of his household. But Nabal is saved and outclassed by the wisdom of his wife Abigail, who negotiates peace with King David, whom Nabal so thoughtlessly offended. This verse also reinforces the stories in the central section of Numbers 11–21, where those who rebel and complain not only trouble their families but the well-being of Israel as well. As Numbers and the psalmist remember these events, rebellious Israel is said to "fall in the wilderness" (Num 14:29, 32; Ps 106:26–7).

The horticultural imagery of 11:28 returns in verse 30 with "the fruit of the righteous is a tree of life." The same phrase occurs in 3:18 and 15:4 (see commentary). The second line literally reads, "But the wise take lives." To take a life ordinarily means to kill someone (Prov 1:19; Ps 31:13; Ezek. 33:6; Jon. 4:3).[7] Some scholars and translations (cf. NRSV) thus choose to

---

7. See Fox, *Proverbs 10–31*, 545.

emend the Hebrew word "wise," *hakam*, to "violence," *hamas*: "violence takes away lives." But other ancient manuscripts support the Hebrew text, and "take lives" does mean to save life in Genesis 12:5. It appears that the phrase expresses a point with irony—just as wickedness and violence take lives in killing, so the wise can take lives by saving them from this fate.

Verse 31 brings the chapter to a close, restating the major theme of future retribution. Christians can find in this verse the eschatological hope that God will vindicate the righteous and judge the wicked; however, it is far from clear that Israel had a sense of the resurrected life at this stage in her history.

LIVE the Story

City, Community, Poverty

In Proverbs 11:12 we read, "Whoever derides their neighbor has no sense." Verse 9 voices a similar concern for the neighbor, that is, one who is near and known to us. The point of these sayings is not to elevate our obligation to our friends over people we do not know. Indeed, similar sayings in 14:21, 31 and 17:5 speak more broadly to "the poor," which includes a class of people that we may not know personally (see commentary on these passages). The root issue here is respect for fellow image bearers. As Van Leeuwen observes, to "damage the bond of common humanity [is] to sever ourselves from our own flesh."[8]

Beyond its concern with our neighbor, chapter 11 has an even more focused interest in the health of the city and society. Commenting on Proverbs 11:10–11, Van Leeuwen describes the chapter's emphasis on "public arenas of commerce (11:1, 15, 24–26) and the sociopolitical commonweal (11:9–14, 24–26)."[9] Contrary to much of the way modern culture almost religiously idealizes individual rights, these proverbs demand that we reckon with the inevitable social consequences of individual conduct. No person is an island.

In an interesting connection, Stephen Toulmin's book *Cosmopolis* traces the history of the way human cultures have sought to relate the order of nature, "cosmos," to the order of society, "polis."[10] Just as the creation mandate in Genesis 1:26–27 has been used as a justification for humans to use and abuse the environment in whatever way that pleases us, Toulmin argues, the idea of cosmopolis led to its own abuses. The initial respect for balance and

---

8. Van Leeuwen, *Proverbs*, 121.
9. Ibid.
10. Stephen Toulmin, *Cosmopolis: The Hidden Agenda of Modernity* (Chicago: University of Chicago Press, 1990), 67–69, 192–96.

order in society was lost to political theories that justified persecution and domination of fellow humans. Social "order" became shorthand for political idealism in which those in power used class structures to maintain economic stability internally and to justify violence against competing nation states externally. Proverbs condemns these distortions of society at the same time that it looks forward to Yahweh's right ordering of the world

Wendell Berry makes a related point in his discussion on the evolution of education and scientific professions that are increasingly specialized into smaller and smaller theoretical areas of research.[11] Such a world closes itself off to the interrelatedness of things in our natural and social world orders. We must, Berry argues, assume the difficult and dangerous risk of redirecting academic and professional specialization in directions that benefit local environments and local communities. This includes our neighbor and the stranger as well as animals and the land (see 12:10–11).

As the stone that the builders rejected, Jesus is the cornerstone of a new construction project that will right the misuse and abuse of power. Just as Proverbs 11:24–25 commends generosity and promises future prosperity as a reward, Jesus similarly calls on a wealthy man to give his possessions to the poor and set his heart on an eternal reward in heaven (Mark 10:17–22). We might also compare Proverbs 11 to the parable of the master of a house and the tenants of his vineyard in Matthew 21:33–46. The lesson of the parable is not merely recognizing Jesus as "the stone the builders rejected" (21:42) but seeing Jesus as the cornerstone of a new construction project in which we manage the vineyard of human life as a "people who will produce its fruits" (21:43, cf. vv. 34, 38, 41, 43).

The Righteous and the Wicked

As Leo Perdue has observed, Proverbs 11 continues the opposition between the righteous and the wicked in chapters 10–12. Its particular contribution is an "emphasis on divine retribution and the importance of language." It is worth quoting his depiction of moral order at length:

> Righteousness, a character trait that involves orderly and moral behavior, secures the lives of the wise-righteous, provides guidance in ways that are straight, delivers them from death, exalts a city, enables one to keep a confidence, provides safety to a nation, obtains honor for those who embody it, allows the generous to be enriched by their own generosity, enables one to escape punishment, seeks favor, and appears as a tree of life.

---

11. Wendell Berry, "Going to Work" in *Citizenship Papers* (Washington, DC: Shoemaker and Hoard, 2003), 38–41.

The wickedness of the foolish-wicked leads to their destruction, results in disgrace, causes the wicked to be captured by their own schemes, dashes the hope of the wicked, leads to trouble for those who practice it, is used to destroy the neighbor with improper speech, overthrows a city, results in shame, brings harm to the cruel, punishes wicked fools and causes them to suffer want, makes them wither, and takes away lives.[12]

Hebrew wisdom rarely lingers in speculative thoughts about the ethics or ideas of justice, civility, harmony, and order. Instead it paints these ideas into metaphors and the familiar scenes of daily life, constantly contrasting righteousness and wickedness, order and disorder, wisdom and folly, and life and death.

---

12. Perdue, *Proverbs*, 167–68.

¹ Whoever loves discipline loves knowledge,
  but whoever hates correction is stupid.
² Good people obtain favor from the LORD,
  but he condemns those who devise wicked schemes.
³ No one can be established through wickedness,
  but the righteous cannot be uprooted.
⁴ A wife of noble character is her husband's crown,
  but a disgraceful wife is like decay in his bones.
⁵ The plans of the righteous are just,
  but the advice of the wicked is deceitful.
⁶ The words of the wicked lie in wait for blood,
  but the speech of the upright rescues them.
⁷ The wicked are overthrown and are no more,
  but the house of the righteous stands firm.
⁸ A person is praised according to their prudence,
  and one with a warped mind is despised.
⁹ Better to be a nobody and yet have a servant
  than pretend to be somebody and have no food.
¹⁰ The righteous care for the needs of their animals,
  but the kindest acts of the wicked are cruel.
¹¹ Those who work their land will have abundant food,
  but those who chase fantasies have no sense.
¹² The wicked desire the stronghold of evildoers,
  but the root of the righteous endures.
¹³ Evildoers are trapped by their sinful talk,
  and so the innocent escape trouble.
¹⁴ From the fruit of their lips people are filled with good things,
  and the work of their hands brings them reward.
¹⁵ The way of fools seems right to them,

but the wise listen to advice.
¹⁶ Fools show their annoyance at once,
     but the prudent overlook an insult.
¹⁷ An honest witness tells the truth,
     but a false witness tells lies.
¹⁸ The words of the reckless pierce like swords,
     but the tongue of the wise brings healing.
¹⁹ Truthful lips endure forever,
     but a lying tongue lasts only a moment.
²⁰ Deceit is in the hearts of those who plot evil,
     but those who promote peace have joy.
²¹ No harm overtakes the righteous,
     but the wicked have their fill of trouble.
²² The LORD detests lying lips,
     but he delights in people who are trustworthy.
²³ The prudent keep their knowledge to themselves,
     but a fool's heart blurts out folly.
²⁴ Diligent hands will rule,
     but laziness ends in forced labor.
²⁵ Anxiety weighs down the heart,
     but a kind word cheers it up.
²⁶ The righteous choose their friends carefully,
     but the way of the wicked leads them astray.
²⁷ The lazy do not roast any game,
     but the diligent feed on the riches of the hunt.
²⁸ In the way of righteousness there is life;
     along that path is immortality.

Listening to the Story in the Text: Deuteronomy 22:1–4, 6, 7, 10; 25:4; Psalms 1:1–6; 31:19

The major themes that dominate this chapter include good and bad counsel, honesty, wise and foolish speech, the value of public reputation, hard work and laziness, and the rewards given to the righteous and the wicked. Like the tree "planted by streams of water" in Psalm 1, this chapter imagines the righteous with a firm foundation and sure future (cf. 12:3, 7, 12).

The celebration of the woman of "noble character" in verse 4 stands conspicuously apart among the other sayings in this chapter. The use of the phrase "noble character" is rare for women and it echoes the poem to the woman of "noble character" (31:10–31) and Ruth and Boaz (Ruth 2:1; 3:11). The verse also recalls the dominant role of feminine imagery in Proverbs 1–9, particularly the way women in these chapters represent both sexual desire and the desire that leads us down the paths of wisdom or folly. Desires are also a major theme in chapter 13.

Proverbs addresses the well-being of animals only twice (12:10; 27:23–27). The Sabbath laws in Exodus 20 and Deuteronomy 5 require Israelites to rest their animals, and Deuteronomy also stipulates specific laws that proscribe attending to the needs of animals used for labor or those separated from their owners.

EXPLAIN the Story

The sayings in this chapter cover an impressive array of issues, but there are still some patterns that unite the material. As Meinhold notices, verses 1–12 are arranged in a way that alternates between sayings of the "wicked" and the "righteous." Within this grouping Meinhold also sees general patterns that separate the sayings into three groups: 1–3, 5–7, and 10–12.[1]

> [1] Whoever loves discipline loves knowledge,
>   but whoever hates correction is stupid.
> [2] Good people obtain favor from the LORD,
>   but he condemns those who devise wicked schemes.
> [3] No one can be established through wickedness,
>   but the righteous cannot be uprooted.

Proverbs 1–9 revolves around the role of desire in coming to wisdom: we love in order to know. Indeed, the path of wisdom is grounded in love, wisdom, righteousness, and the hatred of their opposites (cf. 1:22; 3:12; 8:21, 36; 9:8).

12:1–3 In 12:1 desire is expressly counterintuitive; one does not naturally desire discipline and chastening. However, there is a sense in which we should. Consider the modern university with its increasingly exquisite student centers, luxurious dormitories, lazy rivers rivaling theme parks, and exclusive health club facilities. It increasingly caters to learning in ease and comfort. Compare this vision to the ancient tradition of monasteries with their pursuit of simplicity and self-denial and which comes closer to the biblical vision of learning.

---

1. Meinhold, *Sprüche*, 203.

Concern with the "good" is a theme that appears over sixty times in Proverbs and four times in this chapter (vv. 2, 9, 14, 25). Following the general tone of chapters 10–15, 12:2 reinforces the character-consequence pattern in which the good people merit favor and wicked doers merit judgment.

Verse 3 echoes verses 7 and 12 by contrasting the firm rootedness of the righteous to the vulnerability and ephemerality of the wicked. Psalm 1 similarly contrasts rooted trees "by streams of water" with the wicked who are "like chaff that the wind blows away" (1:3–4). Psalms and Proverbs continually return to this botanical image of roots that symbolize health and safety (cf. Pss 46:5, 11; 55:22; 93:1; 96:10; 112:6; Prov 10:7; 12:7, 12).

> ⁴ A wife of noble character is her husband's crown,
>   but a disgraceful wife is like decay in his bones.

12:4 This verse stands out in a chapter almost exclusively concerned with matters of righteousness and wickedness. Sayings involving women occur in many places in chapters 10–29, but this saying is distinct in the way it calls to mind the feminine and nuptial imagery in chapters 1–9 and 31. This lesson of the power of human affections stands as a well-timed reminder that wisdom *follows* the orientation of the heart.

> ⁵ The plans of the righteous are just,
>   but the advice of the wicked is deceitful.
> ⁶ The words of the wicked lie in wait for blood,
>   but the speech of the upright rescues them.
> ⁷ The wicked are overthrown and are no more,
>   but the house of the righteous stands firm.

12:5–7 As noted at the start of this chapter, the language and images of Psalm 1 echo throughout Proverbs 12, verses 5–7 in particular. The "thoughts" (NIV "plans") of the righteous are contrasted to the "advice of the wicked," (v. 5), which stands parallel to the counsel of the wicked and delight of the righteous in Psalm 1:1–2. The "speech of the upright" resembles the one who "meditates," literally "mumbles," God's torah "day and night" (Ps 1:2; Prov 12:6; cf. 12:23; 13:16; 17:27–28). Both passages also compare the transitory and fleeting future of the wicked to the rootedness and blessing of the righteous (12:7; Ps 1:4–6). Whatever the relationship between these passages, the common message is that the righteous direct their thoughts, speech, and relationships in the community to enduring, rather than temporal ends.

These verses also provide an apt summary of the major themes in the story of Joseph and his brothers in Genesis. In the spirit of the plans of the wicked in 12:5, Joseph's brothers explicitly "plotted" against Joseph in murderous terms of his "blood" (Gen 37:18, 26, 31). Reuben clearly offers upright words to deliver his brother from death (37:26). The Joseph story as a whole revolves around the fate of the house of Jacob: whether it will act wisely or foolishly.

> [8] A person is praised according to their prudence,
>   and one with a warped mind is despised.
> [9] Better to be a nobody and yet have a servant
>   than pretend to be somebody and have no food.
> [10] The righteous care for the needs of their animals,
>   but the kindest acts of the wicked are cruel.
> [11] Those who work their land will have abundant food,
>   but those who chase fantasies have no sense.

12:8–11 These verses are linked together by several themes. Verses 8–9 address the relative pros and cons of public opinion. Wisdom typically results in a good public reputation, though Ecclesiastes 8:10 and 9:14–15 describe familiar situations where this does not prove to be true. Beyond the fickle nature of public opinion, what is most important is a person's true character (v. 9).

Verses 9–11 concern wisdom of agricultural and domestic life in the ancient world and contain the only two uses of the Hebrew root *'bd* in this chapter, translated "servant" and "work." Verse 9 is also one of only three better-than sayings in chapters 10–15; the vast majority of which occur in chapters 16–29 (cf. 3:14; 8:11, 19; 12:9; 15:16–17; 16:8, 16, 19, 32; 17:1; 19:1, 22; 21:9, 19; 22:9; 25:7, 2; 27:5, 10; 28:6; see commentary at 19:1). Proverbs 12:10 is a rare situation where the book addresses the human treatment of animals. (See Live the Story below.)

> [12] The wicked desire the stronghold of evildoers,
>   but the root of the righteous endures.

12:12 Verse 12 bridges the material before and after: the "stronghold" fits with the motif of land and property in verses 9–11, the "root of the righteous" follows 12:3, and the focus on evildoers leads into the section addressing evil speech in 12:13–18. The emphasis on "desire" here (cf. 1:22; 6:25; 21:20) reinforces the determining role of our passions and affections in our pursuit of wisdom. Whereas popular Christianity often speaks sentimentally about the human heart, this saying reinforces the mysterious ways our physical bodies are attached to the physical reality of the world we live in.

> [13] Evildoers are trapped by their sinful talk,
>   and so the innocent escape trouble.

¹⁴ From the fruit of their lips people are filled with good things,
  and the work of their hands brings them reward.
¹⁵ The way of fools seems right to them,
  but the wise listen to advice.
¹⁶ Fools show their annoyance at once,
  but the prudent overlook an insult.
¹⁷ An honest witness tells the truth,
  but a false witness tells lies.
¹⁸ The words of the reckless pierce like swords,
  but the tongue of the wise brings healing.
¹⁹ Truthful lips endure forever,
  but a lying tongue lasts only a moment.
²⁰ Deceit is in the hearts of those who plot evil,
  but those who promote peace have joy.

12:13–20 Verses 13–14 and 15–20 surround the inner saying in verses 15–16 about the fool. The outer verses imagine the power and consequences of human speech: our words can trap us, bear fruit, bring rewards, be valued and rewarded for their honesty, and can either bring violence or healing. The warnings about the power of the human tongue in James 3:1–12 all appear here as well.

The inner verses imaginatively depict the behavior of fools. While speech is not explicit, each of these sayings pictures a situation where speech is happening. On the one hand, fools selfishly rely on their own opinion and perspective and refuse to listen to counsel (that is, spoken to them, v. 15; cf. Prov 3:5; 26:12). On the other hand, fools exhibit impatience and immaturity in the face of difficulty and embarrassment—most likely from what they say (see commentary on 12:23 below).

²¹ No harm overtakes the righteous,
  but the wicked have their fill of trouble.

12:21 This verse departs from the themes of speech in verses 13–23 both implicitly and explicitly. It does maintain the consistent emphasis of contrasting the fates of the righteous and the wicked (cf. 3, 7, 12, 28). The imagery in these cases bears drawing out. We are meant to picture "harm" as a pursuer that poses no threat to the righteous, who seemingly stands rooted and firm. Meanwhile, the wicked are pictured as idle, even weighed down by "trouble."

²² The Lord detests lying lips,
  but he delights in people who are trustworthy.

²³ The prudent keep their knowledge to themselves,
  but a fool's heart blurts out folly.

12:22–23 The NIV's "detests" in 12:22 is again translating the Hebrew *toebah* "abomination." The translation may simplify the reading level, but it also risks eclipsing the fact that this word appears only in Deuteronomy and Proverbs (see the commentary below for 3:32, 6:16; and 8:7). The use of *toebah* in Proverbs stands as a constant reminder that the way of wisdom is parallel to, and often identical with, the law. Honesty is an obvious example of a common virtue.

Verse 23, according to Heim, is a partial repetition of 12:16, only with the order of the lines reversed and a play on similar senses of the Hebrew *kasha*, "cover" or "conceal."[2] One "covers" or "overlooks" an insult in verse 16. The wise here covers knowledge in the sense of knowing when not to reveal too much. Similarly, the way fools "show their annoyance at once" (v. 16) resembles the babbling heart of the fool in verse 23. By creatively repeating these phrases in verses 16 and 23, the author adds structure to the sayings.

²⁴ Diligent hands will rule,
  but laziness ends in forced labor.
²⁵ Anxiety weighs down the heart,
  but a kind word cheers it up.
²⁶ The righteous choose their friends carefully,
  but the way of the wicked leads them astray.
²⁷ The lazy do not roast any game,
  but the diligent feed on the riches of the hunt.
²⁸ In the way of righteousness there is life;
  along that path is immortality.

12:24–28 One could divide this section into smaller divisions, but that would overlook the united role of the themes of diligence, laziness, righteousness, and folly. 12:25 does not appear to fit this pattern, but its emphasis on speech—the power of a kind word to heal anxiety—fits with the emphasis on speech throughout the rest of the chapter and the reminder that wisdom leads to joy (cf. v. 20).

Verse 25 is the only time "forced labor" appears in Proverbs. We find it most often in the context of the Pentateuch, Joshua, and 1 Kings, where it speaks to the labor Israel placed on peoples of Canaanite nations rather than dispossessing the people entirely as God had commanded Israel to do. It is

---

2. Heim, *Poetic Imagination*, 315–19.

impossible to know if the author of this proverb had this in mind, but the historical lesson fits. If Israel had "diligent hands" in following God's statutes, they would have ruled their land more decisively. Whereas 12:25 sounds as though it is addressed to ruling classes, verse 27 teaches a similar lesson about diligence and laziness by using images of the working class—the hunter. The rewards of diligence are particular to each sphere and age of life and can be discerned by wisdom.

The lesson in 12:27 sits between the brackets of verses 26–28, which revisit the common themes of the way, the path, righteousness, and wickedness. As is common in Proverbs, the wise and righteous have good friendships while the foolish and wicked are either friendless or attract friends who provide bad counsel (vv. 5–6).

LIVE the Story

Animal Rights?

Beneath a single proverb lives a story or sometimes a whole world of complex and interconnected ideas. Proverbs 12:10 is just such a proverb: "The righteous care for the needs of their animals."

While only two proverbs speak to the needs of animals (cf. 27:23), many other biblical passages address human care of non-human creatures (cf. Exod 23:4–5; Lev 25:7; Deut 22:1–4, 6–7; 25:4). Deuteronomy 25:4 says, "Do not muzzle the ox while it is treading out the grain." Like the proverb, this seems to favor animal rights. Drawing on the Old Testament worldview, we can come to a few important conclusions about how we should assign value to non-human life.

First, non-human creatures have more theological significance in the story of God's redemption than we tend to allow for them. What we casually refer to as the covenant with Noah is actually a covenant "with every living creature that was with you—the birds, the livestock and all the wild animals, all those that came out of the ark with you—every living creature on earth" (Gen 9:10). God is saving a whole physical world, not just people or disembodied souls. Notice a striking parallel in Mark 1:13 where Jesus goes into the wilderness to be tempted by Satan. Like Noah, Jesus was "with the wild animals," fulfilling the image of peaceful relationships in Isaiah 11:1–9. Furthermore, the wilderness in Mark and floodwaters in Genesis are also inhospitable places of chaos, which become sources of new creation, paralleling the first creation out of chaos (Gen 1:1–2).[3]

---

3. See Richard Bauckham: *The Bible and Ecology: Rediscovering the Community of Creation* (Waco, TX: Baylor University Press, 2010), 126–29.

Moreover, non-human life has a vocation or calling to "be fruitful and increase in number," (Gen 1:22), no different that our own human calling (Gen 1:26–30). Terrence Fretheim describes a "mutuality of vocation" between humans and non-human creation.[4] For example, in God's response to Job in Job 38–41, God appeals to his protection and provision of the wild animals, seas, and forests in order to assure Job of his divine power and compassion. God is pictured as a father and mother, tending to the whole world of creation, sun, stars, oceans, and wild animals, all which exist outside the realm of human control.

It could be objected that our freedom to name and kill the animals is an indication of absolute power over them. Leon Kass observes, "[the] argument for the moral equality of man and animals refutes itself: Only such a *uniquely* dignified being can appreciate the splendor of other species and can respond to their needs with moral self-restraint."[5] Animals, moreover, ruin our land, eat their young, and even devour us without a moral bat of the eye.

But Kass also sees that our gifts of self-consciousness, language, and imagination serve primarily to make us uniquely *responsible* for the flourishing of the non-human world—animals, trees, and lands—all the while recognizing our mutual dependency as creatures of God. Wild animals were free to prey on other animals, but humans were limited to eating herbivores (Deut 14:1–21; Lev 11:1–46). Furthermore, the prohibition to not eat the "lifeblood" of the animal is a reminder of the sacredness of the life of all creatures (cf. Gen 9:4; Lev 17:14; Deut 12:23).

To "care for" the needs of our animals (Prov 12:10) should lead us to question some of our industrial farming, particularly as industrial and medical innovations used to maximize the market value of an animal corresponds to the deprivation of the quality of life and dignity of these same animals.[6] Wisdom is the resource we desperately need to find our footing as we take responsibility for the ecology of the earth. And it should be remembered that Paul applies the law concerning the ox in 1 Corinthians 9:9–10 to the mercy and compassion that should be shown to those who labor for the church.

Public Opinion and Shame

It has been argued that ancient Israel operated more within the honor-shame ethos of Eastern cultures than the guilt-fear ethos of Western nations like our

---

4. Terrence Fretheim, *God and World in the Old Testament: A Relational Theology of Creation* (Nashville: Abingdon, 2005), 269–84. See also Bauckham, *The Bible and Ecology*.

5. Leon Kass, *The Hungry Soul: Eating and the Perfecting of Our Nature* (Chicago: University of Chicago Press, 1994), 118 (emphasis original).

6. See Baukham, *The Bible and Ecology*, 139.

own.[7] That is, Israel's society controlled or moderated behavior by the use of shame and fear of being ostracized from one's family and peers. A guilt-based society, meanwhile, is governed more by penalties and fear of retribution. A person can be guilty of wrongdoing without feeling a sense of shame or dishonor. They can also be shamed without doing anything wrong.

In Proverbs, both of these cultural manifestations are at work: the hope of reward and the fear of punishment (1:19, 33; 2:20–22; 5:7–14; 21, etc.) and the power of cultural shame and dishonor (3:4; 10:5; 12:8; 27:21; 31:23, etc.). As 12:8 makes clear, appearances can be misleading and what really counts is the character beneath the surface.

The growth of social media in the last century should lead us to reflect more critically on the cultural power of shame. Indeed, the internet creates a self-perpetuating platform that encourages us to present images and ideas to be liked, retweeted, commented upon, and reposted. We can build up the social capital of many friends and the ability to post. Dave Egger's novel *The Circle* is an important social commentary on this behavior, providing an enlightening perspective on the damage social media can do to relationships and society as a whole.

In the Sermon on the Mount Jesus warned us, "Woe to you when everyone speaks well of you, for that is how their ancestors treated the false prophets" (Luke 6:26). Similarly, Paul's first letter to the Corinthians points to Jesus' death on the cross as a critique of the honor-shame dynamics in ancient societies. Public opinion remains important, of course (Acts 6:3; 1 Tim 5:10), but only insofar as the reputation speaks truthfully about the human character beneath.

The Healing Power of Words
"The tongue has the power of life and death, and those who love it will eat its fruit" (Prov 18:21). Speech is a dominant theme in Proverbs; it can bring down a city or build it up, ruin friendships or strengthen them, mock or bless, and deceive or be truthful.

Human language also has an immense power to heal, replenish, and counter the effects of a broken world (10:11; 12:25; 13:14; 15:4, 26, 30; 16:24; 25:25). In 12:18 healing words are presented in contrast to rash words that "pierce like swords." Proverbs 12:25 returns to this image, signaling the power of speech to counteract anxiety. As Waltke says, "Whereas anxiety knocks a person out of commission, the personal and kind, pleasant and sweet, timely and thoughtful word restores him with encouragement and hope."[8]

---

7. See Van Leeuwen, *Proverbs*, 125.
8. Waltke, *Proverbs 1–15*, 541.

Kathleen Norris also speaks of "the power of words to continually astonish and invigorate us and even to surpass human understanding."[9] Norris' words resemble parts of James 3:6–17:

> The tongue also is a fire, a world of evil among the parts of the body . . . With the tongue we praise our Lord and Father, and with it we curse human beings, who have been made in God's likeness. Out of the same mouth come praise and cursing. My brothers and sisters, this should not be . . . But the wisdom that comes from heaven is first of all pure; then peace-loving, considerate, submissive, full of mercy and good fruit, impartial and sincere.

Like Proverbs, the wisdom in James reflects on the destructive power of the tongue. Like wisdom from God in Proverbs, the wisdom in James that comes from God equips us to speak words that bring love, bear fruit, and protect the truth. Wise speech results from education and practice. It is the life-long labor of studying the power of language, corralling our desires, and practicing the virtues of that wise speech.

9. Kathleen Norris, *Dakota: A Spiritual Geography* (Boston; New York: Houghton Mifflin Company, 1993), 172.

CHAPTER 18

Proverbs 13:1–25

 LISTEN to the Story

¹ A wise son heeds his father's instruction,
    but a mocker does not respond to rebukes.
² From the fruit of their lips people enjoy good things,
    but the unfaithful have an appetite for violence.
³ Those who guard their lips preserve their lives,
    but those who speak rashly will come to ruin.
⁴ A sluggard's appetite is never filled,
    but the desires of the diligent are fully satisfied.
⁵ The righteous hate what is false,
    but the wicked make themselves a stench
    and bring shame on themselves.
⁶ Righteousness guards the person of integrity,
    but wickedness overthrows the sinner.
⁷ One person pretends to be rich, yet has nothing;
    another pretends to be poor, yet has great wealth.
⁸ A person's riches may ransom their life,
    but the poor cannot respond to threatening rebukes.
⁹ The light of the righteous shines brightly,
    but the lamp of the wicked is snuffed out.
¹⁰ Where there is strife, there is pride,
    but wisdom is found in those who take advice.
¹¹ Dishonest money dwindles away,
    but whoever gathers money little by little makes it grow.
¹² Hope deferred makes the heart sick,
    but a longing fulfilled is a tree of life.
¹³ Whoever scorns instruction will pay for it,
    but whoever respects a command is rewarded.
¹⁴ The teaching of the wise is a fountain of life,
    turning a person from the snares of death.

¹⁵ Good judgment wins favor,
    but the way of the unfaithful leads to their destruction.
¹⁶ All who are prudent act with knowledge,
    but fools expose their folly.
¹⁷ A wicked messenger falls into trouble,
    but a trustworthy envoy brings healing.
¹⁸ Whoever disregards discipline comes to poverty and shame,
    but whoever heeds correction is honored.
¹⁹ A longing fulfilled is sweet to the soul,
    but fools detest turning from evil.
²⁰ Walk with the wise and become wise,
    for a companion of fools suffers harm.
²¹ Trouble pursues the sinner,
    but the righteous are rewarded with good things.
²² A good person leaves an inheritance for their children's children,
    but a sinner's wealth is stored up for the righteous.
²³ An unplowed field produces food for the poor,
    but injustice sweeps it away.
²⁴ Whoever spares the rod hates their children,
    but the one who loves their children is careful to discipline them.
²⁵ The righteous eat to their hearts' content,
    but the stomach of the wicked goes hungry.

Listening to the Text in the Story: Deuteronomy 21:18–21; 25:1–3; Hosea 12:8

The natural background for the proverbs about discipline is among the laws and practices of the Jewish household. Deuteronomy in particular provides for quick and severe punishment of children and social misfits (21:18–21; 25:1–3). Such practices are part of every culture and should not surprise us. See more in "Corporal Discipline" in Live the Story below.

An old proverb says, "Money is a bottomless sea in which honor, conscience, and truth may be drowned." Old Testament prophets also often appeal to false assurances of wealth (Hos 12:8; Zech 11:5; cf. Prov 13:7).

EXPLAIN the Story

The sayings in this chapter move repetitively through several groups of topics set in slightly new contexts.

The chapter divides into four sections:

13:1–6 or 7	Desire, speech, and wealth
13:7 or 8–11	Wealth and speech
13:12–19	Wisdom and counsel
13:20–25	Counsel, ultimate ends, desire

Heim and Waltke are among scholars who highlight the themes and catchwords that overflow from chapter 12 and into chapters 14–16: specifically "wisdom" (vv. 1, 10, 14, 20), "desire," or "life," *nephesh* (vv. 2, 3, 4, 8, 9, 19, 25), "longing," *awah* (vv. 4, 12, 19), and "counsel," "instruction," and "advice" (vv. 1, 10, 13, 14, 15, 17, 18, 20, 24). The chapter pivots around good and bad counsel and the power of human desire or appetite. We have discussed desire in the Introduction and the commentary on Proverbs 6 and 11 above (cf. Prov 19:2), just as we have also considered the important nature of authority or tradition in Proverbs—all human knowledge comes through properly vetted sources. The pressing questions in this chapter are, therefore, "To whom will you listen?" and "What will you choose to satisfy the deep longing of your heart?" These questions are taken up in the final section.

¹ A wise son heeds his father's instruction,
   but a mocker does not respond to rebukes.

13:1 Verse 1 echoes the lectures from the father in chapters 1–9 and at 10:1 with the start of the individual sayings. In this way verse 1 serves to introduce all of the sayings through 15:5. The father represents wise authority figures in general, so the repeated sayings train the son in the skill of following the proper intellectual and religious authority, as counselors and fathers sometimes prove to be foolish and misleading (cf. 13:20, 24).

² From the fruit of their lips people enjoy good things,
   but the unfaithful have an appetite for violence.
³ Those who guard their lips preserve their lives,
   but those who speak rashly will come to ruin.
⁴ A sluggard's appetite is never filled,
   but the desires of the diligent are fully satisfied.
⁵ The righteous hate what is false,
   but the wicked make themselves a stench
   and bring shame on themselves.
⁶ Righteousness guards the person of integrity,
   but wickedness overthrows the sinner.

13:2–6 Waltke notes the focus on speech and wealth in this section.[1] All of the verses also illustrate ultimate consequences for a range of behaviors.

In 13:2–3 we see that our speech or words can bring us temporary satisfaction (good or evil) as well as determining our ultimate fate. "Appetite," *nephesh*, in verse 2b can also mean "life" or "throat," which anticipates those who "guard their lips"— another means of speech—and "preserve their lives," *nephesh* (v. 3; cf. 21:23).

Verses 4–5 speak to controlling desires. We were created to enjoy the earth and wisdom is the God-given means to choose proper pleasures and avoid forbidden ones. Righteousness can be characterized as hatred—a passionate rejection of things that are evil (v. 5a, cf. 8:13).

The ultimate consequences in 13:6 draw this section to a close using the catchword "guard" from verse 3 and "righteousness" and "wickedness" in verse 5 (cf. 11:5).

[7] One person pretends to be rich, yet has nothing;
    another pretends to be poor, yet has great wealth.
[8] A person's riches may ransom their life,
    but the poor cannot respond to threatening rebukes.
[9] The light of the righteous shines brightly,
    but the lamp of the wicked is snuffed out.
[10] Where there is strife, there is pride,
    but wisdom is found in those who take advice.
[11] Dishonest money dwindles away,
    but whoever gathers money little by little makes it grow.

13:7–11 The theme of wealth in 13:7 creates a bridge between verses 6 and 8, resembling some of the themes in 10:15; neither verse comments directly about the moral integrity of the poor or rich person.[2] Commenting on verse 7, Gladson notes a tone of pluralism within wisdom literature regarding human understanding of retribution. Such verses have a "riddle-like character" that mirrors our experience of wealth and poverty in everyday life.[3] Just as apparent inequities can be misperceived, so too can the reasons for wealth and poverty be hidden from sight (cf. Acts 8:10).

Verse 8 continues the train of observations on wealth and poverty in verses 7, 10, and 12. As in 13:7, we do not know if these are righteous or wicked people, only that wealth has undeniable advantages. Heim describes verses 1b and 8b as translinear parallelisms, which are nearly identical sayings that add unity to a larger set of sayings.

1. Waltke, *Proverbs 1–15*, 552. Cf. Heim, *Grapes of Gold*, 160–61.
2. Cf. Clifford, *Proverbs*, 137.
3. Gladson, *Retributive Paradoxes*, 286.

Verse 9 has no lexical connections to verses 7–11, though it may connect to verses 2–6 because of its concluding tone on the righteous and wicked. Van Leeuwen indicates that light in Proverbs is a "metaphor for life, vitality, and goodness" in contrast to death, sickness, and punishment (cf. 20:20; 24:20).[4] "Pride" in 13:10 describes the self-inflated attitude of the fool who rejects good counsel. Such pride leads to strife and division.

Verse 11 closes the section starting in verse 7, echoing the deceptiveness of wealth in verse 7 but also affirming the wisdom of virtue in saving income.

> [12] Hope deferred makes the heart sick,
> but a longing fulfilled is a tree of life.
> [13] Whoever scorns instruction will pay for it,
> but whoever respects a command is rewarded.
> [14] The teaching of the wise is a fountain of life,
> turning a person from the snares of death.
> [15] Good judgment wins favor,
> but the way of the unfaithful leads to their destruction.
> [16] All who are prudent act with knowledge,
> but fools expose their folly.
> [17] A wicked messenger falls into trouble,
> but a trustworthy envoy brings healing.
> [18] Whoever disregards discipline comes to poverty and shame,
> but whoever heeds correction is honored.
> [19] A longing fulfilled is sweet to the soul,
> but fools detest turning from evil.

13:12–19 Verse 12 reaffirms a central tenant in Proverbs that humans are creatures of constant longing and desire. In this case delayed hope, a type of desire, inflicts us with aching sickness. The immediate context illustrates many other sides of desire. Verse 11 shows that there is wisdom in satisfying our desires gradually rather than through greed or desperation. Verse 19 adds a moral judgment to the waiting in verse 12: those who are wise and righteous resist evil and wait for the appropriate desire to be fulfilled. Fools crave evil. The "tree of life" in verse 12 is a common metaphor in ancient Near Eastern wisdom literature and is probably not a direct reference to Genesis 2–3. Nevertheless, both trees imagine a good, divinely given satisfaction to our longings.

Verses 13–14 return to the topic of receiving counsel (cf. v. 10). The words

---

4. Van Leewen, *Proverbs*, 132.

"instruction," "command," and "teaching" also appear often in Deuteronomy, many times from parents to children (cf. 4:6; 6:6–9; 30:11–15). While Proverbs 1–9 intentionally echoes Deuteronomy at many points, the parallel is less direct here, as these verses have in mind the teaching of the wise and not the law of Yahweh.

Verses 12–19 have several devices that hold the sayings in this section together. The middle of the passage is united by the "fountain of life" in verse 14 and the "tree of life" in verse 12, with verse 14 extending the content of verse 13 as well. In addition to the parallels noted in verses 11 and 19, the similarities in verses 13 and 18 regarding counsel create an outward framework. Heim suggests that verse 16 sits at the center of this frame, summarizing the cluster of verses as a whole: the wise person does everything with knowledge and counsel (13–14, 17–18), but fools show their folly in everything by rejecting instruction (13) and persisting in evil (15).[5]

> [20] Walk with the wise and become wise,
>   for a companion of fools suffers harm.
> [21] Trouble pursues the sinner,
>   but the righteous are rewarded with good things.
> [22] A good person leaves an inheritance for their children's children,
>   but a sinner's wealth is stored up for the righteous.
> [23] An unplowed field produces food for the poor,
>   but injustice sweeps it away.
> [24] Whoever spares the rod hates their children,
>   but the one who loves their children is careful to discipline them.
> [25] The righteous eat to their hearts' content,
>   but the stomach of the wicked goes hungry.

13:20–25 To "walk with the wise" (v. 20) is to live a life dependent upon and in submission to the wisdom of the community. The wise, moreover, not only submit their judgments to others, they know how to discern between wise and foolish counselors.

Verses 21–23 speak to rewards. The first and last words in the Hebrew of 12:21–22 form a chiasm: sinners-good-good-sinner. While sinners may build up wealth in this world, their benefits end at death. By contrast, the righteous pass on their inheritance, which includes material goods, skillful living, and faith in God. The paradox in 12:23 reminds us that there are exceptions to this rule—sometimes even the few possessions of the poor are taken away. This verse reflects the conditions and purposes of the Sabbath and Jubilee

---

5. Heim, *Grapes of Gold*, 167.

laws in providing rest and food and justice for the needy (Deut 15:1–21; Lev 25:1–55; cf. Deut 24:17–22).

Verse 24 reminds the reader that the Old Testament commends stripes or lashes for disobedience and foolishness (Prov 22:15; 23:13–14; 29:15; cf. Prov 19:18; 29:17; Deut 21:18–21). Adults are included as proper recipients of beatings (Prov 10:13; 18:6; 19:29; 26:3). In Proverbs the call for severe and immediate punishment reinforces the bi-polar nature of wisdom: wisdom and righteousness stand in stark contrast to folly and wickedness (see Live the Story).

Verse 25 is tied to verse 23 by the word "food" and to other parts of the chapter through the theme of satisfied desire, *nephesh*. The chapter ends with a final emotional appeal to get wisdom.[6]

 LIVE the Story

Authority and the Desires of the Heart

Chapter 13 sews together the themes of counsel and desire. As anyone who has been a parent or teacher knows, desire is usually a more powerful motivator than reason. The principle applies to sinful adults as well. The story in Genesis 3 depicts Adam and Eve using reason to justify listening to a new authority and satisfying their yearning desire for the fruit of the forbidden tree. Almost all of the passages addressing desire in this chapter (vv. 1, 2, 3, 4, 8, 9, 10, 12, 14, 19, 20, 25) contrast the impetuousness and impatience of the fool seeking pleasure to the righteous having their desires satisfied as the result of diligence, wisdom, and righteous behavior. It must also be recognized that good counsel has the power to shed light on our distorted and selfish desires.

Sex and wealth are the two most prominent objects of desire in Proverbs, and we find them in the New Testament as well. Notice the passage in Revelation 3:17, which is within God's warning to the church at Laodicea, "You say, 'I am rich; I have acquired wealth and do not need a thing.' But you do not realize that you are wretched, pitiful, poor, blind and naked." In a separate string of sayings, which sound like proverbs, Paul appeals to the nature of self-deception and possessions, "If anyone thinks they are something when they are not, they deceive themselves" (Gal 6:3; cf. Matt 16:26; Luke 12:16–21; 16:19–26). Paul and Jesus take our longing for wealth and set it on our eternal inheritance in Christ (Matt 6:19–21; Eph 1:13–14).

---

6. Ibid., 169.

Hope and Waiting

"Hope deferred makes the heart sick" (13:12a). Time is a powerful force. A friend recently quoted Proverbs 13:12a after his overseas flight home was delayed a second time. Verse 10b confirms what we already know: that a longing becoming satisfied is pleasurable. Yet reading the verse against the backdrop of the whole chapter, we see that the wise and righteous have an intuitive sense of patience and willingness to wait for rewards (cf. 13:11; cf. 14:29; 15:18; 16:32; 25:17).

What Proverbs assumes about patience, the book of Psalms states emphatically. The beginning of Psalm 13 may be the most clear example when it asks the question "How long?" four times in a row (1–2; cf. Pss 35:17; 67:3; 74:10; 89:46; Hab 1:2). Claus Westermann comments, "Here, time itself becomes a destructive force, wearing down a man's ability to hold out and intensifying the suffering to an inhuman level."[7] Fox observes an important corollary: other people's hopes are a sacred thing and should not be trifled with (cf. Prov 3:28).[8]

In his *timeless* work on the sacred, Mircea Eliade observes that humans, whether religious or non-religious, all experience the mystery, sameness, and visceral nagging of living in time.[9] Consider Hump Day, TGIF and even Thursday, Friday's little sister. Birthdays, weekends, mid-weeks, holidays, and vacations all serve to create a sense of relief and rescue from the homogeneity of time and its gnawing and destructive force.

Christian worship, grounded in the rituals and ceremonies of the Old Testament, instinctively embeds worshipers in a *primordial enactment of sacred time*. Jews celebrate Passover each year as if they are with Moses in Egypt. Christians share in the sacred mystery of Christ's presence in the Lord's Supper in the same way. Such worship actualizes the past in the present and consecrates "today" with the sacredness of the past and the hope of the future. To paraphrase Augustine, "God's eternity is today."

Christian time goes beyond the Jewish actualization of the past. In our present time we have already been "raised with Christ" and have our lives "hidden with Christ in God" as we wait until we "appear with him in glory" (Col 3:1–4; cf. Rom 8:19, 23, 25; 1 Cor 15:51–54; Rev 22:7). In Christ Jesus, the sacred of the past and the future have broken into the present and made their home in the church who waits in the *already* for the *not yet*.

---

7. Claus Westermann, *Living Psalms*, BCOTWP (Grand Rapids: Eerdmans, 1989) 71, in John Goldingay, *Psalms*, vol 1, Psalms 1–41 (Grand Rapids: Baker, 2006), 205.

8. Fox, *Proverbs 10–31*, 566.

9. Mircea Eliade, *The Sacred and the Profane: The Nature of Religion* (Orlando: Harvest Harcourt, 1987), 68–72.

Corporal Discipline

Proverbs 13:14 raises the controversial topic of parents disciplining their children—corporal punishment if we reject the possibility that the "rod" might have a figurative meaning.

While we do not find explicit reference to physical discipline in the New Testament, the principals of the parents' discipline and children's obedience are assumed throughout. Ephesians 6:1–4 and Colossians 3:20–21 both encourage churches probably full of gentile converts to adopt the practice of correcting children in the Lord, a practice drawn from the teachings in the Old Testament. We also find that the New Testament constantly depicts Christians as children of God. The book of 1 John plays on the parent-child metaphor more than any other book. What must be emphasized is that our concept of Christian faithfulness and obedience to God is only as strong as our sense of parental responsibility, authoritative discipline, and submission and obedience within the family and community. But what does this mean for parenting today?

For one, there is the matter of human psychology. We now know that non-violent forms of discipline can be equally effective in motivating behavior. In fact, praise or reward is a more effective motivator than punishment.[10] This should have some part in shaping our philosophy of correcting wrongdoing.

At the same time, the Christian is concerned with more than just behavioral outcomes. Wisdom is instruction in the *ways of things in the world*, most significantly the moral orders of right and wrong. Often, the things we are certain about are often dead wrong (Prov 16:25; 26:3), and painful discipline is an important way to illumine our self-deception. That said, pain can come through other channels than physical discipline.

William Webb's thoughts on corporal punishment are particularly helpful in correcting some of our naïve assumptions about the Bible and discipline. For example, Scripture sets no age limits, endorsing corporal discipline for children and adults.[11] The Bible also views bruising as a natural and even desired consequence of discipline (Prov 20:30; Neh 13:25; cf. Song 5:7). In making human discipline comparable to divine discipline, the Bible qualifies punishment as an expression of love *and* anger (Deut 8:5; 2 Sam 7:14; Prov 3:11–12; Ps 6:1; Heb 12:5–7).

These surprising facts about discipline help us recognize that not all biblical practices are normative for all time.[12] The Bible's acceptance of slavery and

---

10. Schroeder, *Three Faces of Desire*, 40–41.

11. William Webb, *Corporal Discipline in the Bible: A Redemptive-Movement Hermeneutic for Troubling Texts* (Downers Grove, IL: InterVarsity, 2011), 25–54.

12. Ibid., 57–93.

conduct in warfare are recognized to be immoral and illegal today (cf. Exod 21:20–21; Deut 21:10–14). Yet in their ancient context these laws were comparatively mild. Some Egyptian and Assyrian laws, for example, allowed for as many as one hundred, two hundred, or more lashes for an offense, compared to the Bible's limit of forty (Deut 25:3). Likewise, there is no comparison in the ancient world with the Bible's requirements that Israel provide relief and care for slaves every one, three, seven, and forty-nine years.

In reflecting on discipline, Christians must think critically about the purposes of punishment, such as education, spiritual formation, and public deterrence. We must also think carefully how our philosophy of discipline heralds good news. How might it uniquely express both God's holiness and justice, and also his love, compassion, and forgiveness? And how might it bring us face to face with the innocent one who bore God's stripes and welcomed God's wrath meant for us (Isa 53:5; 1 Pet 2:24)?

CHAPTER 19

Proverbs 14:1–35

 LISTEN to the Story

¹ The wise woman builds her house,
  but with her own hands the foolish one tears hers down.
² Whoever fears the LORD walks uprightly,
  but those who despise him are devious in their ways.
³ A fool's mouth lashes out with pride,
  but the lips of the wise protect them.
⁴ Where there are no oxen, the manger is empty,
  but from the strength of an ox come abundant harvests.
⁵ An honest witness does not deceive,
  but a false witness pours out lies.
⁶ The mocker seeks wisdom and finds none,
  but knowledge comes easily to the discerning.
⁷ Stay away from a fool,
  for you will not find knowledge on their lips.
⁸ The wisdom of the prudent is to give thought to their ways,
  but the folly of fools is deception.
⁹ Fools mock at making amends for sin,
  but goodwill is found among the upright.
¹⁰ Each heart knows its own bitterness,
  and no one else can share its joy.
¹¹ The house of the wicked will be destroyed,
  but the tent of the upright will flourish.
¹² There is a way that appears to be right,
  but in the end it leads to death.
¹³ Even in laughter the heart may ache,
  and rejoicing may end in grief.
¹⁴ The faithless will be fully repaid for their ways,
  and the good rewarded for theirs.
¹⁵ The simple believe anything,

but the prudent give thought to their steps.
¹⁶ The wise fear the LORD and shun evil,
　　but a fool is hotheaded and yet feels secure.
¹⁷ A quick-tempered person does foolish things,
　　and the one who devises evil schemes is hated.
¹⁸ The simple inherit folly,
　　but the prudent are crowned with knowledge.
¹⁹ Evildoers will bow down in the presence of the good,
　　and the wicked at the gates of the righteous.
²⁰ The poor are shunned even by their neighbors,
　　but the rich have many friends.
²¹ It is a sin to despise one's neighbor,
　　but blessed is the one who is kind to the needy.
²² Do not those who plot evil go astray?
　　But those who plan what is good find love and faithfulness.
²³ All hard work brings a profit,
　　but mere talk leads only to poverty.
²⁴ The wealth of the wise is their crown,
　　but the folly of fools yields folly.
²⁵ A truthful witness saves lives,
　　but a false witness is deceitful.
²⁶ Whoever fears the LORD has a secure fortress,
　　and for their children it will be a refuge.
²⁷ The fear of the LORD is a fountain of life,
　　turning a person from the snares of death.
²⁸ A large population is a king's glory,
　　but without subjects a prince is ruined.
²⁹ Whoever is patient has great understanding,
　　but one who is quick-tempered displays folly.
³⁰ A heart at peace gives life to the body,
　　but envy rots the bones.
³¹ Whoever oppresses the poor shows contempt for their Maker,
　　but whoever is kind to the needy honors God.
³² When calamity comes, the wicked are brought down,
　　but even in death the righteous seek refuge in God.
³³ Wisdom reposes in the heart of the discerning
　　and even among fools she lets herself be known.
³⁴ Righteousness exalts a nation,

> but sin condemns any people.
> [35] A king delights in a wise servant,
>   but a shameful servant arouses his fury.

Listening to the Text in the Story: Exodus 35:30–38:31; Leviticus 5:14–19; 7:1–5; Deuteronomy 10:12–20

As seen elsewhere in the commentary, the family house and house-building (14:1 and 26) draw upon the theology of God's "house" as a place of prayer and protection as well as the metaphor of the house as the life we live (Exod 35:30–38:31; 2 Chr 2:1–7:10; Prov 3:19–20; 24:3–4; Pss 127–128).

After three chapters of its absence, this chapter returns to the theme of "the fear of the LORD" (14:2; 26, 27). While there are times that wisdom and law should be carefully distinguished, the fear of the Lord in Proverbs goes hand in hand with the vision of righteousness in the law (Exod 20:18–21; Deut 10:12–20). One cannot help but read these proverbs and recall the initiation of God's covenant with Israel at Mount Sinai and the entry into the promised land at Moab.

Finally, "amends for sin" (v. 9) is, more literally, "guilt," which recalls the guilt offerings in the Law (Lev 5:14–19; 7:1–5). See more in the commentary below.

EXPLAIN the Story

In the introduction to chapters 10–29 we observed that almost all of the sayings in chapters 10–15 are antithetical proverbs that revolve around the opposition between the righteous and the wicked and wisdom and folly. The sayings in chapters 10–12 emphasize righteousness and wickedness, while the vocabulary of wise/wisdom and foolish/folly is denser in chapters 13–15. Chapter 14 also initiates a string of royal sayings that continue through chapter 16.

Whereas chapter 13 seemed to have a fairly well-defined structure, this chapter seems to be composed of more small groupings of proverbs that have common catchwords and themes.[1]

> [1] The wise woman builds her house,
>   but with her own hands the foolish one tears hers down.
> [2] Whoever fears the LORD walks uprightly,
>   but those who despise him are devious in their ways.

---

1. But cf. Waltke, *Proverbs 1–15*, 583 who divides the chapter into four sections: 1–7; 8–15; 16–32; 33–35.

³ A fool's mouth lashes out with pride,
> but the lips of the wise protect them.

14:1–3 The first phrase in 14:1 could be translated "the wisest of women" or "the wise among women," resembling "wisdom [who] built her house" in 9:1. Chapter 9 concerns cosmic Woman Wisdom, but this emphasizes a literal woman as in 31:10–31, particularly the references to "hands" (14:1b; 31:13, 19–20, 31). This woman stands alongside the man in 24:3–4 who builds his house and imitates the pattern in which Yahweh made the creation in 3:19–20. Also, as in the depiction of Dame Folly in Proverbs 9:13–18, so too a foolish woman by her own work can tear down a house and a life.

"Fears the LORD" in 14:2 is noteworthy. For one, it imagines a life of uprightness and law-keeping (Deut 10:12, 20). The "fear of the LORD" is also the beginning of wisdom and the means to resist Dame Folly (1:7; 9:10) as well as the trait that most distinguishes the valiant woman (31:30). In addition to the "fear of the LORD" and the repetition of "hands," Proverbs 9, 14, and 31 also mention the "house" (9:1, 14; 14:11; 31:27); a concern for the needy (14:21–21; 31:21); a person's steps (9:6; 14:7–8); recalcitrant "scoffers" (9:7–8; 14:6); care for speech (9:7–9; 14:3, 5); and inheritance to children (14:26; 31:15, 21, 27–28).

Verse 3 is an antithetical saying that once again unites wisdom and folly with speech that protects and speech that evinces pride.

⁴ Where there are no oxen, the manger is empty,
> but from the strength of an ox come abundant harvests.

14:4 This verse stands alone. The word *bar*, "empty," could mean "corn/grain" or "clean/pure." So the second half of 14:4a could be "the manger is empty/clean" or "the manger has grain," though the latter is a less likely match for 14:4b. Adding another level of complexity, *bar* is followed by *rab*, "abundant," reversing the consonants and creating a chiasm. Furthermore, *bar* can work in both concrete and metaphorical senses,[2] which suggests that *bar* may be used to signify not only emptiness but something clean as well. The basic lesson is that you can't have your cake and eat it too.

⁵ An honest witness does not deceive,
> but a false witness pours out lies.
⁶ The mocker seeks wisdom and finds none,
> but knowledge comes easily to the discerning.
⁷ Stay away from a fool,

---

2. *NIDOTTE* "brr," 1:772–74.

for you will not find knowledge on their lips.
⁸ The wisdom of the prudent is to give thought to their ways,
    but the folly of fools is deception.
⁹ Fools mock at making amends for sin,
    but goodwill is found among the upright.

14:5–9 These verses are gathered around various types of wisdom: speech, intellect, and attitude. The "honest" witness in 14:5 parallels the "honest" witness in verse 25. Emphasizing the opposition in these sayings, Fox comments, "honesty and deceit are indivisible qualities."[3]

In verse 6 we are reminded that the scoffer is frequently portrayed rejecting counsel and contrasted to the wise who listens to advice and gets knowledge (cf. 1:22; 9:7–8; 13:1; 15:12, 19:25, 29; etc.).

Verses 7–8 is a rare admonition among a long list of sayings.[4] The call to "stay away," is literally "walk," which ties this verse to the "ways" in verse 8. Together, verses 7–8 depict the wise person as one who accepts counsel and thinks carefully about her thoughts and activities (cf. v. 15). The theme of deception in verses 5 and 8 also serves to give unity to these sayings.

Verse 9a literally says "fools scorn guilt." Commentators wrestle with the meaning of "guilt" in this context. Is it guiltiness? Ceremonial uncleanness? Guilt offerings (Lev 5:14–19; 7:1–5)? In reality, what we have is a beautifully succinct and powerful proverb that leaves readers pondering the implications in just this way. Fools mock the idea of guilt many ways and at all sorts of times. Fools also live in a kind of defensive mood that instinctually denies culpability. The "upright" by contrast receive favor. Whether "goodwill" means their own favor, favor from others, or both, is likewise left to the reader to ponder.

¹⁰ Each heart knows its own bitterness,
    and no one else can share its joy.
¹¹ The house of the wicked will be destroyed,
    but the tent of the upright will flourish.
¹² There is a way that appears to be right,
    but in the end it leads to death.
¹³ Even in laughter the heart may ache,
    and rejoicing may end in grief.
¹⁴ The faithless will be fully repaid for their ways,
    and the good rewarded for theirs.

---

3. Fox, *Proverbs 10–31*, 574.
4. Van Leeuwen, *Proverbs*, 139–40.

14:10–14 Verses 10–13 combine sayings about future consequences (vv. 11–12) with contemplative proverbs about the heart (vv. 10, 13). The final verse (11:14) applies the catchword "heart" to the theme of consequences and includes the "way" from 11:12.

The sayings in 14:10 and 13 lead us to contemplate the mysteries of the human heart and the way grief often reveals loneliness. Such loneliness can be seen in a literal translation of 14:10a, "the heart knows the bitterness of its life." Wisdom does not hide from these hard realities of life.

Verse 11 imagines the outcomes that come to the "house" or "tent" of the wicked and the upright (cf. 11:28). As noted in 14:1 above, these dwellings symbolize a human life and echo the consequences that dominated the rhetoric of chapters 1–9.

Verse 12 also emphasizes consequences with a warning about the limitations of human understanding (cf. 16:25). The saying is an imprecise parallel as "right" (12a) is not the opposite of "death" (12b). The inexactness in the parallels serves to create a surprise and accentuate the lesson about self-deception. Verse 14 draws the sayings together. "Faithless" in the NIV is literally a "devious" or "backsliding heart." (See further in Live the Story.)

¹⁵ The simple believe anything,
    but the prudent give thought to their steps.
¹⁶ The wise fear the LORD and shun evil,
    but a fool is hotheaded and yet feels secure.
¹⁷ A quick-tempered person does foolish things,
    and the one who devises evil schemes is hated.
¹⁸ The simple inherit folly,
    but the prudent are crowned with knowledge.

14:15–18 These four sayings are littered with terms that describe the relative patience/haste and concern/apathy of the thoughts of the "prudent" and "wise" and the "simple" and "foolish." Those who "give thought to their steps," (v.15) and "fear the LORD" (v. 16) are contrasted to those who are too quick to believe things (v. 15): the "quick-tempered,"[5] "overly trusting" (v. 16), and those "scheming evil."[6] The consequences of these two groups are spelled out in 11:18. While Proverbs rarely speaks explicitly about patience, it is implicit to wisdom throughout the collection (see Live the Story in Prov 13).

¹⁹ Evildoers will bow down in the presence of the good,
    and the wicked at the gates of the righteous.

---

5. I rely on Heim's arguments (but changing his wording slightly), *Grapes of Gold*, 179.
6. These are alternative translations to the NIV "fool" who is hotheaded (v. 16) and "devise" (v.17).

²⁰ The poor are shunned even by their neighbors,
    but the rich have many friends.
²¹ It is a sin to despise one's neighbor,
    but blessed is the one who is kind to the needy.
²² Do not those who plot evil go astray?
    But those who plan what is good find love and faithfulness.

14:19–22 Similar to 14:15–18, these sayings are held together by the term "good" in 14:19 and 22. There is also a preponderance of the sound "sh" throughout all of the sayings that gives them assonantal unity.

Verse 19 extends the consequences in 14:18 but uses key terms that set up the next three sayings.

Verses 20–21 both begin with a clause that includes "neighbor." 14:20 expresses a stark, sad reality, which we hear more strongly in the Hebrew than the NIV: the poor are "hated even by their neighbors" while "the rich are loved by many" (author's translation).

Verse 21 provides a warning and exhortation, which serve as a corrective—wise and sensitive behavior acts as a counter injustice. The image of despising one's neighbor anticipates the one who "oppresses the poor" in 14:31 (cf. 17:6). These verses are discussed together in Live the Story below.

Verses 21–22 return to the intellectual and reflective language in 14:15–18. The wise and the foolish engage in deliberate direction of their thoughts—one toward kindness resulting in good, and the other toward evil and going "astray."

²³ All hard work brings a profit,
    but mere talk leads only to poverty.
²⁴ The wealth of the wise is their crown,
    but the folly of fools yields folly.
²⁵ A truthful witness saves lives,
    but a false witness is deceitful.
²⁶ Whoever fears the LORD has a secure fortress,
    and for their children it will be a refuge.
²⁷ The fear of the LORD is a fountain of life,
    turning a person from the snares of death.

14:23–27 The pairs in verses 23–24 and 26–27 surround a central saying in 25. Verses 23–24 continue and complete the sayings about wealth and poverty begun in 14:20–21. Verse 20 stated a harsh reality and 14:22 balances the reality with a warning about caring for the poor. Verse 23 then provides advice for avoiding poverty. Finally, 14:24 repeats "wealth/rich," 'sr, from verse 20 as a final encouragement to be wise by working hard (23), which will result in attracting friends (20) and honor (24).

The saying on honesty in 14:25 is slightly out of place. In the larger context it returns to the theme of honesty in 14:5 and 8 while drawing on vocabulary throughout the chapter, such as "witness," "life/lives," *nephesh* (v. 10), "lies" (v. 8), and "deceit/deception" (v. 5).

The statements about "the fear of the LORD" in 14:1–2, 16, and here in 26–27 are probably thematic and structural markers for the chapter. The point is that those who fear the Lord are those who hear these sayings and do them. These final two sayings in the set seek to compel the reader through assurances of security, blessings, and life.

> ²⁸ A large population is a king's glory,
>   but without subjects a prince is ruined.
> ²⁹ Whoever is patient has great understanding,
>   but one who is quick-tempered displays folly.
> ³⁰ A heart at peace gives life to the body,
>   but envy rots the bones.
> ³¹ Whoever oppresses the poor shows contempt for their Maker,
>   but whoever is kind to the needy honors God.
> ³² When calamity comes, the wicked are brought down,
>   but even in death the righteous seek refuge in God.
> ³³ Wisdom reposes in the heart of the discerning
>   and even among fools she lets herself be known.
> ³⁴ Righteousness exalts a nation,
>   but sin condemns any people.
> ³⁵ A king delights in a wise servant,
>   but a shameful servant arouses his fury.

14:28–35 Two sayings about the king (28, 35) enclose these final verses, all of which draw upon the sayings in the previous twenty-seven verses. Verse 28 repeats the theme of a good reputation, which runs throughout chapters 13–14. Like the rich person who has "many friends" (14:20), the king with "a large population" has "glory"—a word that often signifies dressing in holy array (1 Chr 16:29; 2 Chr 21:21; Pss 29:2; 96:9). The poor person who is "hated" by neighbors parallels the "prince without subjects [who] is ruined."

Verses 29–30 display what Waltke calls a pairing of "outward physiognomy and inward counterpart," though the NIV removes most of the bodily references.[7] Verse 29, a close variant of 14:17, says that those who are "long nosed"

---

7. Walkte, *Proverbs 10–15*, 605.

(NIV "patient") have "great understanding," while those of "quick-tempered" spirit exhibit "folly." In 14:30 the "heart at peace" "gives life to the body" and "envy rots the bones." Proverbs thus shows the intricate connections between bodies, actions, and emotions (cf. Prov 15:18; Matt 12:34).

Verse 31 is a stronger form of 14:21. The second line could be read "whoever is kind to the needy honors God" or "is honored." Since it is the creator who is cursed in verse 31a, it seems more likely that it is God who is honored by compassion. Both statements are nevertheless true.

Verse 32 states the alternative consequences that go to the "righteous" and the "wicked" (cf. 14:11, 19). The second half of 14:33 has a textual problem. The NRSV reads "But [wisdom] is not known in the heart of fools." If we stay with the NIV, the sense could be that wisdom cannot be completely obscured or that wisdom is made evident by foolish behavior.

In 14:34–35 the nation is in view rather than the individual. The verses recall sayings in 14:11, 21, and 22. One individual, namely the king (v. 35), stands as the exemplar for the nation. When 14:35 is read in juxtaposition to verse 34, a righteous king will treasure a "wise servant" while a "shameful servant" will prompt his anger. In the end, the individual relationships within a kingdom determine the strength of the whole.

 LIVE the Story

Kindness and Contempt

According to this chapter, we "sin" and show "contempt for [our] Maker" when we mistreat our fellow human beings (vv. 21, 31). The reference to "Maker" grounds our ethical actions within God's ordering of creation (cf. 11:12–13; 17:5; Job 30:15–23), an image we see lived out in Jesus' ministry.

As Genesis 1 makes clear, we are made in the image and likeness of God. In the *imago Dei*, every one of us is a steward of God's work and his reputation. It must be said that this privilege of representing God was not lost in the fall but is reaffirmed for children of Adam in Genesis 5:1–3 as well as when God lays out the death penalty for murder in his meeting with Noah; the motivation for punishment is that we still bear his image.

Moreover, whatever our different estates in life, we are equal image-bearers of God. Herein lie the roots to Christian thinking about rights, but not in the abstract and defensive ways of asserting rights today. The Bible speaks of rights as the basis for our obligations within a community, not our claims against it. Because God cares for image bearers graciously, so we are to do with one another (Pss 72:4, 112:4; John 13:15). Exodus 22:27 and Proverbs

3:27–33 commend care for the neighbor in need (cf. 14:21, 31). Jesus continually embodies this spirit, especially in the presence of the poor, disabled, and marginalized in society. He sought out the poor, blind, and lame as well as women, widows, and children. He ate with sinners, taxcollectors, and gentiles, and sought the company of the low and forgotten above the great and powerful (e.g., Matt 9:9–13; 15:21–28; Mark 7:24–30; 8:22–26; 10:13–16; Luke 7:1–17, 36–50; 8:40–53; 13:10–17; 14:12–14).

Liberation of the Heart

The word *leb*, "heart," appears almost one hundred times in the book of Proverbs. The heart thinks, conspires, fears, remembers, imagines, loves, aches, and more. The heart is the source of all human thought, emotion, and action (4:23; cf. Matt 12:34). The heart is also mysterious and deep and distorted by the fall (Jer 17:9–10). It can deceive us and be used to deceive others (14:13–14).

Proverbs 14:10 and 13 speak honestly about the pain and loneliness of the heart. The heart's "bitterness" can be seen in Naomi's lament to Ruth and Orpah, which arises out of the loss of Naomi's husband and children, her wandering in a foreign land, and God withholding mercy (Ruth 1:13, 20). Despite the love of her daughters-in-law, Naomi is alone, cut off from healing communion with God and family.

Jean Vanier, the founder of l'Arche communities, has spent most of his life working with people with severe mental and physical disabilities.[8] In these contexts he claims to have discovered the inevitable loneliness of the human spirit. In being alone we meet the full extent of our finite nature, but we also discover that we have been made with a deep desire for God. Only through our loneliness, therefore, can we come to discover the true beauty of our human nature. Are not Vanier's insights confirmed for us in Jesus' cry of dereliction: "My God, my God, why have you forsaken me?" (Mark 15:34). Dying alone, Jesus experienced the most grievous suffering in our human experience.

Jesus' suffering *for his people* reminds us that in our loneliness we also discover our calling to pursue covenant community with our fellow human beings, to bring love and belonging to one another (1 John 4:7). Similarly, it is Ruth's courageous faith and determination that allow Naomi to be reunited with God and her family and community (4:15). Above all, in our loneliness and sorrow we share in the sufferings of Christ, which Paul considers a privilege and a joy (Eph 3:13; see also Heb 4:14–16; 1 Pet 4:13). The cross and dying that seem to the world to be the way of foolishness are seen in Christ to be the doorway to hearts of joy from everlasting to everlasting.

---

8. See Jean Vanier, *Becoming Human* (New York: Paulist Press, 1998).

LISTEN to the Story

¹ A gentle answer turns away wrath,
  but a harsh word stirs up anger.
² The tongue of the wise adorns knowledge,
  but the mouth of the fool gushes folly.
³ The eyes of the LORD are everywhere,
  keeping watch on the wicked and the good.
⁴ The soothing tongue is a tree of life,
  but a perverse tongue crushes the spirit.
⁵ A fool spurns a parent's discipline,
  but whoever heeds correction shows prudence.
⁶ The house of the righteous contains great treasure,
  but the income of the wicked brings ruin.
⁷ The lips of the wise spread knowledge,
  but the hearts of fools are not upright.
⁸ The LORD detests the sacrifice of the wicked,
  but the prayer of the upright pleases him.
⁹ The LORD detests the way of the wicked,
  but he loves those who pursue righteousness.
¹⁰ Stern discipline awaits anyone who leaves the path;
  the one who hates correction will die.
¹¹ Death and Destruction lie open before the LORD—
  how much more do human hearts!
¹² Mockers resent correction,
  so they avoid the wise.
¹³ A happy heart makes the face cheerful,
  but heartache crushes the spirit.
¹⁴ The discerning heart seeks knowledge,
  but the mouth of a fool feeds on folly.
¹⁵ All the days of the oppressed are wretched,

but the cheerful heart has a continual feast.
¹⁶ Better a little with the fear of the LORD
    than great wealth with turmoil.
¹⁷ Better a small serving of vegetables with love
    than a fattened calf with hatred.
¹⁸ A hot-tempered person stirs up conflict,
    but the one who is patient calms a quarrel.
¹⁹ The way of the sluggard is blocked with thorns,
    but the path of the upright is a highway.
²⁰ A wise son brings joy to his father,
    but a foolish man despises his mother.
²¹ Folly brings joy to one who has no sense,
    but whoever has understanding keeps a straight course.
²² Plans fail for lack of counsel,
    but with many advisers they succeed.
²³ A person finds joy in giving an apt reply—
    and how good is a timely word!
²⁴ The path of life leads upward for the prudent
    to keep them from going down to the realm of the dead.
²⁵ The LORD tears down the house of the proud,
    but he sets the widow's boundary stones in place.
²⁶ The LORD detests the thoughts of the wicked,
    but gracious words are pure in his sight.
²⁷ The greedy bring ruin to their households,
    but the one who hates bribes will live.
²⁸ The heart of the righteous weighs its answers,
    but the mouth of the wicked gushes evil.
²⁹ The LORD is far from the wicked,
    but he hears the prayer of the righteous.
³⁰ Light in a messenger's eyes brings joy to the heart,
    and good news gives health to the bones.
³¹ Whoever heeds life-giving correction
    will be at home among the wise.
³² Those who disregard discipline despise themselves,
    but the one who heeds correction gains understanding.
³³ Wisdom's instruction is to fear the LORD,
    and humility comes before honor.

Listening to the Text in the Story: Proverbs 30:7–8, 10–33; Psalms 50; 139; Job 26–28, 38–41; Isaiah 1:10–17; Amenemope 9.5–8; 16.11–14

Chapter 15 returns to the relationship of wisdom, law, and ritual sacrifice. In the Old Testament, God never condemns ritual practice or sacrifice; rather he rejects the hypocrisy of the worshiper who is far from God, involved in immoral behavior, or oblivious to the needs of the poor and marginalized (Ps 50:7–23; Isa 1:10–17; Amos 5:21–24; Mal 3:16–18). Some scholars still hold that wisdom stands opposed to Israel's covenant religion with its cultic offices and rituals.[1] But Proverbs repeatedly assumes the normativity of ritual practice and prayer (7:14; 14:4, 9; 15:8, 29; 28:9; 30:7–9).

This chapter also leads us to reflect on the mysterious ways of the world (15:3, 11). Proverbs 30:10–33 revels in the wonder of human life in this world, much like the speeches in Job 26–28 and 38–41. God's knowledge spans the vastness of creation and the world of the dead (Job 26:6; 28:22; 41:11) to the intricacy of the human being in all its parts (Ps 139). These concerns will emerge in the commentary below.

This chapter also has many significant parallels with ancient Near Eastern sources. For example, the saying in 15:1 resembles this saying in Ani (Any): "A rude answer brings a beating / Speak sweetly and you will be loved."[2] Furthermore, the language of what "detests" or is an "abomination" to a god (cf. 15:8, 9, 26) is also found in Sumerian sayings to Utu.[3] The better-than sayings in 15:16–17 could also be based on Amenemope 9.5–8.[4] These and many more parallels shows the universal concerns of wisdom in the ancient world.

EXPLAIN the Story

There is little question that this chapter has been edited with catchwords and a tapestry of common themes, yet the structure is more open or flowing than other parts of the collection in chapters 10–29. Chapter 15 gathers many of its themes from chapter 10.[5]

---

1. See "Wisdom and Law" in the Introduction.

2. M. Lichtheim, *AEL*, 2:140.

3. Longman, *Proverbs, Zondervan Illustrated Bible Background Commentary*, 5:485.

4. See Fox, *Proverbs 10–31*, 596.

5. Van Leeuwen, *Proverbs*, 148.

Theme	10:1	15:5, 20
Theme	10:2–3	15:6, 6–17
Theme	10:17	15:5, 10, 12, 31–32
Theme	10:27	15:33

The chapter also has several variant repetitions that are found elsewhere in Proverbs (15:8, 13, 14, 16, 17, 18, 20, 22, 33). Furthermore, the divine name Yahweh appears nine times here (36 percent of the verses) and is the densest concentration of the name outside of chapters 3 and 16. Yahweh appears in a repeating structure of a single verse, a verse pair, two single verses, a verse pair, and a single verse (3, 8–9; 11, 16, 25–26, 33).

> 15:1 A gentle answer turns away wrath,
>   but a harsh word stirs up anger.
> 2 The tongue of the wise adorns knowledge,
>   but the mouth of the fool gushes folly.
> 3 The eyes of the LORD are everywhere,
>   keeping watch on the wicked and the good.
> 4 The soothing tongue is a tree of life,
>   but a perverse tongue crushes the spirit.

15:1–4 Except for verse 3, this section addresses speech. 15:1 provides a transition from the wise servant of the king in 14:35 to examples of wise speech in 15:1–2 and 4. The wise servant is one who thinks carefully about his words (cf. Eccl 10:4; Prov 25:15). Abigail exemplifies the power of gentle speech in talking David down from his angry designs against her husband Nabal (1 Sam 25:10–31), a point David later praises with gratitude (vv. 32–34). Verse 4 reinforces this point about grace of speech (cf. Eph 4:25). For more on the phrase "crushes the spirit," see verse 13 below. Verse 2 offers visual ways of imagining two sides of speech: one "adorns knowledge" and the other "gushes folly." The verb translated "adorns" is the same Hebrew word translated "good" in verse 3.

Verse 3 speaks to God's omniscient wisdom, a theme that appears again in 15:11. The "eyes of the LORD" is used several times in the Old Testament as a way of capturing God's observation of every human activity (Deut 11:12; Ps 34:16; Prov 5:11; 22:12; Zech 4:10).

> 5 A fool spurns a parent's discipline,
>   but whoever heeds correction shows prudence.
> 6 The house of the righteous contains great treasure,
>   but the income of the wicked brings ruin.

[7] The lips of the wise spread knowledge,
    but the hearts of fools are not upright.
[8] The LORD detests the sacrifice of the wicked,
    but the prayer of the upright pleases him.
[9] The LORD detests the way of the wicked,
    but he loves those who pursue righteousness.
[10] Stern discipline awaits anyone who leaves the path;
    the one who hates correction will die.
[11] Death and Destruction lie open before the LORD—
    how much more do human hearts!
[12] Mockers resent correction,
    so they avoid the wise.

15:5–12 These verses are united by the themes of rejecting and accepting counsel (5, 10, 12), the "heart" (7, 11), and things that are an "abomination to the LORD" (9–10).[6]

Verses 5, 10, and 12 all address examples of accepting and rejecting counsel. The parents' discipline in verse 5 echoes the instructions in chapters 1–9 (cf. 1:8; 4:1; 6:20). Parents' teachings are reinforced by the discipline of the wise in 15:12. Set in the middle of these three sayings, 15:10 presents the negative consequences for rejecting counsel: "stern discipline" and death (cf. v. 5). This trio of sayings reinforces the *traditioning* authority in Proverbs; wisdom comes through authorities in the community and is subject to our willingness to listen and learn from others.

Verses 8–9 assumes the central position in verses 5–12. "Sacrifice" and "prayer" in verse 8 are probably not two different kinds of worship but two parts that represent the whole act of worship.[7] Proverbs is not a ritual book, but it addresses acts of prayer and sacrifice in several contexts (8:29; 14:4, 9; 7:14; 15:29; 21:27; 28:9; 30:7–9).

The theme of worship in verse 8 parallels "death" in 15:10, which leads to the mysterious abodes of Sheol and Abaddon[8] in 15:11 (cf. v. 24). Verse 8 also assumes that God knows the true motives of the worshiper, which echoes what the Lord knows about "human hearts" in 15:11. (See "Wisdom, Worship, and Prayer" in Live the Story.)

[13] A happy heart makes the face cheerful,
    but heartache crushes the spirit.

---

6. NIV "the LORD detests."
7. Fox, *Proverbs 10–31*, 591.
8. NIV "death and destruction."

¹⁴ The discerning heart seeks knowledge,
    but the mouth of a fool feeds on folly.
¹⁵ All the days of the oppressed are wretched,
    but the cheerful heart has a continual feast.
¹⁶ Better a little with the fear of the Lord
    than great wealth with turmoil.
¹⁷ Better a small serving of vegetables with love
    than a fattened calf with hatred.

15:13–17 The first three verses (13–15) focus on the heart, though verses 13 and 15 are also paired with the themes in verses 16–17.

Based on a parallel saying in Proverbs 18:14, Heim argues that a "crushed spirit" in 15:13 is one of the most severe forms of human pain (cf. 17:22).[9] In Ecclesiastes 7:3–4, Qohelet turns sayings like this and 14:13 into what Seow calls "ludicrous" statements about human mortality and suffering.[10]

This central verse in 15:15 adopts food and feasting as metaphors for the benefits of having a "cheerful heart." Verse 15a acknowledges the inevitability of human suffering. The focus in this verse on the integrity of the human being is picked up from 15:8, 10–11 above. The food metaphor, meanwhile, connects the saying to verses 14 and 17.

Verses 16–17 present two better-than sayings related to various sides of contentment (cf. v. 15). Whereas many passages like 15:6 align righteousness and wisdom with wealth, Proverbs remains constantly aware that wise and righteous people will often suffer and be in poverty and that wisdom is necessary for finding contentment in these situations.

¹⁸ A hot-tempered person stirs up conflict,
    but the one who is patient calms a quarrel.
¹⁹ The way of the sluggard is blocked with thorns,
    but the path of the upright is a highway.
²⁰ A wise son brings joy to his father,
    but a foolish man despises his mother.
²¹ Folly brings joy to one who has no sense,
    but whoever has understanding keeps a straight course.
²² Plans fail for lack of counsel,
    but with many advisers they succeed.
²³ A person finds joy in giving an apt reply—
    and how good is a timely word!

---

9. Heim, *Poetic Imagination*, 371.
10. Seow, *Ecclesiastes*, 246. Cf. Longman, *Proverbs*, 317.

15:18–23 These verses contrast six pairs of people. The repetition of acoustic sounds connects 15:17 to 15:18–19 (*aruha-erek-orah*, where the *h* and *k* sounds are very similar in Hebrew).

In 15:18, "patience" (Hebrew "long nosed") speaks to the inner disposition imagined in 15:17. Verse 19 picks up the theme of the way or path from verses 21 and 24 depicting the sluggard who becomes trapped while the "upright" find a "highway" or smooth path (cf. 22:4).

Verse 20 compares the wise to the foolish, but the mention of "father" and "mother" should not go unnoticed. The father and mother appear in 1:8; 6:20; 10:1; 15:13; and 31:10–31. As Waltke has observed, the parents continually reappear at the "seams" of the major divisions in Proverbs.[11] The "joy" of the father in 15:20 is ironically set against the "joy" that the simpleton finds in folly (v. 21).

Verse 22 continues the contrast between receiving and rejecting counsel (vv. 5, 10, 12, 31, 32). Notice that Proverbs prefers counselors that come in large numbers (cf. 11:14; 24:6); wisdom is enriched and strengthened by human contact with a breadth of cultural and personal perspectives.

Verse 23, like 26:4–5, treasures the right word at the right time and right place. The focus on time and fittingness appears again in the famous poem in Ecclesiastes 3:1–9, though with a tone of acquiescence.

The table below is adapted from Heim in order to demonstrate how catchwords provide unity to 15:24–27 and 28–33.[12]

Verse	"life" (*ḥayyim, nephesh*)	"house" (*bayit*)	YHWH	speech	"hear" (*shm*)	"heart" (*leb*)
24	Yes					
25		Yes	Yes			
26			Yes	Yes		
27	Yes	Yes		Yes		
28				Yes		Yes
29			Yes	Yes	Yes	
30				Yes	Yes	Yes
31	Yes			Yes	Yes	
32	Yes			Yes	Yes	Yes
33			Yes	Yes		

11. Waltke, *Proverbs 15–31*, 632. See "Structure" in the Introduction.
12. Heim, *Grapes of Gold*, 201–2.

24 The path of life leads upward for the prudent
  to keep them from going down to the realm of the dead.
25 The Lord tears down the house of the proud,
  but he sets the widow's boundary stones in place.
26 The Lord detests the thoughts of the wicked,
  but gracious words are pure in his sight.
27 The greedy bring ruin to their households,
  but the one who hates bribes will live.

15:24–27 Apart from 15:26, which isolates motives, these sayings all speak to behaviors and their consequences. The consequences—life and death—are spelled out in verses 24 and 27, which enclose the group of sayings.

The sayings are also united by the metaphors of ways and houses, which dominate chapters 1–9 as well. The "path of life" in 15:24 reiterates the way/path metaphor in verses 9, 10, 19, and 21. Like the path and way, the "house" (v. 25) and "household" (v. 27) symbolize lives of wisdom and righteousness and folly and wickedness.

Verses 25–26 are Yahweh-sayings, describing Yahweh's actions in judgment (v. 25) and his insight into human motives (v. 26). The "thoughts of the wicked" in verse 26 are an "abomination" (author's translation) to Yahweh (cf. 15:8–9).[13] Meanwhile, the "house of the proud" looks back to the houses of the wise and foolish women in 14:1.

Without a husband, the widow is an easy target for ruthless neighbors who would assume ownership at the unprotected borders of her land. Yahweh's protection of the widow's property (v. 26) shows his concern for the weak in society (cf. Deut 19:14; Prov 22:28; 23:10).

28 The heart of the righteous weighs its answers,
  but the mouth of the wicked gushes evil.
29 The Lord is far from the wicked,
  but he hears the prayer of the righteous.
30 Light in a messenger's eyes brings joy to the heart,
  and good news gives health to the bones.
31 Whoever heeds life-giving correction
  will be at home among the wise.
32 Those who disregard discipline despise themselves,
  but the one who heeds correction gains understanding.
33 Wisdom's instruction is to fear the Lord,
  and humility comes before honor.

---

13. NIV "detests."

15:28–33 The table above demonstrates several semantic patterns among these verses, notably speech, listening, and the heart. Verse 28 reinforces the virtue of patience in speech. Yet, as Fox rightly notes, the virtue of patience is not "self-evidently" true, since a fool may have an evil intent in waiting (1:11, 18; 12:6) and "conceal[ing] his hostility" (cf. 10:18; 26:26).[14] Patient speech should be motivated by an interest in the good of our neighbor.

Verse 29 returns to Yahweh hearing "prayer" as in verse 8. The favor Yahweh shows here parallels verses 25–26.

Blessings of good news and well-timed words have appeared already in 15:1, 2, 4, and 7 (cf. 25:25; 29:13), as they do here in 15:30. A literal translation of verse 30a is "bright eyes, happy heart . . . " The NIV adds that the light comes from a "messenger's eyes" in a desire to eliminate ambiguity and align the saying with verse 30b. But the light could describe a subjective or psychological experience: i.e., the state of one's heart can be seen in the eyes. Proverbs often intentionally creates these types of problems in order to force the reader to work out possible meanings.

Verses 31–33 commend receiving wise counsel. "Wisdom" is personified in 15:33, giving her own counsel to "fear the LORD," which, if listened to, will yield more wisdom (1:7; 9:10).

LIVE the Story

God's Searching Wisdom

Proverbs contains many sayings that encourage contemplative responses (see 14:10 and 13 above). Proverbs 30 is a dense collection of such sayings, for example, "There are three things that are too amazing for me, four that I do not understand" (30:18).

God's all-knowing wisdom makes for a common subject for contemplation (15:3, 11; 16:2; 17:3; 24:12). Similar passages are found throughout the Old Testament (Deut 29:29; Pss 7:9; 139; Jer 17:9–10; cf. Rev 2:23). The two contemplative sayings in chapter 15 describe God's knowledge of our intentions for right and wrong (v. 3) and our hearts (v. 11).

God's knowledge of the "heart," *leb*, deserves special attention because this word occurs nine times in this chapter, more often than in any other chapter in Proverbs. The heart represents a complex part of human nature: it has the power of communication (v. 7), emotion (v. 13), discernment (vv. 14, 28, 32), folly (v. 21), and joy (v. 30). Jeremiah 17:9–10 describes

---

14. Fox, *Proverbs 10–31*, 603.

a sickness of sin that keeps us from knowing our own hearts.

But Proverbs sounds a hopeful note to this problem. Commenting on verse 11, Murphy says, "If such mysterious places as Sheol, the realm of Death, and the resting place of the shades are not beyond God's ken, certainly humans are no puzzle."[15] Not only does God know our hearts, but he has placed wisdom within communities to give us access to what is otherwise hidden from our sight (20:5).

In the New Testament, Paul underscores the impenetrability of the deep motives and thoughts of our hearts. But Paul also assures us that the Holy Spirit acts as an interpreter and a mediator between our hearts and the father (1 Cor 2:11; Rom 8:27).

Wisdom, Worship, and Prayer

Chapter 15 sits at the center of Proverbs where the book turns to a succession of Yahweh-sayings and proverbs concerning the king. Many scholars suspect that these more religious and royal sayings were added to an earlier collection. While that is possible, we cannot know for certain. More importantly, the consistent testimony in the Old Testament is one in which wisdom, worship, and prayer go together (cf. Ps 90:12).

We have already mentioned how those with skills to build the temple and the tabernacle—those most central places of prayer and worship—were gifted with wisdom for their task (cf. Exod 28:3; 31:3, 6; 35:26, etc.; 1 Kgs 7:14; 1 Chr 28:21). Significantly, wisdom is the skill necessary to prepare for worship. In this light, we can note a further connection between the beauty and artistry of Israel's tabernacle and temple and the prayer and sacrifice that occurred in them. One implication of this seems to be that when we worship we are involved in observing and participating in artistic representation of eternal realities. If these things are made by wisdom, then wisdom must at least be a part of the imaginative and reverential activity of worship.

Solomon and David are also both depicted as kings of prayer, sacrifice, and wisdom (2 Sam 22:1–51 and 1 Kgs 3:6–15; 8:1–66). The passage in 1 Kings 1–11 is most often thought of in terms of the succession from David to Solomon and Solomon's prayer for wisdom. A very large part of the succession, which begins in 2 Samuel 22, is made up of prayer. First Kings 4 and the Psalter, in fact, testify to David's and Solomon's particular skill in writing psalms of prayer. The fact that David's words are cited almost word for word in Proverbs 30:5, just before the prayer in 30:7–9, is also illustrative of the relationship between wisdom and prayer (see Proverbs 30).

---

15. Murphy, *Proverbs*, 112.

LISTEN to the Story

¹ To humans belong the plans of the heart,
　　but from the LORD comes the proper answer of the tongue.
² All a person's ways seem pure to them,
　　but motives are weighed by the LORD.
³ Commit to the LORD whatever you do,
　　and he will establish your plans.
⁴ The LORD works out everything to its proper end—
　　even the wicked for a day of disaster.
⁵ The LORD detests all the proud of heart.
　　Be sure of this: They will not go unpunished.
⁶ Through love and faithfulness sin is atoned for;
　　through the fear of the LORD evil is avoided.
⁷ When the LORD takes pleasure in anyone's way,
　　he causes their enemies to make peace with them.
⁸ Better a little with righteousness
　　than much gain with injustice.
⁹ In their hearts humans plan their course,
　　but the LORD establishes their steps.
¹⁰ The lips of a king speak as an oracle,
　　and his mouth does not betray justice.
¹¹ Honest scales and balances belong to the LORD;
　　all the weights in the bag are of his making.
¹² Kings detest wrongdoing,
　　for a throne is established through righteousness.
¹³ Kings take pleasure in honest lips;
　　they value the one who speaks what is right.
¹⁴ A king's wrath is a messenger of death,
　　but the wise will appease it.
¹⁵ When a king's face brightens, it means life;

his favor is like a rain cloud in spring.
¹⁶ How much better to get wisdom than gold,
  to get insight rather than silver!
¹⁷ The highway of the upright avoids evil;
  those who guard their ways preserve their lives.
¹⁸ Pride goes before destruction,
  a haughty spirit before a fall.
¹⁹ Better to be lowly in spirit along with the oppressed
  than to share plunder with the proud.
²⁰ Whoever gives heed to instruction prospers,
  and blessed is the one who trusts in the LORD.
²¹ The wise in heart are called discerning,
  and gracious words promote instruction.
²² Prudence is a fountain of life to the prudent,
  but folly brings punishment to fools.
²³ The hearts of the wise make their mouths prudent,
  and their lips promote instruction.
²⁴ Gracious words are a honeycomb,
  sweet to the soul and healing to the bones.
²⁵ There is a way that appears to be right,
  but in the end it leads to death.
²⁶ The appetite of laborers works for them;
  their hunger drives them on.
²⁷ A scoundrel plots evil,
  and on their lips it is like a scorching fire.
²⁸ A perverse person stirs up conflict,
  and a gossip separates close friends.
²⁹ A violent person entices their neighbor
  and leads them down a path that is not good.
³⁰ Whoever winks with their eye is plotting perversity;
  whoever purses their lips is bent on evil.
³¹ Gray hair is a crown of splendor;
  it is attained in the way of righteousness.
³² Better a patient person than a warrior,
  one with self-control than one who takes a city.
³³ The lot is cast into the lap,
  but its every decision is from the LORD.

Listening to the Text in the Story: Job 28; 37–42; Psalms 2, 72, 101; Proverbs 1–9; 30; Ecclesiastes 6:7; 37:5; 72; 101; 1 Kings 2; *Ludlul Bel Nemeqi*

Psalms 2, 72, and 101 all depict Israelite kings who represent Yahweh in their rule over Israel. The "Lord and . . . his anointed" and "his son" (2:2, 7, 12; 72:1) execute justice, judgment, and vengeance against wickedness and unrighteousness (2:9, 12; 72:2–18; 101:5–8). In Proverbs 16, Yahweh and the king come alongside in an almost nearly identical fashion.

Proverbs 16 also repeatedly emphasizes themes from Proverbs 1–9, such as "wisdom," the "way," "the fear of the Lord," the centrality of the "heart," and the "wicked" and the "fool."

Chapter 16 also speaks to the limits of human wisdom—especially in the context of divine judgment. These themes appear elsewhere in Job and Proverbs 30 and many ancient Near Eastern texts. This passage comes from the Babylonian *Ludlul Bel Nemeqi*:

> What seems good to one's self could be an offence to god,
> What in one's own heart seems abominable
> Could be good to one's god!
> Who could learn the reasoning of the gods in heaven?
> Who could grasp the intentions of the gods of the depths?
> Where might human beings have learned the way of a god? (2:33–38)[1]

EXPLAIN the Story

In the introduction to chapters 10–29 we observed the strong signs of transition between chapters 10–15 and 16–29. On one hand, the overwhelming density of antithetical proverbs ("this *but* that") gives way to an emerging mosaic of sayings that are better-than, contemplative, synonymous, semi-synonymous, and uneven. On the other hand, we also meet the largest group of Yahweh sayings (15:33–16:11) and royal proverbs (vv. 10–15). The royal sayings are followed by sayings for the common people (vv. 16–24). A third fact to consider is that this chapter marks the center of the book as a whole (see commentary at 16:17).

These sayings divide fairly neatly into the following sections:

16:1–11	Yahweh sayings
16:10–15	Royal sayings
16:16–20	Sayings of the people

---

1. Translation from *BTM*, 314–14, cited in Fox, *Proverbs 10–31*, 607.

[1] To humans belong the plans of the heart,
   but from the LORD comes the proper answer of the tongue.
[2] All a person's ways seem pure to them,
   but motives are weighed by the LORD.
[3] Commit to the LORD whatever you do,
   and he will establish your plans.
[4] The LORD works out everything to its proper end—
   even the wicked for a day of disaster.
[5] The LORD detests all the proud of heart.
   Be sure of this: They will not go unpunished.
[6] Through love and faithfulness sin is atoned for;
   through the fear of the LORD evil is avoided.
[7] When the LORD takes pleasure in anyone's way,
   he causes their enemies to make peace with them.
[8] Better a little with righteousness
   than much gain with injustice.
[9] In their hearts humans plan their course,
   but the LORD establishes their steps.

I discuss these verses in smaller groupings in the commentary that follows.

16:1–9 Taken as a whole, verses 1–9 reveal how easily the human heart can be deluded, naïve, or led astray by impure motives (see "God's Searching Wisdom" in Proverbs 15). This tone of 16:1–9 encourages the reader to rely on divine assistance on the path through life. Verses 1–3, 7, and 9 deal with the paradoxical relationship between human plans and divine sovereignty—a frequent concern in Proverbs (3:5; 12:15; 19:21; 20:24; 21:2, 30–1; 27:1). We also find a progression of thought in each of the sayings in this chapter.

Hearts plan, but Yahweh's answer is definitive. Verse 2 reveals that Yahweh judges the motives in our planning. To avoid having our plans frustrated or being misled by our motives, verse 3 guides us to commit all our works to Yahweh. Verse 7 then explains the rationale for verse 3—Yahweh establishes our plans because he finds pleasure in our motives and faithfulness. Verse 9 essentially repeats 16:1 and thus closes the cluster of sayings (cf. Ps 37:5; 1 Pet 5:6–7).

Not only does 16:4 support the doctrine of divine retribution—God's supernatural punishment of evildoers—but it also pictures God using evil for his own ends. As Fox notes, the phrasing of verse 4b creates something of a surprise and an insult; God's interest in the day of judgment ranks higher than his concern for the wicked.[2] The context does not require us to believe that God creates wicked people simply to do evil to, or judge, them. Otherwise, all the appeals to be humble and commit our ways to Yahweh would be largely meaningless. Indeed, Proverbs often expresses matters in rhetorical overstatement, e.g., "I in turn will laugh when disaster strikes you; I will mock when calamity overtakes you . . . Then they will call to me but I will not answer; they will look for me but not find me" (1:26, 28). Surely the broader context in chapter 1 shows that this is a dramatic statement to provoke a response in us. Jesus often speaks in a comparative style: "If your right eye causes you to stumble, gouge it out and throw it away" (Matt 5:29). It is in the nature of such aphorisms to embellish matters to provoke a response. We should regard this passage as being much like Romans 9:19–24, which attempts to encourage our sense of humility and wonder in the fact of the mystery of an all-powerful God who judges evil and the wicked (cf. Prov 4:26).

Verse 5 resembles 11:21 and is also a variant of the condemnation of pride in 16:18.

Verse 6a says "love and faithfulness" cover sins, which parallels Yahweh's covenant faithfulness in Exodus 34:6. But, sitting alongside 16:6b, it seems just as likely that human "love and faithfulness" are in view, as in Proverbs 3:3 and Hosea 4:1–3.

Verse 8 is close to 15:16, only "the fear of the LORD" has been replaced with "righteousness." This may be intended to create a surprise, since the reader would expect the same phrase.[3] This kind of intricate change in wording is one of many signs of careful editorial activity at this midway point in Proverbs.

[10] The lips of a king speak as an oracle,
    and his mouth does not betray justice.
[11] Honest scales and balances belong to the LORD;
    all the weights in the bag are of his making.
[12] Kings detest wrongdoing,
    for a throne is established through righteousness.
[13] Kings take pleasure in honest lips;
    they value the one who speaks what is right.
[14] A king's wrath is a messenger of death,

2. Fox, *Proverbs 10–31*, 611.
3. So Heim, *Poetic Imagination*, 383.

but the wise will appease it.
¹⁵ When a king's face brightens, it means life;
   his favor is like a rain cloud in spring.

16:10–15 Four important points should be noted about this passage. First, "justice" in verses 8, 10, and 11 link this section together with verses 1–9.[4] Second, this link is strengthened by the apparent misplacement of verses 10 and 11—the king in the Yahweh section and Yahweh in the king section. Third, verses 10–15 offer a close parallel to the prayer of David in Psalm 101; both passages tie together Yahweh, piety, justice, and kingship. Fourth, the actions and values of the king mirror the actions and values of Yahweh in verses 1–9. (See more in Live the Story.)

Verses 14–15 deserve particular attention. In what sense are we to understand the "messenger of death" (v. 14)? In other words, is this righteous anger, or is it more like the anger of Saul and Solomon who sent out Doeg and Benaiah, respectively, to execute the vengeful death on their adversaries (1 Sam 22:6–19; 1 Kgs 2:25–46)? While these questions are hard to answer, the emphasis is on the wisdom that is able to appease an angry king (v. 14b).

Verse 15 expands the previous verse. The light of the face of Yahweh has positive connotations as in the Aaronic blessing in Numbers 6:24–27 (cf. Pss 4:6; 44:3), as do the lighted eyes of a friend or messenger (Prov 15:30). Even though kings often succumb to a short temper, the wise know the great benefits that come from brightening his spirit.

¹⁶ How much better to get wisdom than gold,
   to get insight rather than silver!
¹⁷ The highway of the upright avoids evil;
   those who guard their ways preserve their lives.
¹⁸ Pride goes before destruction,
   a haughty spirit before a fall.
¹⁹ Better to be lowly in spirit along with the oppressed
   than to share plunder with the proud.

16:16 This better-than saying relativizes material wealth, preferring wisdom and insight to silver and gold. The tone here extends from the better-than sayings in 15:16–17, while the reference to "gold" and "silver" echo earlier passages in Proverbs (Prov 3:14; 8:10, 19; cf. 1 Kgs 10:21–22).

16:17 This verse marks the midway point in Proverbs, combining several sayings from elsewhere in the book (13:3; 19:6; 21:23). Verse 17 adds

---

4. See Whybray, *Composition*, 89.

"highway" and "ways," likely to tie the saying into the surrounding context in the chapter (cf. 16:6, 25).

16:18–19 The cluster of proverbs in verses 16–19 ends with parallel sayings about pride and humility and riches and poverty. Pride usually leads to calamity or ruin; but the path of humility sometimes leaves the humble living among the "oppressed." The sayings prioritize internal virtues over transient material outcomes (cf. Prov 3:5, 7; 6:17; 11:2; 15:25; 18:12).

> [20] Whoever gives heed to instruction prospers,
>   and blessed is the one who trusts in the LORD.
> [21] The wise in heart are called discerning,
>   and gracious words promote instruction.
> [22] Prudence is a fountain of life to the prudent,
>   but folly brings punishment to fools.
> [23] The hearts of the wise make their mouths prudent,
>   and their lips promote instruction.
> [24] Gracious words are a honeycomb,
>   sweet to the soul and healing to the bones.

16:20–24 "Yahweh" in verse 20, which last appeared in verse 11, helps highlight the start to a new set of themes. All four verses are joined by words related to speech: a "word" (v. 20), "called" (v. 21), "lips" (vv. 21–23), and "instruction" (v. 23).[5] The sayings also emphasize "intellectual" vocabulary: "wise," discerning," "prudent," etc.[6] Altogether, the sayings commend wise speaking *and* wise listening. Meanwhile, verse 20 sets the sayings in the context of trust in the Lord. Furthermore, "sweet," "fountain of life," and "honeycomb" (vv. 21, 22, 24) all recall the sayings about the healing power of speech in chapter 15 (vv. 1–2, 4, 7, 23, 26, 30–31; cf. 24:13–14).

> [25] There is a way that appears to be right,
>   but in the end it leads to death.
> [26] The appetite of laborers works for them;
>   their hunger drives them on.

16:25–26 16:25 repeats 14:12 and resumes the theme of the limits of human wisdom from 16:1–9 and the "way" in verse 17. Verse 26 observes the obvious fact that most of our labor is driven by our need to eat. The affluence in modern, Western culture is a rare exception to the rule. "Laborer" and "work" both come from the root 'ml—a word that often caries a negative connotation (cf.

---

5. "Word" = NIV "instruction;" "sweet lips" = NIV "gracious words" (v. 21); and "instruction" = NIV "punishment" (v. 22).
6. See Heim, *Grapes of Gold*, 218–19.

Prov 24:2; 31:7). The saying leaves the reader to contemplate the relationship between work, need, and desire. As Leon Kass observes, "For lack, experienced as desire, is the spur to all aspiration, to action and awareness, to having life at all."[7]

[27] A scoundrel plots evil,
       and on their lips it is like a scorching fire.
[28] A perverse person stirs up conflict,
       and a gossip separates close friends.
[29] A violent person entices their neighbor
       and leads them down a path that is not good.
[30] Whoever winks with their eye is plotting perversity;
       whoever purses their lips is bent on evil.
[31] Gray hair is a crown of splendor;
       it is attained in the way of righteousness.
[32] Better a patient person than a warrior,
       one with self-control than one who takes a city.
[33] The lot is cast into the lap,
       but its every decision is from the LORD.

16:27–33 This final cluster of proverbs describes a sequence of six different types of people, four negative and two positive. The characterizations are also imaginatively portrayed in a sequence of three specific persons and four people described by bodily metaphors.

27	"A man malicious . . ."	30	"eye" and "lips"
28	"A man perverse . . ."	31	"gray hair"
29	"A man violent . . ."	32	"long nose"
		33	"lap"

The first three characters invoke scorn and condemnation for the deceit, division, and violence in their speech. The "path that is not good" in 16:29 recalls the "way" that "leads to death" in 16:25.

Verse 30 creates a pivot in this group of sayings. It continues this series of sayings about unsavory characters in verses 27–29, but it starts a series of people imagined by bodily metaphors in 30–33. But in terms of content, 16:30 fits with the group of condemned characters (27–30) preceding examples of model behavior (31–32). The sophisticated rhetoric and imagery work to provoke a response (see "Human Oglers" in Live the Story).

---

7. Leon Kass, *The Hungry Soul: Eating and the Perfection of our Nature* (Chicago: The University of Chicago, 1999), 27.

Verse 33 retains the sequence of bodily terms ("lap") while drawing the chapter to a close with a common refrain that God is sovereign in his knowledge of our hearts and his judgment of our actions. In the words of Thomas à Kempis, "Man proposes, God disposes."[8]

LIVE the Story

Human Limits

In his book *For the Life of the World*, Orthodox theologian Alexander Schmemann speaks of our instinct to refuse to submit our human reason to the mysteries of God. And in seeking to know more on our own sure ground, we come to know less of those things that are firmly grounded.[9] Gerhard von Rad similarly devotes a whole chapter of his *Wisdom in Israel* to the limits of human wisdom. "It is," von Rad says, "a question not of something which a man does not know, but ought to know and perhaps even could know, but of something he can never know" (cf. 16:1–3, 9, 33; 19:14, 21; 21:30–1). He continues, "Wisdom can never become the object of trust, never become that upon which a man leans in life" (cf. 3:5, 7; 26:12; 27:1; 28:11, 26).[10] The limits of wisdom are discussed further in the commentary on chapter 30.

The teachers of wisdom do not leave us to merely bow to fate, and they never recommend abandoning wisdom because of its limits. Rather, they continually remind us of the central tenet of wisdom, which is to know how to live within human limits—moral and intellectual. Fox rightly says, "While no one can fathom the divine wisdom or control God's will by the exercise of his own wisdom and virtue, one *can* conform to God's standards."[11] Paul similarly warns against confidence in human wisdom, all the while encouraging the pursuit of godly knowledge (1 Cor 8:1–13). For us Jesus is wisdom from God (1 Cor 1:24) in whom we know how to live and act (Col 1:9–10) and have access to all wisdom, revelation, and the love and peace that transcend human knowledge (Eph 3:19; Phil 4:7). In this way Christ holds together a paradox that we don't have in the Old Testament. In his life, death, and resurrection he reveals the full knowledge to which wisdom could only point. And yet what he reveals still lies beyond the limits of the imagination.

---

8. Thomas à Kempis, *The Imitation of Christ: A New Reading of the 1441 Latin Autograph Manuscript* (Macon, GA: Mercer University Press, 2007), 20.

9. Alexander Schmemann, *For the Life of the World: Sacraments and Orthodoxy*, rev. 2nd ed. (Crestwood, NY: St. Vladimir's Seminary Press, 1973), 117–51.

10. Von Rad, *Wisdom in Israel*, 102–3. See also pp. 97–110, 113–38.

11. Fox, *Proverbs 10–31*, 606 (emphasis original).

Gods, Kings, and Subjects

Within Proverbs 16:1–24 lay a rich theology of divine-human relations and human vocation. Verses 1–9 and 11 introduce a series of reflections on divine action and divine knowledge beginning with verses 1–2, which address us by our most basic creational names *adam* and *ish* ("a man;" cf. v. 7). The chapter then moves fluidly from sayings of Yahweh (1–9), to the king (10–15), to common subjects (11–24). Moreover, verse 11 is a Yahweh saying among the royal sayings, which serves to establish God as the standard for the king's justice.[12] The sayings in 1–9 and 10–15 are also linked by the placement of two more terms usually used in connection with Yahweh: *toebah*, "abomination," among the royal sayings (16:12), and *retson/ratsah*, "pleasure," in both sets of sayings (16:7, 13, 15). Heim comments that these "descriptions . . . reinforce the king's close affinity to the Lord."[13]

Thus, as the chapter progresses from Yahweh to king to subject, each role/person exemplifies the behavior of its successor.[14] As in the doctrine of the *imago Dei* in Genesis and the pairing of the king and Yahweh in Psalms (1–2; 8; 45; 69; 111; etc.), God, king, and subjects are tied together organically in their identity and purpose. Wise human agents are a "kingdom of priests" doing God's work in the world (Exod 19:6; cf. 1 Pet 2:9; Rev 1:6). Christ is our representative king in whom we reign and in whose power and authority we go about our ministry in his reconciliation of all things (2 Cor 5:16–21). For this reason Paul commends us to lives of holiness in the pattern of the divine: "Follow my example, as I follow the example of Christ" (1 Cor 11:1). Not only should we see this as an exhortation to look for a model of living through Paul's life to the life of Christ, but we should also look beyond us to children and children's children to whom we are responsible to reveal Christ in our walk.

Human Oglers

The late novelist and essayist David Foster Wallace once wrote,

> Fiction writers as a species tend to be oglers. They are born watchers . . .
> viewers . . . But fiction writers tend at the same time to be terribly self-
> conscious. Devoting lots of productive time to studying closely how peo-
> ple come across to them, fiction writers also spend lots of less productive
> time wondering nervously how they come across to other people.[15]

---

12. Heim, *Grapes of Gold*, 211.
13. Ibid., 214–15.
14. See Van Leeuwen, *Proverbs*, 157–58.
15. David Foster Wallace, "E Unibus Pluram: Television and U.S. Fiction" in *A Supposedly Fun Thing I'll Never Do Again* (New York: Little, Brown & Company, 1997), 21.

Thinking about how other people act and look naturally disposes us to look in the mirror, which is the immediate effect of Proverbs 16:27–32.

The threefold sequence of "man" as the first word (in Hebrew) in verses 27–29 forms a vivid image of ruthless fellows, arousing our ire and hatred. Yet the turn to "Whoever winks with their eye . . ." (v. 30) slows the pace of these lines, drawing our attention to the specific actions of a winking eye and pursed lips. The images force us to embody their behaviors, even if reluctantly (try thinking about pursing lips without pursing your lips).[16] This response phenomena is discussed further in Live the Story in Proverbs 22 and 25. The subtle changes in style and imagery in this chapter move us from external ogling to self-conscious reflection and transformation.

The poem creatively closes with two embodied images: "gray hair," and "long noses" (NIV "patient"). These are pictures we would all prefer of ourselves to those in the previous characters. Proverbs continually puts us in the place of the fiction writer: we study ourselves and others in order to become wise, righteous, patient, and self-controlled. (See also "Brief Interviews with Wicked and Righteous Men" in Live the Story in Prov 29).

---

16. See See David Freedberg and Vittorio Gallese, "Motion, Emotion and Empathy in Esthetic Experience," *Trends in Cognitive Sciences* 11.5 (2007): 201.

LISTEN to the Story

¹ Better a dry crust with peace and quiet
   than a house full of feasting, with strife.
² A prudent servant will rule over a disgraceful son
   and will share the inheritance as one of the family.
³ The crucible for silver and the furnace for gold,
   but the LORD tests the heart.
⁴ A wicked person listens to deceitful lips;
   a liar pays attention to a destructive tongue.
⁵ Whoever mocks the poor shows contempt for their Maker;
   whoever gloats over disaster will not go unpunished.
⁶ Children's children are a crown to the aged,
   and parents are the pride of their children.
⁷ Eloquent lips are unsuited to a godless fool—
   how much worse lying lips to a ruler!
⁸ A bribe is seen as a charm by the one who gives it;
   they think success will come at every turn.
⁹ Whoever would foster love covers over an offense,
   but whoever repeats the matter separates close friends.
¹⁰ A rebuke impresses a discerning person
   more than a hundred lashes a fool.
¹¹ Evildoers foster rebellion against God;
   the messenger of death will be sent against them.
¹² Better to meet a bear robbed of her cubs
   than a fool bent on folly.
¹³ Evil will never leave the house
   of one who pays back evil for good.
¹⁴ Starting a quarrel is like breaching a dam;
   so drop the matter before a dispute breaks out.
¹⁵ Acquitting the guilty and condemning the innocent—

the LORD detests them both.

[16] Why should fools have money in hand to buy wisdom,
   when they are not able to understand it?

[17] A friend loves at all times,
   and a brother is born for a time of adversity.

[18] One who has no sense shakes hands in pledge
   and puts up security for a neighbor.

[19] Whoever loves a quarrel loves sin;
   whoever builds a high gate invites destruction.

[20] One whose heart is corrupt does not prosper;
   one whose tongue is perverse falls into trouble.

[21] To have a fool for a child brings grief;
   there is no joy for the parent of a godless fool.

[22] A cheerful heart is good medicine,
   but a crushed spirit dries up the bones.

[23] The wicked accept bribes in secret
   to pervert the course of justice.

[24] A discerning person keeps wisdom in view,
   but a fool's eyes wander to the ends of the earth.

[25] A foolish son brings grief to his father
   and bitterness to the mother who bore him.

[26] If imposing a fine on the innocent is not good,
   surely to flog honest officials is not right.

[27] The one who has knowledge uses words with restraint,
   and whoever has understanding is even-tempered.

[28] Even fools are thought wise if they keep silent,
   and discerning if they hold their tongues.

Listening to the Text in the Story: Psalms 12:6; 37:16; Jeremiah 9:7; Isaiah 1:24–26, 48:10; Zechariah 13:8–9

EXPLAIN the Story

The book of Proverbs was structured with pedagogical interests in mind: it begins with a combination of provocative and cosmic poems in chapters 1–9, progresses to a repetition of familiar patterns in the sayings in chapters 11–15, and then introduces a variety of increasingly difficult sayings in chapters 16–30.

The vast majority of scholars recognize these patterns within these sections of Proverbs, and yet few scholars acknowledge that the structure has such thoughtful educational ambitions: first to inspire and motivate, second to establish the basic rules, and third to instill skill through increasingly complex drills.

In Proverbs 15 and onward, we see a variety of subjects that incorporate previous proverbs into new sayings. Knut Heim has shown that Proverbs consistently recombines topics and individual lines from one place into new sayings in other places. In this light, it makes sense that, as we advance beyond chapter 15, we encounter more and more repeated sayings and less predictability and easily structured groups of sayings. Proverbs 17 is the first chapter to have very little discernable structure.[1] Its sayings flow seamlessly from the material in chapters 15–16 and touch on a surprisingly wide range of familiar subjects: family (vv. 1, 2, 6, 21, 25), speech (vv. 1, 2, 4, 5, 7, 14, 20, 27, 28), discernment (vv. 4, 10, 27), wisdom and folly (7, 10, 12, 16, 21, 24, 24, 28), friends and neighbors (vv. 9, 17, 18), grief and sorrow (vv. 21–25), messengers (vv. 11, 14), a "bribe" (v. 8), the heart (vv. 19, 20, 22), things not fitting (v. 2), and testing.

In sum, in interpreting this chapter and the rest of 16–30, it will be productive to look for the educational objectives that arise in the combination of topics and repeated lines.

> [17:1] Better a dry crust with peace and quiet
> than a house full of feasting, with strife.
> [2] A prudent servant will rule over a disgraceful son
> and will share the inheritance as one of the family.
> [3] The crucible for silver and the furnace for gold,
> but the LORD tests the heart.
> [4] A wicked person listens to deceitful lips;
> a liar pays attention to a destructive tongue.
> [5] Whoever mocks the poor shows contempt for their Maker;
> whoever gloats over disaster will not go unpunished.
> [6] Children's children are a crown to the aged,
> and parents are the pride of their children.

17:1–6 Waltke and Heim observe a section of sayings running from 16:31–17:6, capped at either end by the catchword *'ateret*, "crown." Heim further observes sustained attention to topics of family, testing, and speech in 16:31–17:9.[2] I have chosen to focus on the topics of family and testing in verses 1–6.

---

1. Heim, *Grapes of Gold*, 226.
2. Ibid., 228–29.

Verses 1–3 could all be labeled "contemplative," as each saying demands that the reader reflect on some matter of value or mysterious aspect of the world. The saying in 17:1 repeats the emphasis on contentment in 15:16–17 and 16:8 (cf. Ps 37:16). However, the NIV "feasting" could be also translated "contentious sacrifices,"[3] in which there is a certain irony in people coming to make peace with God and yet being divided against one another.

Verse 2 shows an example of a social paradox where a lowly person displaces a rightful heir (cf. 19:10; 30:22). Biblical laws favor the protection of family inheritances (Lev 25:8–55; Num 27:1–11; 36:1–12), and so the proverb may say more about the proper conduct of sons than it promises servants a hope of another family's inheritance. 17:3 follows naturally as a reminder that God tests and sees beneath the surface of our actions to our hearts (cf. 15:11; 16:1, 9; 19:21; 20:5; 21:1). The metaphor of testing in a furnace is common (Ps 12:6; Isa 1:24–6; 48:10; Jer 9:7; Zech 12:8–9).

Verse 4 resembles the sayings in 16:27–32, in which the reader observes others as an exercise in self-reflection—here regarding our resistance to falsehood and destruction.

Verse 5 repeats a sentiment expressed in 14:21 and 31 (see commentary and Live the Story in ch. 14). What we do to image-bearers, we do to the creator (cf. 3:12; 19:17: 22:2). This resembles Jesus' sayings in Matthew 25:35–46 that what we do "for one of the least of these" we do for God who claims them. Verse 6 returns to the celebration of old age and the mutual joys that grandparents, parents, and children share in relation to one another.

⁷ Eloquent lips are unsuited to a godless fool—
    how much worse lying lips to a ruler!
⁸ A bribe is seen as a charm by the one who gives it;
    they think success will come at every turn.
⁹ Whoever would foster love covers over an offense,
    but whoever repeats the matter separates close friends.

17:7–9 Waltke describes this section as a janus, looking forward and back.[4] Falsehood and speech (v. 7) looks back to the previous context (vv. 1, 2, 4, 5). "Eloquent" could be translated "excessive," indicating one who says too much (cf. 10:19). The open-ended phrase "unsuited" appears again in 19:10 and in 26:1, where it introduces a list of circumstances that do not fit. Wisdom is largely a matter of hermeneutics or discerning patterns and appropriateness.

The NIV attempts to resolve ambiguity in 17:8. "One who gives it [a bribe]" is "its owner." The owner could refer to the briber or the bribee. In fact,

3. Fox, *Proverbs 10–31*, 623–4.
4. Waltke, *Proverbs 15–31*, 47–49.

it could be both, as the bribe is valued by both parties and brings "success" to each of them in their own way. (See the "Power of a Bribe" in Live the Story.)

In 17:9 one who loves overlooks an offense—even seven times seven times (cf. Matt 18:21–35; cf. 1 Cor 13:5). The end of 17:9b, "separates close friends," repeats part of 16:28. Proverbs cares about relationships: the family in verses 1–8 and friends and neighbors in 17:9, 17–18.

> ¹⁰ A rebuke impresses a discerning person more
>   than a hundred lashes a fool.
> ¹¹ Evildoers foster rebellion against God;
>   the messenger of death will be sent against them.
> ¹² Better to meet a bear robbed of her cubs
>   than a fool bent on folly.

17:10–12 Two sayings about folly surround a central saying about justice. Verse 10 echoes many other sayings that teach the wisdom of listening to the advice of others (12:15; 15:31–32; 19:25). "Evildoers," by virtue of their placement here, are fools who disregard God's authority and power. The "messenger of death" is a common motif, often associated with an angel who renders a judgment of death, or death itself (cf. 16:14; 1 Sam 19:14–15; 2 Kgs 6:32; Pss 35:5–6; 78:49).[5]

In 17:12 a "bear robbed of her cubs" does not imagine sorrow but rage and violence that is somehow better than a fool in his worst state.

> ¹³ Evil will never leave the house
>   of one who pays back evil for good.
> ¹⁴ Starting a quarrel is like breaching a dam;
>   so drop the matter before a dispute breaks out.
> ¹⁵ Acquitting the guilty and condemning the innocent—
>   the LORD detests them both.
> ¹⁶ Why should fools have money in hand to buy wisdom,
>   when they are not able to understand it?

17:13–16 These verses are another loosely connected group of sayings. The disregard for justice in verse 13 echoes verse 11 and anticipates verse 15, and all of them imply some level of divine retributive justice. The latter saying (v. 15) repeats the rule in Deuteronomy 25:1, emphasizing God's strong emotional orientation to matters of justice.

Several passages in this chapter use elements of nature (vv. 1, 12, 14) and human industry (vv. 3, 6, 8, 19, 22) as object lessons for wisdom. Starting

---

5. See Ibid., 52.

arguments is like "breaching a dam." Proverbs 26:17 expresses a similar lesson comparing quarrels to "one who grabs a stray dog by the ears."

As expressed in 17:16, money is often used as a metaphor to express the value of wisdom (cf. 4:5, 7; 16:16; 20:14). Just as someone would not buy what they do not need or cannot use, so wisdom is not "fit" for fools (cf. 17:7). The NIV "not able to understand" can be literally translated "has no sense [heart]," which anticipates "has no sense [heart]" in verse 18, the "heart is corrupt" in verse 20, and the "cheerful heart" in verse 22.

> ¹⁷ A friend loves at all times,
>> and a brother is born for a time of adversity.
> ¹⁸ One who has no sense shakes hands in pledge
>> and puts up security for a neighbor.
> ¹⁹ Whoever loves a quarrel loves sin;
>> whoever builds a high gate invites destruction.
> ²⁰ One whose heart is corrupt does not prosper;
>> one whose tongue is perverse falls into trouble.

17:17–20 Verses 17 and 18 play on two related meanings of *rea*: "friend" and "neighbor." The first saying observes the mysterious gift of a friend who becomes as a member of the family (cf. 18:24; 27:10). Verse 18 reflects on the important distinction between such a friend and a neighbor or fellow citizen who is nevertheless too distant to warrant accepting risks on their behalf. While Proverbs commends generosity, it warns against gambling on unknowns and risk that jeopardizes family wealth (6:1–5; cf. 11:15; 20:16; 22:26; 27:13).

The two negative instances of "love" in verse 19 reverse the positive use of "love" in verse 17. Also, while the terms for "quarrel" here and in verse 14 are different, the principle is the same. The meaning of "high gate," literally "high door," is difficult to interpret; given the surrounding context, the "door" is probably a metaphor for the mouth and "high" a description of its pride (cf. 12:12; 11:27; 13:24).

Verse 20 is another saying about a corrupt heart (cf. vv. 16, 18), which undergirds "perverse" speech that leads only to undesired consequences (cf. 10:31–32).

> ²¹ To have a fool for a child brings grief;
>> there is no joy for the parent of a godless fool.
> ²² A cheerful heart is good medicine,
>> but a crushed spirit dries up the bones.
> ²³ The wicked accept bribes in secret
>> to pervert the course of justice.

²⁴ A discerning person keeps wisdom in view,
  but a fool's eyes wander to the ends of the earth.
²⁵ A foolish son brings grief to his father
  and bitterness to the mother who bore him.

17:21–25 Some commentators view verses 21–28 as the final cluster of sayings in the chapter. To be sure, the themes and language are fluid enough to allow us to organize the material in various ways. This section breaks with an alternative form of proverbs in verse 26.

Verses 21 and 25 cap this group of sayings through the repetition of "father," fool," and "begetting" (omitted in the NIV). The sayings reverse the pride held by parents, grandparents, and children in verse 6 to show the "grief" that comes to a family with foolish children.

In 17:22 the "cheerful heart" signifies an inner attitude or conscious spirit of rejoicing, which Qohelet repeatedly calls for in his *carpe diem* sayings (cf. Eccl 2:10; 3:12, 22; 5:18; 8:15; 10:19; 11:8–9).

Verse 23 returns to the themes of bribe and justice (vv. 8, 13, 15). Legal rules in the Pentateuch also qualify bribes as a matter of injustice (cf. Exod 23:8; Deut 16:19). (See Live the Story below.)

The language in 17:24 does not translate directly into English. Waltke suggests that the Hebrew wording "before his face" (NIV "in view") "connotes . . . personal responsibility" in contrast to the fool who lacks a conscientious appreciation for the world right in front of him.[6]

²⁶ If imposing a fine on the innocent is not good,
  surely to flog honest officials is not right.
²⁷ The one who has knowledge uses words with restraint,
  and whoever has understanding is even-tempered.
²⁸ Even fools are thought wise if they keep silent,
  and discerning if they hold their tongues.

17:26–28 Verse 26 provides an example of litotes, or understatement that provokes counter-reactions: "Not good" and "not right" speak to grievous injustices (cf. commentary at 19:2, 10 and 26:1).

Verse 27 reads more literally, "The holder of words knows knowledge; and one with a cool spirit has understanding." The saying leads us to imagine two people very much along the lines of the people depicted in 16:27–32 and 17:4 (see commentary at 16:27).

Verse 28 is a parallel saying, which teaches that caution and patience are virtues essential to wisdom.

---

6. Waltke, *Proverbs 15–31*, 62.

The Power of a Bribe

Proverbs addresses bribery on four occasions. Most of us probably recognize a bribe as money or a gift given to compel someone to something unjust or immoral—usually in a political or judicial context. But a closer look at the ethical nature of the bribe makes this act more complicated than we might imagine.

For one, bribes are not only political and judicial acts, but actions carried out in every sphere of human life. As the legal scholar John T. Noonan observes, the bribe is something we discover in "action or thought, conduct or language—in criminal prosecutions, in the text of laws, in administrative rules, in political slogans, in confessions, homilies, editorials, news, stories, and diaries."[7] Bribes have been most frequent historically among politicians, judges, and journalists. The US Constitution only names two crimes—treason and bribery. The health of a nation and a society is easily threatened by this crime.

Noonan describes the bribe as having four dimensions: (1) an inducement by the briber, (2) intending improper influence, (3) in a public function, and (4) an action carried out gratuitously by the bribee. To determine whether something is a gift or a bribe, we have to apply each of these dimensions to the particular situational and cultural setting.[8] Significantly, apart from the requirement for the act to influence a public function, each part involves a measure of motivation and intent (desire) of the giver or the recipient of the gift.

The Hebrew verb *shohad*, "bribe," comes from a verb "to give a gift," which occurs only twice in the Old Testament (Job 6:22; Ezek 16:33). The noun form occurs twenty-three times and consistently occurs in contexts forbidding the taking of bribes.[9] A bribe perverts justice: it "blinds those who see" and "twists the words of the innocent" (Exod 23:8; cf. Deut 16:18). God refuses to take a bribe so as not to jeopardize his protection of the weak and outcast (Deut 10:17–18; cf. 2 Chron 19:7). Here we can see that the Old Testament always imagines a bribe as influencing a public function.

The four occurrences of *shohad* in Proverbs are primarily concerned with motives or affections. Proverbs 17:8 literally describes the bribe as a "magic stone in the eyes of its owner; wherever he turns he prospers." The bribe here

---

7. John T. Noonan, *Bribes* (New York: Macmillan, 1984), xi.
8. Ibid.
9. M. A. Grisanti/J. C. McCann, "*shd*," *NIDOTTE* 4:75–76.

motivates the heart with an almost supernatural power, both in the desire for the gift itself and for the change the gift can bring about. Proverbs 21:14 says that "A gift given in secret soothes anger, and a bribe concealed in the [bosom] pacifies great wrath." Interestingly, neither of these two sayings directly condemns bribery in any judicial sense; instead, each illumines the motives and desires of those involved in such transactions and has a way of democratizing the bribe, or taking an offense common to kings and judges and making them applicable to all people.

So how does Proverbs' teaching on the bribe apply to us? In her study of virtue and vice, Rebecca Konyndyk DeYoung observes, "In both our giving and our getting, greed corrodes the virtue of generosity and leads us to ignore the claims of justice."[10] And so bribery brings to the surface deeper issues of our ability to tame our desires for wealth, opportunity, privilege, and, above all, control. The bribe also exposes the vices of envy and covetousness that fight against the virtue of contentment (cf. Prov 13:25; 15:16–17). DeYoung continues, "The hallmark of well-entrenched greed, then, is a willingness to use people to serve our love for money [or power, position, notoriety], rather than the use of money [power, etc.] to serve our love for people."[11]

Given the sinful nature of our hearts (Gen 8:21), is it ever possible to give a gift without undue influence or some hope for a gratuitous benefit? In a biblical sense, no—all gifts involve the fallible intentions of the heart. But, as David Daube astutely observes, "we can distinguish between inevitable fallibility of a general kind and conscious, crass misconduct . . ."[12]

Proverbs 21:14 leaves open the possibility that using a bribe to assuage anger might be morally justifiable, but it must be taken alongside the rest of Proverbs, particularly 6:35. Proverbs' silence on morality in such cases is part and parcel with the nature of the book, which requires us to answer the matter not for personal benefit or comfort but in a way that best fits within the scope of wisdom as a whole.

Judas's Bribe and Kiss

All four Gospels capture the shocking event of Judas's betrayal of Jesus through a bribe of thirty silver pieces and a deceitful kiss in the garden (Matt 26:14–16, 47–56; cf. Mark 14:10–11; 43–50; Luke 22:3–6, 47–53; John 13:2, 27, 30; 18:3–11). The scene is a window into the great mystery of sinful and

10. Rebecca Konyndyk DeYoung, *Glittering Vices: A New Look at the Seven Deadly Sins and Their Vices* (Grand Rapids: Brazos, 2009), 101.
11. Ibid., 109.
12. David Daube, "A Corrupt Judge Sets the Pace," in *Daube on Roman Law*, ed. Calum Carmichael and Laurent Mayali (Berkeley, CA: The Robbins Collection, 2013), 35–52.

rebellious human hearts. On the one hand, the bribe given "in secret" reveals Judas's willingness to distort "justice" (Prov 17:23). In Proverbs 17:8 the bribe is a "charm" and a false promise of "success." This leads us to wonder at the deluded, manipulative, and selfish motives that led Judas to such treachery, especially after having been a close companion of the incarnate Son of God (cf. Prov 17:23). On the other hand, Judas's kiss is an act of one who "separates close friends" (17:9) and a stark image of "an enemy [who] multiplies kisses" (27:6). The close friendship is the source of the worst form of betrayal.

But in the providence of God, Judas's hand in Jesus' death is the act that leads to the cancelling of sin and the death of death. Jesus thus stands in complete contrast to Judas and the others who deny him as well. He was the friend who would not accept a bribe, would not pervert justice, and would offer his life to redeem all betrayal and unfaithfulness.

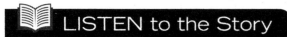

¹ An unfriendly person pursues selfish ends
    and against all sound judgment starts quarrels.
² Fools find no pleasure in understanding
    but delight in airing their own opinions.
³ When wickedness comes, so does contempt,
    and with shame comes reproach.
⁴ The words of the mouth are deep waters,
    but the fountain of wisdom is a rushing stream.
⁵ It is not good to be partial to the wicked
    and so deprive the innocent of justice.
⁶ The lips of fools bring them strife,
    and their mouths invite a beating.
⁷ The mouths of fools are their undoing,
    and their lips are a snare to their very lives.
⁸ The words of a gossip are like choice morsels;
    they go down to the inmost parts.
⁹ One who is slack in his work
    is brother to one who destroys.
¹⁰ The name of the LORD is a fortified tower;
    the righteous run to it and are safe.
¹¹ The wealth of the rich is their fortified city;
    they imagine it a wall too high to scale.
¹² Before a downfall the heart is haughty,
    but humility comes before honor.
¹³ To answer before listening—
    that is folly and shame.
¹⁴ The human spirit can endure in sickness,
    but a crushed spirit who can bear?
¹⁵ The heart of the discerning acquires knowledge,

265

for the ears of the wise seek it out.
[16] A gift opens the way
    and ushers the giver into the presence of the great.
[17] In a lawsuit the first to speak seems right,
    until someone comes forward and cross-examines.
[18] Casting the lot settles disputes
    and keeps strong opponents apart.
[19] A brother wronged is more unyielding than a fortified city;
    disputes are like the barred gates of a citadel.
[20] From the fruit of their mouth a person's stomach is filled;
    with the harvest of their lips they are satisfied.
[21] The tongue has the power of life and death,
    and those who love it will eat its fruit.
[22] He who finds a wife finds what is good
    and receives favor from the LORD.
[23] The poor plead for mercy,
    but the rich answer harshly.
[24] One who has unreliable friends soon comes to ruin,
    but there is a friend who sticks closer than a brother.

Listening to the Text in the Story: Psalms 20:2; 54:3

The broad range of topics in Proverbs 18 yields an endless list of parallel passages in the Bible. Among these, two Old Testament themes deserve emphasis here. The saying in Proverbs 18:10 resembles many Psalms where Yahweh is depicted as a strong fortress and his name as a place of safety (Pss 2:12; 20:1–2; 44:5; 54:3; 91:2; 118:10). Also, the false trust in riches in Proverbs 18:11 is present in Psalms (20:7; 33:16–18; cf. Isa 31:1). Other themes emerge in the commentary below.

EXPLAIN the Story

Amidst a wide variety of sayings in this chapter we find a strong concentration concerning speech (4, 6, 7, 8, 13, 20, 21, 23), friends, quarrels, divisions (1, 6, 17, 18, 19, 24), and justice (5, 17, 18, 19, 23). While the content of the chapter shifts at many points, the chapter is held together by several literary structures and catchwords.

¹ An unfriendly person pursues selfish ends
   and against all sound judgment starts quarrels.
² Fools find no pleasure in understanding
   but delight in airing their own opinions.
³ When wickedness comes, so does contempt,
   and with shame comes reproach.
⁴ The words of the mouth are deep waters,
   but the fountain of wisdom is a rushing stream.
⁵ It is not good to be partial to the wicked
   and so deprive the innocent of justice.

18:1–5 This first section focuses on speech, community, and division within community. The material in chapter 17 also noticeably influences this section and verses 6–9.

The saying about selfishness and division in 18:1 sets the context for the first nine verses and, more loosely, for everything through verse 24, which closes the chapter with a reflection on friendship and acquaintances who foster division. Verse 2 makes a slight shift from selfishness to self-confidence. The selfish "opinion" [NIV] is the Hebrew word *leb* "heart"—a theme repeated in 18:12 (cf. 3:5; 11:12; 26:12).

The saying in 18:3 presents several layers of ambiguity. Does the first line suggest that wicked people show outward "contempt," or does their behavior make them contemptible to others? Both could be true. The second line may just be a parallel thought—those who "shame" are reproached. But, given the near synonymity of "contempt" and "shame," Longman sees continuity in the two lines: after "contempt," "insults will follow."[1] Compare a counter-saying in 22:10.

Verse 4 is another challenging saying. The NIV opposes "deep waters" to a "rushing stream." Yet the contrastive word "but" is not present in Hebrew, and it seems more likely the two lines are synonymous sayings about the speech of the wise, which are deep in richness and abundant in giving life (cf. vv. 8, 20, 21 and 17:27, 28).

In verse 5 the selfishness and division expressed elsewhere in this chapter are imagined in light of the judicial consequences that result for the "innocent" (cf. 17:26). We saw the phrase "not good" in 17:7 and 26; it appears again in 19:2; 20:23; 25:27; 28:21 and resembles sayings that express things "not fitting" (see 19:2, 10; 26:1).

---

1. Longman, *Proverbs*, 354.

⁶ The lips of fools bring them strife,
   and their mouths invite a beating.
⁷ The mouths of fools are their undoing,
   and their lips are a snare to their very lives.
⁸ The words of a gossip are like choice morsels;
   they go down to the inmost parts.
⁹ One who is slack in his work
   is brother to one who destroys.

18:6–9 Verses 6–7 are paired sayings, which is most evident in the chiastic movement from lips/mouths to mouths/lips in the four sequential lines. The nature of the "beating" in verse 6b could refer to the fools' punishment or else social unrest fools bring about. 18:7 warns that foolish speech can boomerang to the speaker.

Verses 8–9 portray two vivid pictures of foolish and sinful behavior that divide a community. Speaking to the phrase "Gossip [is] like choice morsels" (18:8), Van Leeuwen describes gossip as "junk food" and Longman calls it "irresistible"—we crave rumors and spreading them.[2]

In 18:9 the one "slack in his work" injures those around him (cf. 28:24). The word *baal mashit* at the end of the verse is uncertain and could be translated "chief of killers"[3] or "head vandal." Both suggest patently destructive behavior.

¹⁰ The name of the LORD is a fortified tower;
   the righteous run to it and are safe.
¹¹ The wealth of the rich is their fortified city;
   they imagine it a wall too high to scale.
¹² Before a downfall the heart is haughty,
   but humility comes before honor.
¹³ To answer before listening—
   that is folly and shame.
¹⁴ The human spirit can endure in sickness,
   but a crushed spirit who can bear?
¹⁵ The heart of the discerning acquires knowledge,
   for the ears of the wise seek it out.

18:10–15 Verse 14 aside, this cluster is united by themes of pride, listening, and self-confidence. Verse 14 can still be tied in through its emphasis on the inner spirit, which is also in verses 12 and 15.

---

2. Van Leeuwen, *Proverbs*, 173; Longman, *Proverbs*, 356.
3. So Heim, *Grapes of Gold*, 244.

Verses 10–11 juxtapose two contrary dispositions, with "fortified" appearing in both sayings. As noted in the introduction to this chapter, God's name and his character as a tower or refuge are common themes in the Psalms. In contrast to the "righteous" who flee to Yahweh for safety in verse 11, the "rich" trust in their own "wealth." Although the rich believe their wealth is a "wall too high to scale," it provides no assurance to match the refuge Yahweh provides (cf. 21:22).

Verse 12 looks backwards and forwards to other sayings of pride and downfall (cf. 15:33; 16:18).

Verse 14 stands somewhat alone, though its concern with our inner dispositions finds many parallels in this chapter. The saying teaches that, on the one hand, the human spirit is resilient, even during sickness, but second, like the fleeting wealth of the righteous (11), our spirit can be crushed and break (cf. 12:25; 17:22).

Verses 13 and 15 present two sayings that comment on humility and listening. Both sayings anticipate the timeless lines in the prayer of St. Francis, "O, Divine Master, grant that I may not so much seek . . . to be understood as to understand." Verse 15, meanwhile, demonstrates the way our "ears" follow the disposition of our "heart."

> [16] A gift opens the way
>   and ushers the giver into the presence of the great.
> [17] In a lawsuit the first to speak seems right,
>   until someone comes forward and cross-examines.
> [18] Casting the lot settles disputes
>   and keeps strong opponents apart.
> [19] A brother wronged is more unyielding than a fortified city;
>   disputes are like the barred gates of a citadel.

18:16–19 Verses 16–17 present seemingly unrelated topics, except that they both speak to the seats of power in ancient society. Verse 16 is among other sayings about bribes and gifts, in this case bribes and gifts that less privileged individuals use to access people in power (cf. Gen 12:7; Prov 15:27; 19:6; 21:14). But bribes and power players have their limits (Prov 6:35; Jas 2:1–7). Verse 17 commends discretion in judgment, much like the voice of caution in 18:13. Standing alongside verse 16, it tempers the security that is felt in the presence of power brokers. See the discussion of bribes in Live the Story in Proverbs 17.

Consistent with the major theme of division in society in this chapter, 18:18 recommends the time-tested throw of the dice to settle a stalemate. Fox suggests that the word for "opponents" implies stubbornness.[4]

---

4. Fox, *Proverbs 10–31*, 644.

Verse 19 is difficult and probably a corrupt transmission of the original text. Any translation will be somewhat tentative. The saying does seem to pick up the imagery of the refuge in verses 10–11, imagining a "brother wronged" who ostracizes himself as a refuge against his community. Psalms 55 and 133 use voices of prayer to portray the positive and negative sides of this same social reality.[5]

> [20] From the fruit of their mouth a person's stomach is filled;
>   with the harvest of their lips they are satisfied.
> [21] The tongue has the power of life and death,
>   and those who love it will eat its fruit.
> [22] He who finds a wife finds what is good
>   and receives favor from the LORD.
> [23] The poor plead for mercy,
>   but the rich answer harshly.
> [24] One who has unreliable friends soon comes to ruin,
>   but there is a friend who sticks closer than a brother.

18:20–24 The combination of "fruit" and speech ("mouth," "lips" and "tongue") in verses 21 and 22 unite the first two sayings in this cluster. The sayings seem to move from practical consequences of speech—satisfaction in daily life (v.20)—to ultimate consequences of life and death (v. 22). "Tongue" is a feminine noun that is often associated with "fruit," "love," and "life and death,"—themes that pervade Proverbs 1–9. Several scholars thus suggest that "tongue" here is a metaphor for wisdom and/or Woman Wisdom (cf. 2:18–19; 4:6; 5:19; 8:17, 19, 35–6). The pattern is certainly noteworthy.

Except for the possible allusion to wisdom and wives in verse 21, 18:22 seems to be out of context in this chapter. Still, like verse 21, the saying has universalistic overtones that fit with other sayings in this chapter and the rest of Proverbs as well (cf. v. 10; 12:4, 19:14; 31:10–31).

Verse 23 is another proverb about speech: "plead," "answer," and the power of the tongue. The saying laments the power gaps among disparate social classes in the world (cf. 11:24; 14:31; 18:10; 22:7). Elsewhere Proverbs promises divine recompense for these inequalities (21:13).[6]

The ambiguity of the Hebrew in verse 24a allows for many possible translations: "There is one who has shouting friends," "One with many friends soon comes to ruin," and "There are companions who pretend to be friends."[7] The second line is clear: one should value faithful companions over and against being overly social (cf. 18:1; Jas 5;19–20).

5. As noted by Longman, *Proverbs*, 359.
6. See Van Leeuwen, *Proverbs*, 173.
7. Fox, *Proverbs 10–31*, 647.

Jesus, James, and Wisdom

The book of James emphasizes many of the major themes in this chapter: foolish speech (1:19; 3:1–12), coveting riches (1:9–11; 4:2; 5:1–5), access to people of power (2:1–7), and friends and community (2:8–16; 3:16; 4:1–17; 5:19–20). While the New Testament book of James has a certain quaint appeal for Bible studies and sermons, its emphasis in the church and Christian theology is greatly overshadowed by the writings of Paul and, to a lesser extent, Peter and John.

But consider that the James who penned this book was also the oldest of Jesus' brothers, who rose to the position of the bishop of Jerusalem—*the* founding church of all Christianity. On two occasions James gives authoritative direction to Paul and other church leaders for their work with missionary churches (Acts 15:13–29; 21:18–25). James' authority at the time of the writing of the New Testament ought to give evangelicals pause, especially in our tendency to prefer Paul's teachings on "grace and works" in Romans 3–4 to James in 2:14–26. For both writers salvation is by faith through grace; but in both books that faith is dead without works to accompany it (cf. especially Rom 12:1–15:4).

More importantly, Richard Bauckham observes that,

> More than any other New Testament writer, James is a teacher in the style of Jesus, a creative exponent of the wisdom of Jesus, a disciple who, "having been fully trained" in his teacher's wisdom, has become himself a teacher of wisdom "like his teacher" (Luke 6:40).[8]

James gives us privileged insight into Jesus' personhood and teachings.[9] Neither James nor Jesus "avoid[s] seeking disadvantage" or suffering. Oddly, neither of them addresses idleness or childrearing as we find in Proverbs.[10]

Proverbs 18 allows us to see how James and Jesus echo, but also go beyond, the teachings of Proverbs. Relying on Bauckham's insights, we consider three interrelated points.[11]

First, Proverbs often employs an indirect teaching method, presenting descriptions of people and situations that invite reflection on issues of morality

---

8. Richard Bauckham, *James: Wisdom of James, Disciple of Jesus the Sage* (London; New York: Routledge, 1999), 30.

9. See commentary Introduction for more on James and its relationship to Proverbs and the teachings of Jesus.

10. Bauckham, *James*, 95–96.

11. Ibid., 100–05.

and wisdom (see 16:27–33). James, however, explicitly describes Scripture as a mirror that demands self-examination and a change of life (1:22–25). James' rhetoric has an urgency that is motivated by the certain return of the Messiah to bring judgment and establish his kingdom.

Second, Jesus and James also approach ethics in a more unified and comprehensive way. For example, the eight statements addressing speech in Proverbs 18 are only loosely inter-connected, and only verse 21 speaks in terms of ultimate ends. James and Jesus share an intense vision of moral purity and "wholeness," and their statements on speech are drawn together to characterize all speech as truth speaking (Jas 1:19–27; 3:1–12; 4:11–12; 5:9, 12; Matt 5:34–7).

Friends, Enemies, and Community

A third, and much more complex, concern in the sayings of Jesus and James is the nature of social and family relationships. As noted above, Proverbs 18 speaks often about community, warning against quarrelsome and selfish individuals and giving insight to the value of close friends (1, 6, 17; 18, 19, 24). The chapter also reflects almost neutrally on access to positions of power (18:16).

We know from ancient history and Scripture that the earlier church had conflicts between leaders and the worshiping body (1 Cor 3; Phil 4:2–3; James 4:1–2; 1 John 2:19). The New Testament epistles constantly give instructions to maintain unity in the body of Christ. But where Proverbs' teaching tends toward practical observations, James addresses his audience boldly as the "nucleus of ongoing Messianic renewal of the people of Israel . . . [and] the world."[12] Given its mission, this new body must be "a counter-cultural community, in which solidarity, especially with the poor, should replace hierarchy and status, along with the competitive ambition and arrogance (3:14, 16: 4:1–2, 16), and the exploitation of the poor (5:1–6) that characterize dominant society." This explains why Proverbs' emphasis on the "son" gives way to James' emphasis on "brothers and sisters" (1:2, 19, 2:1, 14, etc.).[13]

Such reflections on the book of James allow us to see that the New Testament in no way "moves beyond" Old Testament wisdom and its instructions on morality and practical living. On the contrary, because Jesus has definitively defeated evil and death and established his church as his agent of reconciliation in the world, he actually opens up the wisdom tradition to a new level of intensity and depth. As the church goes about its mission to the world, wisdom becomes a critical means of grace.

---

12. Ibid., 105.
13. Ibid., 102.

¹ Better the poor whose walk is blameless
    than a fool whose lips are perverse.
² Desire without knowledge is not good—
    how much more will hasty feet miss the way!
³ A person's own folly leads to their ruin,
    yet their heart rages against the LORD.
⁴ Wealth attracts many friends,
    but even the closest friend of the poor person deserts them.
⁵ A false witness will not go unpunished,
    and whoever pours out lies will not go free.
⁶ Many curry favor with a ruler,
    and everyone is the friend of one who gives gifts.
⁷ The poor are shunned by all their relatives—
    how much more do their friends avoid them!
Though the poor pursue them with pleading,
    they are nowhere to be found.
⁸ The one who gets wisdom loves life;
    the one who cherishes understanding will soon prosper.
⁹ A false witness will not go unpunished,
    and whoever pours out lies will perish.
¹⁰ It is not fitting for a fool to live in luxury—
    how much worse for a slave to rule over princes!
¹¹ A person's wisdom yields patience;
    it is to one's glory to overlook an offense.
¹² A king's rage is like the roar of a lion,
    but his favor is like dew on the grass.
¹³ A foolish child is a father's ruin,
    and a quarrelsome wife is like
    the constant dripping of a leaky roof.

¹⁴ Houses and wealth are inherited from parents,
   but a prudent wife is from the LORD.
¹⁵ Laziness brings on deep sleep,
   and the shiftless go hungry.
¹⁶ Whoever keeps commandments keeps their life,
   but whoever shows contempt for their ways will die.
¹⁷ Whoever is kind to the poor lends to the LORD,
   and he will reward them for what they have done.
¹⁸ Discipline your children, for in that there is hope;
   do not be a willing party to their death.
¹⁹ A hot-tempered person must pay the penalty;
   rescue them, and you will have to do it again.
²⁰ Listen to advice and accept discipline,
   and at the end you will be counted among the wise.
²¹ Many are the plans in a person's heart,
   but it is the LORD's purpose that prevails.
²² What a person desires is unfailing love;
   better to be poor than a liar.
²³ The fear of the LORD leads to life;
   then one rests content, untouched by trouble.
²⁴ A sluggard buries his hand in the dish;
   he will not even bring it back to his mouth!
²⁵ Flog a mocker, and the simple will learn prudence;
   rebuke the discerning, and they will gain knowledge.
²⁶ Whoever robs their father and drives out their mother
   is a child who brings shame and disgrace.
²⁷ Stop listening to instruction, my son,
   and you will stray from the words of knowledge.
²⁸ A corrupt witness mocks at justice,
   and the mouth of the wicked gulps down evil.
²⁹ Penalties are prepared for mockers,
   and beatings for the backs of fools.

Listening to the Text in the Story: Psalms 1; 14; Matthew 18:21–35

Proverbs continually returns to the images of "getting," "grasping," and "laying hold" of wisdom and knowledge (1:5; 3:18; 4:5–7; see 19:8 below). These physical metaphors imagine the search for wisdom sexually, economically, and as a matter of finding and guarding hidden treasure. The intensity and urgency in these images are meant to compel us to in our search.

⚡ EXPLAIN the Story

Among the wide variety of sayings in this chapter, internal structures can be found among major themes and catchwords: wealthy and poor classes (1, 4, 6, 7, 10, 12, 17, 22), ways and paths (1–3), desire (2, 6, 8, 22), Yahweh (3, 14, 17, 21, 23), and education (25–29).

¹ Better the poor whose walk is blameless
   than a fool whose lips are perverse.
² Desire without knowledge is not good—
   how much more will hasty feet miss the way!
³ A person's own folly leads to their ruin,
   yet their heart rages against the LORD.
⁴ Wealth attracts many friends,
   but even the closest friend of the poor person deserts them.
⁵ A false witness will not go unpunished,
   and whoever pours out lies will not go free.
⁶ Many curry favor with a ruler,
   and everyone is the friend of one who gives gifts.
⁷ The poor are shunned by all their relatives—
   how much more do their friends avoid them!
Though the poor pursue them with pleading,
   they are nowhere to be found.
⁸ The one who gets wisdom loves life;
   the one who cherishes understanding will soon prosper.
⁹ A false witness will not go unpunished,
   and whoever pours out lies will perish.

19:1–9 Verses 1–3 address "ways" and "paths." Verses 1–2 describe non-moral or matters that require careful interpretation (see Live the Story below). Proverbs often promises wealth as a result of seeking wisdom (cf. 3:16; 8:18), and yet the better-than saying in 19:1 provides the necessary caveat that wealth is not a sign of wisdom and righteousness any more than poverty signals folly and wickedness; the true measure of wisdom lies beneath the surface. Verse 2 provokes the imagination with understatement ("not good" = bad); our desires are immensely powerful and require careful direction with wisdom (cf. v. 22). "Hasty feet" that "miss the way" (v. 2b) parallel unguided desires (v. 1a).

Verse 3 may be an extreme example of unconstrained desire in verse 2.[1] The NIV "their ruin" is literally a "perverted way," keeping with the theme of ways/paths in 1–2. The "heart [that] rages against [Yahweh]" is ambiguous and thus able to describe both the rebellion of the fool (3a) as well as the fool's anger in blaming Yahweh for his consequences (3b).

The observations in 19:4, 6, and 7 all express sad realities about wealth and poverty. Even family members and the closest of friends avoid those who become poor. While the observations initially sound detached, the images evoke sympathy for those economically and socially marginalized (cf. 18:16, 23–24). Verse 6 is probably spoken tongue in cheek, since currying favor with the wealthy describes the very brown nosers and rear-end-kissers that people despise. The sympathy for the poor in verses 4, 6, and 7 is further compounded by the negative portrayals of liars and false witnesses in verse 5.

Verse 8 is the first of several sayings about wisdom and folly interspersed throughout this chapter (cf. 11, 13, 15, 20, 25, 27). The call to "get wisdom" echoes a common refrain in Proverbs (cf. 1:5; 4:5, 7; 16:16; 17:16: 18:15; 23:23). The NIV "will soon prosper" is literally "find good," which reinforces the metaphor of the diligent search (cf. 16:20; 17:20; 18:22).

The saying in 19:9 about falsehood and justice sits alongside similar sayings in 19:5 and 28.

> [10] It is not fitting for a fool to live in luxury—
>   how much worse for a slave to rule over princes!

19:10 This verse seems to stand somewhat apart from its context, though it echoes several other sayings about what is "not good" and "not fitting" (see 18:5 and Live the Story below). The image of the fool and the slave resemble the upside-down sayings in Proverbs 30:21–23. Though there is almost nothing most of us can do to alleviate these backwards circumstances, part of wisdom is learning to accept the reality of exceptions to God's intended order for the world.

> [11] A person's wisdom yields patience;
>   it is to one's glory to overlook an offense.
> [12] A king's rage is like the roar of a lion,
>   but his favor is like dew on the grass.
> [13] A foolish child is a father's ruin,
>   and a quarrelsome wife is like
>   the constant dripping of a leaky roof.
> [14] Houses and wealth are inherited from parents,
>   but a prudent wife is from the LORD.

---

1. Cf. Van Leeuwen, *Proverbs*, 178.

19:11–14 These verses collect a group of proverbs about wisdom, family, power, humility, and wealth. Verse 11 commends the wisdom of forgiveness and patience (cf. 14:29; 15:18; 16:32; 25:15). Jesus radicalizes this ethic of forgiveness in Matthew 18:21–35.

Verse 12 may be a concrete example of verse 11, using the king to illustrate the two sides of forgiveness. Power, favor, and wrath are often combined in Proverbs (14:35; 16:13, 15; 18:16; 19:6; 20:2, 28; cf. 1 Kgs 12:1–15).

Verses 13–14 pick up the theme of the fool in verse 10 and reflects examples of order and disorder in the house and family life (cf. 18:11, 22; 19:18, 26, 27). Proverbs elsewhere speaks of the fleeting nature of wealth (1:13; 6:31; 11:4; 18:11) and the desire for a wise wife (12:4; 31:10–31).

[15] Laziness brings on deep sleep,
   and the shiftless go hungry.
[16] Whoever keeps commandments keeps their life,
   but whoever shows contempt for their ways will die.
[17] Whoever is kind to the poor lends to the LORD,
   and he will reward them for what they have done.
[18] Discipline your children, for in that there is hope;
   do not be a willing party to their death.
[19] A hot-tempered person must pay the penalty;
   rescue them, and you will have to do it again.

19:15–19 Verse 15 applies images of hunger and aimless living to promote the virtue of diligent work (cf. 6:4–11; 15:19; 20:4; 22:13, Eccl 10:8; etc.; see commentary on 26:13–16).[2] Waltke reasonably assumes that this verse describes the son in 19:13 based on the parallels of "deep sleep" and the "foolish son" in 10:5 and 19:13–15.[3]

The admonition to keep "commandments" in verse 16 appears ten times in Proverbs, seven in relation to the family (2:1; 3:1; 4:4; 6:20, 23; 7:1–2) and three in other contexts (10:8; 13:13, 19:16; cf. Eccl 8:5; 12:13). Given the emphasis on family in this chapter (especially v. 18), it's safe to assume the family is at least partially in view.

Verses 17 and 18 both share partial lines with 23:13–14, suggesting that the juxtaposition here is intentional (cf. also 14:25; 24:11). Children and the poor are social groups dependent on those with greater resources.

The hyperbole to "rescue" (protect) someone from death expresses the

---

2. Heim, *Grapes of Gold*, 257–58 argues persuasively that "deep sleep" should be taken to represent "apathy" or some such extension beyond its literal meaning.

3. Waltke, *Proverbs 15–31*, 108–9.

urgency of discipline in 19:19, but this verse also concedes that anger may go beyond all correction.

> [20] Listen to advice and accept discipline,
>   and at the end you will be counted among the wise.
> [21] Many are the plans in a person's heart,
>   but it is the LORD's purpose that prevails.
> [22] What a person desires is unfailing love;
>   better to be poor than a liar.
> [23] The fear of the LORD leads to life;
>   then one rests content, untouched by trouble.
> [24] A sluggard buries his hand in the dish;
>   he will not even bring it back to his mouth!

19:20–24 Heim cites a number of themes and catchwords that loosely connect 19:16–23.[4] Verses 20–21 both address *esah*, "advice," "purpose." The plans and advice of wise counselors and Yahweh take precedence to the individual passions of the "heart."

Verse 22 presents difficulties. Verse 22a reads literally, "The desire of the person is his kindness." It is also possible to translate the word for *hasdo*, "his unfailing love" as "his shame."[5] Thus, in addition to the NIV, possible translations include:[6]

NIV note	"Greed is a person's shame"
Fox	"A man's kindness is his fruit"
Van Leeuwen	"A person's self-gratification is his shame"
Waltke	"What people desire in a human being is his unfailing love"

Waltke believes his translation better matches the second line (22b), "better to be poor than a liar."[7] But this is too subjective a preference, as uneven lines are common in Proverbs. It should also be noted that *ta'awat*, "desire," is portrayed both positively and negatively (cf. 10:24; 11:23; 13:12, 19; 18:1; 21:25, 26), so Waltke needs to say more in support of his point.

On the other hand, the proximity of this verse to the negative *ta'awat* in 18:1 and 21:25, 26, and the negative portrayal of human desires in this

---

4. Heim, *Grapes of Gold*, 262–63. 19:24 echoes the "sluggard" in 19:15.

5. *Hsd* I means "shame" or "sin" in 14:24 and 25:10 as compared to the more common *hsd* II, "unfailing love" in 3:3; 11:17, etc.

6. Fox, *Proverbs 10–31*, 658; Van Leeuwen, *Proverbs*, 181, Waltke, *Proverbs 15–31*, 92.

7. Waltke, *Proverbs*, 93.

chapter in general, give some weight to translation in the text in the NIV note and Van Leeuwen. In the end, the phrase is unusual, and I believe the author was sufficiently intelligent to have intended the ambiguity or else eliminated it if he did not.[8] Proverbs deprived of allusions cease to be poetry.

Verse 23 combines the motto of Proverbs (cf. 1:7, 9:10; and v. 25 below) with a line from 16:6b. The fear of Yahweh and controlled desire go together.

Verse 24 returns to the "sluggard" from verse 15 (cf. 26:15). The saying humorously mocks the lazy person who cannot satisfy his own desire (cf. Judg 7:6; 1 Sam 14:26).

> [25] Flog a mocker, and the simple will learn prudence;
>   rebuke the discerning, and they will gain knowledge.
> [26] Whoever robs their father and drives out their mother
>   is a child who brings shame and disgrace.
> [27] Stop listening to instruction, my son,
>   and you will stray from the words of knowledge.
> [28] A corrupt witness mocks at justice,
>   and the mouth of the wicked gulps down evil.
> [29] Penalties are prepared for mockers,
>   and beatings for the backs of fools.

19:25–29 These verses are a tight cluster of sayings that address issues of discipline and which are capped on both ends by *les*, "mock" and "mocker" (25, 28, 29). The sayings can also be heard echoing the vocabulary and themes in Proverbs 1:1–8.

Verse 25 draws on the "simple" and "discerning" in 1:4–5, thus placing the sayings of the prologue into the concrete surroundings of this chapter (cf. 17:10). Clifford comments on the contrast between the "beating" needed to instruct the "simple" and the mere "gesture" that teaches those who are "discerning."[9]

Verses 26–27 return to the family (cf. 7, 13, etc.) with two lessons about the "son" (not translated in the NIV in v. 26): one who "robs" his parents and the other who "listen[s]" and keeps "knowledge" (cf. v. 25; 22:6). It becomes especially clear that the family sayings in the chapter are interwoven with images of wisdom and folly in the community—perhaps the son when he is grown and on his own.

"Witness" from verses 5 and 9 appears again in verse 28 while "justice" repeats the same Hebrew root for "penalties" in verse 29. Verse 28 is further adorned by the homonyms *beliyya'al*, "corrupt," and *yeballa'*, "gulps," in 28a

---

8. Especially in light of the catchwords and wordplay evident throughout the chapter and especially vv. 25–29.

9. Clifford, *Proverbs*, 179.

and b. At the same time the verse creatively flows into the surrounding proverbs; it presents a striking image of a mouth that ravenously consumes "evil" as it spews for folly.

Verse 29 closes the chapter with a final judgment saying, though one can see that the themes in the cluster beginning at verse 25 continue through to 20:4. The violent punishments in verse 29 are obviously an extreme measure, meant to arouse our desire to avoid the paths of folly and mockery.

LIVE the Story

Hermeneutics and Wisdom

"There are no mistakes, only lessons." Or, as another contemporary proverb has it, "practice makes perfect." Wisdom is never just a body of knowledge, but defines the skill of knowing how things fit: the right thought, action or inaction, and speech or silence that best meet the needs of the moment. And this kind of learning involves testing—trial and error.

Beginning in Proverbs 17, we encounter more than two dozen sayings that describe this hermeneutical aspect of wisdom. These sayings include things that are "not fitting" (17:7; 19:10; 26:1) and "not good" (17:26; 18:5; 19:2; 20:23; 25:27; 28:21). The poem in 26:1–12 is an extended series of reflections on fittingness, including one of the most memorable sayings in Proverbs:

> ⁴ Do not answer a fool according to his folly,
>   or you yourself will be just like him.
> ⁵ Answer a fool according to his folly,
>   or he will be wise in his own eyes.

Dilemmas are an inevitable part of life. Should I take this job or that one? Should I buy this house? Drop this course? Say "yes" or "no"? Do I go to the office party or the church potluck? Have Thanksgiving with my in-laws or a ski trip with close friends? Tell my friend what I think of her dress? Tell my child that their artwork is beautiful when it's not? We simply hate to make decisions that might be wrong, hurt someone's feelings, or scar our reputation.

And yet, these decisions are unavoidable in life. The theologian Oliver O'Donovan explains that dilemmas arise, "because the moral field is pluriform. It does not arise out of the adequacy or inadequacy of the moral code . . ."[10] In other words, dilemmas are not the result of not having enough rules, but arise because the world is too complex and diverse for one moral

---

10. O'Donovan, *Resurrection*, 198.

code to address everything adequately. And so we have to go about life deciding which rule and which principle makes the most sense in each situation, whether practically, morally, or socially.

Ethicists use the term "casuistry" to describe this process of deliberation between options. Many of the laws in Deuteronomy are casuistic in this way, providing familiar scenarios and judgments to go with them. The laws only speak to a small fraction of actual circumstances that we live in life and so the law simply provides a marker that helps the community come to a wise and just judgment. Here O'Donovan comments again, "'Casuistry,' as it is called, is not just a matter of solving problems, but of growing in wisdom."[11] These varied individual situations may trouble us, but they are essential to our growing in wisdom. Ambiguous value judgments are particularly rewarding in this regard because of the unique demands they place on us as we deliberate.

A Man's Desire is His Unfailing Love: Poetry and Wisdom

> For what is to be said of the attempt to translate poetry into prose? This kind of translation is, more than any other, like the underside of a carpet,
>
> "And shews the stuff but not the workman's skill . . . "[12]

Poetry rendered in prose is what Douglass Templeton describes as "the substitution of a reflection for the sun in glory" and "the language of emotion" replaced by "the language of thought."[13] The scientific age inspired a modern culture with an intense desire for the pure givenness of things and resists contingency and ambiguity at every level. But even mathematics is not the objective and disembodied science that we often imagine it to be.[14]

Recognizing these nuances in the scientific way of knowing should make us all the more sensitive to the imaginative ways of knowing that are engendered in poetry. Far more than prose, poetry alludes, plays, disguises, and evokes. Just consider some of the following lines when they are translated directly from the Hebrew:

> The poor are hated even by their neighbors
> but the rich are loved by many (14:20)

---

11. Ibid., 191.
12. Hamann in Templeton, *New Testament as True Fiction*, 176, cited in full in the commentary introduction.
13. Ibid.
14. See, e.g., the discussions in George Lakoff and Rafeal Nuñez, *Where Mathematics Comes From: How the Embodied Mind Brings Mathematics into Being* (New York: Basic Books, 2001).

The light of the eyes rejoices the heart
a good report fattens the bones (15:30)

A bribe is a magic stone in the eyes of its owner
wherever he turns he prospers (17:8)

The desire of a man is his shame [unfailing love]
and [but] it is better to be poor than a liar (19:22)

As we discuss these points in the commentary, each of these sayings has an ambiguity or terseness that is resolved or smoothed out by almost all English translations (cf. also 11:26; 12:10; 18:4; 30:1, 15a). Such making of prose out of poetry flattens the texts and stunts the imaginative process. Are the poor really "hated" in 14:20? Whose bright eyes are we to imagine in 15:30? Who is the owner of the stone in 17:8: the briber or the bribee? Does *hsd* mean "shame" or "unfailing love" in 19:22? Or is it both?

Abiding in these puzzles is a major part of the exercise of learning wisdom. As Knut Heim says in conclusion to his message and seminal study on repetition in Proverbs, "What has been written with imagination must be read with imagination."[15] The same can be said for much of the New Testament writings, especially on the lips of Jesus:

> Because you have so little faith. Truly I tell you, if you have faith as small as a mustard seed, you can say to this mountain, "Move from here to there," and it will move. Nothing will be impossible for you. (Matt 17:20)

> Nothing outside a person can defile them by going into them. Rather, it is what comes out of a person that defiles them. (Mark 7:15)

> I have much more to say to you, more than you can now bear. (John 16:12)

Jesus' wisdom in these sayings shows us that our pursuit of understanding has limits.

In a similar vein, Paul reveals that God's wisdom, knowledge, peace, and love ultimately surpass all understanding (Rom 11:33; Eph 3:19; Phil 4:7). Where does this leave us? At least two conclusions can be made. First, we cannot fully attain to the knowledge of God in this life, and so we must always strive to know him and the fullness of his revelation in Christ. The promise of knowing him better leads us ever forward. Second, we must also recognize that there is something nourishing, necessary, and unavoidable about this ambiguity in life. And this leaves us clinging to the risen one.

---

15. Heim, *Poetic Imagination*, 645.

Christological Prefiguring in Proverbs

The greatest affinity with Proverbs in the New Testament is found in James (see Live the Story in 18:1–24) and in Jesus' sayings. Notice that in Matthew 18:21 Peter asks Jesus how often one is required to forgive a neighbor. Jesus responds with this memorable saying, "I tell you, not seven times, but seventy-seven times" (18:22). Jesus then turns to a parable about a "king" who settles debts that are owed to him. The king shows mercy to a man brought to him who owed him an insurmountable debt. But when the released man goes to exact punishments on his debtors, the king recalls him in order to punish the debtor severely. Proverbs similarly combines teachings on forgiveness and overlooking a matter just before a saying about the "rage" and "favor" of a king (19:11–12). Jesus embodies the coming of a merciful, divine king who is slow to anger and ready to forgive. But Jesus also foretells a coming judgment for those who, having been forgiven, refuse to extend forgiveness to our neighbor (Matt 18:35).

CHAPTER 25

Proverbs 20:1–30

 LISTEN to the Story

¹ Wine is a mocker and beer a brawler;
 whoever is led astray by them is not wise.
² A king's wrath strikes terror like the roar of a lion;
 those who anger him forfeit their lives.
³ It is to one's honor to avoid strife,
 but every fool is quick to quarrel.
⁴ Sluggards do not plow in season;
 so at harvest time they look but find nothing.
⁵ The purposes of a person's heart are deep waters,
 but one who has insight draws them out.
⁶ Many claim to have unfailing love,
 but a faithful person who can find?
⁷ The righteous lead blameless lives;
 blessed are their children after them.
⁸ When a king sits on his throne to judge,
 he winnows out all evil with his eyes.
⁹ Who can say, "I have kept my heart pure;
 I am clean and without sin"?
¹⁰ Differing weights and differing measures—
 the LORD detests them both.
¹¹ Even small children are known by their actions,
 so is their conduct really pure and upright?
¹² Ears that hear and eyes that see—
 the LORD has made them both.
¹³ Do not love sleep or you will grow poor;
 stay awake and you will have food to spare.
¹⁴ "It's no good, it's no good!" says the buyer—
 then goes off and boasts about the purchase.
¹⁵ Gold there is, and rubies in abundance,

but lips that speak knowledge are a rare jewel.
[16] Take the garment of one who puts up security for a stranger;
    hold it in pledge if it is done for an outsider.
[17] Food gained by fraud tastes sweet,
    but one ends up with a mouth full of gravel.
[18] Plans are established by seeking advice;
    so if you wage war, obtain guidance.
[19] A gossip betrays a confidence;
    so avoid anyone who talks too much.
[20] If someone curses their father or mother,
    their lamp will be snuffed out in pitch darkness.
[21] An inheritance claimed too soon
    will not be blessed at the end.
[22] Do not say, "I'll pay you back for this wrong!"
    Wait for the LORD, and he will avenge you.
[23] The LORD detests differing weights,
    and dishonest scales do not please him.
[24] A person's steps are directed by the LORD.
    How then can anyone understand their own way?
[25] It is a trap to dedicate something rashly
    and only later to consider one's vows.
[26] A wise king winnows out the wicked;
    he drives the threshing wheel over them.
[27] The human spirit is the lamp of the LORD
    that sheds light on one's inmost being.
[28] Love and faithfulness keep a king safe;
    through love his throne is made secure.
[29] The glory of young men is their strength,
    gray hair the splendor of the old.
[30] Blows and wounds scrub away evil,
    and beatings purge the inmost being.

Listening to the Text in the Story: Genesis 9:28–39; Psalms 14; 53; Jeremiah 17:9–10

The incident with Noah and his sons after Noah had become drunk parallels a long list of such stories in the Old Testament. We discuss these below.

Much like Proverbs 20:9, Psalms 14 and 53 both speak to human sin and unrighteousness, using wisdom language and rhetorical questions:

The fool says in his heart, 'There is no God." (14:1; 53:1)
Do all these evildoers know nothing? (14:4; 53:4)

Jeremiah 17:9–10, meanwhile, reflects on the hidden and inward depths of human thoughts, desires, and emotions. These are common themes in Psalms and Proverbs and of particular interest in this chapter.

EXPLAIN the Story

Another seemingly arbitrary collection of sayings contains many common themes and loosely connected structures. In particular, several topics from chapter 19 flow into the beginning of this material and, in several instances, themes that appear at the beginning of this chapter return again toward the end.

Topic	Ch. 19	20:1–15	20:16–30
Mockers	25, 28, 29	1	
Wisdom		1	19, 26
King winnowing		2	26
King's terror	12	2, 8	
Honor/reputation		3	29
Sloth	15, 24	4, 13	
Inner thoughts/intent		5, 6, 9	18, 20, 24, 27, 30
Unfailing love		6	28 (2x)
Blessing		7	21
Marketplace		10, 14	15, 16, 17, 23

  ¹ Wine is a mocker and beer a brawler;
       whoever is led astray by them is not wise.
  ² A king's wrath strikes terror like the roar of a lion;
       those who anger him forfeit their lives.
  ³ It is to one's honor to avoid strife,
       but every fool is quick to quarrel.
  ⁴ Sluggards do not plow in season;
       so at harvest time they look but find nothing.

20:1–4 This cluster that ends with the "sluggard" (v. 4) probably closes the section that begins with the "sluggard" in 19:24. Acts of folly prevail in this material with the "mocker" as the main culprit. Heim argues that the respective behaviors to be avoided by the "son" (19:27) parallel the warnings to "fledgling courtiers" in 20:2: honesty (19:28), politeness (19:29), alcohol (20:1), and anger (20:2–3).[1]

Verse 1 warns against the destructive effects of beer and wine. Proverbs 31:4–7 provides the same warning for rulers in particular (cf. Eccl. 10:16–17). Wine is also portrayed in a positive light in 3:5 and 9:6. See more in Live the Story below.

Verses 2–3 warn against unchecked anger—both for kings (v. 2) and in a general sense (v. 3).

Verse 4 echoes sayings against the sloth in 19:15, 24 and 20:13 (cf. 10:4–5). It does not merely comment on generic activity, as sloth can often be present in busyness in anything but the right thing. Rather, wisdom values work that knows how to plan and take advantage of the lessons that come down in tradition, whether that be in farming, business, seafaring, etc.

> [5] The purposes of a person's heart are deep waters,
>   but one who has insight draws them out.
> [6] Many claim to have unfailing love,
>   but a faithful person who can find?
> [7] The righteous lead blameless lives;
>   blessed are their children after them.

20:5–7 These verses contains three sayings about reliable types of people. The cluster also compares outward appearances and inner realities/intentions. "Deep waters" (v. 5) are hidden depths of the heart. Some scholars interpret the image negatively, in the sense that our deepest inner thoughts are corrupt or evil.[2] A similar ambiguity exists in 18:4. But if the sense is negative, one would probably expect a stronger statement in 5b, such as the lines in 6b, 8b, and 21b. Indeed, verse 6a seems to restate a neutral observation flowing from verse 5 and then turn to a warning to beware that the hiddenness of the heart can belie the words of the lips in 6b.

Verse 7 states a traditional affirmation of blessing for the righteous throughout their generations (cf. 13:22; 14:26; 17:6). Verse 21 warns children not to abuse their inheritance. Readers are sometimes surprised or alarmed by the idea that someone could be "blameless." This question is addressed in Live the Story below.

---

1. Heim, *Poetic Imagination*, 459–60.
2. See Waltke, *Proverbs 15–31*, 131. Cf. also Fox, *Proverbs 10–31*, 664–65, who, surprisingly, argues that drawing out the these thoughts is not to be imagined as anything difficult since drawing water from a deep well is no harder than a shallow well. Fox seems to assume that the metaphor speaks to water depth and not the depth of its surface. Either way, Fox's reasoning is forced given the imagery in Job 28:1–11 and the basic thrust in both contexts. See Van Leeuwen, *Proverbs*, 185.

[8] When a king sits on his throne to judge,
   he winnows out all evil with his eyes.
[9] Who can say, "I have kept my heart pure;
   I am clean and without sin"?
[10] Differing weights and differing measures—
   the LORD detests them both.
[11] Even small children are known by their actions,
   so is their conduct really pure and upright?
[12] Ears that hear and eyes that see—
   the LORD has made them both.

20:8–12 These verses are set apart by the themes of judgment and "eyes" in verse 8 and 12 and the common concern for inner intentions of the heart. "Eyes" in verse 12 also provides a bridge to verse 13.

Paralleling 20:2 and 26, verse 8 portrays the king as a model of Yahweh's rule and judgment as described in 20:10 and 12.[3] A king's "eyes" that "winnow" or "scatter" evil is a metaphor for discerning judgment.

Verse 9 echoes the observations in verses 5–6—rhetorical questions that bring us face to face with the sin and corruption deep within all of us.

Verses 10 and 12 are Yahweh sayings that reinforce God's knowledge of hidden things and his sovereignty in judgment to include knowing and judging the king who rules as his representative (cf. 8).

Verse 11 presents some difficulties. Most translations take 11b as a statement, "as to whether what they do is pure and right." This sounds like Matthew 7:20, "by their fruit you will recognize them." But in the proverb "conduct" and "actions" are virtual synonyms, which makes the statement so circular that it says little. The 2011 NIV changes its older version by phrasing 11b as a question, "So is their conduct . . . ?"[4] This adds more force by implicating all children with adults as sinners (cf. 6, 9). One possible insight into this passage is the notion of the age of accountability among children "who do not yet know good from bad" (Deut 1:39; cf. Isa 7:15). All societies must wrestle through the knotty challenge of knowing when a child acts with the knowledge and responsibility of an adult, or to be tried as an adult as we say. The talmudic literature also recognizes this problem and establishes that a person must be twenty years old before being tried as an adult. In this light

---

3. Van Leeuwen, *Proverbs*, 186, describes "leap-frog connections" to vv. 10 and 12.

4. Perhaps based on Waltke's suggestion, *Proverbs 15–31*, 120 (cf. 137–38), that *im*, "so," in 11b is used to present two synonymous questions in Job 6:12. Yet another translation arises from the possibility that *nkr*, "to recognize," is really a homonym meaning "to play another person," or "to feign." This would yield the reading "A boy may playact in his deeds, but is his conduct . . . ?" See here Clifford, *Proverbs*, 183–84.

one should consider Fox's suggestion that the saying is about the future: a child's behavior now indicates what he will be like when grown.[5] Even if a child is not held accountable as an adult now, it doesn't mean that his actions are not an indicator of his intentions and his future behavior. The saying also reinforces the virtue of parental discipline when children are young.

> [13] Do not love sleep or you will grow poor;
>   stay awake and you will have food to spare.
> [14] "It's no good, it's no good!" says the buyer—
>   then goes off and boasts about the purchase.
> [15] Gold there is, and rubies in abundance,
>   but lips that speak knowledge are a rare jewel.
> [16] Take the garment of one who puts up security for a stranger;
>   hold it in pledge if it is done for an outsider.
> [17] Food gained by fraud tastes sweet,
>   but one ends up with a mouth full of gravel.

20:13–17 These verses are capped on both ends by food sayings and appear to be grouped around ethics in the marketplace, particularly in light of hidden intentions of buyers and sellers.

Verse 13 resembles the saying about laziness and lack of food in verse 4. "Stay awake" is "open eyes" in Hebrew, which plays on "eyes" in verses 8 and 12. The theme of food returns in 20:17 with a concern about the deceptiveness of food gained unjustly (cf. 9:17–18).

Verse 14 in Hebrew begins tersely, *ra' ra'*, "bad bad" or "evil evil," which parallels "stone stone" and the saying about marketplace deception in 20:10. Verse 15 serves as an aside that reflects on the rarity and value of true and honest speech. Elsewhere wisdom is said to be more valuable than these same treasures (3:15; 8:11, 31:10).

Verse 16 repeats similar warnings found in 6:1; 7:9; 11:15; 17:18; and 22:26–27. In this context mercy has its limits and the pursuit of justice its own dangers.

> [18] Plans are established by seeking advice;
>   so if you wage war, obtain guidance.
> [19] A gossip betrays a confidence;
>   so avoid anyone who talks too much.

20:18–19 Heim provides a number of arguments for grouping these sayings with 20:14–17.[6] Of note, a variety of alternative meanings of the

---

5. Fox, *Proverbs 10–31*, 667.
6. Heim, *Grapes of Gold*, 277–78.

Hebrew *arb*, "pledge," "sweet," and "avoid," are played upon throughout this section (20:16, 17, 19). But links like these can be used to suggest other legitimate structures as well. I have chosen to isolate verses 18–19 based upon the fact that the themes related to the food/marketplace in 14–17 are not here. I also follow Heim's observation that verses 18–19 are paired by the opposition of good public speech (v. 18; cf. 24:6) and harmful speech in secret (v. 19).

> ²⁰ If someone curses their father or mother,
>   their lamp will be snuffed out in pitch darkness.
> ²¹ An inheritance claimed too soon
>   will not be blessed at the end.
> ²² Do not say, "I'll pay you back for this wrong!"
>   Wait for the LORD, and he will avenge you.
> ²³ The LORD detests differing weights,
>   and dishonest scales do not please him.
> ²⁴ A person's steps are directed by the LORD.
>   How then can anyone understand their own way?
> ²⁵ It is a trap to dedicate something rashly
>   and only later to consider one's vows.

20:20–25 These verses are something of an arbitrary grouping, combining family sayings, Yahweh sayings, and concerns with inner intentions. These themes flow into the next section and chapter as well.

Verses 20–21 form a proverb pair about honor and inheritance in the family. Note that inheritance, conduct, and deceitful children all appear earlier in the broader context (vv. 7, 11) and culminate here in two sayings that portray the family undone by disrespectful and greedy children. The metaphor of an extinguished lamp in 20:20 occurs elsewhere (see 13:9 and 24:20).

Verse 22 is the first of a series of five Yahweh sayings that fold into king sayings—a pattern that continues through 21:4 and is first seen in 16:1–9, 10–15. The patterns are a reminder that modern verse and chapter divisions are helpful conventions that can sometimes obscure other structures. This verse (22) discourages hasty threats while encouraging trust in Yahweh's judgment. Verse 23, echoing verse 10 and the prevailing sense of Yahweh's sovereign intervention in these chapters, continues the line of thought in verse 22 to assure the reader of Yahweh's commitment to just judgment.

20:24–25 Although verse 25 does not use the term Yahweh, its dedications and vows assume worship of Yahweh. These verses thus form a complementary pair, beginning with submission to Yahweh's hand in directing our lives and followed by honoring God in what we speak and vow in his name. Prudent speech is also a subject in verses 14, 20, and 22, and implicitly in 17.

> ²⁶ A wise king winnows out the wicked;
>   he drives the threshing wheel over them.
> ²⁷ The human spirit is the lamp of the LORD
>   that sheds light on one's inmost being.

20:26–27 Yahweh and the king, particularly with respect to the intentions of a king's heart, remain in focus from 20:26 to 21:4. Verse 26 echoes verse 2 and largely repeats verse 8. A wise king is like Yahweh in knowing how to discern evil and keep justice.

In 20:27 the "spirit," *neshamah*, that belongs to humans is the vital breath of life than animates every creature (Gen 2:7; 7:22; Deut 20:16). The metaphor seems to indicate that God's breath within us is his "lamp" by which he sees our inward parts. More simply put, because he made our depths, he knows them too. The father's "command" serves as a "lamp" for the child to walk in wisdom (Prov 6:23).

> ²⁸ Love and faithfulness keep a king safe;
>   through love his throne is made secure.
> ²⁹ The glory of young men is their strength,
>   gray hair the splendor of the old.
> ³⁰ Blows and wounds scrub away evil,
>   and beatings purge the inmost being.

20:28–30 In many ways these verses draw this section to a close and echo the beginning of the chapter.[7] A king's "throne" in 20:28 is established by "love and faithfulness." "Love and faithfulness" are also attributed to God (e.g., Exod 34:6; Ps 25:10) and people (Prov 3:3; cf. Gen 24:49; 47:29; Josh 2:14). "Love" is repeated twice here and is the same word translated "unfailing love" in 20:3. "Love and faithfulness" also closely parallels doing "what is right and just" in 21:3. In this way we see many clear signs throughout the Old Testament that extend the character and actions of Yahweh to the king and all humanity.

The "glory" and "splendor" of young men and old in 20:29—though using a different word—follows the "honor" of peaceful people in 20:3.

The chapter ends in 20:30 with a picture of violent judgment that combines the judgment of God and kings and the theme of inner depths of the heart throughout this section of sayings.

---

7. Though, as noted, most themes in the current context continue through 21:4.

Wine Is a Mocker

> Wine is a mocker and beer a brawler. (20:1)

Alcohol saturates modern television, cinema, and magazine ads, especially anywhere near sports and women. These images of happy, beautiful friends having barbecues and toasting in bars elide alcohol's long list of casualties among our families, workplaces, and college campuses. Proverbs 20:1 provokes us to ask what the Bible has to say about drinking (cf. 23:19–20; 29–32; 31:4–5).

Beer and wine are paired twenty times in the Old Testament, expressing a range of positive and negative attitudes toward libations. On the positive side, wine was an indispensable part of festivals. Similarly, Woman Wisdom's memorable feast in Proverbs 9:1–6 twice mentions her preparations of wine. As the *Encyclopedia Judaica* notes, "complete abstinence was associated with turning away from civilization (Jer 35)."[8] The Nazarite vow (Num 6), which requires abstention from drink, also abstains from cutting hair and attending funerals, both clear marks of social participation.[9]

So while wine is a virtue biblically central to community life, drunkenness is its forbidden vice. The rebellious son in Deuteronomy is characterized as a "glutton and drunkard" (Deut 21:20). Consistent with Proverbs 20:1, Daube has observed a pattern among a dozen major stories in the Old Testament in which the drunk, while doing no harm or violence to others, is consistently the object of harm, violence, or sexual mistreatment, or barely escaping one of these. Amnon is killed by his brother Absalom after getting drunk at a festival (2 Sam 13:1–39); Ben-Hadad is defeated by Ahab after getting drunk and losing sense of his faculties (1 Kgs 20:12–16); and, having been rescued by his wife Abigail, Nabal (which means "fool") dies shortly after a drunken feast (1 Sam 25:36). To this list we can add Lot, Noah, Judah, Joseph's brothers, Elah king of Israel, and more.[10]

The New Testament also consistently warns against drunkenness (Eph 5:18; 1 Tim 3:8; Titus 2:3), and the book of Revelation parallels Proverbs'

8. Jeffrey Howard Tigay, et al. "Drunkenness." *Encyclopaedia Judaica*, ed. Michael Berenbaum and Fred Skolnik, 2nd ed., vol. 6 (Detroit: Macmillan Reference USA, 2007), 26–28. Also available at the Gale Virtual Reference Library, http://gale.com.

9. Ibid.

10. David Daube, "Wine in the Bible (Part I: Drunkenness)" in *Biblical Law and Literature: Collected Works of David Daube*, ed. Calum Carmichael, vol. 3 (Berkeley, CA: University of California at Berkeley, 2003), 501–12.

use of wine as a symbol of adultery, sin, apostasy, and judgment (Rev 14:8, 10; 16:19). But, like the Old Testament, the New Testament also affirms fermented drink as a gift from God. The wine at the feast of Cana on the "third day" in John's Gospel parallels the bringing forth of fruit from the land on the third day of creation in Genesis. Wine here is a fertile symbol of Jesus' kingdom (John 2:1–11). Wine is also central to the Lord's Supper and the gathering of God's community both now and when we drink it "new" with our Lord in his Father's kingdom (Matt 26:26; Mark 14:25; cf. Isa 25:6). Wine may be the principal metaphor of the kingdom. It is a gift of God and, in this life, must be used with wisdom rather than banned as immoral.

Blameless and Innocent? Who's Afraid of Romans?

Christians today have an uneasy relationship with the word "righteousness." On the one hand, passages like Proverbs 20:6; Psalms 14; 53; and Romans 3 seem to make it clear that "no one is righteous." Similarly, Romans 3 presents its arguments in a series of rhetorical questions in order to demonstrate that Jews and gentiles alike are all under the condemnation of sin. Paul even paraphrases Psalms 14 and 53 in Romans 3:10–12.

And yet Proverbs, which uses the word "righteous" almost seventy times, far more often than not assumes that righteous people exist and that we meet them in our everyday lives (see 20:7 above). The stories of Noah, Job, and David in Psalm 18 are among many other passages that have no problem labeling people "righteous." The words *tam*, "blameless," and *yasar*, "upright," though used less often in Proverbs, fall into these same categories (cf. Job 1:1, 8; 2:3).

What Christians need in this area is greater sensitivity to language, rhetoric, and context in the Bible. Paul clearly helps us to see that every human stands guilty of sin and unrighteous *as a whole* in our standing under the law. Several sayings in Proverbs 20 likewise affirm a depth of true righteousness that is typically hidden from our sight (5, 6, 9, 24, 27, 30).

But wisdom also demands that we seek to acknowledge and affirm people who are righteous in the sense that they seek to follow God, speak well (10:11), benefit society (10:21), (with obvious exceptions) have success in life (11:28, 30), are good for family (13:22), and a benefit to society (29:2). Christopher Wright summarizes this well,

> The frequent claim made by various psalmists to have lived according to God's law are neither exaggerated nor exceptional. They arise from the natural assumption than ordinary people can indeed live in a way that is broadly pleasing to God and faithful to God's law, and that they can do so

as a matter of joy and delight. This is neither self-righteousness nor a claim
to sinless perfection, for the same psalmists are equally quick to confess
their sin and failings . . . [11]

Wisdom exhorts us to identify these kinds of "righteous" people because
they make good friends, pastors, deacons, politicians, neighbors, and spouses.
And so, wisdom is consistent with the whole of the Bible in calling us to
recognize righteous people, seek them out, bless them, and imitate them. At
the same time, the sense of our inability to achieve and maintain righteousness leads us into greater dependence on the righteous one. Not only has
Jesus granted us righteousness in the eyes of the father (2 Cor 5:31), but we
become—as Israel was always intended to be—the righteousness of God in
the eyes of the nations (Gen. 18:17–19; Isa 48:18; 56:1). In our lives we thus
embody Christ's righteousness both in the message we say and the works we
do (Eph 4:24; 5:9; 6:14; Jas 3:18). And in doing so we cast a light back upon
the righteousness of Christ himself, who fulfilled what was required in Israel's
covenants and reversed the curse of Adam's first sin.

---

11. Christopher Wright, *Deuteronomy* NIBC (Peabody, MA: Hendrickson, 1996), 290.

¹ In the LORD's hand the king's heart is a stream of water
    that he channels toward all who please him.
² A person may think their own ways are right,
    but the LORD weighs the heart.
³ To do what is right and just
    is more acceptable to the LORD than sacrifice.
⁴ Haughty eyes and a proud heart—
    the unplowed field of the wicked—produce sin.
⁵ The plans of the diligent lead to profit
    as surely as haste leads to poverty.
⁶ A fortune made by a lying tongue
    is a fleeting vapor and a deadly snare.
⁷ The violence of the wicked will drag them away,
    for they refuse to do what is right.
⁸ The way of the guilty is devious,
    but the conduct of the innocent is upright.
⁹ Better to live on a corner of the roof
    than share a house with a quarrelsome wife.
¹⁰ The wicked crave evil;
    their neighbors get no mercy from them.
¹¹ When a mocker is punished, the simple gain wisdom;
    by paying attention to the wise they get knowledge.
¹² The Righteous One takes note of the house of the wicked
    and brings the wicked to ruin.
¹³ Whoever shuts their ears to the cry of the poor
    will also cry out and not be answered.
¹⁴ A gift given in secret soothes anger,
    and a bribe concealed in the cloak pacifies great wrath.
¹⁵ When justice is done it brings joy to the righteous

but terror to evildoers.

¹⁶ Whoever strays from the path of prudence
   comes to rest in the company of the dead.

¹⁷ Whoever loves pleasure will become poor;
   whoever loves wine and olive oil will never be rich.

¹⁸ The wicked become a ransom for the righteous,
   and the unfaithful for the upright.

¹⁹ Better to live in a desert
   than with a quarrelsome and nagging wife.

²⁰ The wise store up choice food and olive oil,
   but fools gulp theirs down.

²¹ Whoever pursues righteousness and love
   finds life, prosperity and honor.

²² One who is wise can go up against the city of the mighty
   and pull down the stronghold in which they trust.

²³ Those who guard their mouths and their tongues
   keep themselves from calamity.

²⁴ The proud and arrogant person—"Mocker" is his name—
   behaves with insolent fury.

²⁵ The craving of a sluggard will be the death of him,
   because his hands refuse to work.

²⁶ All day long he craves for more,
   but the righteous give without sparing.

²⁷ The sacrifice of the wicked is detestable—
   how much more so when brought with evil intent!

²⁸ A false witness will perish,
   but a careful listener will testify successfully.

²⁹ The wicked put up a bold front,
   but the upright give thought to their ways.

³⁰ There is no wisdom, no insight,
   no plan that can succeed against the LORD.

³¹ The horse is made ready for the day of battle,
   but victory rests with the LORD.

Listening to the Text in the Story: Genesis 18:19; Psalms 33:16–17; 119:121

In one of Yahweh's several appearances before Abraham, we overhear a conversation about Abraham with Yahweh and his heavenly visitors (Gen 18:1–33). The passage reminds Israel that they were chosen from the beginning to "do what is righteous and just." The call is frustrated in its context by the sins of Sodom and Abraham's own family doing wickedness.

The author of Psalm 119, meanwhile, appeals to having "done what is right and just" as a basis for being protected from those who pursued him (v. 121). In keeping with Live the Story in Proverbs 20, these passages underscore the fact that God's chosen people in every age are designed to act boldly in addressing injustice and righting the wrongs in the world.

EXPLAIN the Story

The following outline builds on Heim's chiastic structure for this chapter, demonstrating how the end mirrors the beginning.[1]

> A Yahweh sayings (1–3)
> A1 King and Yahweh in leadership (1)
> A2 Justice and Sacrifices (3)
>   B Diligence (5)
>   B1 False speech and demise (6)
>   C Nagging wife (9)
>   C' Nagging wife (19)
>   B1' Wise speech and safety (23)
>   B' laziness (25)
> A2' Wickedness and Sacrifices (27)
> A1' Armies and Yahweh in victory (31)
> A' Yahweh sayings (27, 30–31)[2]

As is typical, the smaller sections in this chapter flow into one another and the rest of Proverbs. Besides Yahweh sayings, this chapter also stands out for its emphasis on righteousness and justice (cf. 1:3 and Live the Story in Prov 20).

> [1] In the LORD's hand the king's heart is a stream of water
>   that he channels toward all who please him.
> [2] A person may think their own ways are right,
>   but the LORD weighs the heart.
> [3] To do what is right and just
>   is more acceptable to the LORD than sacrifice.
> [4] Haughty eyes and a proud heart—
>   the unplowed field of the wicked—produce sin.

---

1. Heim, *Grapes of Gold*, 288.

2. For a convincing explanation for why vv. 25–26 interrupt the Yahweh sayings at the end of the chapter, see Ibid., 284.

21:1–4 The Yahweh and royal sayings in chapter 20 continue in these first four verses.

Verse 1 clearly acknowledges God's hand behind the king, giving him "divinely enhanced judicial perspective" (cf. 8:15).[3] This parallels God's hand in military victory at the end of the chapter (v. 31). This verse also reflects on the mysterious intersection of human freedom and divine sovereignty (cf. 16:9).

Van Leeuwen is probably correct in saying that verses 2–4 reflect primarily on the king, particularly since kings are the primary keepers of justice (v. 3).[4] But the sayings are also connected through the common parallel of "right" (v. 2) and "right and just" (v. 3) and the fact that both sayings address false intentions and actions alongside God's standard for true righteousness. See Live the Story below for reflections on 20:3.

Verse 4 stands as a negative parallel to 20:3.[5] Verse 4b is unclear in the original. Available Hebrew manuscripts contain both *ner*, "lamp," and *nir*, "tillage" or "cultivated field."[6] Both translations make sense,[7] but Fox seems to be right that the lamp, as a metaphor for what guides our way in life, is a better parallel for 4a.[8] Fox is supported by the fact that "lamp" also occurs in close context in 20:20, 27 and the notion of sight is already present in the "eyes" in verse 4. We find a comparative piece of folklore in Jotham's parable about trees and bramble in Judges 9:7–15.

> [5] The plans of the diligent lead to profit
>   as surely as haste leads to poverty.
> [6] A fortune made by a lying tongue
>   is a fleeting vapor and a deadly snare.
> [7] The violence of the wicked will drag them away,
>   for they refuse to do what is right.
> [8] The way of the guilty is devious,
>   but the conduct of the innocent is upright.

21:5–8 These verses portray observations of two righteous people (5a, 8b) framing four wicked people (5b-8a).

Verses 5–6 present a pair of sayings about profit in the marketplace. Hard work and its profits contrast with "haste" and "poverty" (cf. 6:18; 13:11 and related sayings in 15:25; 16:3; 19:2, 21; 28:20). Verse 6 expands on the

---

3. Ibid., 286.
4. Van Leeuwen, *Proverbs*, 192.
5. Meinhold, *Sprüche*, 348.
6. Following Waltke again, the 2011 NIV updates its older "lamp" to "unplowed field."
7. For a concise comparison see Clifford, *Proverbs*, 189.
8. Fox, *Proverbs 10–31*, 680.

image in 21:5b: hasty and careless work results in transient wealth that is quickly lost.

Verses 7–8 present the final three people in a list of six. Violent people fall to their own vices (7, cf. 13 and Matt 26:52). Those who "refuse" justice (7b) mirror those who "refuse" hard work in 21:25. We find a creative wordplay in the center of 21:8 that accentuates the opposition between the "devious," *zar*, "guilty" person,[9] and the *zak*, "pure" person who is "upright."

9 Better to live on a corner of the roof
   than share a house with a quarrelsome wife.
10 The wicked crave evil;
   their neighbors get no mercy from them.
11 When a mocker is punished, the simple gain wisdom;
   by paying attention to the wise they get knowledge.
12 The Righteous One takes note of the house of the wicked
   and brings the wicked to ruin.

21:9–12 These verses concern matters in the family house as well as related social settings.[10] Most of the sayings in 21:10–17 put us in the middle of interactions between the righteous and the wicked.

Verse 9, like 21:19, stands out from the surrounding context and serves as a structural marker (see outline above). Similar markers can be seen in 11:16, 22; 12:4; 18:22; 19:13. Furthermore, similar sayings about the quarreling wife occur in 19:13; 25:24; 27:15. Contentious spouses and disobedient children are the two threats to the well-being of a house (family life).[11]

Verses 10–12 display three developing scenes: a public injustice, people learning from public discipline, and people executing public discipline for injustice. The first scene (10) contains wordplay between the "evil," *ra*, desired by the wicked and the "neighbor," *rea*, who shows the wicked no "mercy." The craving of the wicked is taken up again in verses 17 and 25. Themes of compassion and withholding mercy occur throughout Proverbs (14:21, 31; 19:17; 28:8).

Verses 11–12 address various "modes of learning."[12] One can even see a frame of two scenes of inattentiveness (vv. 10, 13) surrounded by two scenes of attentiveness and growing in wisdom and righteousness (11–12). The word *ubehaskil* could be translated "when a wise person prospers" rather than, "by

9. This could also be translated "strange;" see Van Leeuwen, *Proverbs*, 193.
10. It is worth consulting Heim, *Grapes of Gold*, 293–96, who sees vv. 9–19 as a cluster enclosed by the two sayings of the "quarrelsome wife."
11. Clifford, *Proverbs*, 190.
12. Van Leeuwen, *Proverbs*, 193.

paying attention" (NIV), in which case the good fortune of the wise offers yet another mode of learning. In 21:12, the "righteous one"[13] witnesses the acts of the wicked and responds by bringing "the wicked to ruin."

> [13] Whoever shuts their ears to the cry of the poor
>   will also cry out and not be answered.
> [14] A gift given in secret soothes anger,
>   and a bribe concealed in the cloak pacifies great wrath.
> [15] When justice is done it brings joy to the righteous
>   but terror to evildoers.

21:13–15 These verses echo several themes in the chapter but focus primarily on justice and judgment. Verse 13 parallels verses 7 and 10 in the way the sinful actions of the wicked return to them in their fall. He who lives by the sword will die by the sword.

Verse 14 is enigmatic. On the whole, the Old Testament condemns bribes (see Live the Story in Proverbs 19 above). But verse 14 seems to commend bribes, particularly in the way they calm anger and wrath, which—in Proverbs—are antithetical to wisdom. The idea in mind here can be seen in an anecdote about the German pastor Dietrich Bonhoeffer. Bonhoeffer participated in conspiracies to assassinate Adolf Hitler and yet when he attended a rally with his friend and biographer Eberhard Bethge, Bonhoeffer had the presence of mind to offer the Nazi salute to Hitler, saying to Bethge, "put up your hand, you fool." [14] There are times when pacifying wrath and irrational uses of power are necessary for a greater good.

The first line of 21:15 could also be read, "The righteous rejoice in doing justice," which is the preference of many scholars. Following a string of situations involving observations of justice and injustice, this verse reflects on two kinds of emotions or satisfaction we have in observing justice acted out in the public square (cf. 10:28–29).[15]

> [16] Whoever strays from the path of prudence
>   comes to rest in the company of the dead.
> [17] Whoever loves pleasure will become poor;
>   whoever loves wine and olive oil will never be rich.

---

13. The NIV capitalizes "Righteous" and "One," assuming this refers to Yahweh. But the king and other wise people are in the more immediate context. English readers should be aware that Hebrew does not have capitalization and such changes are more a matter of interpretation than translation, though the two are intertwined.

14. The story comes from Douglas Templeton, "There are Lies, Damned Lies and Romanticism: A Classic Approach to the Problem of Theoria," *Theology in Scotland* 16.1 (2009): 51–66.

15. See Fox, *Proverbs 10–31*, 129.

¹⁸ The wicked become a ransom for the righteous,
   and the unfaithful for the upright.

21:16–18 Verses 16 and 17 are a proverb pair about two foolish people and the consequences they reap. The sayings begin with a Hebrew word for "man," *adam* (16) and *ish* (17), translated "whoever" by the NIV. Verse 16 articulates matters in general terms: man/humans who stray from prudence will join the gathering of the dead. In the Pentateuch *qahal*, "gathering,"¹⁶ almost always signifies the assembly of Israel—whether in the desert or at the tabernacle (cf. Exod 12:6). *Qahal* is only used twice more in Proverbs, both times for the community of the faithful (5:14; 26:26). In this context *qahal* signifies the cosmic hoard of the dead in 7:27 and 9:18.

Verse 17 repeats a common warning about gluttony, cautioning here that it leads to poverty—a theme picked up in verses 20 and 25–26 below.

¹⁹ Better to live in a desert
   than with a quarrelsome and nagging wife.
²⁰ The wise store up choice food and olive oil,
   but fools gulp theirs down.
²¹ Whoever pursues righteousness and love
   finds life, prosperity and honor.
²² One who is wise can go up against the city of the mighty
   and pull down the stronghold in which they trust.
²³ Those who guard their mouths and their tongues
   keep themselves from calamity.

21:19–23 Verse 19 is a variant of verse 9 (see above). Verses 20–29 have very little evidence of individual clusters, so this grouping is somewhat arbitrary.

Verses 20–23 are sayings about the wise and the righteous, enclosed by two sayings related to control of the mouth with regard to food and speech (cf. 19:28). "Wise" appears in verses 20 and 22. The saying in 21:20 echoes 21:17 and other proverbs in this chapter related to greed and wealth. Storehouses and savings sometimes symbolize power and greed, but here they stand as virtues that hold off gluttony. Verse 20b could be read as saying that "fools" consume the storehouses of the "wise" (cf. v. 22).

Verse 21 commends those who *radap*, "pursue" or "chase," "righteousness and love," assuring them of finding "life, righteousness, and honor."¹⁷ The verse echoes David in Psalm 23:6, who rejoices that the same *hesed*, "love," will *radap*, "pursue," him all of his days. Just as love was reciprocal between

---

16. NIV, "company."
17. NIV, "life, prosperity, and honor."

God, Woman Wisdom, and humanity in Proverbs 8:22–36, it is here as well.

The "wise" in 21:22 can bring down the strength of the city. Given the possibility that the "fools" in verse 20 are understood as swallowing the savings of the "wise," it is possible that this group of the "wise" represent a source of help to their besieged counterparts. The trust of a strong city here anticipates hope in the battle horse in 21:31.

In 21:23 "guard" and "keep" are the same Hebrew word, accentuating the parallels between wise speech and safe living.

> [24] The proud and arrogant person—"Mocker" is his name—
> behaves with insolent fury.
> [25] The craving of a sluggard will be the death of him,
> because his hands refuse to work.
> [26] All day long he craves for more,
> but the righteous give without sparing.
> [27] The sacrifice of the wicked is detestable—
> how much more so when brought with evil intent!
> [28] A false witness will perish,
> but a careful listener will testify successfully.
> [29] The wicked put up a bold front,
> but the upright give thought to their ways.

21:24–29 Verse 24 turns sharply from the four righteous characters in the previous cluster to pick up the proud person from verse 4, adding to his character behaviors of mocking and anger.

Verses 25–26 contain a pair of sayings about the "sluggard." Themes here resemble earlier sayings in the chapter: the craving of the wicked (10), the "death" of fools (6), and the wicked who "refuse" to do justice (7). Verse 7 is a particularly close parallel that reinforces the link between wickedness, laziness, and injustice. Verse 26 provides a contrast to the "righteous," whose self-control (cf. 20) goes hand-in-hand with generosity.

As noted in the outline at the start of this chapter, verses 27 and 30–31 stand in balance to the Yahweh sayings in verses 1–3. While "Yahweh" does not appear, many scholars observe that *toebah*, "abomination,"[18] typically implies a connection to Yahweh. "Sacrifice" clearly assumes a connection with God. This saying echoes the proverb about sacrifices and justice and righteousness in verse 3 (see more at v. 30 below).

Verse 27 also introduces an aside in which the "wicked" are contrasted to the "upright" in verses 28–29. The "wicked" are inherently deceptive as

---

18. NIV, "detestable."

witnesses (28), which parallels the duplicity of their "bold front" (29). The "upright," by contrast, exhibit conscientiousness in listening "carefully" before testifying and thinking before speaking.

> [30] There is no wisdom, no insight,
>   no plan that can succeed against the LORD.
> [31] The horse is made ready for the day of battle,
>   but victory rests with the LORD.

21:30–31 These verses are Yahweh sayings connected to 21:27. Verse 30 employs a superlative list of threes—"no wisdom," "no insight," or "no plan"—to make an epistemological point: no human intellectual genius can stand next to Yahweh in his wisdom. Verse 31 makes the same point with regard to weapons of war, which signify inability of the best of human technology to compete with Yahweh's power. Placed alongside verses 27–29, a broader statement emerges: no deceptive manipulation of cultural institutions, technological skill or human craft, or ritual sacrifice can compare to Yahweh's wisdom, escape his notice, or stand against his plans.

LIVE the Story

Victory Through Technology

One of the major themes in this chapter is the contrast between human ingenuity and intelligence and divine wisdom and justice (cf. 20:22, 27, 30–31). Whether participating in ritual behavior to gain favor or depending on education, science, and technology to secure our path through life, humans are inescapably prone to autonomy and manipulation (cf. Pss 20:7; 25:7; 33:16–17).

One might argue that technology plays an even more powerful role today than in the world of ancient Israel. Our technology in many ways protects us from everything from extremes in weather patterns and common diseases to risk in financial markets and surprise invasions from foreign countries. This rapid acceleration of technological advancements has coincided with a simultaneous "desacralization of nature" in which supposed scientific "facts" can be distinguished from the less significant "values," such as ethics or "oughts," and religion or beliefs.[19] God and faith are, in essence, sidelined and subordinated to science and reason, and humans replace God as the owners and master of creation.

The technological impulse was evident in ancient culture as well. Aaron undoubtedly showed genius and skill as well as awareness of hip religious

---

19. Stephen Monsma, ed. *Responsible Technology: A Christian Perspective*, Calvin Center for Christian Fellowship (Grand Rapids: Eerdmans, 1986), 27–28.

fads when he fashioned the golden calf—an object of worship that displaced
Yahweh and his work in saving Israel (Exod 32:1–9). But today most people
are born accepting as fact that humans are all-knowing and autonomous and
that technology is a neutral sphere of life. Neither of these assumptions is
true and both rely on assigning values and purposes to people, society, and
nature—values to which people are as religiously committed as the values of
a Christian, Jewish, Buddhist, or other believer.[20]

And so science and technology should be recognized for the religious
power they have gained in culture that is able to replace God and his authoritative ordering of nature. Science and technology are also both subject to
often-overlooked limits. Matthew Dickerson observes four such limitations.[21]
One, human knowledge is limited; we are far from knowing everything about
the world and so we may have reasoning that is "valid," i.e., logical, but not
"sound," because we have made a false assumption based upon something we
do not know. Two, much in scientific and technological reasoning is inductive
in that, given limited information, we are forced to choose between equally
viable possibilities or solutions. These inductive choices often prove to be
wrong. Three, all human reason is limited by the constraints of human language. Language is indeed a remarkable human skill, but everyone experiences
the gaps and confusion that arise in our daily speech with others and the same
happens in the world of "pure reason." And most importantly, human reason
is inescapably shaped and influenced by the power of our desires. We have
seen several proverbs that reinforce this power of our desires and motives to
lead us to choose the wrong thing and to act unwisely.

That said, technology and human learning are not inherently evil and
certainly not something to be avoided. Indeed, God's invitation to be caretak-
ers of the creation in Genesis 1–2 is a command to make things out of culture.
Further, as we will see in the work of the valiant woman in chapter 31, wisdom has a distinct place in joyfully pursuing those technologies that best suit
God's order. The work of this valiant woman anticipates the work and person
of Jesus Christ. It is easy to forget that his work is very often framed in the
language of building and the technology of creation: Jesus is the full revelation
of the *creator God* (John 1:12), "all things have been created through him and
for him" (Col 1:16; cf. John 1:3), and his redemption is working to reconcile
"all things, whether things on earth or things in heaven" (Col 1:20). The
technology of great vineyards, walls, houses, and cities, moreover, symbolizes
the intricacy and power of his coming kingdom.

---

20. Ibid., 24–36, 112–13.
21. Matthew Dickerson, *The Mind and the Machine: What it Means to be Human and Why
it Matters* (Grand Rapids: Brazos, 2011), 183–87.

¹ A good name is more desirable than great riches;
    to be esteemed is better than silver or gold.
² Rich and poor have this in common:
    The Lord is the Maker of them all.
³ The prudent see danger and take refuge,
    but the simple keep going and pay the penalty.
⁴ Humility is the fear of the Lord;
    its wages are riches and honor and life.
⁵ In the paths of the wicked are snares and pitfalls,
    but those who would preserve their life stay far from them.
⁶ Start children off on the way they should go,
    and even when they are old they will not turn from it.
⁷ The rich rule over the poor,
    and the borrower is slave to the lender.
⁸ Whoever sows injustice reaps calamity,
    and the rod they wield in fury will be broken.
⁹ The generous will themselves be blessed,
    for they share their food with the poor.
¹⁰ Drive out the mocker, and out goes strife;
    quarrels and insults are ended.
¹¹ One who loves a pure heart and who speaks with grace
    will have the king for a friend.
¹² The eyes of the Lord keep watch over knowledge,
    but he frustrates the words of the unfaithful.
¹³ The sluggard says, "There's a lion outside!
    vI'll be killed in the public square!"
¹⁴ The mouth of an adulterous woman is a deep pit;
    a man who is under the Lord's wrath falls into it.
¹⁵ Folly is bound up in the heart of a child,

but the rod of discipline will drive it far away.

16 One who oppresses the poor to increase his wealth
   and one who gives gifts to the rich—both come to poverty.
17 Pay attention and turn your ear to the sayings of the wise;
   apply your heart to what I teach,
18 for it is pleasing when you keep them in your heart
   and have all of them ready on your lips.
19 So that your trust may be in the LORD,
   I teach you today, even you.
20 Have I not written thirty sayings for you,
   sayings of counsel and knowledge,
21 teaching you to be honest and to speak the truth,
   so that you bring back truthful reports to those you serve?
22 Do not exploit the poor because they are poor
   and do not crush the needy in court,
23 for the LORD will take up their case
   and will exact life for life.
24 Do not make friends with a hot-tempered person,
   do not associate with one easily angered,
25 or you may learn their ways
   and get yourself ensnared.
26 Do not be one who shakes hands in pledge
   or puts up security for debts;
27 if you lack the means to pay,
   your very bed will be snatched from under you.
28 Do not move an ancient boundary stone
   set up by your ancestors.
29 Do you see someone skilled in their work?
   They will serve before kings;
   they will not serve before officials of low rank.

Listening to the Text in the Story: Leviticus 25; Deuteronomy 15:4, 11; Psalm 10; Isaiah 5:8–10; 58:6–11; Amenemope III.8–IV.1; XX.21–XXI.8; XXVI.6

The Old Testament concedes that there will always be poor among us (Deut 15:11; cf. Matt 26:11), but it also goes to great lengths to make Israel responsible for relieving the plight of the poor and vulnerable (e.g Lev 25; Deut 15:1–18; 24:17–22; Prov 22:1, 2, 9, 16, 22, 28; Isa 5:8–10, etc.).

Furthermore, while the Bible commands us to share with the poor (Deut 16:16–17; Prov 22:9), it also protects the borders and boundary markers of private property (Num 32:33; 34:2, 12; Deut 19:14; 32:8; 1 Kings 21:1–29; Prov 15:25; 22:28; 23:10). That said, land and property ultimately belong to Yahweh and are given as a covenant gift (Exod 23:31; 34:24) and withdrawn when the covenant is broken (Is 10:13).

The most significant parallels between Proverbs and the Instruction of Amenemope occur in 22:17–24:22. As discussed at various points in this commentary, many scholars assume that Proverbs is dependent on Amenemope at this point. But there are enough differences between the two books for this to be anything more than a suspicion. Common content does not mean common origin. Furthermore, as I argue throughout the commentary, wisdom sayings are so prevalent throughout cultures of the ancient world that it makes sense to assume that these texts are just an indication of our common human experience in the world. Several specific parallels are discussed in the commentary in chapters 22–24.

EXPLAIN the Story

[1] A good name is more desirable than great riches;
    to be esteemed is better than silver or gold.
[2] Rich and poor have this in common:
    The LORD is the Maker of them all.
[3] The prudent see danger and take refuge,
    but the simple keep going and pay the penalty.
[4] Humility is the fear of the LORD;
    its wages are riches and honor and life.
[5] In the paths of the wicked are snares and pitfalls,
    but those who would preserve their life stay far from them.
[6] Start children off on the way they should go,
    and even when they are old they will not turn from it.

Verses 1–16 end the Solomonic collection that begins at 10:1 (though cf. a partial restart at 15:1). More will be said about this after 22:16 below. The sayings in verses 1–16 are loosely connected, as can be seen in the various ways scholars have tried to organize them: Meinhold (1–4, 5–6, 7–14, 15, 16), Waltke (1–9; 10–16), Heim (1–5; 6–16).

22:1–6 The first pair of sayings in verses 1 and 2 qualify the privileges and benefits of wealth. Verse 1 emphasizes the superiority of a good reputation to wealth and privilege (cf. Eccl 7:1). As Van Leeuwen observes of verse 2, the "intent is to qualify and mitigate economic divisions that humans are prone to make so much of, thereby denying the humanity that binds them together and to their Maker."[1] In this way the saying restores dignity to the poor and marginalized.

Besides verse 4, all of the verses in 3–6 speak specifically to "ways" and "paths," with the first two sayings (3, 5) setting up the last (6). Wise people take "refuge" while the "simple" wander into trouble (3; cf. 27:12), and the "wicked" take a path strewn with fatal dangers, while those concerned for their lives keep away from such people (cf. 18:24). Verse 6 then exhorts parents to supply the wisdom their children need to walk wisely and find life.

Despite the absence of *way* language, verse 4 fits naturally among these sayings. First, it embodies the heart and disposition of those who stay on safe paths. It also fleshes out the safe place and refuge of verses 3, 5, and 6 as a life of "riches and honor and life."

The 2011 NIV of verse 4a reads, "Humility is the fear of the LORD," an update to the version of 1984, "Humility and the fear of the LORD." These are certainly different ideas, and the earlier translation may be better for "the fear of the LORD" goes beyond humility to include a worldview (2:5), "[hating] evil" (8:13), knowing God (9:10), and a whole way of wise living (31:30). The immediate point of the verse seems to fit with Waltke's translation, "Humility—the-fear-of-the-Lord sort," that is, an attitude of learning needed by the "simple" and "children" who hear such sayings.[2]

> [7] The rich rule over the poor,
>   and the borrower is slave to the lender.
> [8] Whoever sows injustice reaps calamity,
>   and the rod they wield in fury will be broken.
> [9] The generous will themselves be blessed,
>   for they share their food with the poor.

22:7–9 Continuing with the themes of wealth and social class, these verses state a reality (7), a threat of consequences for those who propagate inequalities (8), and promise of blessings for those who resist them (9). In Matthew 26:52 Jesus memorably tells the disciples, "for all who draw the sword will die by the sword." This image of ironic means and ends appears in various forms throughout Proverbs (17:13; 18:7; 19:3; 20:17; 21:25; 22:8; cf. Job 4:8).

The consequences and blessings are not guarantees, of course, but rather serve to undergird God's moral ordering of the world (cf. 16, 22, 28 below).

---

1. Van Leeuwen, *Proverbs*, 197–98.
2. Waltke, *Proverbs 15–31*, 193.

"Generous" in the NIV and other translations is literally "a good eye"—in other words, one who sees or takes notice of the needy in the world. "Eyes" appears again in verse 12, referring to Yahweh who watches to protect "knowledge" and counter injustice.

¹⁰ Drive out the mocker, and out goes strife;
     quarrels and insults are ended.
¹¹ One who loves a pure heart and who speaks with grace
     will have the king for a friend.
¹² The eyes of the LORD keep watch over knowledge,
     but he frustrates the words of the unfaithful.
¹³ The sluggard says, "There's a lion outside!
     I'll be killed in the public square!"
¹⁴ The mouth of an adulterous woman is a deep pit;
     a man who is under the LORD's wrath falls into it.
¹⁵ Folly is bound up in the heart of a child,
     but the rod of discipline will drive it far away.
¹⁶ One who oppresses the poor to increase his wealth
     and one who gives gifts to the rich—both come to poverty.

22:10–16 This cluster consists of two sayings concerning social relations (10–11), a central Yahweh saying (12), and four types of foolish or wicked people (13–16).

Verses 10–11 resemble the sayings in Proverbs 26:4–5. Verse 10 is a reminder that social order sometimes requires confrontation and even forcefully expelling the "mocker," while verse 11 shows that confrontation must be balanced by kindness and speech that leads to social and even political favor.

Verse 12 returns the "eyes" of the "generous" person in verse 9, also imagining the "eyes" of Yahweh that see all. In this case, Yahweh "watch[es] over knowledge," where "knowledge" serves as a metonymy for the wise person in all his attributes—likely the one described in verse 11.[3] In its context the saying provides a reminder that, alongside our efforts to preserve social order, Yahweh is the ultimate standard for, and keeper of, justice.

In terms that are humorous, grotesque, and violent, verses 13–16 depict four kinds of wicked fools. The humorous mockery of the sluggard (v. 13) resembles sayings in 19:24 and 26:13. Clifford observes that lines a and b end with assonantal terms: *ari*, "lion," *eraseah*, "I will be killed." Verse 14 restates sayings about "foreign" women in chapters 1–9 (2:16–19; 5:3–6; 6:24–26; 7:25–27), here in terms of the woman's speech and the one who listens to

_____
3. See Heim, *Grapes of Gold*, 310.

her who is doomed to death (9:16–18; cf. 23:27). Corporal discipline of the child in 20:15 supports the pro-discipline saying in verse 6.[4] Verse 16 offers a warning against mistreating the poor and seeking favor with the rich. The saying appears to be a bridge, as its emphasis on poverty echoes throughout both divisions of this chapter (2, 7, 9, 22–23) and its warning about bribery resembles other sayings about gaining favor with the social elite (1, 11, 29).

> [17] Pay attention and turn your ear to the sayings of the wise;
>   apply your heart to what I teach,
> [18] for it is pleasing when you keep them in your heart
>   and have all of them ready on your lips.
> [19] So that your trust may be in the LORD,
>   I teach you today, even you.
> [20] Have I not written thirty sayings for you,
>   sayings of counsel and knowledge,
> [21] teaching you to be honest and to speak the truth,
>   so that you bring back truthful reports to those you serve?

The collection of 22:17–24:34 contains almost forty sayings, which Clifford calls a "professional ethical guidebook," that fall into three distinct sections: "young people ambitioning a career" (22:17–23:11), "concerns of youth" (23:12–35), and "destinies of the good and the wicked" (24:1–34).[5]

22:17–21 The opening quatrain introduces the sayings from 22:22 to 24:22 and moves from (a) a call to learn wisdom with the whole of our human faculties (17–18), to (b) the fundamental refrain of the fear of, and trust in, Yahweh (19; cf. 3:5; 1:7; 9:10), and (c) a concluding assurance from the father.

Verses 20–21 present two major challenges. First, the Masoretic Text reads *silsom*, which means "three days" or "formerly," but many scholars and most translations follow the emendation *salisim*, "thirty." Technical points of Hebrew syntax are beyond the scope of this commentary,[6] but, contrary to many scholars, I do not believe either reading can be eliminated entirely— "formerly" fits perfectly well with the father's sayings to the son in Proverbs 1–9 and this section of Proverbs (22:17–23:11) has also been shown to have significant parallels with the Egyptian writings of Amenemope, where a father writes thirty sayings to a son. The number thirty carries symbolic meaning in Egyptian writings, which makes the translation "thirty" just as plausible as "formerly." Nevertheless, scholarly efforts to fit the material in chapters 22–23

---

4. See commentary above at 13:24 and Live the Story at the end of that chapter on corporal discipline.
5. Clifford, *Proverbs*, 199, ends these sections at 24:22 and starts a new section with seven sayings in 24:23–34, (p. 216). See 24:23 in the commentary below.
6. See Fox *Proverbs 10–31*, 709–12 and Waltke, *Proverbs 15–31*, 219–20.

into thirty sayings is strained, to say the very least. Thus, even if "thirty" is borrowed as a play on the wisdom of Amenemope, the editors did not feel constrained to hold their collection of sayings to only thirty.

The father's words in 22:21 present a further challenge. While the father's assurances in Proverbs 1–9 make all-encompassing promises, such as long life, prosperity, protection, and exaltation, the father's promise here is narrow, if not obscure.[7] He seems to assure the son that all these teachings will serve only to make him a faithful witness or reliable representative for future employers. It may simply be the case that the writer has followed a similar assurance in Amenemope rather than aligning it more closely with Proverbs 1–9.

> [22] Do not exploit the poor because they are poor
>   and do not crush the needy in court,
> [23] for the LORD will take up their case
>   and will exact life for life.
> [24] Do not make friends with a hot-tempered person,
>   do not associate with one easily angered,
> [25] or you may learn their ways
>   and get yourself ensnared.
> [26] Do not be one who shakes hands in pledge
>   or puts up security for debts;
> [27] if you lack the means to pay,
>   your very bed will be snatched from under you.

22:22–27 These verses contain three pairs of sayings that resemble the instructions in Amenemope. The sayings also share many parallels with the legal rules in the Pentateuch (Exod 22:20–26; Deut 19:14; 24:10–13; 27:17). Only the middle saying (vv. 24–25) does not speak to matters of justice.

Verses 22–23 seek to allay taking advantage of the poor by promising that Yahweh will defend their cause. Clifford says, "Paradoxically [the poor] have a more powerful protector than the rich could afford" (cf. 7, 16).[8] A more literal translation of the Hebrew in verse 23 demonstrates its witty and memorable form: "For Yahweh will contend their contention and he will rob the robbers of life."

Verses 24–25 provide a match to the saying in verse 10, which commands expelling the "mocker" and quarreler. This latter pair warns if we have friendships and associations with those prone to anger their vices will inevitably rub off on us.

---

7. Cf. also Longman, *Proverbs*, 416, who describes this verse as "enigmatic" and Murphy, *Proverbs*, 170, who says that there is "no apparent reason [this assurance] should be mentioned at this point."

8. Clifford, *Proverbs*, 207.

The warning in 22:26–27 against the "pledge" or "security" is repeated in various ways in Proverbs (see commentary on Prov 6:1–15; 11:15; and Listen to the Story in chapter 6:1–19). In a turn on this financial warning, Job appears to ask God to provide a "security" or "pledge" since he has no friends to walk with him in his suffering and false accusations (Job 17:3).

> [28] Do not move an ancient boundary stone
>   set up by your ancestors.
> [29] Do you see someone skilled in their work?
>   They will serve before kings;
>   they will not serve before officials of low rank.

22:28–29 Verse 28 is the second of three sayings that uphold the rights of land ownership through boundary markers (cf. 15:25: 23:10). The Mosaic laws also continually reinforce this same protection of land inheritance and boundaries (Lev 25:8–34; Num 27:1–11; 36:1–12; Deut 19:14; 27:17; cf. Job 24:2; Hos 5:10). The saying applies equally to anyone's possession that might be manipulated in an exchange or a sale.

Chapters 22:28 and 23:10 enclose a longer section of sayings that address the sage whose skill in the crafts of wisdom will gain access to "kings" and the rich (v. 29; cf. Gen 39:1–41:57; Dan. 1:1–2:49; Esth. 5:1–14; 7:1–8:17). But this privilege must be guarded as he is only fit to enjoy the wealth as a guest.

 LIVE the Story

Discernment and Danger
Several sayings in this chapter depict negative consequences in intense images (vv. 3, 5, 10, 14, 22–28), fitting with the general pattern in which Proverbs states the consequences for wickedness and folly in extreme terms of danger and wrath. Common examples include coming to ruin, falling, falling into a pit, death, wrath, terror, condemnation, blows, stripes, beatings, flogging, being hated, falling into thorns, and going hungry. In chapters 1–9 these threats are found in the mouth of Woman Wisdom (1:26–31; 9:1–6).

Such warnings are also prevalent among the prophets, who speak in terms of Yahweh's judgment,[9] and even more so among the psalms (2:4–5; 7:13–15; 10:2, 15; 17:13; 21:10–12; 34:21–22; 35:1–28; etc.). In this light, Proverbs 22:22–23 bears a striking resemblance to Psalm 10.

---

9. See Murphy, *Proverbs*, 10–11.

Psalm 10	Proverbs 22
In his arrogance the wicked man hunts down the [poor], who are caught in the schemes he devises. . . . Arise, LORD! Lift up your hand, O God. Do not forget the [poor]. . . . Break the arm of the wicked man; call the evildoer to account for his wickedness that would not otherwise be found out.	Do not exploit the poor because they are poor and do not crush the needy in court, for the LORD will take up their case and will exact life for life.

The NIV renders the Hebrew *ani* "weak" and "helpless" in Psalms, but "poor" in Proverbs. These are all legitimate translations of *ani,* but readers of English Bibles might easily overlook the fact both texts show Yahweh returning punishment on those who abuse the same needy persons.

Two issues bear further discussion in regards to this extreme rhetoric. First, we should ask why these biblical books appeal to such language when we know that the consequences for the wicked in this life are often minimal or non-existent. The reason for this most likely lies in the area of cognitive and psychological sciences and what we call left-brain and right-brain thinking. While modern neuroscience has shown that these lateral distinctions are greatly oversimplified, we do know that human thought and persuasion involve logical, creative, and embodied experience.[10] Psalms, Proverbs, and the prophets all appeal to this fuller aspect of our human identity; our bodily and sensory life aligns with what we know to be true logically about God's just rules for the world. (See "Shock, Surprise, and Moral Shaping" in Live the Story in chapter 25).

Second, while Psalms and the prophets share their grounding in the blessings and curses of Israel's covenant, Proverbs says almost nothing about the covenant. While a lot has been made of this distinction between wisdom and law/covenant, more recent scholarship is beginning to put less emphasis on differences or oppositions between these two types of writing (see "Wisdom and Law" in the Introduction). Moreover, as we have shown in discussions throughout this commentary, Proverbs is grounded in the larger created order

---

10. See Freedberg and Gallese, "Motion, Emotion and Empathy," 197, 198, who say that "the physical responses seem to be located in precisely those parts of the body that are threatened, pressured, constrained or destabilized" in the work of art, and "Our capacity to pre-rationally make sense of the actions, emotions and sensations of others depends on embodied simulation, a functional mechanism through which the actions, emotions or sensations we see activate our own internal representations of the body states that are associated with these social stimuli . . ."

of God's world, where wisdom points to the safe and upright way to navigate life. Israel's law and covenant are one particular social, moral, and legal system set up within and in agreement with this larger created order.

Poor Pressure

The image of oppressing the poor "because they are poor" in Proverbs 22:22–23 resembles the prohibitions in Deuteronomy 24:10–15, which protect the poor from the manipulations of the rich, specifically with regard to shaming the poor man by entering his house (10–11) or depriving the poor of basic rights by keeping his or her cloak overnight (12–13).[11]

Something along these lines also appears to be at the heart of the exchange between Ahab, king of Israel, and Ben-Hadad, king of Aram, in 1 Kings 20:1–12.[12] Having defeated Ahab in battle, Ben-Hadad first demands that Ahab hand over his "silver and gold" and "the best of [his] wives and children" (20:3). Ahab agrees to surrender all that he has, only to have Ben-Hadad make the further demand of entering Ahab's "palace and the houses of [his] officials" to take his spoils (6). Ahab demurs at this point, most likely because Ben-Hadad is determined to shame Ahab and his officials at a point of weakness and vulnerability.

Practically, this kind of leverage and manipulation occurs in every layer of society. Large corporations often strong-arm smaller producers into reducing the prices on their merchandise so that the corporation can control supply and profit in the retail market. Most suppliers have little choice but to comply. Similarly, the growing power of online retailers is placing increased pressure on low-wage employees who deliver packages into the evenings and on Sundays and holidays.

At the level of the city, the poor and the weak are increasingly cut off from the benefits of higher society as urbanization leaves affordable housing in the worst neighborhoods, with the worst schools, and poorest social conditions. And within each of our families and places of work there are traditions and rituals that penalize the youngest, the new employee, the "rookie," and the "lowest on the totem pole."

The gospel decisively upends these cultural and social trends. The washing of the disciples' feet (John 13:1–20) and Jesus' parable of the laborers in the vineyard (Matt 20:1–16) are two of Jesus' many actions and teachings that resist our inclinations to overlook the marginalized in society around us: "So the last will be first, and the first will be last" (Matt 20:16). At the personal

---

11. The somewhat coincidental penalty for the foolish creditor losing his "bed" in Prov 22:26–27 may suggest a remote relationship between these passages in Deuteronomy and Proverbs.

12. These connections can be found in Daube, *Biblical Law and Literature*, 531–33.

level every one of us can live in a way that remains aware of the overlooked, the needy, and the neglected in our midst. But how do we respond to the systemic problems in our world as a whole? This is a much more difficult question and one that cannot be answered with any specificity here. What can be said is that Christians should pursue their vocations with a deep and driving conviction that we must fight to resist the structures that lead to social gaps in our culture. And then we must think, pray, and labor creatively to form new structures to replace those that are failing us.

LISTEN to the Story

¹ When you sit to dine with a ruler,
  note well what is before you,
² and put a knife to your throat
  if you are given to gluttony.
³ Do not crave his delicacies,
  for that food is deceptive.
⁴ Do not wear yourself out to get rich;
  do not trust your own cleverness.
⁵ Cast but a glance at riches, and they are gone,
  for they will surely sprout wings
  and fly off to the sky like an eagle.
⁶ Do not eat the food of a begrudging host,
  do not crave his delicacies;
⁷ for he is the kind of person
  who is always thinking about the cost.
"Eat and drink," he says to you,
  but his heart is not with you.
⁸ You will vomit up the little you have eaten
  and will have wasted your compliments.
⁹ Do not speak to fools,
  for they will scorn your prudent words.
¹⁰ Do not move an ancient boundary stone
  or encroach on the fields of the fatherless,
¹¹ for their Defender is strong;
  he will take up their case against you.
¹² Apply your heart to instruction
  and your ears to words of knowledge.
¹³ Do not withhold discipline from a child;
  if you punish them with the rod, they will not die.

¹⁴ Punish them with the rod
and save them from death.
¹⁵ My son, if your heart is wise,
then my heart will be glad indeed;
¹⁶ my inmost being will rejoice
when your lips speak what is right.
¹⁷ Do not let your heart envy sinners,
but always be zealous for the fear of the Lord.
¹⁸ There is surely a future hope for you,
and your hope will not be cut off.
¹⁹ Listen, my son, and be wise,
and set your heart on the right path:
²⁰ Do not join those who drink too much wine
or gorge themselves on meat,
²¹ for drunkards and gluttons become poor,
and drowsiness clothes them in rags.
²² Listen to your father, who gave you life,
and do not despise your mother when she is old.
²³ Buy the truth and do not sell it—
wisdom, instruction and insight as well.
²⁴ The father of a righteous child has great joy;
a man who fathers a wise son rejoices in him.
²⁵ May your father and mother rejoice;
may she who gave you birth be joyful!
²⁶ My son, give me your heart
and let your eyes delight in my ways,
²⁷ for an adulterous woman is a deep pit,
and a wayward wife is a narrow well.
²⁸ Like a bandit she lies in wait
and multiplies the unfaithful among men.
²⁹ Who has woe? Who has sorrow?
Who has strife? Who has complaints?
Who has needless bruises?
Who has bloodshot eyes?
³⁰ Those who linger over wine,
who go to sample bowls of mixed wine.
³¹ Do not gaze at wine when it is red,
when it sparkles in the cup, when it goes down smoothly!

^{32} In the end it bites like a snake
   and poisons like a viper.
^{33} Your eyes will see strange sights,
   and your mind will imagine confusing things.
^{34} You will be like one sleeping on the high seas,
   lying on top of the rigging.
^{35} "They hit me," you will say, "but I'm not hurt!
   They beat me, but I don't feel it!
When will I wake up
   so I can find another drink?"

Listening to the Text in the Story: Genesis 39:1–41:57; Leviticus
15:47–55; Ruth 3; 2 Kings 5:1–27; Jeremiah 32:1–15; Amenemope
IX.14–X.5; XIV.4–XV.10; XXIII.13–20; Kagemeni (Kagemni)
I.7–11, 59–60; Ptahhotep 119–126; Ani IV.7–10

As can be seen in the list above and more passages cited in the commentary below, Proverbs 22:17–24:34 resonates with an immense range of ancient Near Eastern and biblical texts. Of particular note are the similarities between Amenemope and Proverbs. For example:

Amenemope	Proverbs
VII.12 Do not move the markers on the borders of fields	23:10a Do not move an ancient boundary stone (cf. 22:28a)
VII.15 nor encroach on the boundaries of a widow	23:10b or encroach on the fields of the fatherless
IX.11 Do not set your heart on wealth IX.14 Do not strain to seek increase	23:4 Do not wear yourself out to get rich
XIV.5–8 Do not covet a poor man's goods. Nor hunger for his bread; a poor man's goods are a block in the throat it makes the gullet vomit.[1]	23:3 Do not crave his delicacies, for that food is deceptive 23:6 Do not eat the [bread] of a begrudging host, do not crave his delicacies 23:8a You will vomit up the little you have eaten

A fuller view of these parallels between Amenemope and Proverbs 22:17–24:34 reveals many similarities and differences. On this point Heim wisely

---

1. "Instruction of Amenemope," trans. Miriam Lichtheim, *COS* 1:47:117–18.

counsels, "there are so many similarities that coincidence can be ruled out" and yet, "there are so many differences that we can conclude with confidence that Proverbs has not simply copied *Amenemope* but has adapted it creatively to craft new variants and paragraphs."[2]

In 2 Kings 5:1–27 we read about Elisha and Gehazi who go to Naaman the leper, commander of the Syrian army. The story illustrates the power of envy and jealousy that reach even the hearts of the Lord's prophets. We take this up in Live the Story below.

EXPLAIN the Story

On the whole, the material in this chapter addresses matters of envy, gluttony, and drunkenness, along with various sayings about justice, wisdom, and adultery. The chapter also falls in the middle of the sayings of the wise from 22:17 to 24:29, which has twenty-two sayings that employ the "do not . . ." form of prohibition, far more than any other portion of Proverbs aside from chapter 3, which has twenty such constructions. Chapter 3 also depicts the father speaking to matters of wealth, envy, generosity, and justice. The warnings against gluttony and drunkenness in chapter 23 provide a counterbalance to positive images of the blessing of abundant crops and wine in chapter 3. The wisdom of Proverbs thus naturally avoids thin moral absolutes; creation is a good gift of God and must be enjoyed within limits.

It also helps to notice the alternating patterns of general sayings about parental discipline and sayings about particular dangers.

Particular	1–11	Envy, food, and drink
General	12–16	Harsh discipline and intimate instruction
Particular	17–21	Envy and drunkenness
General	22–26(27)	Discipline, wisdom, intimacy
Particular	(26) 27–35	Adultery and drunkenness

[1] When you sit to dine with a ruler,
    note well what is before you,
[2] and put a knife to your throat
    if you are given to gluttony.
[3] Do not crave his delicacies,
    for that food is deceptive.

---

2. Heim, *Poetic Imagination*, 551.

⁴ Do not wear yourself out to get rich;
　　do not trust your own cleverness.
⁵ Cast but a glance at riches, and they are gone,
　　for they will surely sprout wings
　　and fly off to the sky like an eagle.
⁶ Do not eat the food of a begrudging host,
　　do not crave his delicacies;
⁷ for he is the kind of person
　　who is always thinking about the cost.
"Eat and drink," he says to you,
　　but his heart is not with you.
⁸ You will vomit up the little you have eaten
　　and will have wasted your compliments.
⁹ Do not speak to fools,
　　for they will scorn your prudent words.
¹⁰ Do not move an ancient boundary stone
　　or encroach on the fields of the fatherless,
¹¹ for their Defender is strong;
　　he will take up their case against you.

23:1–11 This first *particular* grouping begins with 22:28, which is the first of two sayings about the "ancient boundary stone" (cf. 23:10). The intervening material (22:29–23:9) addresses the proper conduct of the wise sage in the presence of wealthy and powerful hosts, weaving in keywords with slightly different meanings.

The chapter begins with a strangely violent image of putting a "knife" to the *loa*, "throat," when viewing the ruler's sumptuous table. Compare Jesus' "gouge [your eye] out" and "cut off . . . [your hand or your foot]" (Matt 5:29; 19:8–9). Hebrew *loa* plays on the synonym *nephesh* in the second half the verse, which is translated "gluttony" (more literally, "heathen of appetite"). *Nephesh* is used again to mean the inner thought life in verse 7. To "crave delicacies," *awah matam*, in verse 3 is repeated in verse 6, which also echoes the word "food" from verse 1. Meanwhile, *awah*, "long," is another virtual synonym for "throat" and "life." Desire and rational thought are distinct but inseparable concepts in Proverbs and nowhere is this more evident than when we are confronted with the envy of someone living where the grass looks greener and the meat smells richer. Such visions are ultimately "deceptive."³

---

3. Clifford, *Proverbs*, 209, perceptively notices that the unusual phrase "understand completely, consider carefully" (NIV "note well") must signify more than food, but the larger motives of dining with rulers to get an advantage in the first place.

In verses 4–5 financial excess is only a meaningful temptation where there are things to be had like food, wine, luxury, and power. As such, we should view this verse pair as an aside, providing a more general caution against envying the more abstract image of "wealth." "Do not wear yourself out" resembles Ecclesiastes 4:8; 5:13–20.

The command not to "trust your own cleverness" sounds somewhat out of place. Fox makes a plausible argument for translating the line, "Leave off your staring!"[4] Either way, the visible picture of the ruler's table in verse 1 parallels the "eye" (not translated in NIV) that "glance[s] at riches" (v. 5a).[5] The Hebrew manuscripts for verse 5b do not agree, but most scholars see a play on two uses of *uph*, "fly," in the eye that "flies" (NIV "glance[s]") over wealth (5a), and wealth that takes flight like an "eagle" (5b).

Verses 6–8 imagines a specific "host" or ruler (cf. v. 1) who is "begrudging" or "stingy" (literally "bad of eye"). Verse 6b repeats 3a above, only here the risk is greater than the envy imagined at first. Because of the false front of the host, the son in this context is involved in an exchange that proves to be humiliating to the point of making him sick. The land in Leviticus vomits up Israel in response to Israel defiling the land by acting like the sexually abhorrent Canaanites who lived there before them (Lev 18:25–28; 20:22). But compare Jonathan who had the prudence to fast from a meal full of violence and betrayal (1 Sam 20:24–34).

The saying about speech in 23:9 may seem out of place, but it follows naturally from the "wasted . . . compliments" in verse 8.[6] This follows similar warnings about the dangers of speaking to fools (9:7–8; 26:4–5; cf. Matt 7:6).

Verses 10–11 round out this group of sayings that began with a variant of the saying on the "ancient boundary" in 22:28.[7] This saying on the "boundary" provides the additional warning of future divine reckoning (cf. Jer 50:34).

> [12] Apply your heart to instruction
>   and your ears to words of knowledge.
> [13] Do not withhold discipline from a child;
>   if you punish them with the rod, they will not die.
> [14] Punish them with the rod
>   and save them from death.
> [15] My son, if your heart is wise,
>   then my heart will be glad indeed;
> [16] my inmost being will rejoice
>   when your lips speak what is right.

---

4. Fox, *Proverbs 10–31*, 723–24.
5. Cf. untranslated "eye" in NIV of v. 6 as well.
6. See Waltke, *Proverbs 15–31*, 243–44.
7. Heim, *Poetic Imagination*, 535.

¹⁷ Do not let your heart envy sinners,
    but always be zealous for the fear of the LORD.
¹⁸ There is surely a future hope for you,
    and your hope will not be cut off.

23:12–18 The three sayings here (ending in v. 19) combine *particular* and *general* material and reveal an emphasis on deep, embodied ways of life and knowing: *leb*, "heart" (vv. 12, 15, 16, 17, 19); *nephesh*, "life" (v. 14, not translated in NIV) and *kileyah*, "kidney" (v. 16, NIV "inmost being").

Verses 12–14 address family instruction and discipline. On the one hand, the son must accept his father's teaching (v. 12, cf. the mother also in vv. 22, 25). The assurance that the child "will not die" is clearly rhetorical, for careless beatings can kill a person (cf. Exod 21:20). The exaggerated rhetoric continues in the stated hope of "sav[ing] them from death" (v. 14b). Any parent knows that discipline and consequences take on a broad range of intensities, in which physical life and death are rarely in question. While the ancient context assumed physical punishment (see commentary at 13:24), the hyperbole here is to motivate the habit of discipline as a whole, not a particular form of it.

Verses 15–16 echo other sayings throughout the chapter. With their tones of unity and intimacy between a father and son, they provide a contrast to images of violent disciplinary measures above (14–15). This contrast is emphasized through the parallels between the "heart" and "ears" in the former set of sayings and "lips" and "heart" in the latter. Verses 15–16 also pick up on the theme of speech in verse 9 and even more emphatically anticipate the joy and unity between father, mother, and son in verses 24–26.

Verses 17–18 close this central set of instructions by returning to the themes of envy and greed, which pervade the broader context (cf. 22:25–28; 23:1–8, 10; 24:1–2). In a way, the couplet is a concise summary of Psalms 37 and 73 (and parts of Job). The antidote for envy is a fear of the Lord accompanied by the reminder that the wicked will eventually meet their fate; appearances in this life are not indicative of transcendent realities. Verse 17a is a variant of 3:31a, 24:1a, and 24:19a, which replaces "sinners" in 23:17 with "the violent," "the wicked," and "evildoers," respectively. Verse 17b is the only one of these four sayings that says something positive, "but always be zealous for the fear of the LORD." Heim illustrates how this change fits the broader context in verses 13–18. First, the "heart" that doesn't envy in 17a complements the "heart [that] is wise" in 15a. Second, the hope of a future in 18 contrasts the threat to the future in 13–14.[8]

---

8. Ibid., 135–37.

[19] Listen, my son, and be wise,
and set your heart on the right path:
[20] Do not join those who drink too much wine
or gorge themselves on meat,
[21] for drunkards and gluttons become poor,
and drowsiness clothes them in rags.

23:19–21 This trio of sayings is another *particular* (vs. *general*) wisdom instruction, which sits in the center of a group of sayings that explicitly mention the father and mother (vv. 15–26). The chapter also seems to intensify its rhetoric. In verses 1–8 food and wine are merely instrumental agents for a lesson on the theme of envy. In this section, gluttony and drunkenness become paths to poverty and shame. And the final sayings (vv. 29–35) imaginatively demonstrate the ruinous and disastrous power of drunkenness.

[22] Listen to your father, who gave you life,
and do not despise your mother when she is old.
[23] Buy the truth and do not sell it—
wisdom, instruction and insight as well.
[24] The father of a righteous child has great joy;
a man who fathers a wise son rejoices in him.
[25] May your father and mother rejoice;
may she who gave you birth be joyful!

23:22–25 This final arrangement of *general* instructions flows seamlessly into the *particular* sayings that follow in verses 26–35. In the broader context, the warmth and intimacy here resembles verses 14–15. The sayings also draw upon language elsewhere in Proverbs 23:22–23 and in chapters 1–9, 1:8; 6:20; cf. 10:1.

The phrase to "buy . . . truth" in 23:23 is a close variant of the saying "get wisdom" in 4:5, 7 (cf. 16:16; 17:16).[9] The joy experienced by parents of a wise child appears in various ways in 10:1; 17:21; and 23:15–16. One can hardly miss the alternating contrasts between warmth/intimacy/joy and danger/punishment/perishing.

[26] My son, give me your heart
and let your eyes delight in my ways,
[27] for an adulterous woman is a deep pit,
and a wayward wife is a narrow well.
[28] Like a bandit she lies in wait
and multiplies the unfaithful among men.

---

9. On the translation of *qanah* as "get" or "buy" see 4:5–7 above.

23:26–28 The father's words turn on a dime, as it were, from intimacy, "give me your heart,"[10] to the deadly danger of the adulteress as "pit" and "bandit." The "pit" (cf. 7:27; 9:18; 22:14) may be both a metaphor of the vagina and Sheol.

Just as the preceding context (vv. 22–25) echoed Proverbs 1–9, the depiction of the adulteress here does as well, especially chapters 5–7. Furthermore, as argued in the commentary on Proverbs 6:20–7:27 above, wisdom is not merely an incidental means to avoid sexual temptation (or gluttony), but getting wisdom and living by wisdom are themselves best understood through metaphors of the heart, stomach, and loins. Indeed, wisdom's caricature as a lover in chapters 4, 9, and 31 go hand in hand with wisdom as honey (24:13) and better than riches (9:11, 18–19).

> [29] Who has woe? Who has sorrow?
>   Who has strife? Who has complaints?
> Who has needless bruises?
>   Who has bloodshot eyes?
> [30] Those who linger over wine,
>   who go to sample bowls of mixed wine.
> [31] Do not gaze at wine when it is red,
>   when it sparkles in the cup, when it goes down smoothly!
> [32] In the end it bites like a snake
>   and poisons like a viper.
> [33] Your eyes will see strange sights,
>   and your mind will imagine confusing things.
> [34] You will be like one sleeping on the high seas,
>   lying on top of the rigging.
> [35] "They hit me," you will say, "but I'm not hurt!
>   They beat me, but I don't feel it!
> When will I wake up
>   so I can find another drink?"

23:29–35 The son's tendency toward self-deception regarding the danger of the adulteress extends to the lure of wine and strong drink as well. Both are as tempting as they are deadly. Van Leeuwen helpfully notes that this poem consists of six questions, followed by an answer, a command, a series of provocative images, and a final speech by the drunkard.[11] The poem persuades its readers with a variety of means—rhetorical questions, humor, and "physical

---

10. Though lacking much of an argument, Clifford, *Proverbs*, 213, raises the possibility that the son's "heart" signifies "obedience rather than love."
11. Van Leeuwen, *Proverbs*, 208.

horrors" that, amazingly, fail to persuade the simple-minded drunkard who speaks at the end.[12] All of this makes this mother and father's teachings appear all the more reasonable and persuasive.

LIVE the Story

To Stand Before Kings

Who of us can observe the advantage and wealth of others without growing discontent with our own lot? The picture in this chapter of standing before rulers—or others who tempt us with what they are or have—is no stranger to biblical narrative. Joseph, of course, is granted many distinguished positions and yet is remembered in particular for resisting the temptations of Potiphar's wife. The false accusations brought against him initially only serve to justify his vindication and humble rise to a position of power that he did not seek. Esther, Daniel, Hananiah, Mishael, and Azariah (Belteshazzar, Shadrach, Meshach, and Abednego) also resisted the temptation to compromise their faith or abuse their place in royal courts (Esth 5:1–14; 7:1–8:18; Dan 1:1–2:49). Though, let it be noted that they did not overlook an opportunity to use their position for good.

Such upstanding examples stand in sharp contrast to the behavior of Gehazi, the servant of Elisha. In the story, Elisha mediates Yahweh's healing power to the leper Naaman, commander of the Syrian army (2 Kgs 5:1–27). The miraculous healing prompts Naaman, unsuccessfully, to send Elisha away with a gift. Elisha's refusal employed the oath formula "as Yahweh lives." In an ironic turn, Gehazi takes up the same oath formula in his own determination to take advantage of Naaman's timely generosity. Elisha's subsequent judgment of Gehazi rhetorically asks him whether Yahweh's mighty acts are a "time to take money or to accept clothes—or olive groves and vineyards, or flocks and herds, or male and female slaves?" (2 Kgs 5:26). We should view it as no coincidence that the reputations of the prophet and the sage are both measured by their ability to withstand the powers of jealousy and envy.

Jesus teaches humility before those with wealth and power (Luke 14:7–11), just as he is able to resist the temptations of his own rightful power and privilege when he stands before Satan in the desert and Herod and Pilate at his sentencing. Our own turning from greed and desire should stand as a constant reminder of the one who "made himself nothing" that he might be exalted and win life for all (Phil 2:6–11).

---

12. Clifford, *Proverbs*, 213–14.

Envy, Vice, and Virtue: Part I

In the next chapter we will reflect more broadly on the seven capital vices. We pause here to reflect briefly on the anthropological nature of envy and jealousy raised in the context above.

Just what is it that drives our desire to have something that is not ours to begin with? In answering this question, theologians and ethicists often draw on medieval theologians who ceded to us the concepts of virtue and vice.[13] For these medievals, love can seem to be expressed in three similar, but misdirected ways: coveting concerns the *possessions of someone else*; envy relates to who we *are* in relation to someone else; and jealousy describes "loving something, possessing it," and then fearing its loss.[14]

Moreover, envy, coveting, and jealousy are all rooted in our comparisons to others and our subsequent sense of self-loathing or dissatisfaction with our lives and our self-image.

We can see the power of such desires of comparison played out in the recent history of the relationships between wages, production, and consumption. In the nineteenth century, a worker's basic needs for life and sustenance were fairly limited. As such, increases in wages provided little motivation for a laborer to work harder. But around the turn of the twentieth century, economic and political thinkers discovered the psychological power of the nascent consumer economy. In a world where there were an increasing number of products—things to be had—the worker had an incentive to work harder for higher wages.[15] We can hardly miss the seeds of our modern consumer culture. Indeed, most of us are willing to work harder and harder for more and more money to buy things, which hardly qualify as needs. And how do we learn about these things that we desire so deeply? We see them worn, driven, eaten, listened to, etc. in the happy, fulfilled, and beautiful lives of *other people* in modern advertisements. We also see them worn, driven, and the rest by our *friends, neighbors*, and *celebrities*.

To notice our neighbor is to observe, compare, and want; the sequence is inevitable. What we do with the sequence is not. James asks: "What causes fights and quarrels among you?" He answers, "desire," "covet[ing]," and our "wrong motives" for requesting things in prayer (Jas 4:1–3). What is James's remedy? "Submit . . . to God," "resist the devil," "come near to God," and "purify your hearts" (Jas 4:7–8). This is the way to pass by the delicacies of kings, neighbors, and drivers of new BMWs without giving in to desire.

---

13. See Kathryn D. Blanchard, "Jealousy and Envy," in *Dictionary of Scripture and Ethics*, 418–419 and DeYoung, *Glittering Vices*, 41–57.

14. DeYoung, *Glittering Vices*, 43–44.

15. See Crawford, *Shop Class as Soulcraft*, 41–44.

Likewise, Jesus says, "do not store up for yourselves treasures upon earth," (Matt 6:19a), and the writer of Hebrews warns: "Keep your lives free from the love of money and be content with what you have . . ." (Heb 13:5a). We have noted before that while Proverbs often emphasizes wealth as the fruit of a wise and righteous life, we find no parallel assurances in the New Testament. Instead, simplicity, contentment, and sharing dominate its message, along with the hope of an eschatological abundance of wealth and feasting in the new creation. Jesus has secured for us an inheritance that exceeds our imagination, and so we may confidently deny pleasures in this life with the assurance that we will enjoy them in "my Father's kingdom" (Matt 26:29; John 14:1–4).

¹ Do not envy the wicked,
    do not desire their company;
² for their hearts plot violence,
    and their lips talk about making trouble.
³ By wisdom a house is built,
    and through understanding it is established;
⁴ through knowledge its rooms are filled
    with rare and beautiful treasures.
⁵ The wise prevail through great power,
    and those who have knowledge muster their strength.
⁶ Surely you need guidance to wage war,
    and victory is won through many advisers.
⁷ Wisdom is too high for fools;
    in the assembly at the gate they must not open their mouths.
⁸ Whoever plots evil
    will be known as a schemer.
⁹ The schemes of folly are sin,
    and people detest a mocker.
¹⁰ If you falter in a time of trouble,
    how small is your strength!
¹¹ Rescue those being led away to death;
    hold back those staggering toward slaughter.
¹² If you say, "But we knew nothing about this,"
    does not he who weighs the heart perceive it?
Does not he who guards your life know it?
    Will he not repay everyone according to what they have done?
¹³ Eat honey, my son, for it is good;
    honey from the comb is sweet to your taste.
¹⁴ Know also that wisdom is like honey for you:

If you find it, there is a future hope for you,
    and your hope will not be cut off.
¹⁵ Do not lurk like a thief near the house of the righteous,
    do not plunder their dwelling place;
¹⁶ for though the righteous fall seven times,
    they rise again, but the wicked stumble when calamity strikes.
¹⁷ Do not gloat when your enemy falls;
    when they stumble, do not let your heart rejoice,
¹⁸ or the LORD will see and disapprove
    and turn his wrath away from them.
¹⁹ Do not fret because of evildoers
    or be envious of the wicked,
²⁰ for the evildoer has no future hope,
    and the lamp of the wicked will be snuffed out.
²¹ Fear the LORD and the king, my son,
    and do not join with rebellious officials,
²² for those two will send sudden destruction on them,
    and who knows what calamities they can bring?
²³ These also are sayings of the wise:
To show partiality in judging is not good:
²⁴ Whoever says to the guilty, "You are innocent,"
    will be cursed by peoples and denounced by nations.
²⁵ But it will go well with those who convict the guilty,
    and rich blessing will come on them.
²⁶ An honest answer
    is like a kiss on the lips.
²⁷ Put your outdoor work in order
    and get your fields ready;
    after that, build your house.
²⁸ Do not testify against your neighbor without cause—
    would you use your lips to mislead?
²⁹ Do not say, "I'll do to them as they have done to me;
    I'll pay them back for what they did."
³⁰ I went past the field of a sluggard,
    past the vineyard of someone who has no sense;
³¹ thorns had come up everywhere,
    the ground was covered with weeds,
    and the stone wall was in ruins.

> [32] I applied my heart to what I observed
>   and learned a lesson from what I saw:
> [33] A little sleep, a little slumber,
>   a little folding of the hands to rest—
> [34] and poverty will come on you like a thief
>   and scarcity like an armed man.

Listening to the Text in the Story: Exodus 23:4–5; Deuteronomy 1:17;
   Psalms 37; 73; Esther 2:19–23

In contrast to chapters 22–23, scholars find little evidence of parallels to other ancient Near Eastern wisdom in this chapter; the sayings nevertheless resonate with many biblical passages.

The instruction against showing "partiality" in judgment (24:23–24) appears among the laws in the Pentateuch (cf. Lev 19:5; Deut 1:17; 16:16–18), and partiality and favoritism are at the core of what led to the unraveling of the family and nation of Israel: Isaac favors Esau, which prompts Jacob, who carries the identity of Israel, to steal the birthright and upset the family order.[1] Having secured his father's blessing away from the favored son, Jacob favors Rachel to Leah and Rachel's sons Benjamin and Joseph to the sons of his other wives and servants (Gen 25:28; 29:16–18; 37:3; 42:8; cf. 1 Tim 5:21).

EXPLAIN the Story

> [1] Do not envy the wicked,
>   do not desire their company;
> [2] for their hearts plot violence,
>   and their lips talk about making trouble.

24:1–2 This verse pair closes the section that began in 23:29 and returns to the common themes of envy and violence (cf. 3:31; 23:17; 24:17; Pss 37; 73). Verse 1 is more complicated than it might appear. If we take the Hebrew *qana* to signify the modern word "envy," then two different things are being imagined, since true envy includes resentment and repulsion of someone's advantage in life, whereas keeping "company" assumes acceptance of the wicked. The saying thus captures two representative responses to the wicked in the community.

---

1. It should be kept in mind that Jacob is alternatively referred to by both names, Jacob and Israel, reinforcing connection between his life and that of the nation.

The latter type of response in 24:1b—avoiding the "company" of the "wicked"—echoes a modern saying that originated in a quotation from Paul in 1 Corinthians, "Bad company corrupts good character" (15:33). "We are known by the company we keep" and "Show me your friends and I will show you who you are" are but two of many similar modern proverbs (cf. Prov 13:20; 24:6; 28:7; 29:3).

> [3] By wisdom a house is built,
>   and through understanding it is established;
> [4] through knowledge its rooms are filled
>   with rare and beautiful treasures.
> [5] The wise prevail through great power,
>   and those who have knowledge muster their strength.
> [6] Surely you need guidance to wage war,
>   and victory is won through many advisers.

24:3–6 Most commentaries separate verses 3–4 from the surrounding content, but they fit naturally within the themes of community, wisdom, and houses in following verses. This leads Waltke to place the sayings within the larger grouping of 3–12, labeling the section "strength and strategy in conflict."[2] Granting basic thematic unity, it still makes sense to break the sayings at the point at which they turn from explicit references to wisdom in the house and kingdom (3–6), to folly (7–9), and social responsibility (10–12).

Verses 3–4 are close variants of 3:19–20 (see the commentary above and "God Made the Word by Wisdom" in Live the Story in chapter 3). Most scholars comment on the fact that the "house" symbolizes a whole way of life; far fewer of them point to the ontological and theological unity of human life and work and God's divine work in creation. (See Live the Story below).

24:5–7 In terms of language verse 7 goes with the next grouping. But it also fits here as one of three loosely related sayings about wisdom. The Hebrew of verse 5 presents us with difficulties. Longman creatively emends the text to a better-than saying: "A wise person is better than a strong one and a knowledgeable person is better than a powerful one."[3] But the broader context here commends strength and resiliency alongside the wisdom of building a house/life (cf. 10). Further, as Clifford, notes, it is wisdom that makes one implicitly strong in gaining victory on the battlefield.[4] The point here is that wisdom is the key to true and superior strength.

---

2. Waltke, *Proverbs 15–31*, 270.

3. Longman, *Proverbs*, 433.

4. Clifford, *Proverbs*, 214. See also 10:15; 14:26; and 18:10 over against 18:11, 19, 23.

[7] Wisdom is too high for fools;
    in the assembly at the gate they must not open their mouths.
[8] Whoever plots evil
    will be known as a schemer.
[9] The schemes of folly are sin,
    and people detest a mocker.

24:7–9 These verses are held together by the placement of the root ʾwl, "fool" and "folly," in 7 and 9 and the root zmm, "schemer" and "schemes," in 8–9. The sayings all threaten the fool with public humiliation and rejection for his pernicious behavior (cf. 17:6; Ps 21:11).

[10] If you falter in a time of trouble,
    how small is your strength!
[11] Rescue those being led away to death;
    hold back those staggering toward slaughter.
[12] If you say, "But we knew nothing about this,"
    does not he who weighs the heart perceive it?
Does not he who guards your life know it?
    Will he not repay everyone according to what they have done?

24:10–12 "Strength" (10) is taken up again from verse 5 and applied to one's social responsibility to intervene in the sight of injustice. Wisdom not only demands abstaining from "schemes" (7–9) but also seeking the welfare of the city (cf. 11:9–14).

The extreme example of people being led to their "death" in verse 11 is almost certainly figurative since it is nonsense to think that we are only morally required to intervene on behalf of unjust execution.[5] That said, most biblical examples of courageous rescue and cowardly apathy concern physical death: Reuben tries to intervene on behalf of Joseph's life (Gen 37:22, 29); the Hebrew midwives boldly risk their lives for the Hebrew children (Exod 1:15–17); Jonathan seeks to protect David from his father Saul (1 Sam 19:4; 20:26–33); and Mordecai reported a threat on the king's life (Esth 2:19–23; cf. also Prov 7:22–23; Luke 10:25–37; Acts 23:16–22; 2 Tim 4:16–18).

Verse 12 is the first of many sayings in this chapter to use God's judgment (divine retribution) as a motive.

[13] Eat honey, my son, for it is good;
    honey from the comb is sweet to your taste.
[14] Know also that wisdom is like honey for you:

5. See Longman, *Proverbs*, 438.

If you find it, there is a future hope for you,
and your hope will not be cut off.

24:13–14 Following an extended cluster of sayings that portray contrasting scenes of wise and foolish behavior, verse 23 supplies a final, enticing image of the honey-like lure of wisdom. Honey is always used as a symbol of pleasure, usually in the context of future blessing. In the vast majority of poetic texts, honey is a positive representation of wisdom, God's revelation, and sexual pleasure (Prov 16:24; Song 4:11; 5:1; Ezek 3:3; Ps 119:103; Sir 24:19–20). Less often, and yet in a related sense, honey stands for hedonism, and its consumption is obviously far more guarded (Prov 25:16, 27). What must be emphasized here is the way wisdom is far from some sanitized pursuit of rational facts. In this sense, "truth" is better imagined like the behavior at a sumptuous feast than the steps used to solve a math problem (though doing math is more like eating than most of us imagine).[6]

¹⁵ Do not lurk like a thief near the house of the righteous,
   do not plunder their dwelling place;
¹⁶ for though the righteous fall seven times,
   they rise again, but the wicked stumble when calamity strikes.
¹⁷ Do not gloat when your enemy falls;
   when they stumble, do not let your heart rejoice,
¹⁸ or the LORD will see and disapprove
   and turn his wrath away from them.
¹⁹ Do not fret because of evildoers
   or be envious of the wicked,
²⁰ for the evildoer has no future hope,
   and the lamp of the wicked will be snuffed out.
²¹ Fear the LORD and the king, my son,
   and do not join with rebellious officials,
²² for those two will send sudden destruction on them,
   and who knows what calamities they can bring?

24:15–22 The group of sayings in this section is dominated by the motive—or threat—of divine retribution. The pair in 15–16 warns against lying in wait at the "house" and "dwelling" of the righteous. These two locales represent the material sum of a person's life, literally the "pasture" and "resting place," where food is stored and consumed. Juxtaposed to verses 13–14, honey appears safer and more satisfying than hard-earned wealth that does not belong

---

6. Lakoff and Nuñez, *Where Mathematics Comes From.*

to us. Furthermore, the numerical symbolism of the righteous who fall and rise "seven times" suggests great strength, in contrast to the weakness of the coward in verses 10–12. Wisdom requires physical, moral, and emotional strength.

In the commentary on 25:21 we briefly examine the variety of biblical passages that address our responsibility to our neighbor and our enemy. It might wrongly be thought that verses 17–18 suggest God will withhold justice if we rejoice in our enemy's demise. But Proverbs consistently upholds the surety of final divine justice, and so it is more likely that verse 18 assures us that God will not approve of our adding public shame to his own punishment. His withholding is an act of limiting consequences to their appropriate level.[7]

Verses 19–20 return to the prohibition against "envy" with the added reassurance that "evildoers" and "the wicked" have no "future hope," that is they will not escape God's judgment (cf. 23:18; 24:14).

Verses 21–22 pick up the theme of unwanted friends and associates from verse 1 and place it in the broader context of giving honor where it is due. The mutual respect for God and king here appears also in Exodus 22:28 (cf. Prov 15:33–16:15). The instruction is motivated by both human and divine judgment.

[23] These also are sayings of the wise:
  To show partiality in judging is not good:
[24] Whoever says to the guilty, "You are innocent,"
  will be cursed by peoples and denounced by nations.
[25] But it will go well with those who convict the guilty,
  and rich blessing will come on them.
[26] An honest answer
  is like a kiss on the lips.
[27] Put your outdoor work in order
  and get your fields ready;
  after that, build your house.
[28] Do not testify against your neighbor without cause—
  would you use your lips to mislead?
[29] Do not say, "I'll do to them as they have done to me;
  I'll pay them back for what they did."

24:23–29 These sayings call for just behavior, whether by judges (23–25), witnesses (26–29), or—as is typically the case in Proverbs—in the everyday situations of our own private judgment and speech.

The first line in verse 23a marks the final set of "sayings of the wise" that began in 22:17. The sayings fall under the opening command not to "show

---

7. See Waltke, *Proverbs 15–31*, 285.

partiality," literally, "to know a face" (23b). The command against showing "partiality" appears elsewhere in 18:5 and 28:21 (cf. 17:26) and undergirds the criteria for selecting community judges in Deuteronomy (1:16–17; 16:18–19). Verses 24–25 spell out the consequences for unjust and just judgment—local and international shame, and "rich blessing," respectively (cf. 17:15; 20:10).

The sayings in 24:26, 28–29 speak to the conduct of witnesses, beginning with the comparison of an "honest answer" to a "kiss on the lips." The kiss is one of the most intimate expressions, whether between lovers, family, or friends (Gen 50:1; Ruth 1:9; 1 Kgs 19:20; Song 1:2; 8:1). The kisses of Jacob and Judas, accompanied by deception, are a double insult to their recipients (Gen 27:26; Matt 26:48–50). Verse 26 seems to anticipate the mention of false testimony and "lips" in verse 28 (cf. 14:5; 19:5; 25:18). Whereas verse 28 forbids false testimony "without cause" and verse 29 speaks specifically to doing so to get back at the neighbor.

Verse 27 departs from the surrounding context, but it may be placed here to connect the sayings back to the major theme of house building in verses 3–4. The basic lesson here is that any project, initiative, or life (i.e., "house") requires appropriate preparation.

> 30 I went past the field of a sluggard,
>   past the vineyard of someone who has no sense;
> 31 thorns had come up everywhere, the ground was covered with weeds,
>   and the stone wall was in ruins.
> 32 I applied my heart to what I observed
>   and learned a lesson from what I saw:
> 33 A little sleep, a little slumber,
>   a little folding of the hands to rest—
> 34 and poverty will come on you like a thief
>   and scarcity like an armed man.

24:30–34 These verses closely follow 6:6–11, except that the earlier passage teaches the lesson by a comparison between the industrious ant and the lazy sluggard (see commentary above). These kinds of observations are fairly common (cf. 4:3–9; 7:6–23; Ps 37:25–26; Eccl 1:12). As Van Leeuwen notes, the setting stands in sharp contrast to verses 3–4 and 27.[8]

Fox argues that the pedagogy in Proverbs relies on rote learning of the tradition of parents and the wise. He also believes that this observation in verses 30–34 is one of the rare places in Proverbs where we find the experiential

---

8. Van Leeuwen, *Proverbs*, 214.

learning that dominates Ecclesiastes.[9]As a result, Proverbs appears naïve and uncritical while Ecclesiastes voices the mature reality of lived experience. But Fox routinely conflates the rhetoric or self-presentation of these books with the way we, and the biblical writers, actually come to know things. Proverbs does sound like dogmatic instruction, but such instruction will only be persuasive if its claims bear out in everyday life. In this way, the role that experience plays in coming to wisdom is nearly the same in Ecclesiastes and Proverbs (see "Shock, Surprise, and Moral Shaping" in Live the Story in chapter 25). It is worth emphasizing this point in order to relieve Proverbs of overly simplistic caricatures that diminish the sophistication and authority of the book.

LIVE the Story

The Bible also consistently warns against rejoicing in the calamity of our enemy or seeking to do injustice or take vengeance on those who have acted unjustly toward us (cf. Exod 23:4; Lev 19:18; Deut 32:35; Prov 3:27; 24:17–18, 28–29; Rom 12:19–21). Jesus' condemnation of the talionic formula, "eye for eye, and tooth for tooth," (Matt 5:38–48) is more than likely *not* a critique of laws and courts, since being slapped on the cheek (Matt 5:39) is a figure of speech for personal shame, not physical injury. What Jesus calls for in this case is forgiveness and refusal to retaliate personally or in court for harm done by a neighbor or enemy.[10] More than that, Jesus leads us to imagine a new ethic that thinks of the good of our enemy above our own.

House Building and the Stars

It is one thing to say that our life in this world is somehow "like" or analogous to God's own work. But read together, Proverbs 3:19–20 and 24:3–4 reveal a much deeper and more significant connection between our life and work and God's work of creation: that our mundane activities in this world are ingrained in realities that transcend our understanding.

Van Leeuwen helps us to appreciate the importance of this. In his study of ancient Israelite, Mesopotamian, and Levantine cultures, he shows that ancient Near Eastern societies understood human life as ontologically grounded in the creation itself.[11] In other words, more than saying that we are like God, these cultures believed that our visible lives are experienced in relation to the cosmic grooves and rhythms built into the creation itself. And so the moral life is not

---

9. Michael V. Fox, "The Epistemology of the Book of Proverbs," *JBL* 126/4 (2007): 669–84.
10. See Carmichael, *Spirit of Biblical Law*, 124–25.
11. Van Leeuwen, "Cosmos, Temple, House," 67–90.

a list of culturally constructed rules, but a matter of living according to the norms and guides God instituted at creation.[12] Seen in this way, the ethical grooves and rhythms of the creation are set within the natural order of the world—its planetary orbits, rain, wind, and ocean currents (cf. Ps 19).

This connection between creation and human living leads us to view our human calling as one of imitating God, whether in the order and fruitfulness of his work in creation (Gen 1), his just concern for the needy and oppressed (Deut 24:16–22), or his willingness to give his life for the world (Phil 2:5).

Envy, Vice, and Virtue: Part II

Throughout this commentary we have pointed to the connections between the proverbial sayings and the historic list of virtues and vices. In the "sayings of the wise" in Proverbs 22:17–24:1 we see examples of all of the cardinal virtues and every traditional vice except vainglory (sometimes mislabeled "pride," which is a larger concept that underlies all of the vices):

Envy	23:3–8, 17; 24:1
Gluttony	23:1–8, 20–21, 29–35
Avarice (greed)	22:28; 23:10
Sloth	24:30–34
Lust	23:27–28
Anger	22:24; 24:15
Courage	23:13–14, 18; 24:5–6, 10, 19–22
Temperance	23:1–8, 20–21, 26–35; 24:1–2, 13–14
Prudence	22:17, 24–27, 29; 23:9, 12, 17, 22–25; 24:3–4, 27, 30–34
Justice	22:21–23, 28; 23:10; 24:11, 15–16, 23–25, 28–29

Notice on the one hand how the medieval framework of Christian ethics that took many centuries to develop was already present in the sayings in Proverbs. Despite the disordered sense one may get in reading these sayings, the classical vices and virtues demonstrate that they work together to undergird a comprehensive moral framework. For this reason, Proverbs should be read as a whole; each of its 915 sayings are designed to shape the intricate layers in our moral nature.

Just as importantly, as we discussed in the previous chapter, the interweaving of the ethics of virtue and vice in Proverbs helps us appreciate their

---

12. Ibid., 81.

interrelationship: virtues work to tame and direct the underlying desires that make us prone to vice. That is to say that vices are not simply indiscretions of desire but also failures to direct those desires to their appropriate, "virtuous" ends.[13] Wisdom does not say "no" to sex, wealth, power, and food, but "yes" to sex within marriage, feasting balanced by fasting, wealth used justly, and power directed to the common good.

We can easily see the principles of virtue and vice in the teachings of the New Testament. The famous sayings on the mount (or plain) illustrate an intensification of the virtues within Jewish culture: lust, anger, humility, revenge, and hatred and love (Matt 5:1–7:29; Luke 6:17–49). Jesus also embodies the best of these virtue in his life. In his prayer on the Mount of Olives, Jesus models for us the essential root to all virtue, submitting our desires to those of the Father: "yet not my will, but yours be done (Luke 22:42).

---

13. Konyndyk-DeYoung, *Glittering Vices*, 34, 43, 164–65.

LISTEN to the Story

¹ These are more proverbs of Solomon, compiled by the men of Hezekiah king of Judah:

² It is the glory of God to conceal a matter;
    to search out a matter is the glory of kings.
³ As the heavens are high and the earth is deep,
    so the hearts of kings are unsearchable.
⁴ Remove the dross from the silver,
    and a silversmith can produce a vessel;
⁵ remove wicked officials from the king's presence,
    and his throne will be established through righteousness.
⁶ Do not exalt yourself in the king's presence,
    and do not claim a place among his great men;
⁷ it is better for him to say to you, "Come up here,"
    than for him to humiliate you before his nobles.
What you have seen with your eyes
    ⁸ do not bring hastily to court,
for what will you do in the end
    if your neighbor puts you to shame?
⁹ If you take your neighbor to court,
    do not betray another's confidence,
¹⁰ or the one who hears it may shame you
    and the charge against you will stand.
¹¹ Like apples of gold in settings of silver
    is a ruling rightly given.
¹² Like an earring of gold or an ornament of fine gold
    is the rebuke of a wise judge to a listening ear.
¹³ Like a snow-cooled drink at harvest time
    is a trustworthy messenger to the one who sends him;
    he refreshes the spirit of his master.

¹⁴ Like clouds and wind without rain
    is one who boasts of gifts never given.
¹⁵ Through patience a ruler can be persuaded,
    and a gentle tongue can break a bone.
¹⁶ If you find honey, eat just enough—
    too much of it, and you will vomit.
¹⁷ Seldom set foot in your neighbor's house—
    too much of you, and they will hate you.
¹⁸ Like a club or a sword or a sharp arrow
    is one who gives false testimony against a neighbor.
¹⁹ Like a broken tooth or a lame foot
    is reliance on the unfaithful in a time of trouble.
²⁰ Like one who takes away a garment on a cold day,
    or like vinegar poured on a wound,
    is one who sings songs to a heavy heart.
²¹ If your enemy is hungry, give him food to eat;
    if he is thirsty, give him water to drink.
²² In doing this, you will heap burning coals on his head,
    and the LORD will reward you.
²³ Like a north wind that brings unexpected rain
    is a sly tongue—which provokes a horrified look.
²⁴ Better to live on a corner of the roof
    than share a house with a quarrelsome wife.
²⁵ Like cold water to a weary soul
    is good news from a distant land.
²⁶ Like a muddied spring or a polluted well
    are the righteous who give way to the wicked.
²⁷ It is not good to eat too much honey,
    nor is it honorable to search out matters that are too deep.
²⁸ Like a city whose walls are broken through
    is a person who lacks self-control.

Listening to the Text in the Story: Exodus 23:4–5; Deuteronomy 22:4; Job 31:29–32

This chapter contains several admonitions to care for "friends" or "neighbors," which culminate in a saying that requires mercy even to our enemies (9–10, 17, 18, 21). We read elsewhere in the Old Testament of demands for compassionate treatment of fellow humans, especially those in need, and even our enemies (cf. Exod 23:4–5; Deut 22:4). In Job's plea of innocence he cites his care for neighbors, those in need, and enemies (Job 31:29–32).

EXPLAIN the Story

The introduction to Proverbs 10:1–29:27 above highlighted the distinctive clusters of sayings and poems in chapters 25–27. These chapters also stand apart for their density of shocking, often violent images.

In his detailed analysis of these three chapters, Van Leeuwen highlights the positive (+) and negative (-) forms of sayings (S) and admonitions (A) in chapter 25 (e.g., *do/do not*, and *eat/do not eat* too much). As can be seen in his diagram below, verses 2–5 contain positive sayings that introduce the tone and themes in the sayings and admonitions in the rest of the chapter. Each section, moreover, moves between positive and negative groups of sayings.[1]

Introduction		S:+ (vv 2–5)
Body	I.	A:-(vv 6–10)
		S:+ (vv 11–15; except for v 15 which is S:-)
	IIA.	A:-(vv 16–17)
		S:-(vv 18–20)
	IIB.	A:+ (vv 21–22)
		S:-(vv 23–27; except for v 25 which is S:+)

Van Leeuwen also identifies three chiastic structures with several keywords that are carefully placed at the beginnings and ends of the chapter and smaller collections within.[2]

1	v. 2	"glory"			"search"	(+)
	v. 5		"wicked	"righteous"		(+)
	v. 26		"righteous"	"wicked"		(-)
	v. 27	"search"			"glory"	(-)
2	v. 16		"honey"	"to eat"		(+/-)
	v. 27a		"to eat"	"honey"		(-)

---

1. Van Leeuwen, *Context and Meaning*, 64.
2. Ibid., 71.

| 3 | vv. 16–17 | "to eat" | "hate you" *(snk)* | (-) |
| | 21–22 | "your enemy" *(snk)* | "to eat" | (+) |

Even more stylistic detail emerges as the sayings reverse the normal order of topic-comment to comment-topic.[3] For example, "Like an earring of gold or an ornament of fine gold is the rebuke of a wise judge to a listening ear" (v. 12) sounds backwards. As Fox observes,[4] it is more natural to begin with the topic, "The rebuke of a wise judge to a listening ear . . ." and end with the comment "*is like* an earing of gold or ornament of fine gold."

However, most English versions seek to *correct* this order in search of a clearer saying. But as Fox states, the reversed order in Hebrew gives the saying "the feel of a riddle."[5] Clifford adds that such a saying "provokes suspense, making the reader active."[6] We will see the full significance of this ordering in the commentary on chapters 25–28.

[1] These are more proverbs of Solomon, compiled by the men of Hezekiah king of Judah:

25:1 The comparatively flat prose of verse 1 forms a break between the sayings behind and those ahead. It is not that the content of the proverbs changes, but that, as in a staged performance, the editors raise the curtain for the fifth act (1:1; 10:1; 22:17; 24:23; *25:1*; 30:1; 31:1). This helps to emphasize the authoritative foundation of the book.

Waltke points out that Hezekiah and Solomon share many significant parallels that might explain why their names are chosen for the headings in Proverbs. Both kings attained great wealth, centralized Israel's worship, and had gifts brought to them by surrounding nations (1 Kgs 6–9; 2 Kgs 18:1–20:21; 2 Chr 29:1–32:33).[7] It should also be remembered that, because Proverbs pays little explicit attention to Israel's law, covenants, and history, the added appeal to authority is necessary. Solomon "the wise," Hezekiah, and the other figures in these introductions thus primarily serve theological and literary purposes, reminding the people that—in a rightly ordered world—God, king, wisdom, and justice are tightly woven together. This did not hold true in the lives of Solomon and Hezekiah.

---

3. Or what Clifford, *Proverbs*, 223–24, calls "figure (or vehicle)" and "the thing meant (tenor)."
4. Fox, *Proverbs 10–31*, 785.
5. Ibid., 775. Cf. Alter, *Art of Biblical Poetry*, 175–77.
6. Clifford, *Proverbs*, 224.
7. Waltke, *Proverbs 15–31*, 301.

² It is the glory of God to conceal a matter;
    to search out a matter is the glory of kings.
³ As the heavens are high and the earth is deep,
    so the hearts of kings are unsearchable.
⁴ Remove the dross from the silver,
    and a silversmith can produce a vessel;
⁵ remove wicked officials from the king's presence,
    and his throne will be established through righteousness.

25:2–5 As already noted, verses 2–5 set up the major themes in the chapter and contain keywords that close the chapter in verse 27. The first couplet (vv. 2–3) brings together similarities and differences between God and kings. The Old Testament elsewhere contrasts what God knows and conceals and what humans know on earth (cf. Deut 29:29; Ps 115:16; Job 28:1–28). It is a king's "glory" to look into those things which God has hidden (cf. Gen 18:17). Most notably, Solomon looked into a seemingly impossible situation and wisely discerned a just solution (1 Kgs 3:16–28). As in this passage in 1 Kings, the king's wisdom here flows naturally into the judicial sayings in verses 4–5 (cf. Pss 72; 82; 89; 93–97; 104:35; 135–136; Jer 31:35–37).[8]

The king's "unsearchable," *heqer*, heart strikes an unexpected note. As Fox observes, *heqer* is only used elsewhere in Proverbs of God and creation.[9] This saying probably arose among court officials both as a lofty goal and a warning. Nathan showed his skill in discerning David's heart in his ability to elicit confession and repentance (2 Sam 12:1–14; cf. 1 Kgs 20:39–43).

Verses 4–5 move to a statement addressed to royal courts, using dross, silver, and vessels as metaphors for order in the kingdom. The Hebrew ending is cryptic, "a vessel will come out." The NIV seeks a simpler solution in its translation, "a silversmith can produce a vessel." It is possible that the phrase in Hebrew alludes to Aaron's language of the golden calf that just "came out" of the fire in Exodus 34:24, though there is no contextual reason to believe so. The main point seems clear enough: just as dross ruins vessels, bad friends ruin kings.[10] This point is explicit in verse 5a, which encourages the king to purge his courts of the "wicked" (cf. 16:12; 20:28; and 29:14).

⁶ Do not exalt yourself in the king's presence,
    and do not claim a place among his great men;
⁷ it is better for him to say to you, "Come up here,"

---

8. Van Leeuwen, *Context and Meaning*, 75.
9. Fox, *Proverbs 10–31*, 779.
10. Longman, *Proverbs*, 457.

than for him to humiliate you before his nobles.
What you have seen with your eyes
⁸ do not bring hastily to court,
    for what will you do in the end if your neighbor puts you to shame?
⁹ If you take your neighbor to court,
    do not betray another's confidence,
¹⁰ or the one who hears it may shame you
    and the charge against you will stand.

25:6–10 This section could easily be extended to the break in verses 15–16. I select the break where the admonitions turn to sayings. The sections are clearly interwoven.

The saying in verses 6–7ab addresses court officials, but again applies to every social stratum: humility leads to honor, but self-honor leads to shame (cf. 27:2).[11] It may be that Jesus had this saying in mind in his teaching about humility in Luke 14:7–11 (cf. Prov 23:1–8).

The Masoretic Text places the phrase in 7c, "what you have seen with your eyes," with the content in verse 7. Fox combines the sayings through the phrase, "[his nobles] whom your eyes have seen."[12] Similar wording can be found in Proverbs 23:6. Most modern translations follow the LXX and Vulgate, reading verse 7c as the start of verse 8. In favor of this, Deuteronomy 21:7 uses language of eyesight in determining guilt in a murder. According to this reading, visual evidence alone should not lead one to a hasty accusation. The word *rib*, "court," might simply mean "contention" or "dispute" rather than an official legal setting. Other sayings in the surrounding context encourage patience and good legal justification for initiating conflict (cf. 9–10, 15, 18; 26:16, 20–21).

Verses 9–10 continues the theme of disputes, this time calling for sins and conflicts to be handled at the lowest level. Similar teachings appear in Agur's oracle (Prov 30:10) and Jesus' teachings, which exhort us to resolve matters before they become public affairs and before we bring an offering to God (Matt 5:21–23; 23:18). The sayings in verses 10–11 hinge on a familiar principle of ironic reversal—jeopardizing your neighbor's public reputation will result in your own shame (cf. 1:18–19; 10:2; 11:4; 26:27; 28:8–10, 18b, 22).

¹¹ Like apples of gold in settings of silver
    is a ruling rightly given.
¹² Like an earring of gold or an ornament of fine gold

---

11. See ibid., 452.
12. Fox, *Proverbs 10–31*, 778.

is the rebuke of a wise judge to a listening ear.
¹³ Like a snow-cooled drink at harvest time
is a trustworthy messenger to the one who sends him;
he refreshes the spirit of his master.
¹⁴ Like clouds and wind without rain
is one who boasts of gifts never given.

25:11–14 These verses contain four positive sayings related to various types of speech—all of them stated in the riddle form of comment-topic. Verses 11 and 12 both begin with striking images of wealth. As in verse 8, the NIV's "ruling rightly given" assumes a court setting, which may very well be implied. The Hebrew is more subtle, comparing "apples" of gold and silver to "a word rightly spoken" (cf. 10:19; 17:27; Jas 3:2). Both rulings and well-timed words are matters of *fittingness* (cf. 16, 17, 20, and 26:1–12). Note also that the "earing of gold" in verse 12a parallels the "listening ear" in 12b.

Verses 13–14 use weather contradictions as a basis of comparison or comment (cf. also 27). Some scholars and translations, persuaded by the fact that snow does not fall in Israel at harvest time, reduce "snow" to "cold drink"—something that is not unusual. But one does not have to have seen snow on a hot day to imagine how refreshing it would be; you're probably doing it now. Consider our own equally contrived, "when hell freezes over." The unexpected weather makes the point all the more striking. See more on this in Live the Story below.

¹⁵ Through patience a ruler can be persuaded,
and a gentle tongue can break a bone.

25:15 This verse again uses elements of paradox and surprise. It can be dangerous to try the patience of rulers (cf. Is 7:13), but as "the pen is mightier than the sword," so steadfastness is better than might (cf. Eccl 7:8–9; 10:4). The parallel in verse 15b provides a shocking image. In the Old Testament bones are sacred symbols of life and markers for clean and unclean (Gen 2:23; Num 19:16, 18; 2 Sam 5:1; Job 2:5). Breaking a bone is also a sign of a cursing and great suffering (Exod 12:46; Num 9:12; 24:8; Lam 3:4). The unusual image uniquely communicates the power of patience and gentleness.

¹⁶ If you find honey, eat just enough—
too much of it, and you will vomit.
¹⁷ Seldom set foot in your neighbor's house—
too much of you, and they will hate you.

25:16–17 The parallel between "honey" and "eat" in verses 16 and 27 are one of several features that mark this as the center of the chapter (see figures above). These two sayings reinforce the principle of fittingness, or finding the right balance between too much and too little, whether food or companionship. "Vomit" is yet another example of hyperbole and surprising language in the chapter. Van Leeuwen observes that the saying is not aimed at the angry friend, ironically, but at the one who visits too often.[13]

> [18] Like a club or a sword or a sharp arrow
>   is one who gives false testimony against a neighbor.
> [19] Like a broken tooth or a lame foot
>   is reliance on the unfaithful in a time of trouble.
> [20] Like one who takes away a garment on a cold day,
>   or like vinegar poured on a wound,
>   is one who sings songs to a heavy heart.

25:18–20 The admonitions in 16–17 above are again followed by three sayings that employ provocative imagery. Waltke calls the "club," "sword," and "sharp arrow" in verse 18 "three deadly assault weapons,"[14] which the saying uses as a metaphor for bearing false witness, prohibited by one of the Ten Commandments (Exod 20:16). Verse 19 begins with two painful images that characterize an unreliable person. The saying applies equally to people who act unreliably and those who naïvely trust them.

Verse 20 closes this group of sayings with sensations of coldness and burning. The NIV "vinegar poured on a wound" follows the LXX. Some translations (NKJV, NAS, NET, ESV) choose to stay with the MT, "soda," *nater*, in place of "wound."[15] But "wound" makes more sense in light of sayings in the surrounding context that depict pain or discomfort as expressions of harm done to others. To "sing songs to a heavy heart" is unfitting speech (cf. vv. 11–12). Elsewhere, the Old Testament demonstrates the power of speech and song that bless the troubled listener (1 Sam 16:15–23; Job 30:31; Prov 12:25).

> [21] If your enemy is hungry, give him food to eat;
>   if he is thirsty, give him water to drink.
> [22] In doing this, you will heap burning coals on his head,
>   and the LORD will reward you.

25:21–22 A pair of admonitions again follows sayings above. These verses represent yet another surprise in the form of paradox or oxymoron: the pleasure or relief given to an enemy (v. 21) will result in his suffering (v. 22). More is going on here than meets the eye. On the one hand, verse 21 follows

13. Van Leeuwen, *Context and Meaning*, 24.
14. Waltke, *Proverbs 15–31*, 327.
15. The KJV and JPS use "nitre," another word for soda.

legal prescriptions and other proverbs that call for compassionate treatment of strangers (potentially enemies) in need (Exod 23:4; Lev 19:9–18; Deut 24:14–22; Prov 3:27; 10:12; 17:9; 19:11). Verse 22, however, contradicts the biblical teachings that forbid seeking vengeance (Prov 17:13; 20:22; 24:17–18; Pss 11:6; 140:10; Rom 12:17–21). It could be that "burning coals" is a figure of speech for personal shame, or that "you will heap" is a way of speaking to God's future vengeance. But given the irony elsewhere in this chapter as well as nearby sayings that speak to sensitivity to the neighbor (vv. 9, 17, 20), verse 22 may be a creative way of transforming an attitude of bitterness into a loving and compassionate response.

> [23] Like a north wind that brings unexpected rain is a sly tongue—
>   which provokes a horrified look.
> [24] Better to live on a corner of the roof
>   than share a house with a quarrelsome wife.
> [25] Like cold water to a weary soul
>   is good news from a distant land.
> [26] Like a muddied spring or a polluted well
>   are the righteous who give way to the wicked.
> [27] It is not good to eat too much honey,
>   nor is it honorable to search out matters that are too deep.
> [28] Like a city whose walls are broken through
>   is a person who lacks self-control.

25:25–28 The chapter ends with a final list of negative sayings with a single positive saying at their center (v. 25).

Similar to their dislike of "snow in harvest" in verse 13, some commentators seek to emend the meteorological anomaly of rain in verse 23 from a "north wind" to the "west." Whatever the deeper meaning in this weather metaphor it is sure that "slander stirs up anger."[16] Verse 24 is a variant of 21:9 and 19 (see commentary).

Verses 25–26 give us two contrasting water images. Verse 25, the only positive saying in this final grouping, compares the refreshing power of cold water to the hope and comfort found in a good messenger and good message. This anticipates the good news of salvation (Isa 52:7; Nah 1:15; Rom 10:14–15).

Whereas verse 25 imagines water at its best, verse 26 imagines it at its worst. Water that is "muddied" and "polluted" is robbed of its life-giving powers. So, too, the righteous who do not oppose the wicked fail to uphold their role in society.

---

16. Clifford, *Proverbs*, 227.

Verse 27 combines variant half-lines from verses 2–3 and 16 to bring the poem to a close with a flare of poetic skill. Like verses 16–17, the saying encourages modesty both in relation to physical and intellectual appetites. Verse 28 voices another word of modesty and self-control, employing a final image pregnant with allusions to violence and warfare.

 LIVE the Story

Shock, Surprise, and Moral Shaping

Although few scholars make very much of the fact, chapters 25–26 not only contain extended and intricate proverb-poems, they also bring together a large group of violent and shocking images that have been used to form riddles. We may never know how many authors or redactors lay behind these sayings, but we do notice a concentration of artistic and rhetorical skill that sets these chapters apart.

This all reminds us that good poets and narrators are able to manipulate emotions and mold beliefs.[17] This power of combining creativity with urgency is obvious in chapters 1–9 in the way the writers charge the sayings with choices between life and death, wisdom and folly, and two seductive women who appeal to us on each path. Here the rhetoric is more focused on particular moral behaviors that are too easily rationalized in common society.

We tell children to speak gently, but Proverbs surprises us with "a gentle tongue [that] can break a bone" (v. 15). For our "watch what you eat," and "enough sweets," Proverbs leaves us with a vivid sensation of vomiting from having eaten too much (16). "Be reliable" or "trustworthy" are encouraged through the image of unreliable people as "a broken tooth or a lame foot" (19). "Be sensitive," is likewise encouraged by the image of insensitive "songs to a heavy heart," portrayed as one who "takes away a garment on a cold day, or like vinegar poured on a wound." Our "don't make excuses" is imagined as the "sluggard [who] says, 'There's a lion in the road'" (26:13). And the indiscretion of not minding our business gets compared to "one who grabs a stray dog by the ears" (26:17).

Above all we can see that Proverbs' ethical instruction is *embodied*; it assumes an organic integration of heart, head, body, emotion, and desire. This is why none of us has to think twice in connecting the discomfort of a useless foot, a broken tooth, acid on a wound, or a thorn in the hand to social and ethical faults. Knowing this, the poet is able to shape our responses to

---

17. Though dated, Wayne C. Booth's *The Rhetoric of Fiction* (Chicago: University of Chicago, 1961), 169–205, is still one of the seminal works in this area.

each of these behaviors, making them more serious and memorable than they would be otherwise.

Water, Life, Fertility, and the Ordered Society

The proverbs in this chapter also rely on our sense of, and dependency upon, the world around us. So-called nature sayings emerge most prominently in 30:11–33, but they are at work in creative ways here as well, particularly in the poet's use of weather and water. The weather contradictions in verses 13, 14, and 23 all play upon our expectations and needs for water. Verses 25 and 26, meanwhile, provide two contrasting images of refreshing and polluted waters (cf. 5:15–19; 8:29; 17:14; 18:4; 20:5; 21:1; 30:4, 16).

Psalms also relies heavily on familiar images of nature and water, e.g., "a tree planted by streams of water" (1:3); "I am poured out like water" (22:14); "he leads me beside quiet waters" (23:2); "The voice of the Lord is over the waters" (29:3); "my whole being longs for you, in a dry and parched land where there is no water" (63:1); and "Praise him, you highest heavens and you waters above the skies" (148:4) to name but a few. The prophets add hundreds more images like these. And lest we think such nature sayings were conventions of a bygone era, it bears mentioning similar sayings today: blood is thicker than water, water on fire, and water under the bridge.

Still, most people in the western world live at arm's length from the effects of changing weather and dirty water. Our modern advancements have done a lot to shield us from this world, and I for one am grateful for indoor plumbing and filtration systems.

But this growing distance from nature comes at a cost. For, as Wendell Berry observes, *we are our bodies*, which makes us a part of this larger creation we inhabit.[18] It should not go unnoticed that the Bible constantly reorients us to the creation as a means to elicit wisdom, repentance, humility, healing, worship, and a sense of purpose, responsibility, and identity. The further we move from food, land, and water, particularly as nourishers of our bodies, the less we think about our obligations to our bodies, our neighbors, and the earth. Arguments like Berry's have generated an endless chain of green movements, like organic foods, home gardening, humane animal husbandry, buying local foods, and sustainable agriculture. To be sure, much of this movement has taken on a tone of religious fervor, trendy lifestyles, and a highly sentimental and pastoral view of older ways of life.

One can easily err on any one of many sides to this issue. Proverbs respects nature while steering us away from faddish behavior, ambivalent hedonism,

---

18. "The Body and the Earth" in *The Unsettling of America: Culture and Agriculture* (San Francisco: Sierra Club Books, 1986), 97–140.

scientific egoism, and all the errors that go along with them. Proverbs also turns us to nature to renew our sense of wonder, identity, and responsibility. In part this means being in touch with water and land in some tangible way, even if it's a single houseplant. And finally we must seek to bridge our experiences in the world with the hundreds of psalms, proverbs, and biblical passages that rely on nature to shape us into godly, wise, and loving creatures.

Above all we must remember that much if not most of our knowledge of Jesus in the Gospels comes to us through interaction with nature: being baptized in a river, suffering in the desert, walking on water, stilling waters and storms, multiplying bread and fish, healing diseases with mud and spittle, and filling fishermen's nets. All of these interactions remind us of the great mystery of the incarnation, in which Jesus assumed our bodily nature to redeem this world and give us spiritual *bodies*: "And just as we have borne the image of the earthly man, so shall we bear the image of the heavenly man" (1 Cor 15:49).

¹ Like snow in summer or rain in harvest,
  honor is not fitting for a fool.
² Like a fluttering sparrow or a darting swallow,
  an undeserved curse does not come to rest.
³ A whip for the horse, a bridle for the donkey,
  and a rod for the backs of fools!
⁴ Do not answer a fool according to his folly,
  or you yourself will be just like him.
⁵ Answer a fool according to his folly,
  or he will be wise in his own eyes.
⁶ Sending a message by the hands of a fool
  is like cutting off one's feet or drinking poison.
⁷ Like the useless legs of one who is lame
  is a proverb in the mouth of a fool.
⁸ Like tying a stone in a sling
  is the giving of honor to a fool.
⁹ Like a thornbush in a drunkard's hand
  is a proverb in the mouth of a fool.
¹⁰ Like an archer who wounds at random
  is one who hires a fool or any passer-by.
¹¹ As a dog returns to its vomit,
  so fools repeat their folly.
¹² Do you see a person wise in their own eyes?
  There is more hope for a fool than for them.
¹³ A sluggard says, "There's a lion in the road,
  a fierce lion roaming the streets!"
¹⁴ As a door turns on its hinges,
  so a sluggard turns on his bed.
¹⁵ A sluggard buries his hand in the dish;

351

he is too lazy to bring it back to his mouth.
[16] A sluggard is wiser in his own eyes
    than seven people who answer discreetly.
[17] Like one who grabs a stray dog by the ears
    is someone who rushes into a quarrel not their own.
[18] Like a maniac shooting
    flaming arrows of death
[19] is one who deceives their neighbor
    and says, "I was only joking!"
[20] Without wood a fire goes out;
    without a gossip a quarrel dies down.
[21] As charcoal to embers and as wood to fire,
    so is a quarrelsome person for kindling strife.
[22] The words of a gossip are like choice morsels;
    they go down to the inmost parts.
[23] Like a coating of silver dross on earthenware
    are fervent lips with an evil heart.
[24] Enemies disguise themselves with their lips,
    but in their hearts they harbor deceit.
[25] Though their speech is charming, do not believe them,
    for seven abominations fill their hearts.
[26] Their malice may be concealed by deception,
    but their wickedness will be exposed in the assembly.
[27] Whoever digs a pit will fall into it;
    if someone rolls a stone, it will roll back on them.
[28] A lying tongue hates those it hurts,
    and a flattering mouth works ruin.

Listening to the Text in the Story: Leviticus 19:35–37; Deuteronomy 25:13–15; Psalms 7:16; 9:16–17; 32:9; 141:10; Ecclesiastes 10:8–9; Isaiah 56:9–12

Proverbs 26 echoes many familiar sayings and accounts of misfits in the Old and New Testaments. The scoundrel in verses 23–26 closely resembles the duplicitous behavior forbidden in the law (Lev 19:35–37; Deut 25:13–15). Both Proverbs and the law regard this behavior as an "abomination" (see Prov 3:32). The ironic way the wicked fall subject to their plots and schemes (v. 27) first appears in Proverbs 1:18–19 and is a common image in Psalms as well

(Pss 7:16; 9:16–17; 35:7–8, etc., cf. also Eccl 10:8–9). Finally, both the "dog returns to its vomit," and the "fool to his folly," appear in Pharaoh's reversing course after each of the plagues (Exod 8:8–15) and Israel after judgment (Isa 56:9–12). (See more in Live the Story below.)

EXPLAIN the Story

Though this chapter does not have the neat chiastic structure in chapter 25, it is nevertheless a tightly constructed whole of one long poem with several shorter groups of sayings:

26:1–12	Fools and fittingness
26:13–16	The sluggard
26:17–26	Three extended sayings (17–19; 20–22; 23–26)
26:27–28	Concluding sayings

The chapter also contains sound patterns and wordplay that hold the sayings together.

- repetition of consonants *k-s-y-l* in vv. 1–12 (*ksyl* = "fool")
- *sikker*, "drunkard," v. 9 and *soker*, "hire," in v. 10
- end of v. 14 *weatsel al-mittato*, "sluggard on his bed," and start of v. 15 *taman asel*, "sluggard buries his hand"
- *ober mitabber*, "passes," and "one who rushes" in v. 17

As a final point of introduction, I believe some scholars have rightly noticed that Proverbs 26 comments on the main topics in chapters 25. I will highlight this in the commentary below.

[1] Like snow in summer or rain in harvest,
    honor is not fitting for a fool.
[2] Like a fluttering sparrow or a darting swallow,
    an undeserved curse does not come to rest.
[3] A whip for the horse, a bridle for the donkey,
    and a rod for the backs of fools!

26:1–3 These verses introduce the major theme for verses 1–12, which Van Leeuwen describes as "the [fool] in his various relations."[1]

Verse 1 adds another weather contradiction to those in chapter 25. This time two weather patterns, "snow in summer" and "rain in harvest," are compared to honoring a fool. Most scholars simply assume that the *rarity* of these

---

1. Van Leeuwen, *Context and Meaning*, 90.

natural events emphasizes the impropriety of such ill-placed honor. Heim, however, discerns more at work in verse 1a and its two comments in 1b. Snow in summer is indeed rare, but rain in harvest is less so. Furthermore, in the agricultural world rain during harvest would be recognized more for its "disastrous" nature than its rarity.[2] So too, the honored fool spells doom for the community.

Verse 2 is the only verse in the poem that does not mention the "fool," though it follows the more fundamental concern of *fittingness*. A literal translation of the end of the verse yields "does not come." The phrases "to rest" in the NIV and "alight" in other versions have been added for clarity. The original meaning is partially lost to us, but the basic implication of birds in flight is that they do not land or return to the nest; so a thoughtless curse does not "hit home."

While public beatings were common in the ancient world (see 13:24), the deeper point in 26:4 is that the fool acts like a brute beast. Much like ancient fables, wisdom, folly, and animals come together elsewhere in the Old Testament (Gen 3:1–15; Num 22:21–35; Ps 32:9; Prov 30:2; Eccl 3:18–19).

> [4] Do not answer a fool according to his folly,
>   or you yourself will be just like him.
> [5] Answer a fool according to his folly,
>   or he will be wise in his own eyes.

26:4–5 These verses pick up on the topic of speech in 25:20, 23, and 25. These sayings are some of the most cited sayings in Proverbs, partly because they are somewhat controversial. Robert Gordis, for example, believes that the redactors of proverbs juxtaposed two contradictory sayings known to professional sages, much like "Fools rush in where angels fear to tread" next to "To hesitate is to be lost."[3] Others believe that each saying applies to a different situation, which is true in a sense. However, given the context and unity of the poem, these sayings should be read together, as Van Leeuwen does here, "the distinction between fool and wise man is not absolute; precisely when one has 'mastered' the conventional wisdom (as in 26:3,4), he is in danger of becoming foolish."[4] Clifford wisely adds the point: "[g]ranted the discomfort and even danger of such association, someone has to speak up for wisdom."[5]

To be "wise in his own eyes" is an echo from Proverbs 3:7; it appears again in verse 12 and once more in describing the sluggard in verse 16.

> [6] Sending a message by the hands of a fool
>   is like cutting off one's feet or drinking poison.

---

2. Heim, *Poetic Imagination*, 575.
3. Robert Gordis, "Quotations in Wisdom Literature," *Jewish Quarterly Review* 30/2 (1939): 137.
4. Van Leeuwen, *Context and Meaning*, 102.
5. Clifford, *Proverbs*, 231.

[7] Like the useless legs of one who is lame
    is a proverb in the mouth of a fool.
[8] Like tying a stone in a sling
    is the giving of honor to a fool.
[9] Like a thornbush in a drunkard's hand
    is a proverb in the mouth of a fool.
[10] Like an archer who wounds at random
    is one who hires a fool or any passer-by.
[11] As a dog returns to its vomit,
    so fools repeat their folly.
[12] Do you see a person wise in their own eyes?
    There is more hope for a fool than for them.

26:6–12 These verses provide a montage of the fool's damaging potential, absurd nature, and ultimate fate.

The foolish messenger (v. 6) is a counter-comment to 25:13 (cf. 25:25); both verses address the behavior of the sender more than the messenger. The same phrase for "drinking poison" is translated in 4:17 as "drink . . . violence." The NIV assumes a self-inflicted malady, but it may be that the proverb imagines violence as inflicted by the careless sender instead. Unfortunately, the NIV reverses the riddle form of the original (see 25:11 and the introduction to ch 25).

Verses 7–10 speak to a variety of social consequences brought about by the fool. Verses 7, 9, and 10 provide three more sayings in riddle form, illustrating the danger of wisdom in the mouth (7, 9) or actions of fools (10). The sayings naturally flow with the surrounding poem: their message extends the idea in verses 4–5, the "legs" in verse 7 play upon the "feet" in verse 6, and the "drunkard" in verse 9 plays on "drinking" harmful libation in verse 6.

Verse 8 is another violent saying, emphasizing the un-fittingness of the fool in a wise society. The NIV translation "tying a stone in a sling" is uncertain. It could mean either that the stone is tied and therefore unable to release as intended or that any stone in a sling is a movement toward violence and danger. Heim helpfully summarizes the consequences of the fool in verses 6–10 as "laughable inefficiency, annoying inconvenience, and mortal danger to self and others."[6]

Verses 11–12 close the poem on fittingness. Verse 11 displays the gross behavior of dogs instinctively returning to their vomit. Dogs were not house pets in ancient Israel but viewed as wild and dangerous and symbols of

---

6. Heim, *Poetic Imagination*, 582.

uncleanliness (cf. 26:17). Peter draws upon this verse or a similar saying in his condemnation of false prophets and teachers (2 Pet 2:17–22). Verse 12 returns to the normal topic-comment order of sayings and borrows two variants from elsewhere in Proverbs: "Do you see a person" (22:29; 29:20) and "wise in his own eyes" (v. 16; 3:7). Some scholars read this saying literally, suggesting that there is actually some hope for a person "wise in their own eyes." In the present context and first use of the phrase (3:5–7) it is clear that these people are one in the same. The comparative statement is for poetic play.

> [13] A sluggard says, "There's a lion in the road,
>   a fierce lion roaming the streets!"
> [14] As a door turns on its hinges,
>   so a sluggard turns on his bed.
> [15] A sluggard buries his hand in the dish;
>   he is too lazy to bring it back to his mouth.
> [16] A sluggard is wiser in his own eyes
>   than seven people who answer discreetly.

26:13–16 These verses list what Waltke calls a "mirror of sluggards" that follows the "mirror of fools" in verses 1–12.[7] Folly and laziness are also combined in 6:6–11 and 24:30–34. Longman helpfully comments, "Proverbs parodies laziness more than any other form of foolishness."[8] The variant in 22:13 gives an explicit fear of being mauled whereas in 26:13 such a gruesome death is only implied. This is somewhat surprising given the density of violent images in these chapters. It may be that the editor of this chapter imagined the sayings being read sequentially, in which case 26:13 creates a gap that the mind naturally fills in with the memory from 22:13.

Verse 14 critiques the sluggard's addiction to sleep. The verse expands on verse 13 to show the extent to which the sluggard loves idleness. That said, the ancient view of sloth includes both the sleeper and the busybody who avoids the task at hand. These verses similarly describe the spectrum of behavior that seeks to avoid responsibilities: excuse making, sleep, pride, and careless speech.

> [17] Like one who grabs a stray dog by the ears
>   is someone who rushes into a quarrel not their own.
> [18] Like a maniac shooting
>   flaming arrows of death
> [19] is one who deceives their neighbor
>   and says, "I was only joking!"

---

7. Waltke, *Proverbs 15–31*, 355.
8. Longman, *Proverbs*, 468.

26:17–19 These verses are the first of four short poems that make up the second half of the chapter. Verse 17 is closely linked to verses 11–12 through the repetition of keywords "dog" (11) and "stray," which is the same word as "passer-by" in verse 10, as well as the repeated image of an archer (10). Whereas the fool in verse 17 is the victim of his folly, he becomes the perpetrator in verses 18–19. Similar carelessness of the fool can be seen in 10:23, only verse 18 adds wildly violent imagery in keeping with the tone of violence in chapters 25–26 as a whole.

> ²⁰ Without wood a fire goes out;
>   without a gossip a quarrel dies down.
> ²¹ As charcoal to embers and as wood to fire,
>   so is a quarrelsome person for kindling strife.
> ²² The words of a gossip are like choice morsels;
>   they go down to the inmost parts.

26:20–22 These verses expand the topic of the meddling busybody in verse 17 with two intense images. The first portrays gossiping and quarreling as fire, either calmed by their absence (20) or ignited by their presence (21). The second image characterizes the desire for gossip as unconstrained gluttony (cf. 18:8). The lack of control over one's passions always leads to self-destruction, social unrest, and upheaval (cf. 25:28).

> ²³ Like a coating of silver dross on earthenware
>   are fervent lips with an evil heart.
> ²⁴ Enemies disguise themselves with their lips,
>   but in their hearts they harbor deceit.
> ²⁵ Though their speech is charming, do not believe them,
>   for seven abominations fill their hearts.
> ²⁶ Their malice may be concealed by deception,
>   but their wickedness will be exposed in the assembly.

26:23–26 Verses 23–26 illustrate the complexity of human hypocrisy, what Fox calls "feigned friendship."[9] The sayings are united by the three-fold repetition of the words for "heart" (23–25) and "hate/enemy" (24, 26, cf. v. 28). Verse 23 compares outward speech that disguises the heart to the attractive glaze that hides the weaknesses of a vessel. Verses 24–25 move beneath the metaphor to unfold the depths of a foe's hateful deception. The "seven abominations" adds an unexpected and conspicuous touch. "Seven" likely echoes the "seven" wise persons depicted in verse 16, while "abominations" echoes unjust behavior in the law.

---

9. Fox, *Proverbs 10–31*, 800.

²⁷ Whoever digs a pit will fall into it;
   if someone rolls a stone, it will roll back on them.
²⁸ A lying tongue hates those it hurts,
   and a flattering mouth works ruin.

26:27–28 These verses spell out the fate of the fools, quarrelers, haters, and hypocrites in this chapter (cf. 12). Verse 27 threatens the reversal of fortunes to the evildoer. Compare it to the modern saying, "He who throws boomerangs should duck." Except here, the consequences are unavoidable. (For the "pit" see Psalms 7:16; 9:16–17; 35:7–8; 141:10 and Ecclesiastes 10:8–9.) Verse 28 presents challenges in translation, but it appears to be a summary statement about the damage of hateful and duplicitous speech.

 LIVE the Story

Fittingness and Wisdom

As part of a human behavior experiment conducted by the *Washington Post* in 2007, Grammy-Award winning violinist Joshua Bell played a highly complicated Beethoven piece for forty-five minutes during the morning rush hour of one of the busiest metro stations in Washington, DC. Of over 1,000 people who passed by, only seven stopped to watch. Passersbys contributed $30 to hear a piece Bell earned thousands for playing in concert the night before. At the time of this writing nine years have passed, but this moving story is still told to illustrate our modern priorities and lack of taste and appreciation for beauty.

Students of the book of Proverbs, however, could rightly suggest that this story is an example of fittingness: the right time and right place for something. Does it really surprise us that busy people with countless priorities like family, school, meals, meetings, metro connections, and carpool times might have to pass by such a sight without realizing it? Would it surprise us if a neurosurgeon in the middle of surgery decided not to leave because some world-class chef was serving lunch in the hospital café? Surgeons and commuters go about their normal schedules because they fit the grooves of life in this world. There are times for music and meals, but they are not on metro platforms and operating rooms (one hopes anyway).

One of the main reasons that people failed to understand Jesus was a failure to appreciate where he fit in Israel's story. Too many people were looking backwards to a restoration of monarchic Israel and unprepared to grasp that his kingdom encompassed much more than that. The key to understanding Jesus is recognizing that he comes out of Israel to establish a new era.

Something new was on the scene and old things must give way: "No one sews a patch of unshrunk cloth on an old garment . . . Neither do people pour new wine into old wineskins" (Matt 9:16–17). Thus we find that Jesus and his disciples do not fast as others do, do not observe the Sabbath as expected, and they do not retain old categories of Jew and Greek and clean and unclean (cf. Mark 2:18–6; 5:21–43).

Fittingness and Speech

In his introduction to *Mere Christianity*, C.S. Lewis distinguishes between "fighting like animals" and "quarrelling." "Quarrelling means trying to show that the other man is in the wrong. And there would be no sense in trying to do that unless you and he had some sort of agreement as to what Right and Wrong are . . . ."[10] Because of our sinful and finite nature, no human has a monopoly on right and wrong. Therefore we are bound to some degree of quarreling as we search for truth and wisdom, all the while avoiding senseless animal instincts. On the whole, chapter 26 fits well with Lewis's distinction. Verses 3, 5, and 26 all assume public contention and opposition from the just and the wise. Verses 4, 6, 7, 9, 17–19, 20–22, and 23–25, meanwhile, caution against needless arguments and thoughtless speech. Wisdom knows how to maintain the proper balance.

Fittingness and Vocation

Finding our "calling" today usually amounts to pursuing a "passion" and deep "purpose." This self-serving recommendation often leads into a black hole of uncertainty. The principle of fittingness offers a refreshing insight into our pursuit of meaningful work. In his book on work and vocation, Matthew Crawford says, "A good diamond cutter has a different disposition than a good dog trainer. The one is careful, the other commanding. Different kinds of work attract different human types, and we are lucky if we find work that is fitting."[11] Crawford goes on to critique the two major metrics used by universities to sort students: intelligence and demographics.

> But as a young person surveys the various ways he could make a living, and how they might be part of a life well lived, the pertinent question *for him* may be not what IQ he has, but whether he is, for example careful or commanding. If he is to find work that is fitting, he would do well to pause amid the general rush to the gates.[12]

10. C.S. Lewis, *Mere Christianity* (New York, Macmillan, 1952), 17–18.
11. Matthew B. Crawford, *Shop Class as Soul Craft: An Inquiry into the Value of Work* (New York: Penguin, 2009), 72.
12. Ibid., 72–73.

In a similar article in *The New Republic*, Jonathan Malesic responded to a Venn diagram that went viral on social media that encouraged people to pursue their "purpose" at the center of four overlapping circles: what we love, what we are good at, what the world needs, and what pays. Malesic says:

> Getting all four alleged elements of purpose to intersect is incredibly difficult. Even in the best of economic times, people rarely find remunerative work that they also love. And in an economy driven by consumer demand, what the world wants and what it needs may be quite different things.[13]

And so it is that the search for purpose and passion are uniquely unfitting guides for finding work that fits us. Indeed, it is because finding our calling tends to be "incredibly difficult" that we need wisdom to discern the right fit for the right person at the right time (see Live the Story in chapter 31).

Fittingness and Ethics

In chapter 21:14 above, we related the story of Dietrich Bonhoeffer and his friend and biographer Eberhard Bethge and Bonhoeffer's surprising willingness to offer Hitler a Nazi salute. Bonhoeffer, of course, was in the thick of several attempts to have Hitler assassinated, and his actions appear as a compromise in his public display of loyalties in the interest of protecting a strategic plan. Not every occasion for telling the truth is an occasion worth dying for (Exod 1:15–20; Josh 2:1–8). It might be right to resist Adolf Hitler, but it may be that this is not the best place and now is not the right time.

According to Oliver O'Donovan, ethical wisdom is grounded in the principle that every event of "novelty" or new situation we meet in life "manifests the permanence of the created order."[14] Ethical reasoning is thus a matter of *fitting* our ethical decisions into the framework of the permanent created order, which we know primarily through the laws, narratives, and poetry of the Bible.

Most of us are probably inclined to describe Bonhoeffer's situation as an "exception" to the moral rule of not lying. But O'Donovan argues that the language of *exceptions* leads us to think of gaps or weaknesses in the moral code. But this only sends us in search of yet another rule in a long and growing list. So instead of making new rules for each exception, he argues that we should view a moral dilemma as a sign of *our own* lack of knowledge of God's moral order.[15] "Lying" is a thicker and more complex behavior than we first imagine it to be.

---

13. Jonathan Malesic, "Don't Search for 'Purpose.' You Will Fail: The Big Lie Behind A Venn Diagram Meme," *New Republic*, May 28, 2015, http://www.newrepublic.com/article/121915/dont-search-purpose-you-will-fail.

14. O'Donovan, *Resurrection and Moral Order*, 189.

15. Ibid., 195.

Why is this kind of thinking about ethics important? O'Donovan argues that the difference between looking for moral exceptions versus a deeper moral order is the difference between legalism and true morality.[16] Biblical morality looks at the ethical dilemma as God's invitation to peer more deeply and clearly into the order he made for the world. As we handle each ethical decision we are like a farmer who comes to know the lay of his land through years of use.

Jesus often forces this kind of ethical reasoning on those around him. For example, when confronted by the fact that his disciples did not fast like the disciples of John, Jesus answered, "How can the guest of the bridegroom fast while he is with them?" (Mark 2:19). Jesus then goes on to observe no one would sew a new patch on old clothing or put new wine in old wineskins. Jesus and his disciples then collect heads of grain as they journeyed through the grain fields on the Sabbath, provoking a stern rebuke from the Pharisees (Mark 2:23–27) followed by Jesus' pointing to David and his men who ate the consecrated bread of the priests in a time of great need (1 Sam 21:1–6). Just as the Pharisees are blind to the exceptions to the law, they are blind to the lawgiver standing in their midst. Jesus thus mirrors the prophets' judgments against Israel, who only lived at the surface of the laws and overlooked the way the law always points to God's gracious dealings with his people (cf. Hos 6:6; Amos 5:21–24; Matt 23:23–24).

---

16. Ibid., 203.

 LISTEN to the Story

¹ Do not boast about tomorrow,
  for you do not know what a day may bring.
² Let someone else praise you, and not your own mouth;
  an outsider, and not your own lips.
³ Stone is heavy and sand a burden,
  but a fool's provocation is heavier than both.
⁴ Anger is cruel and fury overwhelming,
  but who can stand before jealousy?
⁵ Better is open rebuke
  than hidden love.
⁶ Wounds from a friend can be trusted,
  but an enemy multiplies kisses.
⁷ One who is full loathes honey from the comb,
  but to the hungry even what is bitter tastes sweet.
⁸ Like a bird that flees its nest
  is anyone who flees from home.
⁹ Perfume and incense bring joy to the heart,
  and the pleasantness of a friend
  springs from their heartfelt advice.
¹⁰ Do not forsake your friend or a friend of your family,
  and do not go to your relative's house when disaster strikes you—
  better a neighbor nearby than a relative far away.
¹¹ Be wise, my son, and bring joy to my heart;
  then I can answer anyone who treats me with contempt.
¹² The prudent see danger and take refuge,
  but the simple keep going and pay the penalty.
¹³ Take the garment of one who puts up security for a stranger;
  hold it in pledge if it is done for an outsider.
¹⁴ If anyone loudly blesses their neighbor early in the morning,

it will be taken as a curse.
¹⁵ A quarrelsome wife
    is like the dripping of a leaky roof in a rainstorm;
¹⁶ restraining her is like restraining the wind
    or grasping oil with the hand.
¹⁷ As iron sharpens iron,
    so one person sharpens another.
¹⁸ The one who guards a fig tree will eat its fruit,
    and whoever protects their master will be honored.
¹⁹ As water reflects the face,
    so one's life reflects the heart.
²⁰ Death and Destruction are never satisfied,
    and neither are human eyes.
²¹ The crucible for silver and the furnace for gold,
    but people are tested by their praise.
²² Though you grind a fool in a mortar,
    grinding them like grain with a pestle,
    you will not remove their folly from them.
²³ Be sure you know the condition of your flocks,
    give careful attention to your herds;
²⁴ for riches do not endure forever,
    and a crown is not secure for all generations.
²⁵ When the hay is removed and new growth appears
    and the grass from the hills is gathered in,
²⁶ the lambs will provide you with clothing,
    and the goats with the price of a field.
²⁷ You will have plenty of goats' milk to feed your family
    and to nourish your female servants.

Listening to the Text in the Story: Leviticus 19:35–37; Ruth 1:16–17;
2:10–13; 1 Samuel 18:1–4; 20:1–21:1; Job 2:9–37:24; Psalms 41:9;
55:12–13; Ezekiel 34; Amenemope 19:11–13; 22:5–9

The overwhelming focus on friends and family members in this chapter alerts us to the vast number and variety of biblical passages concerned with the friend: law, narratives, wisdom, prophets, and Gospels. We are given examples of good friends like Ruth and Jonathan as well as traitorous friends (Pss 41:9; 55:12–13). Similarly, this chapter brings to mind the many biblical passages concerned with the shepherd, especially the motif of the shepherd-king in Ezekiel 34. Friends and shepherds will be discussed more closely in Live the Story below.

# EXPLAIN the Story

In comparison to the unified and highly stylized poems in chapters 25–26, this chapter appears almost random. However, many scholars have demonstrated signs of careful editing among the pairs of proverbs.[1]

> [1] Do not boast about tomorrow,
>   for you do not know what a day may bring.
> [2] Let someone else praise you, and not your own mouth;
>   an outsider, and not your own lips.

27:1–2 The two admonitions in this opening verse-pair are followed by seven sayings (vv. 3–9). The admonitions are united by the play on the Hebrew verb *halal*, translated "boast" (v. 1) and "praise" (v. 2), and they address various dimensions of appropriate and inappropriate speech (cf. 26:1–12). Boasting about ourselves or our knowledge of the future and any form of overconfidence are almost always censured (Prov 16:3; Jas 4:13–15; Amenemope 19:11–13; 22:5–9). Jeremiah's exhortation to boast in Yahweh is rhetorical and calls for an admission of humility and dependence (Jer 9:23–24). Paul, however, finds it necessary to establish his credentials to the Corinthians at length (2 Cor 10:12–11:33).

> [3] Stone is heavy and sand a burden,
>   but a fool's provocation is heavier than both.
> [4] Anger is cruel and fury overwhelming,
>   but who can stand before jealousy?

27:3–4 Lines 3a and 4a have identical syntax; both of them set up extreme forms of pernicious behavior. "Provocation" (3b) can also be translated "vexing," using the same verb that describes Peninnah who would "vex" or "provoke" Hannah because of her barren womb (1 Sam 1:6–7). Such taunting can feel heavier than the weight of stones and sand. Verse 4 remarks that the effects of "jealousy" are worse than anger (cf. 12:16; 17:25). Anger is often just the outward expression of deeper emotions.

> [5] Better is open rebuke
>   than hidden love.

---

1. See Van Leeuwen, *Context and Meaning*, 123–43 and Heim, *Poetic Imagination*.

⁶ Wounds from a friend can be trusted,
   but an enemy multiplies kisses.

27:5–6 These verses address correction from a friend. "Open rebuke" is somewhat ambiguous and might allude to public punishment as in 29:15. Even so, Proverbs continually praises those who receive correction, especially in chapters 1–9 (cf. 1:23, 25, 30; 3:11; 5:12, etc.). "Hidden love" (v. 5b) probably indicates not private correction but a rebuke that is never given; withholding correction in the name of love is no love at all. Similarly, verse 6 welcomes the correction of "a friend," but chastises the false "kisses" of an "enemy," literally a "hater." Judas betrayed Jesus with such kisses (Matt 26:48–50).

⁷ One who is full loathes honey from the comb,
   but to the hungry even what is bitter tastes sweet.
⁸ Like a bird that flees its nest
   is anyone who flees from home.

27:7–8 These sayings differ in content, yet both emphasize matters of fittingness. Verse 7 illumines the power that relative degrees of hunger and thirst have on our perception of taste. The point applies to any form of pleasure. The NIV "even what is bitter" (7b) is probably better translated "every bitter thing" or "anything bitter."[2] Furthermore *mar*, "bitter," may be an allusion to the bitterness of the adulteress or forbidden woman in 5:4 and the bitter taste of *mor*, "myrrh," in 7:17, deepening the sense of the saying.

Verse 8 turns to fittingness in relation to place. The saying has broad application, of course, but it is worth noting an echo of the husband who has left home in Proverbs 7:19. The sayings would be distant were it not for the parallel to "bitter" in 27:7 and "myrrh" (same Hebrew root) in 7:17, not to mention the fact that "rebuke" in verse 5 is another of several more examples in this chapter where it appears that the writer chooses language specifically aimed at connecting the content to chapters 1–9. We will see more of these below.

⁹ Perfume and incense bring joy to the heart,
   and the pleasantness of a friend springs from their heartfelt advice.
¹⁰ Do not forsake your friend or a friend of your family,
   and do not go to your relative's house when disaster strikes you—
   better a neighbor nearby than a relative far away.

27:9–10 These verses involve a number of complex issues. Verse 9a is straightforward (cf. Pss 104:15; 133:2). Verse 9b is uncertain and can be

---

2. Waltke, *Proverbs 15–31*, 377; Longman, *Proverbs*, 477.

translated various ways. The NIV captures the overall notion that advice from intimate friends is greatly treasured.

Verse 10 breaks the chain of sayings in verses 3–9 with two admonitions and a third line that offers a comparison. Clifford very helpfully describes the logical flow between these sayings, "Cultivate old family friends and neighbors; do not automatically count on kin in time of trouble, for neighbors and friends are ready at hand."[3] Ruth is a shining example of near friendship when family is far away (Ruth 1:16–28; 2:20).

> [11] Be wise, my son, and bring joy to my heart;
>   then I can answer anyone who treats me with contempt.
> [12] The prudent see danger and take refuge,
>   but the simple keep going and pay the penalty.

27:11–12 Verses 11–12 combine an admonition and a saying, each beginning with a synonym: "wise" (11) and "prudent" (12). Verse 11 underscores the importance of parent-child relationships; an obedient or "wise" son or daughter galvanizes the parent against opposition. Verse 12 gives an example of a child with insight who turns away from danger (cf. 22:3). The introduction of the father and "son" are yet another allusion to chapters 1–9.

> [13] Take the garment of one who puts up security for a stranger;
>   hold it in pledge if it is done for an outsider.
> [14] If anyone loudly blesses their neighbor early in the morning,
>   it will be taken as a curse.

27:13–14 Verse 13 is a close variant of 20:16; only "strangers" (masc. pl.) has been changed here to "stranger" (fem. sg.). The fact that the feminine form is used almost exclusively of the "foreign woman" may be another sign that the variant in 20:16 was adapted here to maintain the connection with chapters 1–9.[4] The saying about a "security" and "pledge," moreover, is also a connection to 6:1–5 (cf. 11:15; 17:18; 22:6).[5] Verse 14 exhibits a second example of faulty friendship and a lack of fittingness in speech. A poorly timed blessing becomes a "curse."

> [15] A quarrelsome wife
>   is like the dripping of a leaky roof in a rainstorm;
> [16] restraining her is like restraining the wind
>   or grasping oil with the hand.

---

3. Clifford, *Proverbs*, 238.
4. Of course, 27:13 may have been the source for 20:16. The point as noted by Heim, *Poetic Imagination*, 495, is that the writers adapt variant sayings to fit their surrounding context.
5. On the link to chapters 1–9, see Van Leeuwen, *Proverbs*, 231.

27:15–16 These verses are another variant, this time of 19:13 and 25:24. Verse 15 reinforces the occasional unreliability of family members (10) with poor judgment and lack of self-control (13–14). Verse 16 provides a further aside about the wife; however, the text is difficult and the translation may be impossible to recover. One possibility is that the one who "restrain[s]" or, better, "hides the storm," will be "called right." Or "his hand will meet oil." Granting that the Hebrew may be lost to us, the point seems to be that this woman will not receive correction (cf. 5).

[17] As iron sharpens iron,
    so one person sharpens another.
[18] The one who guards a fig tree will eat its fruit,
    and whoever protects their master will be honored.
[19] As water reflects the face,
    so one's life reflects the heart.

27:17–19 These verses appear somewhat disconnected, yet they are held together by parallels between natural elements and human body parts/nature in the first and third sayings: "iron" and "face" (NIV "another") in verse 17 and "water," "face," and "heart" in verse 19. For this reason it is unfortunate that English translations so hastily over-translate and dull the poetic resonance of the sayings.

Verse 17 echoes the refrains that praise friendship in this chapter. Verse 18 may very well be a specific example of a loyal servant who acts as a friend to his master. Van Leeuwen discerns that this saying affirms faithfulness among farmers (18a) and servants (18b) in order to show the nobility of all vocations.[6] The content of the sayings may have motivated the collector to add verses 23–27 at the end of this group. Verse 19 seems to speak of an individual and thus depart from social sayings. But a literal translation makes a social setting more likely: "As in water a face to a face, so a man's heart to a man."[7] In other words, people are known through the intimate interaction of friends (cf. 17; 20:5).

[20] Death and Destruction are never satisfied,
    and neither are human eyes.

27:20 Verse 20 is another isolated saying typical of the loose connections in the chapter, especially compared to chapters 25–26. Still, like verses 17 and 19, body parts, in this case "eyes," stand as a symbol for human nature. Furthermore, the insatiability of human desires, also found in 30:15–16

6. Ibid.
7. Fox, *Proverbs 10–31*, 812.

(cf. Num 15:39; Eccl 2:10; 4:8; 6:7–9), introduces the two sayings about refining in verses 21–22.

> ²¹ The crucible for silver and the furnace for gold,
>   but people are tested by their praise.
> ²² Though you grind a fool in a mortar,
>   grinding them like grain with a pestle,
>   you will not remove their folly from them.

27:21–22 These verses close the main body of sayings in this chapter before the epilogue in verses 23–27. As noted above, the topics of refining and testing sound a final caution at the end of this collection. Verse 21 is a variant of 17:3, but, in keeping with the paucity of Yahweh sayings in chapters 25–29, omits the divine name. "Praise" (v. 21b) echoes verses 1–2, perhaps to enclose the sayings.

Verse 22 appeals to the crushing image of mortar and pestle as a way to illustrate that no amount of effort can separate a fool from his folly (cf. 18:2; 26:11–12). The similar saying in 22:15 provides a balance—the use of the rod can remove folly from the youth.

> ²³ Be sure you know the condition of your flocks,
>   give careful attention to your herds;
> ²⁴ for riches do not endure forever,
>   and a crown is not secure for all generations.
> ²⁵ When the hay is removed and new growth appears
>   and the grass from the hills is gathered in,
> ²⁶ the lambs will provide you with clothing,
>   and the goats with the price of a field.
> ²⁷ You will have plenty of goats' milk to feed your family
>   and to nourish your female servants.

27:23–27 These verses resemble the saying about the sluggard in 24:30–34 only, instead of scenes of neglect, these verses depict the fruits of hard work over a long season. The one negative statement comes in verse 24: wealth does not last forever. The lesson is that one should approach life, beginning at the smallest level of the economic cycle, moving through each stage with care (23, 25), and keeping the end goals in mind: clothes to wear, money to spend, and food to eat (26–27). Van Leeuwen and Meinhold suggest that the "crown" in verse 24 and the fact that this poem closes the Solomonic section that began in 25:1–7 imbue this section with royal overtones—the farmer-shepherd doubles as a symbol of the king.[8] See more on this below.

---

8. Van Leeuwen, *Context and Meaning*, 131–143; Meinhold, *Sprüche*, 461. But Cf. Longman, *Proverbs*, 484, who rejects the royal overtones.

 LIVE the Story

Good Friends and Good Family

Chapter 27 conspicuously avoids *eros*, or sexual love, and instead gives close attention to the two loves that C. S. Lewis calls affection and friendship—the loves between family, friends, and neighbors.[9] By friendship, Lewis is speaking about love that is neither biological nor needed for survival.[10] Friendship, in other words, is an unnatural love of commitment between any two people who may share any number of other bonds with others close to them.

Such is Ruth's commitment to Naomi in devoting herself to her mother-in-law out of no absolute need or biological relation: "Where you go I will go, and where you stay I will stay. Your people will be my people and your God my God. Where you die I will die, and there I will be buried. May the LORD deal with me, be it ever so severely, if even death separates you and me" (Ruth 1:16–17). Ruth is indeed a friend closer than biological family in a time of need (Ruth 2:11–12; cf. Prov 27:10).

Jonathan and David offer an equally powerful example of friendship that is closer than a family bond (1 Sam 18:1–4). David's use of marital language in his lament of Jonathan's death (2 Sam 1:26) has prompted some readers to suggest that David and Jonathan shared an erotic love. C. S. Lewis wryly dismisses this as a claim that can neither be proven nor disproven using the following example: "If there were an invisible cat in that chair the chair would look empty; but the chair does look empty, therefore there is an invisible cat in it."[11]

Readers will disagree about the morality of same-sex relationships, but the situation with David and Jonathan should be seen in its fuller context. Everyone loved David, not just Jonathan, and David took many wives, after all, and was, in no uncertain terms, attracted to Bathsheba sexually (2 Sam 11:1–4). David might very well have been bisexual, but only if skepticism is pressed to its limits. Indeed, it should also be noted that when the prophet Nathan risked his life by rebuking David (2 Sam 10:1–13; cf. Prov 27:5–6), not only did David repent, but he honored the prophet by calling one of his son's Nathan (2 Sam. 5:14). David was a man who knew friendship.

Belaboring this point is essential, for as Wesley Hill rightly notes, "friendship" has fallen on hard times. Relying on the insights of Benjamin Myers, Hill blames three myths for the devaluation of friendship: (1) "sex wholly

9. C. S. Lewis, *The Four Loves* (New York: Harcourt, Brace, 1960).

10. Ibid., 63–64.

11. Lewis, *Four Loves*, 60.

explains the depths of our most profound relationships;" (2) the nuclear family is the ultimate significance of the nuclear family—that is, there are no closer bonds than parents, children, and siblings; and (3) our freedom is tied to our happiness—the less burdened we are socially, the happier we will be.[12] This cultural demotion of friendship leads us to characterize the single life as a life of desperate loneliness. During an age where an increasing number of people seek counseling and therapy, and sexual experimentation is considered normal, friendship is rarely seen as a missing piece in the human emotional and psychological puzzle.

Hill goes on to demonstrate that Jesus not only embraced such friendship but transformed it into something greater.[13] As evidence of Jesus' deep bond with his followers, John depicts Jesus weeping over the death of his "friend" Lazarus (John 11:11, 35). When Jesus called himself the "vine" and his disciples the "branches," he explained that this bound the disciples to Jesus as "friends," and thus born into a new fellowship with the Father (15:13, 15). Like the disciples, our friendship with Jesus results in a mystical union: "I in them and you in me—so that they may be brought to complete unity" (John 17:23). And so in Christ we are empowered for newer and stronger friendships than even those enjoyed by Ruth and Naomi and Jonathan and David.

Good Shepherds, Good Kings

The sayings in Proverbs were probably collected to train sages and prepare youths in the royal line of succession. But its sayings nevertheless also apply naturally and easily to popular life. Such is the nature of stories, folktales, and proverbs.

The final agricultural poem in 27:23–27 should thus be imagined speaking to good work in palaces, fields, homes, marketplaces, and shops of craft. That said, it is the *agricultural* model or metaphor that works so well to cross all of these social and vocational lines. This may have something to do with the timeless and holistic nature of the bucolic, as Van Leeuwen calls it.[14] James Rebanks's recent memoir about his life as a shepherd in the Lake District of England suggests such an explanation:

> It is a farming pattern fundamentally unchanged from many centuries ago . . . You could bring a Viking man to stand on our fell with me and he would understand what we are doing and the basic pattern of our farming

12. Wesley Hill, *Spiritual Friendship: Finding Love in the Church as a Celibate Gay Christian* (Grand Rapids, MI: Brazos, 2015), 10–14.
13. Ibid., 45–61.
14. Van Leeuwen, *Context and Meaning*, 137–78.

year. The timing of each task varies depending on the different valleys and farms. Things are driven by seasons and necessity, not by our will.[15]

Echoing Proverbs 27, Rebanks goes on to say: "[m]aking good hay is like a commandment from God if you live here. People once have faced ruin and even famine if they couldn't feed their animals through the winter."[16] Agricultural life involves the mind and the body in work that not only involves the whole lifecycle of food and clothing but is also attended by real and immediate consequences, whether warmth and food or famine and cold.

Perhaps the lack of such wholeness and particularity is what makes "cubicle work" seem so unsatisfying. Working in abstractions, such as populating databases, selling the name or idea behind a commodity as opposed to the commodity itself, or participating in a miniscule part of the work of a company, hospital, school, law firm, etc. are some of the root causes of modern vocational restlessness. To be sure, many people celebrate the new "knowledge worker" and the "creative class" of the rising millennial generation. While we don't need to condemn banking, industry, and large corporations as evil, a biblical understanding of work should leads us to ask critical questions about the assumptions of our day. Matthew Crawford, for example, seeks to expose the false elevation of higher education and accumulation of wealth over the lesser fields of crafts and trades.[17] Besides farming, which is increasingly industrialized, the trades are one of the few places where we still have examples of work that provide clear pictures of wholeness, community, and individual identity.

The agricultural metaphor here also applies naturally to the political realm. To "know the condition of your flocks" (27:23) is to know the state of a kingdom, its people, its economy, and its allies and enemies and their complex and varied interrelationships and interdependencies. For example, Nathan confronted David's sin against Uriah and Bathsheba with a parable about a wealthy sheep thief (2 Sam 12:1–12). Furthermore, David is the first of many shepherds who would fail to care for the flock of Israel—its land, worship, poor and needy, wealth, and justice (Jer 23:1–4; Ezek 34:1–6). And so the promise of a coming shepherd as God's messiah is not a promise of a kind man caring for lambs (Isa 40:11; Jer 34:1–31; 37:24), but a divine king whose death and resurrection renews every marred and fractured dimension of human life: social, political, religious, and agricultural (John 10:1–18).

---

15. James Rebanks, *The Shepherd's Life: Modern Dispatches from an Ancient Landscape* (New York: Flatiron Books, 2015), 32.

16. Ibid., 69.

17. Crawford, *Shop Class*, 143–48.

¹ The wicked flee though no one pursues,
    but the righteous are as bold as a lion.
² When a country is rebellious, it has many rulers,
    but a ruler with discernment and knowledge maintains order.
³ A ruler who oppresses the poor
    is like a driving rain that leaves no crops.
⁴ Those who forsake instruction praise the wicked,
    but those who heed it resist them.
⁵ Evildoers do not understand what is right,
    but those who seek the LORD understand it fully.
⁶ Better the poor whose walk is blameless
    than the rich whose ways are perverse.
⁷ A discerning son heeds instruction,
    but a companion of gluttons disgraces his father.
⁸ Whoever increases wealth by taking interest or profit from the poor
    amasses it for another, who will be kind to the poor.
⁹ If anyone turns a deaf ear to my instruction,
    even their prayers are detestable.
¹⁰ Whoever leads the upright along an evil path
    will fall into their own trap,
    but the blameless will receive a good inheritance.
¹¹ The rich are wise in their own eyes;
    one who is poor and discerning sees how deluded they are.
¹² When the righteous triumph, there is great elation;
    but when the wicked rise to power, people go into hiding.
¹³ Whoever conceals their sins does not prosper,
    but the one who confesses and renounces them finds mercy.
¹⁴ Blessed is the one who always trembles before God,
    but whoever hardens their heart falls into trouble.

¹⁵ Like a roaring lion or a charging bear
   is a wicked ruler over a helpless people.
¹⁶ A tyrannical ruler practices extortion,
   but one who hates ill-gotten gain will enjoy a long reign.
¹⁷ Anyone tormented by the guilt of murder
   will seek refuge in the grave;
   let no one hold them back.
¹⁸ The one whose walk is blameless is kept safe,
   but the one whose ways are perverse will fall into the pit.
¹⁹ Those who work their land will have abundant food,
   but those who chase fantasies will have their fill of poverty.
²⁰ A faithful person will be richly blessed,
   but one eager to get rich will not go unpunished.
²¹ To show partiality is not good—
   yet a person will do wrong for a piece of bread.
²² The stingy are eager to get rich
   and are unaware that poverty awaits them.
²³ Whoever rebukes a person will in the end gain favor
   rather than one who has a flattering tongue.
²⁴ Whoever robs their father or mother
   and says, "It's not wrong,"
   is partner to one who destroys.
²⁵ The greedy stir up conflict,
   but those who trust in the LORD will prosper.
²⁶ Those who trust in themselves are fools,
   but those who walk in wisdom are kept safe.
²⁷ Those who give to the poor will lack nothing,
   but those who close their eyes to them receive many curses.
²⁸ When the wicked rise to power, people go into hiding;
   but when the wicked perish, the righteous thrive.

Listening to the Text in the Story: Exodus 22:24; Leviticus 25:36; Deuteronomy 1:13, 17; 4:1–8; 5:1; 21:20; 23:20–21; 24:14; 2 Samuel 14:4–11; 15:1–6; Psalm 32; Isaiah 5:21; Ezekiel 22:12

In his study of Deuteronomy and Proverbs, Schipper argues that the Deuteronomic law stands behind the editing of Proverbs, particularly chapters 1–9, 28, and 30.[1] The most conspicuous example is the way Proverbs borrows

1. Schipper, *Hermeneutik Der Torah*.

Deuteronomy's mixing of legal and sapiential terms: torah (1:5; 4:8; 4:44; 17:18–20, etc.), "justice/judgments," (1:17; 4:1, 5, 8, etc.), "hear/listen" (Deut. 1:17; 4:1, 6; 5:1, etc.) and "understanding" (1:13; 4:6; 32:29). All of these terms appear in Proverbs 28:1–11. Chapter 28 also alludes to several laws found in Deuteronomy 21–24. (See the commentary below as well as 1:8 and 30:1–9.)

Other Old Testament passages echo throughout this chapter as well: the confession of sin to find mercy (Ps 32; Prov 28:13), those who oppress the poor (Ezek 22:12; Prov 28:3, 8), and those wise in their own eyes (Isa 5:21; Prov 28:11, 26).

 EXPLAIN the Story

Several poetic features separate the first part of the collection of Hezekiah in 25:1–27:27 from 28:1–29:29. To start, the proverb-poems and clusters in the former give way to mostly antithetical sayings (A *but* B) as in chapters 10–15. Second, also like chapters 10–15, we find repeated emphasis on the "righteous" and the "wicked," particularly in key structural locations (28:12, 28; 29:2; 16).[2] Furthermore, four of these structural sayings are nearly identical variants (28:12, 28, 29:2, 29:16), which may very well divide these chapters into four sections. Finally, five of Proverbs' thirteen uses of torah, "law/instruction," occur in these chapters (28:4 [twice], 7, 9; 29:18),[3] and Yahweh, which is absent from chapters 25–26, appears five times in these chapters (28:5, 25; 29:13, 25, 26).[4] It is sometimes argued that chapters 28–29 are a manual for kings. More will be said in Live the Story below.

> [1] The wicked flee though no one pursues,
>   but the righteous are as bold as a lion.
> [2] When a country is rebellious, it has many rulers,
>   but a ruler with discernment and knowledge maintains order.
> [3] A ruler who oppresses the poor
>   is like a driving rain that leaves no crops.
> [4] Those who forsake instruction praise the wicked,
>   but those who heed it resist them.
> [5] Evildoers do not understand what is right,
>   but those who seek the LORD understand it fully.

---

2. See Heim, *Poetic Imagination*, 592–608.

3. It should be noted that the six occurrences of torah are found in chapters 1–9, which reinforces Schipper's arguments noted above and in the context of vv. 1–11.

4. For more structural detail in these chapters, see Murphy, *Proverbs*, 213–14.

⁶ Better the poor whose walk is blameless
    than the rich whose ways are perverse.
⁷ A discerning son heeds instruction,
    but a companion of gluttons disgraces his father.
⁸ Whoever increases wealth by taking interest or profit from the poor
    amasses it for another, who will be kind to the poor.
⁹ If anyone turns a deaf ear to my instruction,
    even their prayers are detestable.
¹⁰ Whoever leads the upright along an evil path
    will fall into their own trap,
    but the blameless will receive a good inheritance.
¹¹ The rich are wise in their own eyes;
    one who is poor and discerning sees how deluded they are.

28:1–11 These verses are united by several keywords: "understanding" (2, 5, 7, 11), torah (4 [2x], 7), and terms for "rich," "poor," and "low" (3, 6, 8, 11).

Verse 1 turns the unfounded fear of a lion in 26:13 to the dread imaged in the curse in Leviticus 26:17 and 36. Fox comments that "[t]he wicked live in constant anxiety."[5] But this should be held in balance with the fact that sometimes the wicked and foolish are apathetic and unaware of their fates (cf. v. 22 and 9:13, 18).

Heim observes the following parallel sequences of keywords and contexts in verses 2–6 and 7–11:[6]

A	*bin* "understanding" v. 2	A'	*bin* "understanding" v. 7
B	oppression of the *dal* "poor" v. 3	B'	oppression of the *dal* "poor" v. 8
C	*torah* as "basis of discernment" v. 4	C'	*ra'* "evil" "as basis of discernment" v. 5
D	effects of "evil" *ra* v. 5	D'	effects of "evil" *ra'* v. 10
E	*ras* "poor" "blameless" better than *asir* "rich" "perverse" v. 6	E'	*dal* "poor" "wise" better than *asir* "rich" and "wise in their own eyes" v. 11

The first line of verse 2 could be translated "for" [or "because of"] the nation's rebellion it has many rulers. But this is not necessary in the context. Hosea 8:1–4 lists the appointing of many rulers as one of a long list of Israel's transgressions in breaking their covenant. By contrast, a wise ruler (literally

5. Fox, *Proverbs 10–31*, 819.
6. Heim, *Poetic Imagination*, 442.

"man") keeps order in the kingdom. Verse 3 nuances the previous saying to say that even a single ruler can implement a system of injustice that provides no security for the weak.

Verses 4–6 set up three comparisons between righteous and unrighteousness people. Verse 4 contrasts those who "forsake" with those who "heed" the torah, which can be translated "instruction" or "law" (cf. Rom 1:28–32). There is something of a false dilemma in English translations at this point, as the whole context in verses 1–11 weaves together language of sapiential teaching and standards of justice such that both meanings can be in play. There is also a strong misconception in popular and scholarly circles that wisdom and law operate in separate spheres of life. They are, in fact, more alike than not. Indeed, verse 5 expands on the legal terminology in places like Proverbs 1:3 and 2:5. Wisdom and understanding lead to the knowledge of "what is right," the same word translated "justice" in other contexts. The end of verse 5 is sometimes legitimately translated "know all," which goes beyond the NIV "understand [justice] fully." Paul expresses a similar contrast in 1 Corinthians 2:14–16. The better-than saying in 28:6 is a close variant of 19:1, which uses "speech" instead of "ways." In 28:6 wealth and poverty are not always aligned with wisdom and folly or righteousness and wickedness (cf. Mark 10:25; Sir. 2:12).

Verses 7–8 list two sayings that share precise parallels in the Mosaic law. In this light we can see that the NIV's translation of torah as "instruction" dulls this connection. The son's consortium with "gluttons" (7) echoes the law in Deuteronomy 21:20. In fact, *zolelim*, "gluttons," is only used in Proverbs and Deuteronomy (cf. also Prov 23:20). The condemnation of unjust transactions by the rich in verse 8 resembles verse 28 and repeats several laws (Exod 22:24; Lev 25:36; Deut 23:20–21; cf. Ezek 22:12). The nature of redistribution appears to be divine rather than human, which fits naturally within the surrounding context of legal themes and language.

Verse 9 is yet another echo from the law, Deuteronomy in particular, which frequently calls Israel to "hear" the torah or "statutes and judgments" (see chapter introduction above). The specific mention of the "ear" that hears the torah is also unambiguously Deuteronomic language (Deut 5:1; 29:3; 31:11–12, 28, 30; 32:1, 44. Cf. Exod 15:26; 24:7 and the commentary at 4:1–8, 5:1, and 8:32–34). On the prayers that are "detestable," literally, "an abomination," see 3:32; 11:1; 12:22; 15:8; 26:25.

Verse 10 again appeals to divine retribution to discourage leading others astray. Similar forms of this warning occur several times (Deut 27:18; Job 12:16; Prov 5:20; 20:1; 26:7; Isa. 28:7; Matt 5:19; Luke 17:1–2).

Verse 11 uses the familiar person who is "wise in their own eyes" (3:7;

26:5, 12) to sound another reminder about the conditional link between wealth, righteousness, wisdom, poverty, wickedness, and foolishness (cf. 6, 8, 20, 29:13). The rich, intelligent, and powerful are prone to take credit for their position in life (cf. Deut 8:17; Isa 5:21). Also, as in 26:4–5, the humble-and-truly-wise see through the proud-and-not-wise.

> [12] When the righteous triumph, there is great elation;
>   but when the wicked rise to power, people go into hiding.
> [13] Whoever conceals their sins does not prosper,
>   but the one who confesses and renounces them finds mercy.
> [14] Blessed is the one who always trembles before God,
>   but whoever hardens their heart falls into trouble.
> [15] Like a roaring lion or a charging bear
>   is a wicked ruler over a helpless people.
> [16] A tyrannical ruler practices extortion,
>   but one who hates ill-gotten gain will enjoy a long reign.

28:12–16 These verses are loosely connected sayings that form a chiasm:

> public power and wealth (12)
>   sayings of personal piety (13–14)
> public power and wealth (15–16)

Verse 12 is the second of four section markers (see introduction above). All four sayings employ images of the wicked and righteous rising/increasing and falling/waning with corresponding effects on the public masses.

Verses 13–14 provide the two inner sayings, which address personal piety and divine favor. Van Leeuwen helpfully comments that Psalm 32, a penitential psalm, "may . . . be the best OT commentary on these two verses."[7] "God" does not appear in the Hebrew, but fits quite naturally with the context. (See more on "A Praying Wisdom" below.)

Verses 15–16 close this cluster with two contradictory sayings about power and wealth. The animal metaphor in verse 15 is close to 19:2 and 20:2. The animal world is often a reliable mirror for human behavior and its excesses (cf. 30:29–31). The NIV "helpless" is the same word translated "poor," which is a keyword in these chapters (cf. 28:3, 8, 11; 29:7, 14). The Hebrew in verse 16 is difficult, and the NIV opts to render the beginning "A tyrannical ruler," rather than "A ruler without understanding" as almost all other translations and commentaries do.[8] The uneven parallel bothers many commentators as "extortion" (16a) is not in the same category as a long life (16b). But as Heim

---

7. Van Leeuwen, *Proverbs*, 238.
8. See also Murphy, *Proverbs*, 213 who follows the LXX: "A prince lacking in revenues . . ."

demonstrates, uneven parallels are the norm in Proverbs (see Introduction).[9] The unevenness is probably intended to match the saying with verses 12–13 and the overriding theme of the rise and fall of the powerful in chapters 28–29.

> [17] Anyone tormented by the guilt of murder
>> will seek refuge in the grave;
>> let no one hold them back.
> [18] The one whose walk is blameless is kept safe,
>> but the one whose ways are perverse will fall into the pit.
> [19] Those who work their land will have abundant food,
>> but those who chase fantasies will have their fill of poverty.
> [20] A faithful person will be richly blessed,
>> but one eager to get rich will not go unpunished.

28:17–20 These verses depict four loosely related comparisons enclosed by two synonyms for "man," *adam* (v. 17) and *ish* (v. 20). The middle sayings each begin with a participle, "the one who . . .", or "whoever."

The line structure in 28:17 is unusual, and interpreters either divide it into two or three lines. The Hebrew in verse 17a describes one who "oppresses the life blood." To "oppress" is the same word translated "extortion" in verse 16, while "life blood" is a figure of speech for murder (cf. Gen 9:6). The image of fleeing to the "grave," literally "pit," may pick up on the law that provided for cities of refuge for unintentional murder (Deut 19:1–10; Exod 21:12–14), except that the proverb reverses the provisions in the law, which demanded justice for premeditated murder. In the larger context of the chapter, common people are given times to avoid wicked people (7, 12, 28, 29:3, 24) and times to oppose them (1, 4, 23; 29:4; 8, 16).

Verse 18 is a saying about the "way," (cf. v. 10) recalling the root metaphors of ways, paths, and houses in chapters 1–9. Verse 18b literally ends, "fall into the one." Some commenters omit the line or attempt to emend it; whatever the original meaning of the line, the larger message is clear and in keeping with chapters 1–9: straight paths lead to life and blessing and twisted paths to divine recompense (cf. 2:8, 12, 13, 15; 20; 3:6, 23; 10:9, etc.).

The sayings in verses 19–20 juxtapose the hard worker and faithful person (vv. 19a, 20a) to the dreamer and one greedy for gain (19b, 20b). Verse 19 is also nearly identical to 12:11, and verses 20 and 12:12, in their respective contexts, both condemn greed. Proverbs consistently maintains the virtue of hard work and patience while condemning haste and envy (see 13:11; 21:5, 25).

9. Heim, *Poetic Imagination*, 642. The NIV's gloss may be an effort to balance the sayings.

²¹ To show partiality is not good—
  yet a person will do wrong for a piece of bread.
²² The stingy are eager to get rich
  and are unaware that poverty awaits them.
²³ Whoever rebukes a person will in the end gain favor
  rather than one who has a flattering tongue.

28:21–23 These verses explore three of the many faces of greed; see more on virtue and vice in Live the Story in chapters 23–24. Line 21a is a variant of 24:23, but 21b is unique and puts "partiality," literally, "to recognize a face," in the context of bribes and greed. The meager bribe of a morsel of bread exposes the power of greed and the vulnerability of justice in human courts. The word "stingy" in verse 22 is "the bad of eye" in Hebrew. The phrase "good of eye" in 22:9 describes the generous person who will be "blessed" over against the miser doomed for "poverty."

"Favor," *hen*, plays on *hon*, "rich," in verse 22. The correction of children, the wise, and the fool are favorite topics in Proverbs (see commentary at 3:12; 9:7–8; 13:24; 26:4–5). This saying applies reproof to the deeper motives of greed and self-interest.

²⁴ Whoever robs their father or mother and says,
  "It's not wrong,"
  is partner to one who destroys.

28:24 This verse is another saying of three lines (cf. 10, 17). These rarer sayings might have been structural markers for chapters 28–29.

The loyalty owed to parents lies at the roots of human origins and Israel's first family (Gen 4:1–10; 9:22–27; 27:18–24), which may explain why honor to parents was included in the Decalogue (Exod 20:12; Deut 5:16). The proverb's concern with theft provides a brief commentary on when Jacob took his birthright and his wife Rachel stole the household idols (Gen 31:34–35). Jesus also condemns the theft of withholding duty to parents (Mark 7:10–13) and, in a parable, demanding an inheritance before the father's death (Luke 15:11–32).

²⁵ The greedy stir up conflict,
  but those who trust in the LORD will prosper.
²⁶ Those who trust in themselves are fools,
  but those who walk in wisdom are kept safe.
²⁷ Those who give to the poor will lack nothing,
  but those who close their eyes to them receive many curses.

28:25–27 These verses explore the relationships between pride, greed, and trust.[10] "Greedy," *rehab nephesh* (25a), which Waltke translates "unconstrained appetite," is inevitably divisive (Jas 4:1–3).[11] Echoing Proverbs 3:5–9, the preventative remedy for intellectual self-confidence and material hoarding is to trust in Yahweh and extend generosity to those in need. DeYoung's thoughts here are an apt summary for these verses, "Like the other vices rooted in pride, greed expresses the do-it-yourself method of finding happiness, instead of the contentedness of receiving the good that God has to give and depending on his provision."[12]

> [28] When the wicked rise to power, people go into hiding;
>   but when the wicked perish, the righteous thrive.

28:28 This is the second of four thematic refrains in chapters 28–29 (see 28:12). Proverbs assumes a privileged and educated readership. These sayings thus repeatedly remind us that we are all complicit in allowing wicked to rise to power and bear the consequences for doing so.

 LIVE the Story

Kings, Power, Justice, and the Ordinary Citizen

Scholars often get mired in debates about whether, or how much of, chapters 28–29 were written for young royals in training for leadership. Is this a manual for kings or commoners? A poetic reading of the chapter, however, provides a more nuanced view, allowing us to see the royal sayings framing the chapter in such a way that the individual sayings about justice and righteousness always apply equally to royal dealings and the common life.

King/ruler explicit:	28:2, 3, 16, 28; 29:2, 4, 12, 14, 16, 26
King/ruler implicit:	28:8, 12, 15
Lion (always associated with king in Proverbs):[13]	28:1, 15–16
High/low, rich/poor:	18:3, 6, 8, 11, 12, 18, 19, 22, 27; 29:3, 7, 13, 23
Emphasis on *torah* (law):	28:4 [twice], 7, 9; 29:18

10. See Fox, *Proverbs 10–31*, 832.
11. Waltke, *Proverbs 15–31*, 398.
12. DeYoung, *Glittering Vices*, 101.

What[13] is significant about this poetic framing is (1) that we are all responsible for the justice and welfare of a nation, including, within limits, whom we allow to rise to power; and (2) that God so ordered the world that God, king, and subject all share the same moral framework.[14] As a result, God's character and actions represent the standard for the king while the king's character and actions set the standard for the individual and community. This is precisely the way the king is depicted in both Psalms and Deuteronomy. As Jamie Grant comments, "As with the king and the reader of Psalms the inculcation of a worldview is encouraged. It is about more than just following the particulars of the 'law,' it is a holistic way of thinking and acting shaped by God's revelation . . . ."[15]

Of course, God's chosen kings and subjects throughout history repeatedly failed to imitate their royal creator. In their place, Jesus takes on flesh and becomes Israel's long-awaited king. This king upholds the just requirements of the law, submits to the will of the Father, and dies and rises again to new life in order to restore justice and moral order to the whole creation. This obedient, crucified, and risen king is our foundation and our model for moral and political life today. Our political structures have changed significantly, but the moral order has not, and so we can confidently imitate Jesus' obedient kingship, knowing that it represents the perfect rule of God the Trinity (John 14:9).

A Praying Wisdom

Scholarly and popular readers alike share the habit of drawing sharp lines between wisdom literature and other genres, particularly anything that has devotional or historical content (see 4–6 above). It is more generous and appropriate to assume that the sages wrote and gathered sayings within a worldview shared with the authors of Leviticus, 1–2 Samuel, Psalms, and Isaiah. The difference between these genres is usually one of emphasis and not opposition, as we can see from the casual reference to prayers and confessions in 28:9, 13–14 (cf. 15:8, 29; 30:6–9). These proverbs about prayer fit naturally within the emphasis on poor and lowly and prideful and exalted in chapters 28–29.

Verses 13–14 sit at the center of the chapter and deserve special attention. As Waltke notices, the pair forms a chiasm with "impenitent" in 13a and "the hardened sinner" in 14b on the outside. Situated in the middle, 13b and 14a

13. See 19:12; 20:12; 28:1, 15–16; 30:30.
14. See Bartholomew and O'Dowd, *Old Testament Wisdom*, 34–35
15. Jamie Grant, *The King as Exemplar: The Function of Deuteronomy's Kingship Law in the Shaping of the Book of Psalms*, Academia Biblica 17 (Atlanta: Society of Biblical Literature, 2004).

emphasize the means to avoid these extremes: worship, confess, repent, and fear God (Isa 1:16f; Hos 14:1; 1 John 1:8f).[16] Furthermore, Van Leeuwen points out that Psalm 32, which most commentators recognize as a close parallel to these verses, ends in a wisdom instruction (32:8–11).[17] In the larger context, the chapters exhort us both to be bold but also humble, prayerful, and trusting in God.

Proverbial Families in the Gospels

In the Gospels Jesus draws upon many legal and wisdom sayings from the Old Testament to shed light on the dynamics of parent-child relationships and to open a window into the work of the kingdom he brings to humanity. The parable of the prodigal son (Luke 15:1–11) portrays both sons in Proverbs 28:7—the one who keeps the law and the one who becomes a companion of gluttons. Meanwhile, Jesus' rebuke of Jewish leaders who forsook obligations to their parents in order to appear holy in the public places (Mark 7:9–13) assigns the condemnation in Proverbs 28:24.

Viewing Jesus' ministry through these two proverbs we come to see, first, that Jesus brings long-awaited judgment to the powerful and hypocritical leaders in society who are as dishonorable children to their divine Father. But, second, Jesus also offers the Father's joyful and happy reception to sons who have squandered life and returned in humility, repentance, and a cry for help.

16. Waltke, *Proverbs 15–31*, 417.
17. Van Leeuwen, *Proverbs*, 238.

LISTEN to the Story

¹ Whoever remains stiff-necked after many rebukes
    will suddenly be destroyed—without remedy.
² When the righteous thrive, the people rejoice;
    when the wicked rule, the people groan.
³ A man who loves wisdom brings joy to his father,
    but a companion of prostitutes squanders his wealth.
⁴ By justice a king gives a country stability,
    but those who are greedy for bribes tear it down.
⁵ Those who flatter their neighbors
    are spreading nets for their feet.
⁶ Evildoers are snared by their own sin,
    but the righteous shout for joy and are glad.
⁷ The righteous care about justice for the poor,
    but the wicked have no such concern.
⁸ Mockers stir up a city,
    but the wise turn away anger.
⁹ If a wise person goes to court with a fool,
    the fool rages and scoffs, and there is no peace.
¹⁰ The bloodthirsty hate a person of integrity
    and seek to kill the upright.
¹¹ Fools give full vent to their rage,
    but the wise bring calm in the end.
¹² If a ruler listens to lies,
    all his officials become wicked.
¹³ The poor and the oppressor have this in common:
    The LORD gives sight to the eyes of both.
¹⁴ If a king judges the poor with fairness,
    his throne will be established forever.
¹⁵ A rod and a reprimand impart wisdom,

but a child left undisciplined disgraces its mother.
¹⁶ When the wicked thrive, so does sin,
 but the righteous will see their downfall.
¹⁷ Discipline your children, and they will give you peace;
 they will bring you the delights you desire.
¹⁸ Where there is no revelation, people cast off restraint;
 but blessed is the one who heeds wisdom's instruction.
¹⁹ Servants cannot be corrected by mere words;
 though they understand, they will not respond.
²⁰ Do you see someone who speaks in haste?
 There is more hope for a fool than for them.
²¹ A servant pampered from youth
 will turn out to be insolent.
²² An angry person stirs up conflict,
 and a hot-tempered person commits many sins.
²³ Pride brings a person low,
 but the lowly in spirit gain honor.
²⁴ The accomplices of thieves are their own enemies;
 they are put under oath and dare not testify.
²⁵ Fear of man will prove to be a snare,
 but whoever trusts in the LORD is kept safe.
²⁶ Many seek an audience with a ruler,
 but it is from the LORD that one gets justice.
²⁷ The righteous detest the dishonest;
 the wicked detest the upright.

Listening to the Text in the Story: Exodus 32:9, 25; Deuteronomy 1:17; Psalm 74:9; Isaiah 28:17 (8b); Lamentations 2:9

Emending Blaise Pascal's hyperbole, it could be said that all of humanity's problems stem from an unwillingness to receive correction from another. Most of this chapter falls under the categories of rejecting and submitting to correction, whether by nations, children, servants, the wise, or the fool. Israel is frequently described as a "stiff-necked" and "stubborn" people, unwilling to heed the words of Yahweh, Moses, and the prophets (Exod 32:9; 33:3, 5; 34:9; Deut 9:6, 13; 10:16; 2 Kgs 17:14; Pss 78:8; 81:12; Prov 1:25, 30; 5:12; Isa 30:1; 46:12; Jer 5:23; 16:12).

⟨⟨⟩⟩ EXPLAIN the Story

As discussed in the previous chapter, chapters 28–29 are linked by the repetition of the refrain in 28:12, 28; 29:2, and 16, as well as the emphasis on high and low, rich and poor, and righteousness and wickedness. Furthermore, as we will see now, sayings about correction, anger, and the emotions are applied in patterns that include kings, children, slaves, and the wise and foolish, as in chapter 28.

Scholars often divide chapter 29 into two parts with verse 16 as the middle point. In this light, notice that, aside from verses 2 and 16, which are structural refrains for chapters 28–29, almost of the sayings in 1–16 *begin* with a masculine singular noun: "man" (seven times, using four synonyms), "king or ruler" (4, 12, 14), "one who cares" (7), and "poor man" (13). Moreover, *ish*, "man," and its common synonyms are keywords for this chapter (see more in Live the Story below). Also, *hokmah*, "wisdom," and *hakam*, "wise," appear in verses 3, 8, 9, and 11.

> [1] Whoever remains stiff-necked after many rebukes
>   will suddenly be destroyed—without remedy.
> [2] When the righteous thrive, the people rejoice;
>   when the wicked rule, the people groan.
> [3] A man who loves wisdom brings joy to his father,
>   but a companion of prostitutes squanders his wealth.

29:1–3 These verses introduce the final set of sayings, which started at 25:1 and ends with the new section heading at 30:1. The reproof imagined in verse 1 is repeated, or else implicit, in verses 3, 8, 9, 11, 15, 17, 19, 21, and 24. The path to wisdom travels within a community where the old and wise guide the young and simple. That said, the truly wise person always remains open to correction (9:8; 13:1).

Verse 3 applies the general principle of instruction to the particular situation of a son who listens to his father and avoids the adulteress and strange woman (cf. 5:8–12; 6:20–7:27). The close parallel in 5:10 makes clear that "wealth" refers to the son's inheritance. As noted above, verse 2 is the third of four refrains (see 28:12). While it is beyond the scope of this commentary, it is worthwhile pointing to Waltke's careful analysis of the poetic symmetry between the first and second lines of these four sayings.[1]

> [4] By justice a king gives a country stability,
>   but those who are greedy for bribes tear it down.

---

1. Waltke, *Proverbs 15–31*, 403–4.

⁵ Those who flatter their neighbors
    are spreading nets for their feet.
⁶ Evildoers are snared by their own sin,
    but the righteous shout for joy and are glad.
⁷ The righteous care about justice for the poor,
    but the wicked have no such concern.

29:4–7 These verses present four loosely connected sayings held together by the repetition of "justice" in verses 4 and 7 and the two traps in verses 5–6. Verse 4 is the first of several sayings that speak to the conduct of kings, princes, and city rulers. The "king" is used as a figure of speech known as synecdoche, in which he represents the whole rule of the city. The king rarely metes out justice at the individual level. The word "bribes" in 4b could also be translated "taxes." In either case, justice stands in contrast to financial corruption.

To "flatter," literally speak "smooth words," in verses 5–6 imagines all kinds of manipulative speech (cf. 2:15; 7:12), which parallels the financial manipulation in the previous verse. The Hebrew is terse and the "net" could be at the feet either of the neighbors or flatterers. Both meanings are possible and the ambiguity might be intentional. Verse 6 clearly imagines a situation where "evildoers" fall into their own trap (cf. 1:19; 26:7; Ps 7:15). Clifford unnecessarily emends "shout for joy" to "runs," believing that it provides a closer parallel to 6a.[2] As we have often observed, imprecise and disjointed parallels are the norm in Proverbs. Scoundrels trapped in their own schemes stand in contrast to the free worship and joy of the righteous.

Verse 7 closes this section, returning to matters of justice in verse 5. A literal translation communicates the starkness of the saying, "The righteous knows the case (rights) of the poor, but wicked do not understand such knowledge." The play on two types of *knowing*—compassionate and aloof—highlight the power of conscience and virtue in determining what we *reason* to be true about the world around us. Note that *din*, "rights," is a very different idea than our post-Enlightenment concept of individual and inalienable rights. This is about the justice owed by the haves to the have-nots.

⁸ Mockers stir up a city,
    but the wise turn away anger.
⁹ If a wise person goes to court with a fool,
    the fool rages and scoffs, and there is no peace.
¹⁰ The bloodthirsty hate a person of integrity

---

2. Clifford, *Proverbs*, 248–50.

and seek to kill the upright.

¹¹ Fools give full vent to their rage,
   but the wise bring calm in the end.

29:8–11 These verses depict four public situations involving anger (literally "heat"), wisdom, and folly. In the outer sayings the wise bring peace. The middle sayings, meanwhile, offer examples where violence and rage cannot be calmed and the only option for the wise is to stay away (cf. 26:17). The Hebrew in verse 8 plays on the image of wind and fire in the mocker who "breathes out" (*puah*) lies and "inflames" the city, unless a sage is there to put it out (cf. Isa 28:17; Ezek 21:31).[3]

The NIV "court" in verse 9 may over-translate what is probably just a "dispute" or "debate" with no judges involved. Furthermore, "fool" in verse 9b is not in the Hebrew, so the saying may simply imagine conflict with no resolution (cf. Eccl 9:17).

Verse 11 mirrors verse 8 as the wise brings control to chaos. Also, the fools who "give full vent," literally "let out wind/spirit," echoes the "mockers" breathing anger in verse 8.

¹² If a ruler listens to lies,
   all his officials become wicked.
¹³ The poor and the oppressor have this in common:
   The LORD gives sight to the eyes of both.
¹⁴ If a king judges the poor with fairness,
   his throne will be established forever.

29:12–14 Contrary to standard Hebrew syntax, the subject appears as the first word in each of these phrases, usually as a sign of emphasis: "ruler," "poor," and "king."[4] Verse 12 emphasizes the king's responsibility both to be wise to flattery (cf. 5) and also to recognize that his behavior will shape his followers and the nation as a whole.

Verse 13, like 22:2, reminds us that our human dignity, grounded in our bearing the divine image, transcends our rank in society. Rank, as exhibited in the surrounding verses, is often a matter of social changes and corrupt practices. Verse 14 again reminds the king of his responsibility, this time that it is grounded in the theological point in verse 13 (cf. Deut 10:18). The word for "poor" in verses 13–14 is only used fifteen times in Proverbs, six of these in chapters 28–29 as a part of a large proportion of sayings that emphasize high/low and rich/poor.

---

3. So Clifford, *Proverbs*, 251. Cf. "blast a city" in Longman, *Proverbs*, 499.
4. Though there are exceptions, Hebrew syntax usually follows the pattern verb-subject-object.

[15] A rod and a reprimand impart wisdom,
   but a child left undisciplined disgraces its mother.
[16] When the wicked thrive, so does sin,
   but the righteous will see their downfall.
[17] Discipline your children, and they will give you peace;
   they will bring you the delights you desire.

29:15–17 These verses offer another cluster of sayings enclosed on both ends, this time by the theme of household discipline. However, as Van Leeuwen also points out, the sayings in verses 15–21 alternate between addressing children and slaves. These were closely aligned groups in the household social and economic system.[5] The central saying in verse 16 is the last of four refrains (see 29:2).

The parental discipline in verses 15 and 17 resembles many others (see commentary at 13:24). The sole mention of the mother's shame in verse 15 matches the shame the son brings to the father in verse 3. A penitent child brings "delights" (v. 17), which is a word that describes food eaten by the wealthy and powerful (Gen 49:20; Lam 4:5).

[18] Where there is no revelation, people cast off restraint;
   but blessed is the one who heeds wisdom's instruction.

29:18 This verse has generated considerable debate as to whether *hazon* should be translated "revelation" or "prophetic vision" and whether *torah* should be translated "instruction" or "law." The two questions should be considered together. First, *hazon* is used thirty-five times in the Old Testament, of which only Psalm 89:19 does not explicitly mention a prophet, though it clearly alludes to Samuel or Nathan (cf. Ps 74:9).[6] Michael Fox comments, "there is no reason to imagine that at any stage the 'wise man' repudiated either [cult or prophecy]."[7] Furthermore, as we have already seen in chapters 2 and 28, *torah* appears to have been carefully combined with other sayings in chapters 28–29. Finally, it should be noted that many of the sayings in this chapter concern royal thrones and public courts. The allusion to a prophetic voice in the community seems most likely, especially in light of the fact that the chapter ends with a return to the theme of the fear of the Lord and the continuity between divine and human rule (vv. 26–27).

---

5. Van Leeuwen, *Proverbs*, 243–44.
6. See John Goldingay, *Psalms*, vol. 2: Psalms 42–89, BCOTWP (Grand Rapids: Baker Academic, 2007), 696. Cf., however, Longman, *Proverbs*, 507, who does not see any prophetic allusion here.
7. Fox, *Proverbs 10–31*, 840.

^{19} Servants cannot be corrected by mere words;
   though they understand, they will not respond.
^{20} Do you see someone who speaks in haste?
   There is more hope for a fool than for them.
^{21} A servant pampered from youth
   will turn out to be insolent.

29:19–21 These verses present yet another cluster created by parallel outer sayings. Also, the sayings all end in words composed only of the Hebrew letters *mem*, *nun*, and various guttural sounds that create acoustic symmetry around *ms* and *ns*.

Verses 19 and 21 appear to work in tandem, first raising a problem and then providing the cause and solution. The first saying portrays a situation that might reflect the "stiff-necked" and the "fool" in verses 1 and 9, neither of whom are corrected by wisdom. The root of rebellion is not epistemological—"though they understand"—but prideful determination (cf. 1, 23). If verse 21 in fact answers this problem, the solution is training a servant from his youth—this implicitly provokes parents and slave-owners to uphold their responsibilities.

Verse 20 gives a lesson applicable to verse 21: teach slowness in speech (Jas 1:19–20). Like 22:29 and 26:12, the form of the saying is intentional understatement, or litotes. Heim comments: "biting sarcasm comes in elegant surprise."[8]

^{22} An angry person stirs up conflict,
   and a hot-tempered person commits many sins.
^{23} Pride brings a person low,
   but the lowly in spirit gain honor.
^{24} The accomplices of thieves are their own enemies;
   they are put under oath and dare not testify.
^{25} Fear of man will prove to be a snare,
   but whoever trusts in the LORD is kept safe.
^{26} Many seek an audience with a ruler,
   but it is from the LORD that one gets justice.

29:22–26 These sayings may be loosely paired by common terms for "man" or "humanity" with verses 25–26, mimicking a pattern in chapter 28 of related sayings grouped around a central verse.

---

8. Heim, *Poetic Imagination*, 543.

ish	the angry person	v. 22
adam	the prideful person	v. 23
	thieves, oaths, traps	v. 24
adam	the fear of man	v. 25
ish	the one who gets justice	v. 26

The first pair in verses 22–23 juxtaposes anger and pride. Verse 22a is a variant of 15:18a, yet it has been combined here with the one who "commits many sins" (verse 22b). This phrase only appears fourteen times in Proverbs, and yet seven are in chapters 28–29 (28:2, 13, 21, 24; 29:6, 16, 22), which is yet another sign that the authors of these chapters were working creatively with a stock set of terms and themes. As a vice, the root of anger is pride, and so the preventative measure for hot-tempered behavior is to develop the virtue of humility (v. 23; cf. 15:33; 16:18–19).

Verse 24 says that the one who "divide[s] plunder" or "shares loot" with robbers "hates his own life" (NIV "accomplices of thieves are their own enemies").[9] Line 24b is more difficult, but "put under oath" most likely refers to a "conditional curse"[10] that a thief takes on his own life when making a covenant with an accomplice. As is typical of the shortsightedness of fools, they cannot see that they will fall into their own pit (Prov 1:10–19; 26:27; 29:6).

The final two sayings (vv. 25–26) before the conclusion highlight the integral relationship between fear and trust (cf. Ps 118:8–9). The "fear of man" could mean fearfulness in general, as in anxiety, or else fear of other humans in their power and position. The latter is more likely given the parallel contrast between human justice and divine justice in verse 26. Chapter 29 leaves behind a picture of a topsy-turvy world: mockers, evildoers, corrupt rulers, recalcitrant servants and children, murderers, fools, and oppressors. In our natural human response to seek help and safety, Proverbs reminds us that Yahweh alone is the guarantor of justice and proper object of trust (cf. 3:5; 22:19).

> [27] The righteous detest the dishonest;
>   the wicked detest the upright.

29:27 This verse provides a fitting conclusion to chapters 28–29 as well as 10–29 (and perhaps even 1–29). For one, we have seen that the themes of righteousness and wickedness, which dominated chapters 10–15, return with surprising frequency in these final two chapters.

---

9. Longman, *Proverbs*, 509; Clifford, *Proverbs*, 247.
10. Fox, *Proverbs 10–31*, 845.

The verse also concludes with two legal terms that place the individual sayings in the larger context of divine justice and cosmic world order of chapters 1–9. First, *toebah*, "detest" or "abomination," which ordinarily speaks to despicable acts of injustice hated by Yahweh, now describes the intense opposition between the righteous and wicked (see 11:1). Second, *awel* goes beyond the NIV "dishonest" to identify a character of "injustice" or "perversity" (cf. Lev 19:15; Isa 61:8).[11] Thus, having just been reminded of the foundational truth that wisdom begins with the fear of Yahweh (25–26, cf. 1:7; 9:10, etc.), this verse echoes the doctrine of the two ways and the determining power of desire in chapters 1–9; the path of wisdom demands a commitment of the deepest human desire and disposition.

LIVE the Story

Wisdom, the Prophetic Vision, and Discipleship

The historic Christian church has always focused its doctrine on the history of redemption, that is, God's work to redeem and heal a broken world. But this emphasis often leaves the wisdom literature looking like an unwanted step-child at worst, or icing on the cake of the gospel at best. These views only encourage us to separate our secular lives from the sacredness of our salvation. But the Bible knows no such division. Our mundane way of life in this world is walked as a righteous and redeemed follower of the saving God (Prov 1:7); sacred salvation and secular practical living form a chord of two inseparable strands.

Chapter 29 reinforces this union with its natural blending of legal, prophetic, and wisdom terms. Consider also Jeremiah's way of describing his rejection by the Israelites: "They said, 'Come, let's make plans against Jeremiah; for the teaching of the law by the priest will not cease, nor will counsel from the wise, nor the word from the prophets. So come, let's attack him with our tongues and pay no attention to anything he says'" (18:18; cf. Lam 2:9). Elsewhere in Jeremiah God chastises Israel with language from Proverbs: "My people are foolish, they do not know me. The sons are fools; they have no understanding. They are wise in doing evil and do not know how to do good" (Jer 4:22).[12] In Jeremiah 8 God makes it clear that for Israel's lack of wisdom, she could not discern her own sin and its consequences (8:4–9). And so here we have a clear picture of wisdom and prophecy working hand in hand. The prophetic vision in 29:18 thus orients us to God's saving work

---

11. David W. Baker, "*'āwel*," *NIDOTTE* 3:342–44.
12. My translation.

in the world, but shows that wisdom is necessary to interpret the times and the prophetic vision correctly (cf. Deut 18:14–21).

It should not escape our notice that Paul prays for wisdom and understanding so that the church might *discern the mystery of the gospel* and *live wise* and righteous lives (cf. Eph 1:17; Phil 1:9–11; Col 1:9). Biblical discipleship today needs to be refreshed with the Spirit of Wisdom—that God-given insight into life and the world made possible by the Son who is "before all things" in whom fullness dwells, and in whom "all things hold together" (Col 1:17).

Brief Interviews with Wicked and Righteous Men
David Foster Wallace, the much celebrated and equally troubled writer who took his own life in 2008, left behind a collection of writings that explore the sinful human condition in ways virtually unmatched in modern fiction. His *Brief Interviews with Hideous Men* assembles a collection of fictional interviews with depraved men who simultaneously capture our attention and disgust us with their gross and perverse desires. One can, of course, find hideous characters in all sorts of shameless writing. But Wallace's work, much like Nathan's judgment parable to David, entertains its audience in order to provoke the kind of deep and honest self-reflection that we are instinctually prone to avoid. Similar examples can be found in the writing of Flannery O'Connor and John Kennedy Toole's Pulitzer Prize winning novel *A Confederacy of Dunces.*

In the commentary on 6:1–19 I suggested that the despicable characters in that chapter invited just this kind of self-reflection, which I played out through a reading of the story of Jacob and his sons under Live the Story.

Chapter 29 offers another opportunity for this type of reflection. For one, the chapter uses *ish* twelve times, over twice the frequency of any other chapter.[13] We also find four more words in this category including the plural *anshe*, "men" (8, 10) and the synonyms *geber* (5) and *adam* (23). Add to this the fact that almost all of these terms are the first word in their respective lines and the emphasis on individual humans is unmistakable.

In contrast to chapter 6:16–19, this chapter juxtaposes despicable men (and women) of wickedness, violence, and folly to faithful men and women righteousness, wisdom, compassion, justice, and humility. This final volley of individual sayings forces us to look beneath virtue and vice to imagine people we know, stories we have heard, and of course, reflections in our own lives. In doing so it shapes our desire to fear God, love wisdom, and detest wickedness (vv. 25–27). I think it is no coincidence that the last two chapters of Proverbs

---

13. A rate of 44.4 percent. Chapter 16 uses *ish* seven times, averaging to 21 percent of the sayings.

leave us with portraits of three wise characters: Agur, King Lemuel's mother, and the valiant woman.

Christ goes beyond the righteous figures in Proverbs to give us a picture of the perfect human life, one in which the divine and the human come together as God fully intends for us. In this way Jesus provides an example of a righteous life for us to follow (cf. John 13:15, 34; Phil 2:5–11). More than that, our very pursuit of a wise and righteous life involves the deeply mysterious and spiritual process of putting off the old self and clothing ourselves with Christ, the Righteous One (Rom 13:14; Col 3:1, 12).

LISTEN to the Story

¹The sayings of Agur son of Jakeh—an inspired utterance.

This man's utterance to Ithiel:
"I am weary, God,
   but I can prevail.
² Surely I am only a brute, not a man;
   I do not have human understanding.
³ I have not learned wisdom,
   nor have I attained to the knowledge of the Holy One.
⁴ Who has gone up to heaven and come down?
   Whose hands have gathered up the wind?
Who has wrapped up the waters in a cloak?
   Who has established all the ends of the earth?
What is his name, and what is the name of his son?
   Surely you know!
⁵ "Every word of God is flawless;
   he is a shield to those who take refuge in him.
⁶ Do not add to his words,
   or he will rebuke you and prove you a liar.
⁷ "Two things I ask of you, LORD;
   do not refuse me before I die:
⁸ Keep falsehood and lies far from me;
   give me neither poverty nor riches,
   but give me only my daily bread.
⁹ Otherwise, I may have too much and disown you
   and say, 'Who is the LORD?'
Or I may become poor and steal,
   and so dishonor the name of my God.
¹⁰ "Do not slander a servant to their master,
   or they will curse you, and you will pay for it.

[11] "There are those who curse their fathers
  and do not bless their mothers;
[12] those who are pure in their own eyes
  and yet are not cleansed of their filth;
[13] those whose eyes are ever so haughty,
  whose glances are so disdainful;
[14] those whose teeth are swords
  and whose jaws are set with knives
to devour the poor from the earth
  and the needy from among mankind.
[15] "The leech has two daughters.
  'Give! Give!' they cry.
"There are three things that are never satisfied,
  four that never say, 'Enough!':
[16] the grave, the barren womb,
  land, which is never satisfied with water,
  and fire, which never says, 'Enough!'
[17] "The eye that mocks a father,
  that scorns an aged mother,
will be pecked out by the ravens of the valley,
  will be eaten by the vultures.
[18] "There are three things that are too amazing for me,
  four that I do not understand:
[19] the way of an eagle in the sky,
  the way of a snake on a rock,
the way of a ship on the high seas,
  and the way of a man with a young woman.
[20] "This is the way of an adulterous woman:
  She eats and wipes her mouth
  and says, 'I've done nothing wrong.'
[21] "Under three things the earth trembles,
  under four it cannot bear up:
[22] a servant who becomes king,
  a godless fool who gets plenty to eat,
[23] a contemptible woman who gets married,
  and a servant who displaces her mistress.
[24] "Four things on earth are small,
  yet they are extremely wise:

²⁵ Ants are creatures of little strength,
   yet they store up their food in the summer;
²⁶ hyraxes are creatures of little power,
   yet they make their home in the crags;
²⁷ locusts have no king,
   yet they advance together in ranks;
²⁸ a lizard can be caught with the hand,
   yet it is found in kings' palaces.
²⁹ "There are three things that are stately in their stride,
   four that move with stately bearing:
³⁰ a lion, mighty among beasts,
   who retreats before nothing;
³¹ a strutting rooster, a he-goat,
   and a king secure against revolt.
³² "If you play the fool and exalt yourself,
   or if you plan evil,
   clap your hand over your mouth!
³³ For as churning cream produces butter,
   and as twisting the nose produces blood,
   so stirring up anger produces strife."

Listening to the Text in the Story: Genesis 1–3; Leviticus 19; Deuteronomy 5:6–21; 2 Samuel 22:31; Ecclesiastes; Job 38; Enuma Elish, Table IV, lines 45–47

Proverbs concludes with three poems: the sayings of Agur (30:1–33), the words of King Lemuel's mother to her son (31:1–9), and the song of the valiant woman (31:10–31). These extended proverb-poems have a narrative-like quality that mirrors the genre of chapters 1–9. As in any book, the beginning and ending provide a framework or lens for reading the book as a whole.[1] In the case of Proverbs, the poems in the frame elevate the tone and tenor of the book: their cosmic imagery makes the sayings relevant across generations and cultures; their parental appeals express urgency and ultimacy; and Agur's message issues a warning about the limits of human wisdom.

On the whole, Agur's passage creates a sharp and unexpected turn. Its autobiographical tone and extended reflections on nature, law, and society stand apart from the generalities of the individual proverbs. But they also

---

1. O'Dowd, "Frame Narrative."

create many links or echoes with familiar passages in the Old Testament and Second Temple literature. These echoes of other texts illumine an otherwise complicated and enigmatic wisdom passage.

First, notice Agur's initial confession, "Surely I am only a brute, not a man; I do not have human understanding. I have not learned wisdom, nor have I attained to the knowledge of the Holy One" (v. 2). Agur radically shifts the overall tone of Proverbs from the preceding chapters. His confession recalls Adam's and Eve's predicament in Genesis when they were outsmarted by a serpent or beast (brute) that was more "crafty" in his ways. The passage also echoes Qohelet's confession in Ecclesiastes: "I also said to myself, 'As for humans, God tests them so that they may see that they are like the animals. Surely the fate of human beings is like that of the animals; the same fate awaits them both: As one dies, so dies the other. All have the same breath; humans have no advantage over animals. Everything is meaningless'" (Eccl 3:18–19). In fact, Ecclesiastes returns to this pessimistic attitude toward knowledge often (Eccl 1:18; 2:13, 14; 7:11, 12), and its autobiographical style also resembles Agur's language in verses 1–9. Very much like Ecclesiastes—and, in contrast to most of Proverbs—Agur has a clear sense of the fall from the ordered and peaceful world of Eden.

The chapter deepens its tone of humility at several points, particularly in the four cosmic questions in verse 4, which ask, "Who has gone up to heaven and come down?" The image of heavenly ascent and descent appear frequently in the Old Testament, as in Deuteronomy when Moses assures Israel that the word, or promise, which he is giving them is, "not up in heaven, so that you have to ask, 'Who will ascend into heaven to get it and proclaim it to us so we may obey it?' Nor is it beyond the sea, so that you have to ask, 'Who will cross the sea to get it and proclaim it to us so we may obey it?'" (30:12–13). This image also appears in the Jacob story in Genesis 28:12, "He had a dream in which he saw a stairway resting on the earth, with its top reaching to heaven, and the angels of God were ascending and descending on it."[2] Jacob is not mentioned in Proverbs, but the final questions in Proverbs 30:4, "What is his name, and what is his son's name?" have led many readers to wonder if this might be a faint allusion to Jacob (renamed Israel), who was known throughout the Old Testament as God's son. A passage in the postexilic Jewish book of Baruch makes this question all the more interesting. Baruch combines language from the stories of the patriarchs with Israel's search for wisdom in the wisdom literature.

> [29] Who has gone up into heaven and taken her [wisdom],
>   and brought her down from the clouds? . . .

---

2. Scholars also point to similar imagery in Job 28; 38–39; Gen 11; 2 Sam 22–23; and Amos 5:8.

[36] He found a way to knowledge,
and gave her to Jacob his servant
and to Israel whom he loved (Bar 3:29, 36 NRSV).

We will return to these questions below. What bears emphasizing here is that the strong divisions between wisdom, law, and prophecy in modern scholarly literature is often overblown, having grown out of speculative reconstructions of Israel's social history (see Introduction). Again and again we find an overlap of common themes and images that unite these books around a commitment to follow the God of creation who is at the same time the God of Abraham, Isaac, Jacob, and Moses. In its surrounding context, Agur's application of these images emphasizes that Israel's unique chosen status has not relieved her from the universal human problem of accessing this divine gift of wisdom.

Agur's humble tone continues in his statement of trust in 30:5. Most scholars agree that this passage is a shortened version of the same confession in David's final prayer in 2 Samuel 22:31 (cf. also Pss 18:30–31;105:19; 119:4; 144:2). The primary difference is that David's prayer refers to "Yahweh" while Agur uses the more general term "Eloah." Possible reasons for this change in the name of God will be discussed below.

The prologue ends with the only prayer in the book of Proverbs (vv. 7–9).[3]

Proverbs 30	Leviticus 19	Deuteronomy 5
[7] "Two things I ask of you, LORD; do not refuse me before I die: [8] Keep **falsehood** and **lies** far from me; give me neither poverty nor riches, but give me only my daily bread. 9 Otherwise, I may have too much and disown you and say, '**Who is the** Lord?' Or I may become poor and **steal**, and so **dishonor the name of my God**.	[11] "'Do not **steal**. 'Do not **lie**. 'Do not **deceive** one another. [12] 'Do not swear falsely by my name and so **profane the name of your God**: **I am the** LORD. [13] "'Do not **defraud** or **rob** your neighbor. 'Do not hold back the wages of a hired worker overnight.	[11] "You shall not **misuse the name of the** LORD your God, for the LORD will not hold anyone guiltless who misuses his name. [16] "Honor your **father** and your **mother**, as the LORD your God has commanded you, so that you may live long and that it may go well with you in the land the LORD your God is giving you.

---

3. Distinguishing between a prayer to God and mere reflections uttered in a monologue is not as simple as some might imagine. The NIV adds the word "LORD" to the original Hebrew of verse 7 to signal the translators' beliefs that this is a prayer. Even if it is not a prayer, this is still the only autobiographical petition of its kind in Proverbs.

Proverbs 30	Leviticus 19	Deuteronomy 5
10 "Do not **slander** a servant to their master, or they will **curse** you, and you will pay for it. [11] "There are those who **curse** their **fathers** and do not bless their **mothers**."	[14] 'Do not **curse** the deaf or put a stumbling block in front of the blind, but fear your God: **I am the** LORD."	[19] "You shall not **steal**. [20] "You shall not give **false testimony** against your neighbor. [21] "You shall not **covet** your neighbor's wife. You shall not set your desire on your neighbor's house or land, his male or female servant, his ox or donkey, or anything that belongs to your neighbor."

Thematically these three passages bear clear resemblances: all warn against falsehood, theft, and cursing our neighbor or family member, all protect the rights of the oppressed classes, and all seek to honor the name of Yahweh. The dual poles of desire between contentment and coveting are also explicit in Proverbs and Deuteronomy and implicit in Leviticus.

At a linguistic level, Deuteronomy and Proverbs use the same words for "steal," (Prov 30:9; Deut 5:19), while the word for "lie" in Proverbs 30:8 is the same as that used twice for taking God's name in "vain" in Deuteronomy 5:1 and "false testimony" in Deuteronomy 5:20. Recent scholarship has in fact renewed the argument that Proverbs 1–9; 28; and 30 draw upon the Torah, Deuteronomy in particular, to shape the beginning and end of Proverbs. Proverbs 30 either explicitly or implicitly calls to mind the third, eighth, ninth, and tenth commandments.[4] Is it possible that one of these passages was used as a template for the others? Not everyone will come to the same conclusion, but what these parallels do make clear is that there are common concerns and foundations for the worldviews exhibited in legal and wisdom literature, even though the perspective or outlook might have changed, particularly as here in Proverbs 30.

Proverbs 30 also contains the largest collection of numerical sayings in the Old Testament. Depending on whether we count the lists in verses 7–9 and 11–14, there are as many as seven numerical sayings in the chapter, in addition to the list of questions in verse 4. Technically, a numerical saying includes a title line with a number and a list.[5] Numerical lists and sayings

---

4. See Meinhold, *Sprüche*, 500 and Bernd U. Schipper, "Das Proverbienbuch und die Toratradition" *Zeitschrift für Theologie and Kirche*, 108/4 (2011): 381–404.
5. See 6:16–19 and "Wisdom, Business, and Economics" in Live the Story for chapter 6.

appear throughout the literature in the ancient world. The sayings in Proverbs 30, which arise from reflection on the wonders of natural and social phenomena, can be found in other cultures. One parallel example appears in the Babylonian creation account in the Enuma Elish, where an inverted numerical list serves to express human reflection on divine mysteries in nature:

> He brought forth Imhulla "the Evil Wind,"
> the Whirldwind, the Hurricane,
> The Fourfold Wind, the Sevenfold Wind,
> the Cyclone, the Matchless Wind;
> Then he sent forth the winds he had brought forth,
> the seven of them.[6]

Most of the lists in Proverbs 30 are what Roth calls "graded numerical sayings," which take the form of x, x+1 (e.g., "There are three things that are too amazing. . . four that I do not understand. . ."). In Roth's study of ancient numerical sayings, he argues that numerical sayings were unique to Semitic poetry, found elsewhere only in Akkadian, Ugaritic, and Aramaic texts. In fact, when these texts in Proverbs were later translated into the non-Semitic Greek Septuagint and Latin Vulgate, the feeling of the incomplete title line "there are three things . . . , and four" often caused translators to change them, modifying the open sense of the poetry to a more complete list.[7] Whatever their precise motives, it is clear that Hebrew poetry invites us to reflect on a sample list that has applications for an endless number of realities.[8]

EXPLAIN the Story

Chapter 30 presents the most challenging sayings in the book: the author or authors of the chapter are unknown, it has the only example of an autobiographical voice (1–9), it has the book's only prayer (7–9), and it speaks of humility and wonder that we do not find anywhere else in the book. The style in the sayings is also the most diverse in Proverbs, combining traditional wisdom sayings with cosmic theophany, prophetic declarations, skeptical poetry, a prayer, and legal discourses. Many scholars overlook this stylistic diversity and thus fail to acknowledge what one scholar calls the choir of competing

---

6. *Enuma Elish*, Tablet IV, lines 45–47, in Roth, *Numerical Sayings*, 28.
7. Ibid., 6.
8. See Ryan P. O'Dowd, "Aesthetic Shaping of Agur's Oracle in Proverbs 30.1–9," Inner Biblical Allusion in the Poetry of Psalms and Wisdom, Society of Biblical Literature (Atlanta: Sheffield Phoenix Press), in press.

genres in Agur's sayings.[9] Like nothing else in Proverbs, this chapter silences and awes us with the dazzling complexity of its artistry and the power in its sayings.

The structure of the chapter also reveals the hand of a sophisticated author or editor. Scholars generally agree about where the chapter divides between distinct voices, topics, and genres, but most also recognize that these features flow over into one another in a way that creates an artistic whole.

As noted in the Introduction, Proverbs engages many conversations that arise throughout in the Old Testament and other ancient Jewish writings. These conversations involve the nature of the good life, the cause of suffering and poverty, and the relationship between law and wisdom. Having been written for an educational setting of some kind, Proverbs 30 tackles these issues with sequences and patterns that make it ideal for study and memorization.

31:1–14 Humble wisdom for a fallen world
>   1–4 Introduction and prologue: humility and wonder
>   5–6 First conclusion and warning from Mosaic Law
>   7–9 Prayer: help keeping the Mosaic Law
>   10 Second warning from Mosaic Law
>   11–14 Four generations: reflections on human cultures

30:15–30 Collected sayings of wonder
>   15a Individual saying about desire and greed
>   15b-16 Numerical saying about endlessness of desire
>   17 Individual warning to respect parents
>   18–19 Numerical sayings of wonder
>   20 Individual statement about the pleasures of sin
>   21–23 Numerical saying about social and natural powers
>   24–28 Numerical saying of wonder in nature and society
>   29–31 Numerical saying about pride and confidence

30:30–33 Concluding warning about pride and renewed call to humility

Assuming that Agur is one of the authors of this chapter, scholars nevertheless disagree about how much of the chapter is to be ascribed to him, from as little as verses 1–4 or 1–9, to as much a 1–14 or the whole chapter. The sharp divisions on this question from the last century have softened in recent years, allowing the literary presentation of the book to play a greater role in the chapter's interpretation. In a compilation of sayings like Proverbs, it is simply impossible to know how many sources lie behind the final work (see

---

9. James Crenshaw, "Clanging Symbols," in *Justice and the Holy: Essays in Honor of Walter Harrelson*, ed. Douglas A. Knight and Peter J. Paris (Atlanta: Scholars Press, 1989), 51–64.

"Authorship and Date" in the Introduction). It helps to recall that the two headings in these final chapters (Agur and Lemuel) fit with the five introductory formulas in chapter 1–29 (Solomon, Hezekiah, etc.) to make a symbolic total of seven. This sixth and penultimate set of sayings unsettles the largely tame world of everything that has been said so far, with an unknown author who has striking things to say about wisdom.

30:1a The opening verse is the most challenging in Proverbs and considered by some to be the most enigmatic text in the Old Testament. Who are Agur, Jakeh, Ithiel, and Ukal? Should some of these be translated as something other than names? As can be seen in the chart below, opinions vary widely.[10]

Hebrew	The Words of Agur, son of Yakeh. An oracle, an utterance of the man. To Ithiel, to Ithiel and Ukal.
NIV	The sayings of Agur son of Jakeh—an inspired utterance. This man's utterance to Ithiel: "I am weary, God, but I can prevail
NASB	The words of Agur the son of Jakeh, the oracle. The man declares to Ithiel, to Ithiel and Ukal:
ESV	The words of Agur son of Jakeh. The oracle. The man declares, I am weary, O God; I am weary, O God, and worn out.
Torrey	Oracle of the man. I am not God, I am not God that I might be capable.
Gemser	Saying of the man: I am incapable O God . . . and can I understand?
Plöger	Utterance of the man who has struggled with God. I have struggled, O God, so that I might grasp it.

Like most English versions, the NIV has simplified the repetition of "oracle, and utterance" and decided to try and find close translations for the final Ithiel and Ukal in the Hebrew.

For several reasons it would be rash to hurry past these difficulties in search of a simpler translation. First, unless there is an obvious alternative, it is generally safer to stay close to the original text. Second, there are reasonable interpretations of the original Hebrew and alternative readings tend more to satisfy the reader's desire for simplicity over against what may be the author's desire to resist simplicity. Third, and related, this whole chapter revolves around difficult questions and enigmas, and so problems with unknown

---

10. A full list can be found in Whybray, *Composition*, 150.

names might well serve a larger purpose. Finally, passages that are quick to eliminate Ukal and the repetition of Ithiel's name tend to overlook the fact that names, divine and human, are the most dominant feature of the first nine verses.

30:1b-4 Agur's opening confession, "I am weary," in verse 1 sets up an equally pessimistic tone in verses 2–3: Agur is "stupid," or, like a brute, does not have the understanding of a man, and does not have knowledge of the Holy One. The claim to not have wisdom or knowledge of God immediately echoes the motto of the prologue in chapters 1–9: "The fear of the Lord is the beginning of knowledge, but fools despise wisdom and instruction" (1:7). It's particularly clear that Agur has reversed the confidence in chapters 2 and 9 in the table below.

Proverbs 30	Proverbs 2
[3] I have not learned wisdom, nor have I attained to the knowledge of the Holy One.	[4] and if you look for it as for silver and search for it as for hidden treasure, [5] then you will understand the fear of the Lord and find the knowledge of God.
	Proverbs 9
	[10] The fear of the Lord is the beginning of wisdom, and knowledge of the Holy One is understanding.

While Proverbs calls for humility at several points (cf. 11:2; 29:23; 30:32), Agur's autobiographical confession engages the reader in a way that elicits reflection on the problem of human limits and frailty.

Scholars disagree about the seriousness of Agur's tone here. Does he really mean that he has no wisdom and no knowledge of God? Or is he speaking rhetorically, demonstrating his own humility before calling for ours? The latter option seems more likely, since Agur not only calls us to believe in and obey God and also because he teaches so many other sophisticated lessons. In this light, Agur's tone stays consistent with lessons elsewhere in Proverbs that the path to wisdom begins with humility and faith (3:5–7; 26:12; 28:26).

In verse 4 Agur delivers his first of many lists in this chapter, this one composed of six questions. The first four questions all begin with "who" and the last two ask for a name. In the discussion above we pointed to several passages outside Proverbs that parallel the first question: "Who has gone up to heaven and come down?" I suggested that the Hebrew wording of ascending and descending to and from heaven matches most closely with Genesis 28:12, which describes the angels of God ascending and descending the ladder in Jacob's dream. It is significant, in this light, that Amos 9:6 and Baruch 3 also allude to heavenly ascent and that they both share Agur's emphasis on names—Jacob, Israel, and Yahweh in particular. Added to that, the image of ascent in Agur and Baruch centers on the search for, and limits of, human wisdom. These strong parallels make it likely that Agur's questions are engaging a common source of anxiety in Israel's postexilic experience: what good is God's law without a temple? And can we still access wisdom in the aftermath of national defeat?

The language and images of the next three questions are unique to Agur, but their content and purpose are similar to the who-questions in the divine speech in Job 38: "Who shut up the sea behind doors when it burst forth from the womb" (v. 8). The questions in Job emphasize God's divine wisdom and power and Job's status as a finite creature. Agur's point is the same: humans, despite our yearning for self-confidence and sense of accomplishment, prove to be frail and naïve in the face of God.

The final two questions in verse 4 ask for names: "What is his name, and what is the name of his son? Surely you know!"[11] The obvious answer to the first question is "Yahweh"—he is the one who laid out the creation and holds it in his hand. What about the name of the son? There is little agreement on this question, but one should not overlook the many signals that point to Jacob-Israel. As we noted in the first question, Baruch, Amos, and Proverbs 30 all connect the image of heavenly ascent to the name Jacob-Israel as they are used interchangeably in the Old Testament.[12] Second, when Jacob wrestles the angel in Genesis 32:27–29, he is denied an answer to his request for the angel's name. Instead, the angel renames Jacob "Israel"—one who wrestled with God and succeeded. Furthermore, Jacob and Israel are referred to elsewhere in the Old Testament as God's son (Cf. Exod 4:22; Deut 14:1; 32:5–6, 18–19; Isa 43:6; 45:11; 63:16; Jer 3:4, 19; 31:20; Hos 11:1).

Above all, notice Agur's consistent pattern of alluding to texts with slight changes of hand, usually withholding names from expected places. These changes force the reader to fill in the gaps of the puzzle. The name pair Jacob-Israel from Genesis 32 naturally fits this answer best. Even if the answer to this question is not "Jacob," Agur labors to get us caught up wondering whether

---

11. In this final phrase, "Surely you know!," many scholars see an intentional borrowing and reversal of God's challenge at the beginning of the divine speeches in Job "Tell me, if you understand" (38:4). Agur could be using this phrase to intensify the power of his own questions and elicit the response of humility that he wants from his audience.

12. The same is true of Esau-Edom.

the "the son" includes me and my people. The obvious answer is yes. Agur will return to this play on names again in verses 5 and 9.

30:5–6 These verses combine two partial citations from the Old Testament. The first (5) is a truncated citation of David's oath after he escaped from his pursuers (2 Sam 22:31), a saying that is repeated in several psalms (Pss 18:30–31; 19; 105; 119:4; 144:2). God and his words are steadfast and reliable.

Keeping with his play on names in this chapter, Agur replaces "Yahweh" in David's oath with "Eloah." This is significant not only because it is the only use of this divine name in Proverbs but also because it is the third name Agur has used for God, so far excluding Yahweh, which is favored in the rest of Proverbs. Again, Agur appears to be modeling the care with his speech that he wants to instill in his pupils, a point that is clear in the second citation in verse 6, "Do not add to his words, or he will rebuke you and prove you a liar." The first part of this saying has been drawn from Deuteronomy 4:2 (cf. Deut 12:32; Rev 22:18–19). This is Agur's first mention of lying (one of Jacob's tragic flaws), yet only the beginning of eight warnings that Agur will give about human speech. Our words always dangerously risk sin, but God's word stands fast.

30:7–9 These verses represent the only prayer in the book of Proverbs, and they bring partial closure to Agur's autobiographical introduction (cf. 8:29; 15:8; 28:9). Some scholars argue that verses 7–8 represent the first graded numerical saying in chapter 30: Agur lists two items, but prays for three. Clearly the prayer to be saved from poverty and riches is interwoven with the prayer for "my daily bread." Whether they are two prayers or one, the larger point is that Agur gives us a model of what we should most desire at the end of our lives: truthful speech and moderation in what we own and desire (cf. 15:16; 19:1, 22). It is as though this verse influenced the Lord's Prayer in the Gospels (see Live the Story below).

Agur's motivation for his prayer is stated in verse 9—he does not want to "disown" God and say "Who is the LORD [Yahweh]?' [or] become poor and steal, and so dishonor the name of my God." Wisdom and morality are not abstract virtues for Agur; his deepest desire is to end his life having lived faithfully before his God.

Until now, Agur had used three names for God and one question asking for God's name. Verse 9 is the first time that he uses the covenant name, Yahweh. But he does so in a question rather than a statement—matching the allusive question in verse 4, "What is his name?" One should not miss the many parallels in this verse and the allusions to Jacob in verse 4. Jacob not only stole his brother's birthright, but he also lied to his father and brother. When Isaac asked him how he returned from his fictional hunt for meat so quickly, Jacob answered, "Yahweh your God gave me success," explicitly profaning God's name in the act.

We should also remember the point above, that 30:7–11 calls to mind six of the Ten Commandments (3, 5, 7–10).[13] Imagining that Agur has Israel's narratives and laws in mind allows us to appreciate how sophisticated the interlacing of this text is. Even if we don't believe that the text was written with Jacob specifically in mind, the point of these first nine verses is clear: wisdom begins with humility, dependence on God's word, and a corralling of human speech and desire.

30:10–14 The autobiographical voice of the first nine verses virtually disappears at this point, leading some to believe a text has been appended to Agur's words. Either way, the themes in the first nine verses resurface at many points, making it clear that chapter 30 stands as an artistic composition in its own right. For one, Agur's request for God to guard his speech flows over into the warnings to give equal measure to the way we address servants and our parents—perhaps representing two poles of the social fabric of an ancient Israelite boy. Furthermore, the vices in Proverbs 30:7–11 follow closely after the language and prohibitions in Deuteronomy's version of the Decalogue (5:11–21). Deuteronomy elsewhere speaks directly to the rights of the servant in the face of a cruel master (23:15–16).

Verses 11–14 list four unrighteous classes of people. The pedagogical force of the chapter is clear in Hebrew as each line begins with the word *dor*, "a generation." Verse 11 continues the warnings against immoral speech, chiding those who curse their fathers and do not bless their mothers. Verses 12–14 portray forbidden sins through physical metaphors: eyes, glances, teeth, and jaws that together express pride, violence, and disregard for the poor and needy.

30:15–33 In the LXX these verses appear after 24:23–24, though other limitations with consistency of the Greek translation of Proverbs lead us to stick with the order of Proverbs in the Masoretic Text.[14] That said, one cannot mistake a clear shift from the ethical focus of verses 1–14 and the turn to reflective or contemplative material in verses 15–33.

The short saying in 15a bridges the four immoral generations with the numerical saying that follows, by way of a short punchy personification, literally "The leech's two daughters: give, give." The brevity of words accentuates the power of the image. With two mouths, each daughter's name depicts her nature and character: greedy, needy, and demanding—feeding on blood, the

13. The sixth Commandment is clearly in view in 30:20.
14. For a brief discussion of these issues see the Introduction and Murphy, *Proverbs*, xxvi.

very symbol of life itself. [15] Following four prideful and ruthless generations, these daughters represent the inherited character of their inherently greedy mother. "Be careful what you are, because your children will be just like you!"[16] In the context of short proverbs, Ezekiel prophesies, "Like mother, like daughter. You are a true daughter to your mother, who despised her husband and her children" (16:44–45). So too, just as the leech image warns parents to model upright living, it cautions children not to reproduce the sins of the previous generation.

Most scholars recognize 30:15b–16 as the first graded numerical list. Such lists combine a sequence of x, x+1 things that, apart from one thing, seem otherwise unrelated (cf. 6:16–19). This list combines four things with insatiable appetites: the grave, the barren womb, the dry land, and fire. The chief puzzle in this list is the barren womb: does it imagine the women's endless desire for a child or the barren womb's desire to remain empty? Waltke suggests that the passage is chiastic: the outside images (grave and fire) destroy life while the inside images (woman and land) are sources of life.[17] But it may also be that the empty womb and thirsty land personify the impotence or failure of these two life sources; the womb has no children and the land no water. If so, all four things share an insatiability that consumes or denies life itself—so too with our desires (cf. 27:20).

Like verses 10, 15, and 20, verse 17 bridges sequential numerical lists. Verse 17 personifies the "eye," which mocks a father and scorns a mother.[18] The proverb imagines the grotesque penalty of the eye being gorged upon by ravens and vultures. Perhaps the proverb was added here after verses 15b–16 because the eye is elsewhere marked for its insatiability (27:20; cf. 23:26). Furthermore, returning to the theme of honoring parents in verse 11, the saying also sustains the emphasis on humility and obedience that saturates this whole chapter.

Verses 18–19 collect four images of things that are "too wonderful," that Agur does not "understand." Perhaps not surprisingly, the Hebrew word for "wonderful" here appears far more often in Psalms and Job than any other books in the Old Testament. At the end of his story Job memorably confesses that he "spoke of . . . things too wonderful for me to know" (42:3). Many familiar psalms use this same term, praising God for his "wondrous works."

The *wonderful* items in Agur's list gradually progress from the animal

---

15. It is possible that the two daughters are metaphors for the leech's two mouths rather than actual offspring. The metaphor plays in both directions.

16. Fox, *Proverbs 10–31*, 867.

17. Waltke, *Proverbs 15–31*, 488.

18. On such bodily metaphors, see 16:27–33.

world—a snake on a rock and an eagle in the sky—to an intersection of humans with nature—a ship on the sea—to the deep mystery of human intimacy—a man with a maiden.[19] It is likely that the emphasis is on the last image, but to know why one must first identify commonalities among the images. The common word in all four pairs is the "way" they relate.

There are several theories for what "way" refers to: (1) things that have mysterious destinations, (2) things that leave no trace, and (3) things that move in a sublime manner. A mysterious destination seems the least likely, given that the way revolves around the interaction of the pairs rather than something else not mentioned. As for the second proposal, the lack of a trace in movement works for the first three examples, but it is almost impossible to apply to the fourth. The obvious connection is the very mystery of the physical movement between these pairs. Just as the Song of Songs uses metaphors to make us imagine the beauty of a sexual relationship, so too does Agur's list leaves the "wonder" of lovemaking to the imagination of the student of wisdom.

Verse 20 is the final interruption to the running list of numerical sayings from 15–31. The NIV begins with "This," but it should probably read "*Thus is the way* of the adulterous woman . . .," signaling a comparison with the "way" of the four previous examples. Fox is among some scholars who suspect that this negative example of an adulterous woman parallels the condemnatory behavior of the unmarried couple in verse 19, but several points can be made against this.[20] First, the contemplation in verse 19 focuses on the way of the man, not the woman. Second, neither the man nor the woman in that verse is explicitly imagined as sinful. Furthermore, Fox's reading would require us to find something in the examples of the snake, the eagle, and the ship that corresponds to the duplicitous or immoral behavior in verse 20. More likely, the flow in Proverbs 30 moves from a mysterious contemplation on nature (18–19) to a contrasting comparison of the way of those who pursue their vices with no sense of guilt or wrongdoing, "She eats and wipes her mouth and says, 'I've done nothing wrong.'" As we observed in Proverbs 9, eating and drinking serve as common metaphors for sexual pleasures (cf. Song 5:1). The adulterous woman reveals that even the ways of sin go beyond our understanding.

---

19. Fox, *Proverbs 10–31*, 872, notes that the Hebrew words used in verse 19 generically designate a man and a "young girl" or "maid," and not a husband and a wife. In Fox's mind sexual intercourse cannot be in view because that would endorse an immoral relationship. But Fox presses the language too far and reads a moral lesson into what is overwhelmingly a contemplative context of lists in verses 18–31. The use of "man" and "maid" allow the poet to emphasize the natural mystery and beauty of sexuality apart from, but not in violation of, the social institution of marriage.

20. Cf. Ibid., 873.

Verses 21–23 gather four things under which the earth "trembles" and "cannot bear up." A few scholars in the past have viewed these images as humorous or mocking in nature. After all, what harm is there in a "godless fool who gets plenty to eat"? However, Van Leeuwen has argued that such assessments miss the larger point of these sayings, which is that all of them represent examples of the social and hierarchical order of he world turned on their heads, calling this "World Upside Down" (WUD) wisdom.[21] The fool who gets too much to eat symbolizes an inversion of normal social structures (Prov 19:10). The slave who becomes king in verse 22a imagines another such inversion of social order, while the two examples in verse 23 depict the disruption of order in the home: "a contemptible woman who gets married" and "a servant who displaces her mistress" (23). This final image parallels the lesson taught in the stories of Sarah and Hagar and Rachel and Bilhah.

The succession from David to Solomon captures both sides of these four sayings where Bathsheba, the Queen mother, speaks for the two rulers in her house to secure the throne away from the foolish Adonijah, an illegitimate heir. As we'll discuss at length in the next section, Agur's sayings repeatedly force us to contemplate images of the world where wisdom is lacking, with a particular focus on social structures: family, society, and kingdom.

The four small creatures in verses 24–28 provide examples where wisdom (sagacity) compensates for insignificance and lack of strength. This is a favorite theme in Old Testament narratives: Jacob outwits Esau and Laban, David defeats Goliath and Saul, and Joshua, Gideon, and Abimelech all defeat superior enemies through wise employment of their forces.[22]

The four beasties in verses 24–28 divide into two pairs. The first pair focuses not on the creatures but on their lack of "strength" and "power": By wisdom, ants have food in winter and badgers find safety in the rocks. The ants bring to mind a common theme in Proverbs that encourages storing up food and care for the wellbeing of the house (6:8; 12:11; 20:13; 27:23–27; 31:15, 21). The second pair has explicitly royal connections: locusts that don't have a king but move in ranks and insignificant lizards that have the run of king's palaces.

Of course, educated and uneducated people alike can hear these sayings and find immediate applications for life. Yet these four creatures also alert us to a deeper undercurrent in Proverbs that seeks to provide particular guidance

---

21. "Proverbs 30:21–23 and the Biblical World Upside Down" *JBL* 105/04· 599–610. Van Leeuwen borrows the term from Franz Delitzsch, who first recognized this principle behind the proverbs in these verses.

22. See David Daube, "Quartet of Beasties," 380–386, who explores the theme of wisdom overcoming size and strength in the Old Testament. Daube reveals how often animal metaphors play a central role in these stories.

to those who rule and a voice of caution to those who put all their hopes in powerful human leaders. (See Live the Story below).

Verses 29–31 present four things that are "stately in their stride" with "stately bearing." As in verses 18–19, three examples from the animal world culminate in the main focus: the human king. Unfortunately, the original Hebrew text of verse 31 has almost certainly been corrupted or lost, making our conclusions about the list's meaning somewhat tentative. We do know that the lion is a common symbol of the powerful king (Gen 49:9–10; Prov 19:12; 20:2). This saying balances the previous list that recognized the success of the small and insignificant things of the earth against all odds. Agur appears to juxtapose two contrary perspectives as part of his lessons on the limits of human understanding. Both the rule and its exception exist in the world God created.

Agur's sayings end in 30:32–33 with a warning that is accompanied by two metaphors that emphasize his point. While it is true that kings have great power (vv. 29–31), it is a serious mistake to act like a fool in acting arrogantly and plotting evil. The pressing of milk into curds parallels the pressing of the nose that results in bleeding and the pressing of anger that produces strife. The privilege of rank and power must be guarded with humility and wisdom.

LIVE the Story[23]

A Forgotten Side of Wisdom

Most of Proverbs provides a parental voice of basic life lessons. Agur, meanwhile, is a taskmaster who offers almost no reprieve from sayings that confront the weaknesses of our human desire and pride and expose the limits of our understanding. Among the topics he visits, the common threads are humility and wonder.

Reflection on these two themes is not foreign soil in Proverbs. The sayings in 16:1–4 make human wisdom and planning subject to God's plans and judgment while contemplating the mystery of God's purposes for the wicked (cf. 20:24; 21:30–31). Proverbs elsewhere reflects on the mysterious nature of gossip and deception (26:22–28). On several occasions the proverbs use honey to expose the seductive power of our sinful desires and the limits of human wisdom (25:27; 27:7).

Yet these topics are only handled briefly with a primary concern of instilling ethical behavior. Agur, on the other hand, is less interested in addressing

---

23. Some of these reflections were previously published online. See "Agur and the American Election," *Comment Magazine*, January 7, 2013, https://www.cardus.car/comment/article/3837/agur-and-the-american-election/.

our ethical conduct than he is with the task of opening up a long, reflective gaze on the theological, social, political, psychological, and spiritual mysteries of life. Silence, reflection, and contemplation have become rare in the modern technological age where we are saturated by images and sounds. But Agur echoes the command in Psalm 46:10, to "be still and know that I am God . . ." Our neglect of this still time of contemplation will rob us of the wisdom Agur has to offer.

Recovering the "Primary" Work of Art

Most Christians have never read Agur's oracle, despite the fact that there are more Bibles and more kinds of Bibles in print today than at any time in history. Our electronic gadgets allow us to read, search, and compare texts almost anywhere at anytime. Yet, actual biblical reading is decreasing. And most readers are selective: New Testament texts are favored to the Old Testament, and stories and messianic prophets are preferred to law and wisdom. I have heard a few sermons on Proverbs, usually chapter 8 or the valiant woman in chapter 31, but never one I can remember on Agur. Agur's own testimony convicts us, for "*every word* of God is flawless" (30:5, emphasis added). Each passage of Scripture has something to tell us about God and about navigating life in this world.

Like Psalms, Job, and Ecclesiastes, Agur's oracle empathizes with students and young people desperately in search of a spouse and a calling. These passages provide a deep treasury of writings that meets us in the highest and lowest points of life and everywhere in between. While these texts do not provide the "answers" to most of our hard questions, they offer a message from God in the form of honest words of an ancient human very much like us. These writers give us words to pray, images and thoughts for reflection, and rebukes for our sinful attitudes. Such deep and wonderful resources given by God to carry us through life and yet they are so seldom read.

Writing in a similar vein, the literary critic George Steiner passionately critiqued the "triumph of the secondary" and a loss of the primary work of art. The majority of us do most of our reading in news reports, websites, texts, tweets, and emails. Self-help books outsell novels and we read more biblical studies than books in the Bible. All of these tend to promote a behavior of "secondary" consumption—information gobbled down. But few of us have the time or aptitude to ingest and feed on the primary works of stories and poetry.[24]

Steiner does not endorse high culture of museums, symphonies, or the opera. Rather, he appeals to people of all backgrounds and cultures to come

---

24. George Steiner, *Real Presences* (Chicago: Chicago University Press, 1989).

into contact with creativity and imagination that put us face to face with the "real presence" of God himself. "[T]here is aesthetic creation," Steiner says, "because there is *creation*."[25] The human artist assumes that there is a supreme artist of all that is. Steiner writes as a Jewish thinker, but he recognizes the unique claim of Christian theology that the word of God is at the same time a means to encounter the Word made flesh.

The fitful poetry in Proverbs 30 offers a form of poetic realism—what it's like to live as a creature in God's vast world: palpable images of blood-sucking leeches and a shameless adulteress; the beauty of human love alongside natural marvels that humble the best of human culture and political ambition; a painful look at the destructive power of desire; and the example of a humble teacher. There are more questions than answers, but one thing stands firm— the creator of this whole world and the word that reveals him to us (30:5).

Instilling a Worldview of Wonder

This commentary has repeatedly emphasized how the structure of Proverbs shapes our view of reality. Chapters 1–9 are elementary—wisdom to help young men make a choice between two ways, two women, and two houses. Reality appears to fit within orderly divisions of right and wrong, just and unjust, and wise and foolish. The hundreds of familiar sayings in chapters 10–29 reinforce this ordered view of the world, with only an occasional instance of ambiguity or disorder (especially chaps. 25–29).

Proverbs 30 turns this pattern upside down, admitting that our experiences of reality will lack any sense of order. Sometimes wisdom cannot be found. Often things go beyond our understanding. And too frequently our vices and passions destroy life itself. As Proverbs progresses, it gradually introduces us to what Gerhard von Rad calls the "fringe of vast, divine mysteries."[26]

This leaves our world in a difficult place. Because of our knowledge of science and mathematics, most of us can manage our bank accounts, work a job, and keep ourselves alive with food. This much of the world appears to have order.

But bigger questions about meaning, God, and ethics seem to have been forever lost in a fog that resists the impressive powers of science and reason. Douglas Adams's bestselling novel *The Hitchhiker's Guide to the Galaxy* aired a typical sentiment of the last fifty years, poking fun at these futile efforts to find truth. The most sophisticated computer ever designed, Deep Thought, works for over half a million years to conclude that the answer to "The Great

---

25. Ibid., 201, emphasis original.
26. von Rad, *Wisdom*, 293–94.

Question. The Ultimate Question of Life, the Universe and Everything" is a startling forty-two—a number!

Of course Deep Thought is too simple a computer to know what the question was that yielded this answer. The play on our inability to get at truth continues to the end of the book with one character casually admitting that the pursuit is hopeless and one ought to give up and "just keep yourself occupied." In our culture of authenticity, such expressive individualism reigns: "be yourself," "do what you love," "pursue happiness," "if it feels good, do it."

These attitudes are fueled by narratives of culture often labeled relativism, consumerism, subjectivism, and pluralism. We live amidst a great suspicion of any meaning or order outside of ourselves and so each of us has to find the meaning and purpose for ourselves. Individual authenticity is the answer.

On the one hand, this has led to a growth in generic spirituality and tolerance of any and every religious belief—a shallow church. On the other hand, this relativist attitude flows naturally into our approach to ethics. This problem may be best summed up Alasdair MacIntyre's aptly titled book *Whose Justice? Which Rationality?*[27] In an argument that lasts four hundred dense pages, MacIntyre labors to get around the modern problem that alternative views of how we reason make it nearly impossible to resolve our disagreements about ethics. We see this debate played out everyday in arguments about the role of government, private gun ownership, same-sex marriage, abortion, and the like. Jiminy Cricket's curt advice "always let your conscience be your guide" tries to get around the problem with a cute saying. The problem is that millions of conscience-followers have found themselves in deep-seated opposition to one another.

Significantly, biblical writings like Agur's oracle, Job, and many psalms (e.g., 73, 90, 131) refuse to let mystery slide into relativism and skepticism. Rather they exhort us to work through mystery in search of wisdom. Oliver O'Donovan describes it this way when he observes that the wonder of the ant, the eagle, the ship, and the man with a woman "display an ordered sense of direction, but precisely how that sense of direction is given does not meet the eye. And it is what does *not* meet the eye that wisdom has its business." He goes on to say that such wisdom is "about the disclosure of creation to the enquiring, believing, and patient observer."[28] Such wisdom does eliminate all of the fog, confusion, and mystery of life and replace it with rational certainty.

---

27. (Notre Dame: University of Notre Dame, 1998.) A more recent and very readable statement of this problem can be found in Michael Sandel's *Justice: What's the Right thing to Do?* (New York: Farrar, Straus and Giroux, 2010).

28. Oliver O'Donovan, "Response to Craig Bartholomew," in *A Royal Priesthood? The Use of the Bible Ethically and Politically. A Dialogue with Oliver O'Donovan* (Grand Rapids: Zondervan, 2002), 113.

A Realistic View of Political Power

On the whole Proverbs portrays a positive view of government and kingship (chs. 1–29), but it ends with passages that remind us of the limits of human rulers and governing systems. This political message would have been clearer in the ancient world where wisdom writings were naturally associated with royalty—kings and their courts of sages and scribes (see Introduction). The book of Proverbs is thus appropriately ascribed to Solomon (1:1), Israel's wise king (1 Kings 3–10). King Hezekiah (25:1) and King Lemuel's queen mother (31:1) are also cited as contributing authors with unambiguous royal connections.

But Agur has an untraceable lineage and, contrary to the claims of some scholars, no sign of any royal connections.[29] Likewise, in contrast to Solomon's confidence in Proverbs 1, Agur begins with a confession of humility, ignorance, and the limits of human wisdom (30:1–9). His oracle elsewhere contemplates the ant, the rock badger, and the locust, who live safely and prosperously despite having no leader (30:25–27). The lizard (v. 28), the fourth and final creature in the list, is a picture of wisdom itself: "unpretentious but infinitely versatile"—a stark contrast to the pretentiousness of the strutting rooster and the king before his people (v. 31).[30] As we will see in the next chapter, the final royal scene in Proverbs (31:1–9) depicts the scolding words of King Lemuel's mother, reproving him for falling victim to the typical abuses of power: women, overindulgence, and neglecting the poor.

Too often modern academic commentaries on Proverbs tend to make a caricature of its pro-Solomonic ideology. But this ignores the strong images in these final two chapters and the obvious fact that the final editors of the Old Testament put this book next to Ruth and Ecclesiastes, books that do little to advance our confidence in ancient kings. On the contrary, a careful reader comes away from these books seeking wisdom rather than power.

Agur, Jesus, and the Foolishness of Wisdom

After Israel's fall, exile, and subjection to Roman rule, the nation was left in a void. Moses and the prophets promised a future, restoration from failure, and hope for the future. Reality suggested otherwise. Wisdom writings like Baruch, Sirach, and the Wisdom of Solomon came into prominence during this Second Temple period, providing a way for Israel to find a new sense of identity. Agur's oracle has its own place in this historical setting. Breaking stride with the first twenty-nine chapters of the book, it presents us with

---

29. The common denominator among ancient collections of wisdom is fathers writing to sons, not royalty. See, Fox, *Proverbs 1–9*, 8–9.

30. Ibid., 115.

puzzling images, a prayer, and a confession. Rather than lifting the fog, Agur teaches the wisdom to make a way through it.

Agur's oracle resembles the teachings of the New Testament at many points. For one, Jesus calls us to a new ethical vision, but he does so far more often through stories and metaphor than rules. As Dale Allison has observed, the memorable Sermon on the Mount in Matthew 5–7 only has one rule.[31]

Most scholars also recognize the strong connection between "give me only my daily bread" and not profaning God's name in 30:8–9 and Jesus' teaching in the Lord's Prayer, "hallowed be your name," and "give us today our daily bread" (Matt 6:9–11; cf. Luke 11:2–3). Wisdom, humility, dependence, and prayer, which seem only tangentially related on the surface, come together in Jesus' life and teaching.

Jesus and Agur also share similar ways of affecting shock and surprise. Matthew presents Jesus somehow going beyond Israel's promises; most of Mark's gospel is shrouded in a secret that stymies human understanding; Luke again and again portrays confused disciples and amazed crowds; and John narrates the gradual revealing of God's glory to Israel and the nations. In each account of Jesus' life, mystery is present.

Agur also anticipates Paul's letters. Agur's path to wisdom begins with humility, an affirmation of wonder, and a fascination with the incomprehensible. In 1 Corinthians Paul opposes the wisdom of the world to "God's wisdom, a mystery that has been hidden and that God destined for our glory before time began" (1 Cor 2:7). In this mystery we discover that God has chosen the foolish, weak, and low to shame the wise and lofty (1:25–28). Where worldly wisdom celebrates learning, "knowledge puffs up" (8:1), true wisdom finds its roots in the reality of Jesus' crucifixion and death (1:22; 2:2).

Paul turns from his critique of human wisdom at Corinth to letters of prayer for Ephesus, Colossae, and Philippi, passionately exhorting these churches to pursue the endless riches of wisdom and knowledge in Christ (Col 2:2–3). Jesus' death and resurrection open the way for wisdom and understanding into the "mystery of his will . . . which he purposed in Christ" (Eph 1:9). The extent of this wisdom staggers the mind with its "incomparably great power" (1:19), "incomparable riches of his grace (2:7), "love that surpasses knowledge" (3:19), and "peace of God, which transcends all understanding" (Phil 4:7).

Like Agur's wisdom, the wisdom of Christ is lowly. It refuses to set its hope on human rulers and earthly political powers. And it bows before the wonders of God in creation. Dale Allison contends that the problem with

---

31. Dale Allison Jr., *The Luminous Dusk: Finding God in the Deep, Still Places* (Grand Rapids: Eerdmans, 2006), 84.

those who did not understand Jesus was not their ignorance, but their lack of imagination.[32] No human way of thinking would conclude that a God hung on a cross would pave the way for the renewal of all things or our dying to ourselves to gain access to that life. As the way of a man with a woman and a lizard in king's palaces, things we do not understand and are inclined to overlook retain a clue to the mystery of God stored up for ages but now revealed in Christ.

---

32. Ibid.

LISTEN to the Story

[1] The sayings of King Lemuel—an inspired utterance his mother taught him.

[2] Listen, my son! Listen, son of my womb!
   Listen, my son, the answer to my prayers!
[3] Do not spend your strength on women,
   your vigor on those who ruin kings.
[4] It is not for kings, Lemuel—
   it is not for kings to drink wine,
   not for rulers to crave beer,
[5] lest they drink and forget what has been decreed,
   and deprive all the oppressed of their rights.
[6] Let beer be for those who are perishing,
   wine for those who are in anguish!
[7] Let them drink and forget their poverty
   and remember their misery no more.
[8] Speak up for those who cannot speak for themselves,
   for the rights of all who are destitute.
[9] Speak up and judge fairly;
   defend the rights of the poor and needy.
[10] A wife of noble character who can find?
   She is worth far more than rubies.
[11] Her husband has full confidence
   in her and lacks nothing of value.
[12] She brings him good, not harm,
   all the days of her life.
[13] She selects wool and flax
   and works with eager hands.
[14] She is like the merchant ships,
   bringing her food from afar.

417

¹⁵ She gets up while it is still night;
    she provides food for her family
    and portions for her female servants.
¹⁶ She considers a field and buys it;
    out of her earnings she plants a vineyard.
¹⁷ She sets about her work vigorously;
    her arms are strong for her tasks.
¹⁸ She sees that her trading is profitable,
    and her lamp does not go out at night.
¹⁹ In her hand she holds the distaff
    and grasps the spindle with her fingers.
²⁰ She opens her arms to the poor
    and extends her hands to the needy.
²¹ When it snows, she has no fear for her household;
    for all of them are clothed in scarlet.
²² She makes coverings for her bed;
    she is clothed in fine linen and purple.
²³ Her husband is respected at the city gate,
    where he takes his seat among the elders of the land.
²⁴ She makes linen garments and sells them,
    and supplies the merchants with sashes.
²⁵ She is clothed with strength and dignity;
    she can laugh at the days to come.
²⁶ She speaks with wisdom,
    and faithful instruction is on her tongue.
²⁷ She watches over the affairs of her household
    and does not eat the bread of idleness.
²⁸ Her children arise and call her blessed;
    her husband also, and he praises her:
²⁹ "Many women do noble things,
    but you surpass them all."
³⁰ Charm is deceptive, and beauty is fleeting;
    but a woman who fears the LORD is to be praised.
³¹ Honor her for all that her hands have done,
    and let her works bring her praise at the city gate.

Listening to the Text in the Story: Ruth; Psalms 111–112; 119;
Ecclesiastes 7:23–29; Lamentations

Proverbs 31:10–31 is an acrostic poem in which each line begins with a subsequent letter of the Hebrew alphabet. Other acrostic poems in the Old Testament include Psalms 9; 10; 25; 34; 37; 111–112; 119; 145; Lamentations 1; 2; 3; 4;[1] and Nahum 1:2–8[2] (cf. Sir 50:13–30). Psalm 112 deserves special attention since it shares several parallels with Proverbs 31: "the fear of the LORD" (Ps 112:1; Prov 31:30), a list of laudable works (Ps 112:4–9; Prov 31:12–27), the absence of fear of temporal events in life and the future (Ps 112:7, 8; Prov 31:21, 25), wisdom combined with generosity (Ps 112:4, 5, 9; Prov 31:20, 26), wealth (Ps 112:3; Prov 31:16, 18, 29), and a connection to children (Ps 112:2; Prov 31:28).[3]

Perhaps most important is the way the "theology" of Yahweh and the people of God in the hymn in Psalm 111 sets up a second hymn concerning the "anthropology" of the righteous follower of Yahweh in Psalm 112.[4] For reasons I will address in verse 10 below, the theology and cosmic invitations in Proverbs 8 set up the anthropology of this woman in 31:10–31. But there is a marked difference here as well in that Psalm 112 is a hymn addressed to Yahweh, whereas Proverbs 31 is a hymn addressed to a woman (see more below).

In many Hebrew manuscripts Proverbs is followed by the book of Ruth. Ruth is the only woman in the Old Testament to be called *hayil*, "valiant" (3:11).[5] Boaz is likewise labeled "valiant" and, at the end of Ruth, the elders of Bethlehem pray that Ruth's entrance into Boaz's house will make his name "valiant" or "established" in Bethlehem, comparing Ruth to Rachel, Leah, and Tamar in Genesis (Ruth 4:11–12). Tamar (Gen 38:1–30) is alluded to in Ruth 2 by way of several parallels: their foreign identity, the surprising preservation of a family line, the return to the "father's" and "mother's" houses, and several unique Hebrew terms.[6] The dominant element among these four women is that of fertility and the growth of the family and nation.[7]

EXPLAIN the Story

Proverbs ends with two distinct poems: the advice of King Lemuel's mother (vv. 1–9) and the noble or valiant woman (vv. 10–31). Scholars generally

---

1. Lamentations 5 has 22 lines (one for each letter of the alphabet), but it strays from the acrostics in chapters 1–4. One might say that the acrostic is there and not there.

2. Also a broken acrostic.

3. See Wolters, *Song of the Valiant Woman*, 5.

4. Cf. John Goldingay, *Psalms*, vol. 3: Psalms 90–150, BCOTWP (Grand Rapids: Baker Academic, 2008), 309.

5. NIV "noble character."

6. See André LaCocque, *Ruth*, Continental Commentary (Minneapolis: Fortress, 2004), 50–139.

7. Ibid., 139. Cf. "procreative strength," Carmichael, *Sex and Religion*, 52.

agree that these passages connect the end of the book to chapters 1–9. The prohibition of giving *hayil*, "strength," to women in 31:3 is contrasted to the woman of *hayil*, "nobility" or "valor," in verses 10 and 29. Over half of all the verses in chapters 1–9 mention women. Furthermore, the "fear of the LORD" is carefully placed at the beginning and the end (1:7; 31:30). And finally, the poems in chapter 31 embody parental, in this case motherly, instruction in wisdom (31:1–2, 26; cf. 1:8; 2:1; 4:3; 6:20, etc.).[8]

31:1–9 It was not uncommon for women to be featured and even admired in ancient wisdom literature, but the advice from Lemuel's mother here is the only known incidence where a queen mother gives advice to a king. This is the first of several signs that this poem offers a subtle critique of royal culture that viewed women as sex objects and intellectually inferior.

The appearance of the phrase "the words of so-and-so" in verse 1 makes this the seventh and final major heading in Proverbs (cf. 1:1; 10:1; 22:17; 24:23; 25:1; 30:1). "Lemuel" could be a proper name or an epithet like "Qohelet" in Ecclesiastes, though Qohelet's identity remains a mystery.

The threefold petition by the mother in verse 2 "Listen . . . listen . . . listen" is striking. Some scholars translate this "No . . . no . . . no" or "what . . . what . . . what." Whether Lemuel might already have violated these commands or is recalling these words from his youth is unknown. The basic point seems to be an emphatic warning paralleling the appeals of the father and mother in Proverbs 2–3. "Son of my vows" (NIV "prayers") recalls Hannah's vow (1 Sam 1:11).

Waltke sees a structural relationship in verses 3–5: verse 3b expands on 3a just as verse 5 expands on in verse 4.[9]

In 31:3 the king should not give his *hayil*, "vigor," or his "ways" to women who will only "ruin kings." These metaphors are sexual, echoing the man destroyed by a woman in 6:33. "Vigor," meanwhile, anticipates the contrasting woman of *hayil* who should be desired (10, 29).

Verses 4–9 address the intersection of wine, strong drink, and kingship (see 20:1 and Live the Story for that chapter). The wealthy and ruling classes were the most likely to have access to strong drink and their drunkenness was likely to harm every strata of society.

While the warnings in verse 4–5 may go without saying, it is surprising to hear alcohol recommended as a sedative for physical and financial woes (6–7). Waltke believes that this advice is sarcastic.[10] But it is more likely that the saying reveals the inevitability of suffering and injustice. The king must

8. Waltke, *Proverbs 15–31*, 502.
9. Ibid., 507.
10. Ibid., 509.

keep his wits to seek justice, limit harm, and care for the casualties of life that often slip through the cracks.[11]

Verses 10–31 represent the book's concluding poem. Whybray comments that many books in the Old Testament have openings and/or closings that indicate how the editors intended for the books to be read, such as Joshua 24; Ruth 4:18–22; 2 Kings 25:27–30; Psalms 1–2; Ecclesiastes 12:9–13; and Hosea 14:9. The links between Proverbs 31:10–31 and verses 1–9 and chapters 1–9 make it likely that this final poem provides just such a *hermeneutical framework* for the book.[12]

In addition to the alphabetic acrostic structure, this passage should be thought of not just as a song, but a "hymn." Wolters lists seven persuasive reasons for this; three are worthy of note. One, the poem takes the shape of a hymn: an introduction and the central character, the praiseworthy deeds of the character, and a call to praise. Two, terms like the *eshet-hayil*, "valiant woman," (v. 10) and *halal*, "praise," resemble language from hymns to heroes in military contexts. Finally, hymns are "poetry of action," and Proverbs 31:13–31 is loaded with verbs of strength and activity.[13]

Clifford further demonstrates that the chiastic structure of the poem focuses all of the sayings on the woman's strong and skillful hands:[14]

> *hayil* "valiant," v. 10a
> > *ba'lah* "her husband," v. 11a
> > > *yadeha shillehah* "her hand she puts," v. 19a
> > > > *kapah tamku* "her palms grasp," v. 19b
> > > > *kapah parsah* "she opens her palms," v. 20a
> > > *yadeha shillehah* "her hand she stretches," v. 20b
> > *ba'lah* "her husband," v. 28b
> *hayil* "valiant," v. 29a

31:10–12 These verses introduce the subject of the hymn in terms that echo throughout Proverbs 1–30 and the rest of the wisdom literature. The valiant woman in verse 10, like Woman Wisdom, is valued as better than "rubies" (8:11). Furthermore, the theme of "finding" echoes the repeated commands for the son to find wisdom (2:5; 3:4; 13), a good wife (12:4), and Qohelet's lament when he could not find wisdom or a woman (Eccl 7:23–29). Job likewise expresses the challenge of finding wisdom, especially in times of crisis (28:1–28). The husband's "trust" (NIV "full confidence") in verse 11 is

---

11. Fox, *Proverbs 10–31*, 887.
12. Whybray, *Composition*, 159–61.
13. Wolters, *Song of the Valiant Woman*, 6–12.
14. Modified from Clifford, *Proverbs*, 273.

a phrase normally reserved for faith in God but is here applied to a woman (2 Kgs 18:22; Ps 118:8–9; Isa 36:5).[15]

31:13–15 Each verse from 13–27 emphasizes a unique dimension of this woman's exceptional work. Verse 13 exhibits *mature skill* alongside *emotional intensity*. To "select" or "seek" "wool and flax" shows her devotion to her skill and "eager hands" express what some translations rightly call "pleasure."

Verse 14 views her work through the perspective of its great *geographical scope*. The term *tahar*, "merchant," is only used twice more in Proverbs, speaking of Woman Wisdom's profit in 3:14 and the merchandise in 31:18. Finally, 31:15 imagines the *duration* of her work. Taken with verse 18, this poem would seem to endorse a long day with little sleep. But passages like Psalm 127:2 and the Sabbath laws make it unlikely that the poem upholds a sleepless work ethic. The point is that she does not waste the hours when most of us are likely to pursue the more unprofitable habits of life; she numbers her days, to paraphrase Moses (Ps 90:12).

31:16–18 These verses provide another trio of this woman's remarkable attributes. Verse 16 celebrates skill in knowing the value and potential of economic resources. Buying a field to plant fruit has deep theological significance in Israel's story (cf. Gen 23:12–13; Isa 5:1–4; Ezek 17:4–6). Contrary to Israel's consistent misuse of the land, this woman brings forth its intended flourishing. Environmental activism today needs to bear in mind the clear biblical teaching that the earth was always for humans to enable its full fruit-bearing potential (Gen 1:28–30; 2:15).

The vigorous work described in verse 17 is more literally to "gird her loins," much as warriors and prophets prepare themselves for daunting tasks (cf. Exod 12:11; 2 Kgs 4:29; 9:1). "Strong" in 17b is one of countless reminders of the power and confidence in her work.

Clifford observes that the two lines in verse 18 are parallel. To see the profit in her labor (18a) complements the lamp that allows her to see and gauge, literally "taste," the material value of her work at the end of each day (18b). Verses 13, 16, and 18 highlight the skill this woman has in discerning the good from the bad. She is like the expert shopper who knows how to pick the perfect melon in a pile, or financier who knows the perfect price for an investment.

31:19–20 The outline above showed the central position of these two sayings in the poem. "Hand" and "fingers" combine finely honed skills with "poor" and "needy" to form a picture of ethical maturity and great compassion.[16] The physical work of her "hand" and "fingers" in verse 19 provide the

15. Waltke, *Proverbs 15–31*, 521.

16. For an illuminating study of the *hapax legomenon kisor* see Wolters, *Song*, 42–56, previously published as "The Meaning of *kîsôr* (Prov 31:19)," *Hebrew Union College Annual* 65 (1994): 91–104.

means for her "hands" and "arms" to be metaphors for works of mercy. The sayings anticipate Paul's command to the Corinthians to use their gifts for the "common good" (1 Cor 12:7).

31:21–25 These sayings are linked at several levels. First, the specific images of the woman's actions (21–22, 24) are paired with two portraits—one of the husband before the elders (23; cf. Isa 61:9) and the second of the woman as she stands before the audience of the poem (25). The sayings also move from the home to public life. Finally, the group as a whole is enclosed by sayings that match clothing activities with attitudes of confidence (21, 25).

The sadly popular slogan "let go and let God" has no place here. This woman fears Yahweh (30) at the same time that she labors to secure herself against the constant threats of poor crops, sickness, poverty, and bad weather. This can be seen especially in the way her diligent work with her hands making clothes and bedding (21–22, 24) mirrors the metaphorical way she clothes herself with "strength and dignity." She works hard because she trusts the Lord. As a result, she has no fear of foul weather or the unknowable future.[17] The poem also implicitly critiques our modern day throwaway culture: "scarlet," "purple," and "linen" are rare materials of the very highest quality. The woman knows the value of a quality garment just as she knows the potential of good land (cf. 16). What is also absent here are signs of our modern consumerist mentality of owning one of everything or chasing the latest faddish trend. The focus here is not buying popular brand names that impress our peers, but quality goods that bring flourishing to daily human life.

31:26–27 The valiant woman's wise speech echoes the wise words of Lemuel's mother (1–9) and Woman Wisdom's invitation for all humanity to hear her wisdom (8:1–11). This is significant because the valiant woman can be seen to connect the wise teaching of mothers (1:8; 6:20; 31:1–9) with an array of actions that draw out the full potential of the created world—the same world attested to by the cosmic woman (8:21–31).

Verse 27 returns a final time to the woman's concrete actions. Wolters argues that the first word in verse 27, *sophiyya*, "she watches over," is a transliteration and pun playing on *sophia*, the Greek word for wisdom. The coincidence may seem far-fetched, but consider that the ambiguous form of this Hebrew participle follows the pattern of words of other ambiguous words such as "clothed" or "to clothe" in verse 25 or "nothing of value" that can be either the object or the subject in verse 11. This is also the only praise in the poem that starts with a participle, and it has been written not in the normal

---

Wolters appeals to linguistic and cultural studies to argue that the distaff is a particular type of "grasped spindle" that requires two hands.

17. Bartholomew and O'Dowd, *Old Testament Wisdom*, 116.

qal form of the verb, *sapah*, but the rarer form *sophiyya*. If Wolters is correct, the pun would have us read the verse, "the ways of her house are wisdom," which clearly echoes ways and houses of wisdom in chapters 1–9 while also serving as a contrast or critique to the idle and intellectual forms of wisdom in Greek philosophy. This wisdom is about the hard and dirty work of turning the base things of nature into a vibrant and verdant culture. Such a saying fits naturally with verse 27b, which imagines her devouring productivity rather than wallowing in sloth.

31:28–31 The closing praise turns from the voice of the narrator to testimonies from the woman's children, husband, and community. Van Leeuwen observes that she is "blessed" because she is, like Wisdom, a source of blessing (3:13–18).[18] Her husband's praise, *halelah*, is the same word used to praise Yahweh in Psalm 112:1, which we hear in English as hallelujah (cf. v. 30b). As a timeless critique to the fleeting and ever-shifting measures of good looks, this woman is most known for her religious faith (cf. 1:7), which is most evident in her virtuous and active life among her community and her family.

Verse 31 brings the book to a close with a saying that looks back across all 31 chapters. "Honor her" is another term of heroic praise, which points us to the determined and consistent labor of her hands (cf. 19–20). Her praise in the city gates also reminds us of the public appeals of Woman Wisdom in 1:20; 8:1–3; and 9:1–6. This point is explored further below.

LIVE the Story

Perhaps no other chapter in Proverbs, or even the Bible, has more to say about work and vocation (calling), especially with regard to women. With chapter 31 being placed at the end of the book, it serves in many ways to remind the reader that all of the sayings are really about our calling to live life well before God.

For the Life of the World and Not Just for Women

Joseph Blenkinsopp has called chapter 31 an "unattainable fantasy about the kind of woman who would make the perfect wife."[19] And yet does it really make sense to end Proverbs with a fantasy poem that leaves men feeling shamed and women intimidated and deflated? Proverbs does indeed load this woman down with all of the qualities of all the best women at all the best

---

18. Van Leeuwen, *Proverbs*, 263.
19. Blenkinsopp, *Sage, Priest, Prophet: Religious and Intellectual Leadership in Ancient Israel*, 35.

times. But this woman serves an even greater role that exemplifies the best of womanhood; she embraces all the best of wisdom for men and for women.

As such there is a better way to read this chapter that keeps us close to the poetic form and larger context in Proverbs. As Christine Roy Yoder has observed, this woman should be identified with the cosmic Woman Wisdom we meet in Proverbs 1–9:

> Both women are hard to find and are more precious than jewels. Both have a house and a staff of young women. Both provide food, prosperity and security. Both are known at the city gates and bestow honor on their companions. Both are physically strong and loath wickedness. Both extend their hands to the needy. They laugh. And both teach; their identities and instructions are associated with "fear of YHWH." . . . This is what life looks like for those who accept wisdom's invitation to dwell in her household (9:1–6).[20]

Yoder rightly observes that this "'women's work' is set apart and named as the beginning, indeed the standard, of faithfulness."[21] And so this picture of a woman, rather than shaming or else overlooking the young man addressed in this book, leads him to be attracted to this character for two interrelated reasons. First, activities like this were not all that uncommon for women when this chapter was written, and so a man could very well look for a woman who would increase his financial status and social standing in the community (11). But the young man would simultaneously be drawn to her because she is such a clear and concrete manifestation of Woman Wisdom in day-to-day life. In this way she is an enticing image for how a wise man should live his own life: full of activity, industry, compassion, creativity, vitality, and faith. She is the book of Proverbs in a concrete form that is attractive to all readers.

Education, Craftsmanship, and Social Hierarchy

In his *Sources of the Self*, Charles Taylor traces the rise and fall of the perception of various forms of human occupations in western cultures.[22] In the ancient Greek world, contemplation was typically held to be superior to manual labor, marriage, childbearing, and the basic maintenance of physical life. One thinks of Plato's emphasis on "mind over matter." This Greek worldview did a lot

---

20. "Proverbs," in *Women's Bible Commentary*, 3rd ed., ed. Carol A. Newsom, Jacqueline E. Lapsey, and Sharon H. Ringe (Louisville: Westminster, 2012), 241. Yoder provides detailed lexical connections between these two women in "The Woman of Substance (*eshet hayil*): A Socioeconomic Reading of Proverbs 10–31," *JBL* 122/13 (2003): 446.

21. Yoder, "Proverbs," 241.

22. Charles Taylor, *Sources of the Self: The Making of the Modern Identity* (Cambridge: Harvard University Press, 1989), 211–33.

to shape the higher ideals of the contemplative and religious life in the early centuries of the church and the rise of monasteries and orders.

But this contemplative ideal gradually came to an end as a result of several changes in western culture. People grew increasing distrustful of religious and political authorities. The world also experienced both the burgeoning new discoveries in the natural sciences and the increased sense of the rights of the individual. The Reformation and Enlightenment mark the climax of this movement, giving way to a new passion to recover the dignity of ordinary life—scientists, craftspeople, traders, and mothers and fathers. Whereas the priest, monk, king, and philosopher were the most esteemed vocations in the Middle Ages, the emerging Protestant ideal celebrated the mundane professions to an equal or even greater degree.

The upside to this shift is that ordinary life became valued as a good in itself; God sanctifies every mundane vocation we participate in as citizens in the world. The valiant woman is the perfect picture of the God-loving human being, extraordinarily skilled in the "secular" professions, and esteemed by the whole community. Not coincidentally, most of Jesus' life on earth was spent not as the messianic savior, but as a carpenter. Mundane work! Walter Ciszek captures the point well:

> He did not fashion benches or tables or plowbeams by means of miracles, but by hammer and saw and by ax and adz. He worked long hours to help his father, and then became the support of his widowed mother, by the rough work of a hill country craftsman. Nothing he worked on, so far as we know, ever set any fashions or became a collector's item. He worked in a shop every day, week in and week out, for some twenty years. He did the work all of us have to do in our lifetimes. There was nothing spectacular about it, there was much of the routine about it, perhaps much that was boring. There is little we can say about the jobs we do or have done that could not be said of the work God himself did when he became man.[23]

The nature of work changed measurably with the onset of the industrial revolution, the mass expansion of technology, and explosion of universities, colleges, and professional training centers. Matthew Crawford has written one of the most helpful summaries of this time period. In chapters entitled, "A Brief Case for the Useful Arts" and "The Separation of Thinking from Doing," Crawford persuasively challenges the modern push to elevate undergraduate education and white-collar degrees over the intellectual challenges

23. Walter J. Ciszek, S.J., *He Leadeth Me* (San Francisco: Ignatius, 1995), 103. I am grateful to Julie Johnson for introducing me to Ciszek's writing.

and moral shaping uniquely embodied in less esteemed "crafts" and "trades."[24] He emphasizes the moral and intellectual significance of our work.

Crawford further shows that those who are highest paid in western society are often skilled in such narrow and particular tasks that they have little sense of the purpose of their work and its interconnectedness to community, responsibility, and the natural environment of God's world. Those who work in the trades, by contrast, are innately tied into the community and how their gifts affect its well-being.

In this way the valiant woman is something of a poster child of crafts and trades. But she is much more than that too. Her work merits praise because she, like Jesus in his earthly life, pursues it with a keen appreciation for the whole of things: faith, human dignity, hard work, justice, patience, compassion, refined skill, and the interrelationships between families and between local and international economies. She is the perfect combination of faith, intellect, and manual skill. Our overburdened and increasingly indebted system of higher education is greatly in need of a renewed vision of the meaning and value of work and the shallowness that attends to our worship of grades and resumes.

Works and Good Works: Secular and Sacred

The appreciation for the ordinary life after the Reformation did not come without consequences. Part of this historical transformation is owed to the Reformers' rejection of mediation of clergy and higher church authority. This distrust of tradition and human authority set in motion the decline of doctrinal depth in the church and the emergence of a new, modern form of belief grounded in personal and emotional connection to God *within* (interiority).[25] As a result the spiritual life came to be set apart from, or in tension with, the natural and political world where we live.

This is merely a form of renewed Gnosticism or a dualism of nature versus grace, which we can see manifesting itself in various ways in the patristic, medieval, Anabaptist, and Reformed traditions. The patristic and medieval view, that grace stands apart from, or in tension with, nature, made it necessary to read Proverbs in allegorical terms. The valiant woman thus has to represent Mary or the church in their spiritual devotion. Planting a vineyard naturally symbolizes the mission to make disciples of all nations. In this way of thinking, Christian vocation in the secular world is done only because it is necessary; it remains beneath the more holy call to seclusion and spiritual contemplation.

---

24. Crawford, *Shop Class*, 11–53.
25. See Andrew G. Walker and Robin A. Parry, *Deep Church Rising: The Third Schism and the Recovery of Christian Orthodoxy* (Eugene, OR: Cascade Books, 2014), 8–16.

In the Anabaptist tradition, Christian vocation is similarly viewed as a call to holy living among the people of God. Our work in the world is distinct from our vocation or, more properly, the vocation of the church. According to Jacques Ellul, Christian work is only positive in its original setting in the garden of Eden. Since the fall it is only "laborious and necessary to survival."[26] The only dignity in work is it keeps us alive. But the wisdom literature, and Proverbs in particular, is conspicuously absent from the writings of Anabaptists like Ellul, John Howard Yoder, and Stanley Hauerwas.[27] One wonders if they recognize that wisdom is a "tree of life" (3:18) who, in her song to a fallen humanity, nevertheless rejoices at the idea of humans taking up their work with her at their side (8:30–36). Somehow, for Proverbs, work done by wisdom in the fear of Yahweh is redemptive and full of grace.

Meanwhile, some of the Reformers adopted a form of "hyper-Augustinianism," which re-centered the gospel from the Catholic understanding of a good news story of God's redeeming kingdom in Christ to narrow doctrinal propositions grounded on "justification by faith" and "grace alone." This narrow gospel created obvious problems for those wanting to affirm the ordinary life since it risked appearing either that our works deserve merit or else that humans might have a hand in God's reconciliation of the world—a problem of intermixing grace and good works.[28] Luther and Melanchthon in particular, who leaned on the valiant woman to make their case for the value of the ordinary life, struggled to reconcile the valiant woman's works with her religious "fear of Yahweh." How could nature and grace comingle in this way? In keeping with Luther's proclivity for making sharp divisions, he articulated his famous antitheses between law and gospel and spiritual and secular, which go hand in hand with his doctrine of two kingdoms and an inner-outer distinction for the life of the Christian.[29] As one can imagine, in their reading of Proverbs 31 Luther and Melanchthon divide the valiant woman's activities between the spiritual—those upholding the first table of the Decalogue (sacred right worship)—and the secular—those upholding the second table (right conduct).[30] Surely one can see that the hyper-Augustinian reading forces a unified piece of poetry into a tight theological grid, dulling and distorting the beauty and integrity of its theology in the process.

---

26. Jacques Ellul, "The Ethics of Freedom," in *Working: Its Meaning and Its Limits*, ed. Gilbert C. Meilaender (Notre Dame: University of Notre Dame Press, 2000), 99.

27. Cf. Douglas J. Schuurman, *Vocation: Discerning our Calling in Life* (Grand Rapids: Eerdmans, 2004), 83–90.

28. Taylor, *Sources*, 246–47.

29. Oliver O'Donovan, *The Desire of the Nations: Rediscovering the Roots of Political Theology* (Cambridge: Cambridge University Press, 1996), 209–10.

30. See Wolters, *Song*, 22–24.

It should come as little surprise that Karl Barth and Dietrich Bonhoeffer, both Lutheran ministers, felt a need to nuance Luther's strong two-kingdom divide in order to justify a religious rejection of the secular Nazi regime—a mixing of the two kingdoms was simply necessary in some way to oppose the sins of citizens in the public square and preserve the common good of humanity. Grace has to overflow into secular politics, as it were.

There are two other major ways of interpreting the valiant woman's work that do not hold nature and grace in strict opposition. The official Catholic tradition holds that the grace that we receive in our sacramental life in the church transforms or sanctifies our mundane work in the world. In other words, grace can be added to nature to elevate it from its secondary and fallen condition to the good it was made to be.[31] In the Dutch Calvinist tradition known as Kuyperianism or neo-Calvinism, we find a common Reformed rejection of ecclesiastical and social hierarchies but also a rejection of the sharp division between nature and grace and secular and sacred. In this tradition the valiant woman's works are a manifestation of her faith in the world. To plant orchards, spin cloth, and sell garments are good and spiritual activities because they participate in the creation mandate to bring the world to flourishing.

Readers will no doubt come to this chapter with a broad range of theological commitments, and if we are to honor this important poem in its form and its context in Proverbs, we will simply have to raise these questions about nature and grace, the sacred and the secular, and the value and meaning of work in a fallen world.

Do What You Love

The valiant woman exudes endless energy. Her hands are busy with joy and laughter and move in a way that reflects confidence in God. She works "with eager hands" (13) and "can laugh at the days to come" (25). One could possibly take away from this that we should "do what we love" with our life; any calling is suitable so long as we are passionate about it—as the sentiment has it today.

But it's important to distinguish the pleasure the valiant woman derives from her work from the source of motivation for that work. Miya Tokumitsu has written a provocative critique of the Do What You Love movement (DWYL). Addressing the likes of Steve Jobs and Oprah Winfrey, Tokumitsu warns,

> The problem is that [DWYL] leads not to salvation, but to the devaluation of actual work, including the very work it pretends to elevate!—and more importantly, the dehumanization of the vast majority of laborers. . . . By keeping us focused on ourselves and our individual happiness, DWYL

---

31. Ibid., 20–22 and Taylor, *Sources*, 223.

distracts us from the working conditions of others while validating our own choices and relieving us from obligations to all who labor, whether or not they love it.[32]

Tokumitsu does not exclude "love" and "passion" from having a role in the job we pursue, but she does situate these goals within the larger interests of the common good.

More needs to be said, of course. As Jeremiah warns us, "the heart is deceitful above all things and beyond cure. Who can understand it?" (17:9). James similarly asks, "What causes fights and quarrels among you? Don't they come from your desires that battle within you?" (4:1–2). These words reconnect us with the major thrust of Proverbs 1–9, where we come to see that the path of wisdom is grounded in the object of our desire (1:8–19; 3:21–35; 6:20–7:27; 9:1–18). Elsewhere in Proverbs we hear, "Desire without knowledge is not good—how much more will hasty feet miss the way" and "Many are the plans in a person's heart, but it is the LORD's purpose that prevails" (19:2, 21; cf. 20:5). The Anabaptist tradition discussed above has good grounds here for resisting the idea of individual callings and looking for joy in our work. The Anglican tradition echoes this suspicion of pursing our passion. In its Book of Common prayer it begins Christian worship with the collect: "Almighty God, unto whom all hearts are open, all desires known, and from whom no secrets are hid; Cleanse the thoughts of our hearts by the inspiration of thy Holy Spirit . . ." To enter into God's presence we need the only one who truly understands our hearts to look in and cleanse them from all their false and deluding passions.

The complexity of desire comes home to roost in the recent movie *End of The Tour* and David Lipsky's book about David Foster Wallace on which the movie is based. When asked about his intended audience, Wallace says: "if there is a sort of sadness—I don't know what, under 45 or something?—it has something to do with pleasure and achievement and entertainment. And a kind of emptiness at the heart of what they thought was going on . . . ."[33] Technology and media offer us an endless stream of pleasure, which only distracts us from the problem that we are lonely and lost.

Wisdom runs counter to this delusional consumption of media and entertainment and our struggle with sadness and desire. While we cannot, and

32. Tokumitsu, "In the Name of Love: Elites Embrace the 'Do What You Love' Mantra. But It Devalues Work and Hurts Workers." *Slate Magazine*, January 16, 2014, http://www.slate.com/articles/technology/technology/2014/01/do_what_you_love_love_what_you_do_an_omnipresent_mantra_that_s_bad_for_work.html.

33. David Lipsky, *Although of Course You End Up Becoming Yourself: A Road Trip with David Foster Wallace* (New York: Broadway Books, 2010), 274.

probably should not, say that our pleasure is irrelevant to our sense of calling, we must recognize that pleasure and joy *follow*, or *flow from*, the work of God in Christ rather than *precede* it. Indeed, in Ephesians we see Paul brimming over with praise and thanksgiving for all that God has done in Christ, "to bring unity to all things in heaven and on earth" (1:10). Then Paul prays for God to give us wisdom to begin to discern this unfathomable mystery (1:17–23). And then he sends us with this vision of redemption to go and bear fruit in every manner of good work.

In the end we come to appreciate the valiant woman and Woman Wisdom as exemplars for our lives in Christ. Their great love for God and for the order and purpose that he wove into the world at creation (8:21–30) gives way to their love for humanity and the work humans are designed to do in the world (8:31; 31:15, 20). And so our path to wise vocations begins with the same deep love for God, for the redeemed order of creation, and for the wisdom God gives to open the eyes of our hearts and set our feet in paths of obedience. Within this worldview we will find the fullest of joy in the work of our hands.

Scripture Index

Psalms

Proverbs

Ecclesiastes

Song of Solomon

Isaiah

Jeremiah

Lamentations

Mark

Luke

Subject Index

Author Index